Acclaim for *Across the Red River*

'Stationed in Rwanda and Burundi in the second half of the
1990s, Jennings, an accomplished anecdotalist, manages to
combine in *Across the Red River* terrifying accounts of his
experiences trapped in fire fights and getting slung out of both
countries with a hilarious ear for dialogue. But he is no less
angry at what was done – and not done – in Burundi . . .
Jennings's broad-brush pastiche [goes] a long way to explain
why Africa is a continent in crisis' *The Times*

'A very brave book. It is brave not just because of the dangers he
faced while reporting on the genocidal killings in Central Africa.
Rather it is brave because for so many of us the problems of
Africa are a thorough turn-off, incomprehensible and insol-
uble . . . Jennings has . . . [an] eye for detail and a novelist's ear
for dialogue. He makes even the supposedly incomprehensible
differences between Hutu and Tutsi tribesmen come alive . . .
Christian Jennings has starkly documented the greatest humanitarian disaster since the Nazi holocaust in readable and
surprisingly humorous prose. He has lifted the stone on the
unreal world of African politics in which a quarter of the GDP
of Burundi comes from humanitarian aid money. And he has
exposed the aid racket' *Daily Mail*

'A highly personalised account . . . Whether visiting massacre
sites, or suddenly realising he has just eaten prawns fished from
Lake Kivus – into which thousands of cholera victims had
recently been dumped – Jennings rips open the baffling politics
behind one of the greatest tragedies of the 20th century' *FHM*

'The book's main value is to shine a light on the "slow-trickle
genocide" in Burundi, possibly the scariest place on earth and
certainly one of the most neglected' *Irish Times*

Christian Jennings was based in Central Africa from 1994–1998, working first for the *Sunday Telegraph* and then as Reuters correspondent for Rwanda, Burundi and eastern Zaire. Most recently he has reported on the Kosovo crisis for *Scotland on Sunday*.

Across the Red River

*Rwanda, Burundi and the
Heart of Darkness*

CHRISTIAN JENNINGS

PHŒNIX

A PHOENIX PAPERBACK

First published in Great Britain in 2000
by Victor Gollancz

This paperback edition published in 2001 by Phoenix,
an imprint of Orion Books Ltd,
Orion House, 5 Upper St Martin's Lane,
London WC2H 9EA.

A CIP catalogue record for this book
is available from the British Library.

ISBN 0 575 40028 5

Typeset at The Spartan Press Ltd,
Lymington, Hants
Printed in Great Britain by
The Guernsey Press Co Ltd,
Guernsey, C.I.

Contents

Contents

List of Illustrations

Thanks and acknowledgements are due to many people on at least three different continents. In London, thanks go to Samantha Bolton and Anne-Marie Huby from Médecins sans Frontières-UK, to Michela Wrong from the *Financial Times* and to Nicholas Kotch from Reuters. In former Yugoslavia I'd like to thank Abdul Hani Aziz from the UN, and in Paris Steven Fox at the American Embassy. In Africa thanks go to Corinne Dufka in Freetown, to David Fox at Reuters in Nairobi, Alexei Sindahije in Bujumbura, Yahya Muvunyi in Kigali and Alistair Lyne in Johannesburg. Also to David Guttenfelder in Tokyo and to Catherine Taillefer in Quebec. In the United States I'd like to thank my former fellow Rwanda correspondent, Chris Tomlinson from the Associated Press.

Hereford, March 1999.

This book is dedicated to the memories of Myles Tierney,
Juan Ruffino, Cedric Martin, Reto Neuenschwander and
all the others who stayed behind.

'This place gives me the creeps,' the buxom English girl said in a low voice.

'There have been massacres and things here, haven't there?' Her disciple, sipping a yellow drink, stared at the photograph. 'Or am I thinking of Ruanda?' She frowned thoughtfully.

'Both Ruanda and Burundi have had their massacres,' her guru said.

The disciple shuddered.

'Mind you,' her guru added, 'they only kill each other as a rule. They never touch Europeans – or hardly ever.'

'In Burundi do the tall ones kill the short ones or the short ones kill the tall ones? I know Burundi does one thing and Ruanda the other.'

'I'm never sure myself,' her guru said.

Her disciple sighed. 'I find African politics so very confusing.'

Shiva Naipaul,
North of South

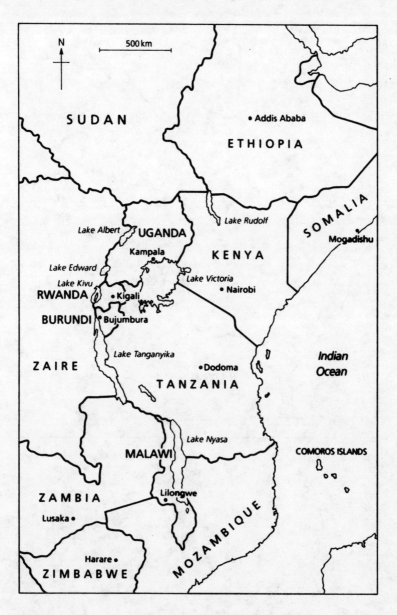

N

500 km

SUDAN

• Addis Ababa

ETHIOPIA

Lake Albert

UGANDA

Lake Rudolf

SOMALIA

Mogadishu

Kampala

KENYA

Lake Edward

Lake Kivu

RWANDA

• Kigali

Lake Victoria

• Nairobi

BURUNDI

• Bujumbura

ZAIRE

Lake Tanganyika

• Dodoma

Indian
Ocean

TANZANIA

Lake Nyasa

COMOROS ISLANDS

MALAWI

ZAMBIA

Lilongwe

Lusaka •

MOZAMBIQUE

Harare •

ZIMBABWE

Central and East Africa

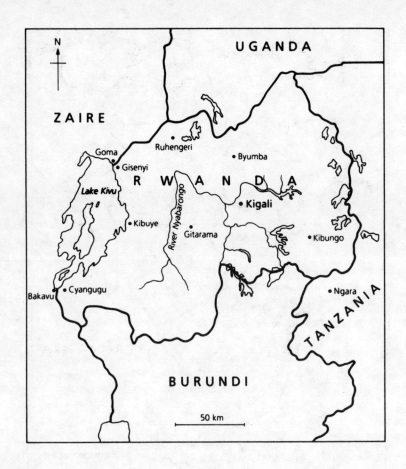

Rwanda

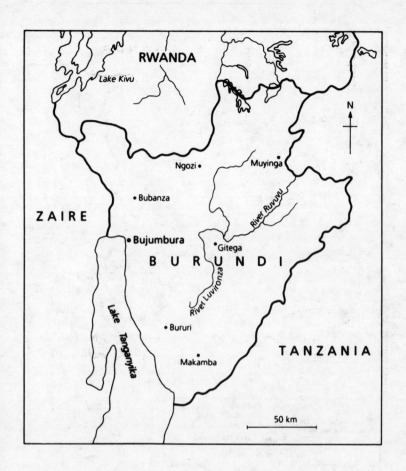

Burundi

The Great Lakes region, showing location of refugee camps in eastern Zaire, November 1996

Part 1

Chapter 1

Killing Starts Tonight

I arrived in Rwanda for the first time on Friday 26 August, 1994. I was carrying one hundred and fifty pounds of equipment, which included a satellite telephone, fifteen thousand dollars, eighteen litres of mineral water, a copy of *The Day of the Jackal* and thirty feet of climbing rope. The temperature in Kigali was ninety degrees. Gregoire Kayibanda airport was almost deserted. The war in Rwanda was over.

The twin-engined Beechcraft which had flown me in from Nairobi's Wilson airport taxied around fast. It let down its steps just long enough for me to dump my equipment. Then I moved out of its propeller wash and it turned and took off again immediately, climbing fast into the blue sky, heading due east for Kenya. I bent down and stowed the Frederick Forsyth novel in a side-pocket of my rucksack. I'd read it about thirty times before, but on the flight in had turned to it to still my nerves. The familiar prose about the calm, capable, chain-smoking assassin had reassured me as I fretted about my first trip to a war zone.

There were rows of jagged bullet holes splattered across the walls of the airport buildings, every pane of glass in sight was shot out, and the side of the smashed control tower had been hit by anti-tank rockets. The only person I could see was a teenage soldier. I assumed he was from the victorious rebel Rwandan Patriotic Front (RPF), which had just invaded the country from Uganda. He was wearing dusty black Wellington boots and an East German camouflage uniform, and was sitting in the shade by the entrance to the terminal building smoking a cigarette. His Belgian FN automatic rifle had a felt-tip pen stuck down the barrel. I slung my flight bag around my neck, picked up my rucksack and the silver flight cases containing the satellite phone and generator, and shuffled very, very slowly towards him beneath my load. He gestured backwards with his head into the dark interior of the building. I staggered in and dumped my kit down in front of a table. Two soldiers carrying heavily customized Kalashnikovs were staring at a photograph of the Princess of Wales in the *Daily Telegraph*. A tall, thin woman wearing a denim shirt and skirt took my passport and looked at it.

'*Bienvenu à Rwanda,*' she said, shaking my hand.

Five minutes later, I was directed over to the other side of the airport complex. By now at the helm of an airport trolley with one uncontrollable wheel, I was pouring with sweat and had three hundred metres to push to the other terminal building. Built in a seventies-style pattern of smoked glass and tan concrete, it too had had every window smashed, and it appeared to be deserted. An effort had been made to start clearing up, for there was not a spot of rubbish anywhere. It was very quiet. Out of the bright sunlight it was cooler. Water from the lavatories had spread over the tiled floor of the arrivals lounge. The door to the Ladies was diagonally colandered with bullet holes and the handle was blown off. Somebody had fired a round through that internationally understood sign showing the outline of a woman in a triangular skirt. What kind of carnage could possibly be inside? I walked in. Nothing. Just a flooded floor and a hand drier into which somebody had emptied half a Kalashnikov magazine. I wondered what they might have been looking for in there. I was curious now. I pushed open the door of one of the cubicles, and my boots squelched on the wet floor. For just such an eventuality, I thought, had I bought the pair of lightweight canvas and leather combat boots I was wearing. There was nothing in the first cubicle, except a hot, dead smell of sweet, burnt gravy. I opened the next door along. I was just looking into the pan, and letting out an enormous sigh of relief to discover nothing more frightening than a couple of cartridge cases at the bottom, when there was a discreet clearing of a throat behind me.

'*Vous cherchez quelque chose, M'sieur?*'

It was the tall woman from immigration. She was standing there looking at me, smirking, her low heels just high enough to raise her half an inch out of the water that covered the floor. I smiled and shrugged.

'I was only looking,' I explained in French.

I walked out, picked up my mountain of luggage, and waddled down the stairs towards the chrome customs desk, where a man was waiting. I heaved my luggage up in front of him. He smiled and said nothing as I took everything out of my rucksack. He sniffed at the petrol in my generator. Then he opened one of my packets of Rowntrees Fruit Pastilles and took out two orange ones, one of which he put in the breast pocket of his silk shirt, and the other in his mouth.

'Who is he, exactly, this one?' he asked the woman, raising his eyebrows in my direction.

'Journalist,' she said. 'English. Found him in the Ladies.'

It took me nearly twenty minutes to repack my rucksack. Knowing practically nothing about conditions in Rwanda, except that it was hot, there had been a war and a genocide, and that the country was in ruins, I had bought enough equipment to last me for days. My experience of working in Africa until then had been limited, but specialist. For four months in 1985 I had served as a French Foreign Legion paratrooper in Djibouti, patrolling the Somalian and Ethiopian borders in open trucks on long-range patrols. That apart, I had spent two weeks on holiday in the Gambia earlier in 1994. It was that April, while I had been lying on a West African beach, that the Rwandan genocide had started five hundred metres from where I now stood. The plane carrying the presidents of Rwanda and Burundi had been shot down by unknown assassins at the other end of the runway, plunging the tiny country into its hundred days of slaughter.

I reckoned that I had at least two good things going for me. I could speak French, and knew how to deal with African soldiers. Remembering my desert patrols in Djibouti with '*La Legion*', I had decided that I had best be prepared for Rwanda. I had borrowed the rucksack and a variety of its contents from a friend who had been an officer in the Special Air Service. I'd then topped up his equipment with an expensive trip to a specialist camping shop in London. It was the kind of outlet frequented not only by professional mountaineers, but also by overzealous members of the Territorial Army, and men who might subscribe to survival magazines. The rucksack was vast and camouflaged. It still had flecks of dried vomit on the carrying straps, from where my friend had been air-sick on a Chinook helicopter during an SAS exercise. Into it, I had loaded an army groundsheet, a poncho, a khaki army sleeping-bag, two saws, each with different-sized teeth, and a small machete. I'd bought mess tins, military 'compo' food, a compass with luminous settings and a small map in a waterproof cover showing the night sky in the southern hemisphere. Food had been a hard choice. I knew that there was a shortage of food in Kigali, and suspected that most shops would be closed. So I had brought some tinned spaghetti and rice pudding, and eight days' worth of vacuum-packed sausages, beans and onions. The orange mixtures sat harshly mummified in their packaging, their expiry date two decades hence. I had a hexamine stove and a week's supply of paraffin tablets, a miniature camping gas cooker and a mosquito net. I also had insect repellent that was so strong it had already half melted the end of my toothbrush after leaking in my sponge-bag. I had elastic bungy cord – black, non-reflective, ex-US Army – for slinging a jungle hammock, two shiny metal carabiners, one pink, one turquoise, and thirty feet of khaki climbing rope with a breaking strain of a thousand kilos. I had two first-aid kits, including full suture equipment, twenty-four disposable hypodermic syringes and a plasma drip set. In case of gunshot wounds, I had four British army field dressings and two boxes of Super Lillets. I had eighteen candles, a torch, two pairs of scissors, a camouflage headband and a sunhat. I'd packed twenty-five square feet of NATO-specification camouflage vehicle netting, two boxes of windproof and waterproof matches, three British army water-bottles, eight changes of clothes and a Swiss army knife. I had been in two minds about bringing half a dozen marine distress flares, eventually deciding against, but, worried that I would not be able to wash, I *had* brought a hundred and fifty individual sachets of moist wipes which I had taken off the BA stewardess on the flight from Heathrow.

As I was repacking my bags, sliding my case of mineral water into the bottom of the rucksack, I asked the customs officer what he had been looking for.

'Oh, I don't know . . . at other airports they search people's bags, so we do it here too.'

I walked across the deserted lobby. The blast holes from hand-grenades and mortars sprayed outwards across the tiles from the point of impact. At one side of the lobby were two empty, looted vendors' kiosks and, in the middle, two large glass display cases. One was occupied by a scraggy, stuffed buffalo, and the other by an eight-foot-high mountain gorilla made out of black soap. In its out-stretched paw was a bar of Sulfo soap, which it proferred like a lavatory attendant waiting patiently for a gentleman customer to finish relieving himself in an expensive hotel. Sulfo Rwanda had built the gorilla out of their own best-selling product, and presented it to the airport in an effort to remind visitors about the plight of the endangered mountain gorillas in the north. Standing by the soap primate was a man wearing brown slacks and a yellow shirt. He walked up to me, took my equipment, put it straight down again, and then pointed at a battered Datsun outside.

'*Taxi, m'sieur?*'

Outside in the sun, the city of Kigali climbed and stretched along the hills in front of me. There was a vivid clash between the blue sky, the green eucalyptus and avocado trees, and the harsh red and brown of the earth. Set on several hills, it looked very beautiful, half of the houses hidden by trees and forests. So this is what a war zone looks like, I thought. The destroyed airport was silent, and no cars passed on the road that led down to the city. It was hotter than ever in the Datsun, its vinyl seats scorching with a hot plastic heat that whipped straight through my trousers and shirt. To make matters more uncomfortable still, I had four thousand dollars in cash stuck to the top of each thigh with insulating tape.

'Where are we going, patron?' asked the smiling driver.

I thought hard. I had no idea. I didn't know where any of the hotels were, nor the headquarters of any of the aid organizations I had contacted before leaving England. Where, I wondered, did I start? The driver looked at me expectantly.

'The UN.'

I was in Rwanda to make a TV documentary whose producers wanted to track down the men responsible for the Rwandan genocide that had left around 850,000 people dead since April. I'd started a new job with a television production company three days before, and had been sent on this mission as the only person in the office who could speak decent French, and had visited Africa, in any context, before. Until that morning I'd known practically nothing about the country, apart from what I'd seen on the news or read in the papers over the preceding four months. I was worried, because this was my first foreign TV assignment, and time was tight.

I had arrived in the Kenyan capital, Nairobi, twenty-four hours before. There'd been a minor car accident in the dark on the way from the airport, but I'd arrived at the hotel in one piece, and straight away telephoned a fixer who, I had been told, could arrange an aircraft charter into Kigali.

I met Rudiger Voggs the following morning on the terrace of the Norfolk, the oldest hotel in Nairobi. In the pre-war days everybody used to stay there. The wood-panelled walls of the Lord Delamere bar were still hung with fading watercolour cartoons of the old set; the long-dead majors in their club ties, the jaunty colonial officers cracking a joke, gin and bitters clenched in dusty hands, the firm-jawed trackers of leopard and lion.

Rudi, as he introduced himself, was white Kenyan, via Germany, but Europe was a long time ago. Now he was a whiff of mid-Atlantic style planted in uptown Nairobi. Physically, he looked like the result of a genetic experiment involving Phil Collins and all three of the Bee Gees. Conversationally, he was firmly stuck on the American West Coast in the mid-seventies. About five foot five, he had silvery grey hair which swept into a bouffant parting at the front, then coasted midway across his ears. It tumbled casually over the upturned collar of his black leather jacket, whose sleeves were turned halfway up his forearm. A red silk shirt was tucked in to tight snow-washed denim jeans, over white lace-up shoes.

'So, man,' he said, sitting in the paisley upholstery of one of the Norfolk's wicker armchairs and ordering coffee in fluent Swahili, 'first time in Nairobi, eh?'

I admitted it was.

'Going into the Kig, eh? Should be groovy.'

He sipped his coffee and lit a Marlboro, turning to glance at a tall, elegant black woman swaying past the hotel entrance.

'Jesus, man,' he sighed, shaking his silver mane as he spooned sugar into his coffee. 'The state of some of the pussy on these streets.'

He tut-tutted. 'You should see it – it's not healthy for a man. Distracts you.'

We talked about Kigali, and he, guessing I was worried about it, reassured me. I passed him the five thousand dollars for the air-charter.

'Yup, this country,' he sighed, looking around him. 'Gets into your bones after a while. But I'm all right. Yeah. I'm all right. I'm getting out at the end of the year. Heading back to Tasmania; that's where my lady is from. Gonna have a good time. Put down some roots near the ocean. Play a lot of golf.'

We sat smoking in companionable male silence, until it was time to go.

'Tell you what, Christian, when you get back in, yeah, you give me a ring. We'll go out, you can meet my lady, we'll go eat seafood, drink some good wine, and then, heh! Take it from there. Party till dawn. You know?'

I said nothing, worrying, as Rudi had said, about going to Rwanda. Then he put me into a black London taxi, known in Nairobi as a 'London-Look', smacking the wing hard with one hand as the driver turned to take me to Wilson, Nairobi's commercial airport. An hour later we were airborne over the Rift Valley, and I was alone with my Rwanda notes in the chill interior of a ten-seater Beechcraft.

Nearly a million people in Rwanda had been killed in two months. In state-sponsored slaughter, one majority tribe, the Hutu, had turned on the minority one, the Tutsi, and tried to exterminate them. The massacres had started on 6 April, the day the plane carrying the Presidents of Rwanda and Burundi was shot down over Kigali airport. From then until June, gangs of Hutu militiamen and soldiers, helped by the Hutu peasant population, had hunted down the Tutsi all across Rwanda. They had killed them in a variety of horrifying ways, with machetes, clubs, hand grenades and automatic weapons. I remembered reading about the massacres at the beginning of May, sitting on a train travelling to Manchester, where I was taking up a job on a Sunday television chat show. The article – I think it was in *The Economist* – had told how hardline politicians from the Hutu government had coerced the peasant population of Rwanda into killing their Tutsi neighbours. The country, no bigger than Wales, had run with blood. Other newspapers had published graphic descriptions of Tutsis, including children, babies and women, being hacked to death at roadblocks, in their houses, on the roads and in the forests and bush of the tiny country.

The explanations for the killings that I read from the pile of press cuttings on my lap seemed to vary. One journalist said that the Hutu had been oppressing the Tutsi for nearly two decades. The genocide – as it was now being called – was the climax of a campaign to incite ethnic hatred. The Hutu had been led by clever, articulate politicians and local officials to believe that they would be slaughtered by the Tutsi if they didn't kill the minority group first. A radio station had broadcast messages urging the Hutu population to kill all Tutsis, to fill mass graves, to finish them off. The killing had been dubbed 'work'. Another article said that the president's plane had been shot down because he was under intense pressure to share power, both political and military, with the Tutsi, and hardliners led by his wife had killed him to prevent this. This article had a photograph of her, a large woman called Agathe Habyarimana, but it was a bad photocopy so she was almost unidentifiable.

A background article about Rwanda told me that it was one of the smallest counties in Africa, that it was mountainous and hilly, and that it exported coffee and tea. On a listing of the world's poorest countries, it ranked in the bottom twelve, and most of the population were employed in agriculture. A picture showed a woman with a basket on her back picking tea. A range of green mountains was behind her, and the sky was a fierce blue. She was smiling. I wondered briefly whether she was still alive. Was she Tutsi or Hutu? How could you tell the difference? Was there any? Tutsis were tall and thin, Hutus short, broad-faced and squat, somebody had said, but intermarriage made the differences hard to spot. The map of Rwanda showed the capital, Kigali, bang in the middle, with roads snaking out through the hills to the other towns. Zaire and Lake Kivu lay to the west, Lake Victoria and Tanzania to the east, Uganda to the north and Burundi to the south. The country was landlocked. It had had the same president – Juvenal Habyarimana – since 1973, and was supposedly democratic, although his Hutu party, the MRND, had suppressed any effective opposition. The army was quite small, and French trained and equipped. It had been fighting a low-level counter-insurgency war against Tutsi guerrillas based in Uganda since 1990. I looked at the front of this background report: published in 1993. So it was out of date, I thought, as I leant my head against the vibrating plastic window of the Beechcraft.

The cover of a recent edition of *The Economist* was illustrated with a photograph of the rotting, skeletal hand of a Rwandan corpse, outstretched in death. 'Who will save Rwanda?' said the headline. The leader article was about proposed military intervention to try and stop the massacres. Nobody apart from the French appeared to be interested in doing anything. At the beginning of the genocide in April, United Nations peacekeepers had even been withdrawn from the country, and no action had been taken against the Hutu militia gangs, the interahamwe. An article written in June showed pictures of French paratroopers driving in trucks across the Rwandan border from Zaire, flying the *tricolore*, and waving to jubilant crowds of peasants. France had decided to act to save the Tutsis, said a French government minister. Other comments in the article said that the French were only intervening in Rwanda because they had trained the army and because the government was sympathetic to French interests.

This I did know about. I'd served in the French Foreign Legion's

Parachute Regiment in the mid eighties and knew that there had been training missions carried out with the Rwandan government army. This was something that had struck me as perfectly routine at the time, as the French seemed to be perpetually engaged in training their African allies. But apparently the French had become involved in instructing the militias and troops who were to carry out the genocide. France was being the pragmatic mistress of *realpolitik* that I remembered from my days in Corsica and Djibouti, saying that her humanitarian mission, code-named *Opération Turquoise*, had only been launched to try and save the remaining Tutsis.

The next newspaper cutting was from one of the British dailies, and the accompanying photograph showed an old woman. She was a Hutu, the caption told me, and she was struggling under the weight of an enormous bundle she carried on her head. At the side of the road beside her lay a corpse face down on the tarmac. She was one of a million and a half mainly Hutu refugees who had fled Rwanda to escape the advance of a Tutsi army that had invaded Rwanda from Uganda. Two great waves of refugees had flooded in to Zaire and Tanzania, the article said, terrified that the advancing Tutsi soldiers would take revenge on them for their part in the genocide. The capital, Kigali, had fallen to the Tutsi rebels on 4 July. The article was dated a few days after the event. At the bottom of the piece was a photograph of the rebel commander, Major-General Paul Kagame. He had a thin black face, wire-rimmed glasses and was wearing a beret that was too big for him. The picture caption read something like 'Lightening advance by strategist Kagame', while the article said that he had been trained in the United States.

After the end of July, the articles I was reading were all concerned with the fate of the Rwandan refugees. They'd fled across the north-western Rwandan–Zairean border into the town of Goma, set on the northern shore of Lake Kivu. A million refugees had dumped themselves down on the volcanic lava beds outside the town, in the shadows of the active volcanoes of the Virunga range. Cholera had struck almost immediately. There was no sanitation, hygiene conditions were very poor and it was impossible to dig latrines in the hard volcanic rock. The only water had to be trucked in from

Lake Kivu, which was, anyhow, contaminated by corpses. Nearly 50,000 people had died in Goma. Aid workers and the UN were calling it the worst humanitarian disaster they had ever seen; others suggested that the cholera epidemic could be an almost biblical revenge cast upon those who had carried out the genocide.

Both these newspaper and magazine articles, as well as British television back home, had been full of pictures of the crisis. Rwandan refugee children dipping buckets into ponds where corpses had been dumped and where humans had defecated. Frantic, bustling aid workers pushing drips into the arms of dying Rwandans, while hundreds of thousands of people crouched diseased and terrified underneath a sky black with volcanic dust. There were photographs of thousands of corpses rolled up in rush matting and laid at the side of the road, of French soldiers bulldozing them into mass graves. The latest articles and photographs were from a week before. They reported that the cholera epidemic had passed its peak, but that the nightmarish, gigantic refugee camps had stayed put.

I looked up. The pilot was saying something from the cockpit, pointing downwards with his thumb.

'Rwanda.'

I looked down. We had come in over the western edge of Lake Victoria, and were flying low. Gone were the vast expanses of the Kenyan plains: we were over much higher, hillier country. There were bright green forests and fields, small collections of huts, vivid red scars of roads branching out from them, and here and there the occasional black mirror of a small lake. My first glimpse revealed a green and fertile country, and the earth was the red of the central African highlands. It looked compact. It felt as though I was flying over a patch of history. There were 850,000 new corpses down there. The pilot made a signal that we would shortly be coming in to land. I packed away my press cuttings, and my pictures of the assorted government ministers, political leaders, generals and militiamen that I had come to Rwanda to track down, and tightened my seat-belt. I wondered what lay ahead. I had no idea where to start. I was looking for the instigators and perpetrators of a genocide whose origins and process I hardly understood, in a country I had never visited. Most had fled with the Tutsi backlash and were scattered in the hellish Hutu refugee camps. My deadline allowed me five days to find them.

Sitting in the battered Datsun taxi two hours later, we made our hot way to the United Nations building. To the taxi driver's obvious pleasure, this route took us via the Red Cross headquarters, two hotels, and a British aid agency, asking directions as we went. He was from Burundi, he explained, and didn't know Kigali. I was from England, I said, and didn't know Rwanda. He said that was fine. We ambled up and down the hills of central Kigali, women and children swaying along the sides of the road, bundles of firewood and jerry-cans balanced on their heads. I noticed deserted trenches and gun-emplacements along the roadside underneath the banana and avocado trees. The car swerved to and fro across the tarmac to avoid holes that had been circled in white paint, and which still contained anti-tank mines. We climbed a hill, the two-lane road divided by a low, scrubby hedge. Traffic had thickened. Four-wheel-drive Toyotas and Land Rovers pulled in and out, overtaking the slower, more heavily laden Rwandan cars. The sides of the vehicles were emblazoned with the flags and stickers of the Red Cross (ICRC), Médecins sans Frontières (MSF), Oxfam and a dozen other organizations.

Ten minutes later we hit our first road-block. We sat in the sun, engine off, and waited for the cars in front of us to trickle past the clutch of Tutsi soldiers from the Rwandan Patriotic Front (RPF), who sat on their upturned crates at the top of the hill. Teenagers, in their trainers, camouflage jackets, and with their Kalashnikovs and South African R-4 assault rifles, they were checking for stolen vehicles. It was a lengthy process, involving the checking of chassis and serial numbers. They were looking for Hutu militiamen trying to slip out of Kigali, my driver told me. After an hour, we arrived at the compound of the British aid organization we'd been looking for, I gave the driver twenty dollars in place of the hundred he asked for and, ten minutes later, a British doctor gave me a lift to the United Nations building. It was set in the Amahoro Hotel, just in front of Kigali's football stadium. There were a lot of British soldiers in evidence, and rows of white UN vehicles parked in the orange dust. I dumped my mountain of equipment in a pile by the entrance and lit a cigarette.

I was just wondering who to ask for when a British major in tropical camouflage uniform walked over, shook my hand, and gestured me towards the main entrance.

'Carlton TV? Heard you'd arrived. Come on in. Beer at the bar. Happy Hour.'

We went past the sentries with assault rifles slung across their chests and their Aldershot tattoos. Maps and lists of orders were posted everywhere. Groups of officers in jungle boots and dusty tropical camouflage moved purposefully. Each door had a three-letter acronym or an abbreviation stencilled on it in red paint. OPS. SIGINT. RSO. MOVCOM. The impromptu bar was full and two soldiers were uncapping bottles of warm Kronenbourg with the energy of stokers feeding the boilers on a battlecruiser. The major raised his hand.

'Beer? Yup?'

Five Kronenbourgs arrived.

'Cheers. Sorry, they're not cold. No power you see – lines still down. Shelling.'

'Canadians are meant to be doing something about it,' chipped in a captain by his side.

'Canadians?' asked the major. 'Oh, yes, good stuff. Power back on – cold beer.'

Other officers came to join our circle. I held my cigarette and two beer bottles in one hand as I shook hands with a blond paratroop major. Two American journalists came over and shook my hand. I explained my mission; both looked surprised when I said I had only five days in which to achieve it. More beer arrived, and we were joined by Samantha Bolton, an Englishwoman with catlike eyes who was the press officer for Médecins sans Frontières. She had just arrived back from Goma.

'You'll need a car, somewhere to stay . . . I suggest you try the Diplomates, most of the other journalists are there. What else? Hmm.'

She pursed her lips.

'Your guilty men. Best try Zaire. Round Goma; but finding them in five days?' She raised her eyebrows and pouted again. 'In Zaire? In those refugee camps? Good luck.'

Five minutes later the beer ran out.

'Need a lift with us?' asked one of the American journalists.

Not a single electric light could be seen as we sped through the complete darkness of a Kigali night. We swung through several roundabouts, down dual carriageways, my cigarette trailing the occasional spark as I held it out of the window in the warm night.

The Hotel Diplomates was also in complete darkness, but I could make out a four-storey modern building with a large garden. Three RPF soldiers lounged in armchairs at the entrance, a belt-fed Chinese machine-gun propped in the dust. They were wearing raincoats and sweaters despite the heat. The hotel manager, a tall man in steel rimmed glasses, told me the only room that was available that hadn't been destroyed in the fighting was the *Suite Presidentielle*, which came in at one hundred and twenty dollars a night. I had no choice. I took it for two nights, paying from the thick wedge of dollars that hung in the blue pouch around my waist. So much for my jungle equipment, airstrip-marking devices and rice pudding, I thought, running jauntily up the stairs.

I had spoken too soon. On the third floor, rows of splattered holes ripped through the concrete walls of the corridor, where it had been hit by machine-gun fire. Dust, glass and lumps of mortar scrunched underfoot near the huge hole in the wall. Brass cartridge cases jangled underfoot in the floaty plaster dust. Opening the door to my suite, I saw that an anti-tank rocket had blown up in one room. A photo hung on the wall of another, showing four mountain gorillas, their faded colours picked out in the light of my torch. Four bullet holes were shot through it. The four dusty, empty rooms had no electricity, no water in the taps, and no glass left in any of the windows. Somebody had crapped on the floor, but it must have been some time ago; even in the cloying, eighty-degree heat, there was no smell. An empty steel helmet lay by the bed, a bullet hole shot through it. On the inside there were dark stains and what looked like the remains of old puff pastry. I lit the candle by the bed, and then, putting my small Maglite between my teeth, I took the steel helmet and attempted to scrape the excrement off the carpet with the brim. It was a more complicated operation than it looked, the weave of the carpet clung tenaciously. My jaws were aching from holding the torch by the time I chucked the helmet and the withered turd through the smashed window into the garden below.

Dinner downstairs on the terrace was by candlelight. It consisted of a very thin omelette and five bottles of Primus lager, warm and sticky.

'It's brewed in Zaire, you know,' said Steve, an English photographer sitting across the white plastic table from me. 'It's got formaldehyde in it.'

'Probably essence of Hutu corpse as well,' said one of the American journalists from Paris. 'Knowing fucking Lake Kivu.'

'Are they still chucking them in the lake?' asked Chris. 'It'll be full in a minute. Like Lake Victoria – how many was it they fished out of there?'

'Forty thousand washed up on the Ugandan shore apparently – Reuters got good pics,' said Steve.

'The way I hear it, nobody's eating fish in Uganda right now,' chipped in one of the Americans.

'Come off it. Would you? Be half of some Tutsi university lecturer from Butare in with your Tilapia and rice,' said someone else.

'Plus his wife and kids asking for a lift,' said Chris.

'Oh fuck off. That's gross.' Steve laughed.

'What's Goma like at the moment?' I asked, changing the subject and mentally brushing off some anecdotes from the French Foreign Legion in case I had to stand my conversational corner. 'Can you move around?'

'Zairean soldiers everywhere. Trying to rip you off all the time,' said Jean-Phillipe, a Swiss man who wrote for *Libération* in Paris. He'd been travelling in Zaire and Rwanda with Steve since April.

'It's five bucks here, ten there, two dollars for this, beer money for that, *donnez, donnez, donnez,*' said American Chris, waving to attract the waiter. 'It's so civilized being back in Kigali.'

The waiter, a very thin Rwandan man in a dirty white shirt and crooked bow-tie, appeared at the edge of the flickering cocoon of candlelight.

'*Messieurs désirez?*'

'*Cinq Primus, s'il vous plaît.*'

He wrote the order on a slip of paper which he laid with the others in a pool of beer at the centre of the table. I leant back, propping my feet on the table struts, listening to the others. Over by the entrance the soldiers were chatting quietly in their armchairs. The sky was blue-black and there were lots of new stars. It was warm.

'Driving around in May, d'you remember?' said Steve. 'Road-block in Kigali? Piles of bodies at the side of the road. Pissed interahamwe militiamen? Leaning in the car window screaming at us? Are you Belgians? *Êtes-vous Belges?*'

'Yeah, I remember,' said Jean-Phillipe. 'Holding a live hand-grenade in front of our faces, saying they were going to pull the pin out if they discovered we were Belgians. Fuck.'

'Or what was his name, you know, the AP photographer? Tall guy? Blond?'

'Dominic?'

'Something like that. Saying they'd been through a road-block where they were chopping up some women. Made them wait inside the car. Half an hour. Chopped off one leg. Then went over and sat in the shade to smoke a fag. Drink some Primus. Then came back and carried on; another arm. Kicked her around some more. Then more Primus. Then another leg.'

'What happened?' I asked.

'Let them through the road-block eventually, but not before they put both legs on the bonnet of their car.'

'Christ. Talk about savage.'

'Or do you remember – *Opération Turquoise*? Down in the south-west? Coming up against those militia guys. Eyes somewhere else; covered in banana leaves. Been killing for six weeks. Tried to get us out of the car.'

'Yeah, and only getting away because we said there was a lorry behind us full of French paratroopers dressed as nuns?'

'Or that small woman from AFP? Really good-looking. The French troops nicked her car – Peugeot 205. Ripped the doors off, said it gave them better firing positions.'

'Christ. Hutus.'

'Fucking savages.'

'Hope they all died of cholera.'

'Probably did.'

'Waiter!'

'*M'sieur?*'

'*Quatre* Primus.'

'More formaldehyde.'

'Essence of Hutu. Fuck it.'

'Who's got a packet of fags I can steal?'

'Buy your own.'

'No dollars left. Ran out in Bukavu – got some more coming in from Nairobi on Tuesday.'

'So, Christian,' asked Chris, turning towards me. 'Goma, eh?'

'Yes. Trying to find government ministers, army bigwigs. The ones who planned it.'

'Which ones?'

'Augustin Bizimungu? And Bizimana. And Bagosora. 'Bout five others too. Commanding officer of the former government army?'

I was slurring. I didn't have my notes.

'Best try the Karibu Hotel,' said Chris. 'Outside Goma, by the lake. But be careful. They don't like whities much up there. Not something I'd try right now.' He paused.

'It can be done, but it's very difficult. You see, all the former military are in those camps, and their commanders are among them. The interahamwe are running those places completely. But try the Hotel Karibu. Some of the big fish are meant to be there.'

I sat at the table thinking, as around me the others got up and left for bed. The city was quiet, the soldiers at the gate silent in their armchairs. I pushed back my plastic beach chair, and the waiter slipped out of the darkness.

'The bill,' he said softly, picking up the soggy wedge of paper from the middle of the table. I paid with a stack of twenty dollar bills and, back in my suite, was asleep minutes after grinding my cigarette butt out on the carpet.

In Kigali, at least, the war was over. But relics of the fighting that had surged backwards and forwards across the city between April and July were everywhere. Drinking my coffee the following morning I could see an unexploded 82mm mortar bomb and a 20mm cannon shell lying in the hotel flower bed ten feet from where I was sitting. Lying next to them in the dark red earth was a Boots No. 7 lipstick. The coffee was almost greenish in hue, while the breakfast omelettes were no different from the dinner ones. My companions at the other tables included the journalists I had met the previous day, and a grey-haired woman picking heartily at a slice of papaya fruit. I'd decided the best way to start my manhunt was to attend the United Nations press conference that took place every morning at the UN head-quarters where I had met the British soldiers the day before. My producer and film crew were coming to Kigali in four days time, and were expecting a comprehensive schedule of interviewees – including our guilty Rwandan government ministers – to be ready for them. I needed to know more about the situation in Rwanda, more about the situation in Goma, and, most importantly, I needed a decent driver and vehicle to take us to Zaire.

A British lance-corporal from 9 Parachute Engineer Squadron was leaning against the sandbags outside the Amahoro Hotel trying to find some shade, when I emerged from the UN press briefing an hour later. I was accompanied by Anne-Marie Huby, a press officer from Médecins sans Frontières. We stood outside the entrance and the soldier looked her up and down with undisguised lust, before gripping his assault rifle and looking away.

Anne-Marie had suggested that I accompany her to a mission station at Kabgayi, thirty-five kilometres south of Kigali, where there had been a series of massacres during April and May. The plan was to drive down the following day. That evening I should go to a party that MSF were holding at their base in the capital, a disused warehouse in the industrial zone. The press briefing had been of little use to me. Aside from Anne-Marie's invitations I'd had two other suggestions of activities that I might like to cover. A press officer from GOAL, an Irish aid agency, wanted me to come and look at the conditions at the centre for traumatized genocide widows. An officer from Major Mike Russell's Para. Engineer detachment thought that I might be interested in seeing what some of the British troops in Rwanda were up to. From the point of view of the news back home, he said, there was a good story to be covered at an orphanage on the outskirts of the capital. The men were involved in heavy digging operations to unblock the lavatories. I could only imagine corpses were involved.

Outside the sandbagged entrance of the Amahoro Hotel my newly hired driver, Melchior, was waiting with his white minibus. I'd found him in the shade of a tree in the Diplomates car-park, a lean man who professed good driving skills and claimed to know the roads of Rwanda 'better than I know my Aunt's garden'. For a four-hour run he was going to charge me seventy-five dollars. I stressed that if the trip I was planning to make that morning went well, he could well have a job for the duration of our filming trip.

The toy parrot perched in a small, golden cage that hung from Melchior's rear-view mirror bounced and swayed as we headed towards the road that led south out of Kigali. We were on our way to Ntarama church, an hour away, where, in April and May, more than 1750 Tutsis had been slaughtered by Hutu gendarmes and militiamen. I wanted to find out if we could film it, as it was the closest and most accessible of three or four massacre sites that had been left untouched. Melchior had said he knew exactly where it was, but within ten minutes of leaving the outskirts of the capital, he was completely lost. As we rolled through the red dust of the track heading south, I had to stop every ten minutes to ask directions from people at the side of the road. We drove like this for half an hour, until we breasted a curve on the edge of a small village. I got out to look at the burnt, smashed buildings. All of them, bar three or four, had the word 'Tutsi' marked on their outside walls in charcoal. The houses were a mess of burnt, smashed rafters, old cooking pots, scraps of clothing and broken chairs and tables. Outside the houses, I stood underneath a large mango tree and looked around for any signs of mass graves, or the remains of the people who must have been taken out and slaughtered. There was nothing to be seen and nobody to ask, so I walked back and asked Melchior. He did not know this area, he said, but he imagined that the inhabitants of the village must have been told to leave their homes and assemble in a church, or school, or hospital, like at Ntarama, where they would then have been killed. As we drove on, the eucalyptus groves and banana plantations around us seemed practically deserted; occasionally we would pass somebody on the road, an old woman with a bundle of firewood on her head, or a farmer walking along carrying a machete, but nothing more. My window was rolled down, and every so often there would blow a hot, sweet smell. On the wind was carried the stench of a mass grave or pile of rotting bodies, lying somewhere out of sight among the banana trees and bush at the side of the road.

Melchior chose to stay with his minibus as we arrived at Ntarama church. He parked in the shade and fiddled with some attachment on his back door. I opened the red metal gate of the chapel compound, and walked up a gentle slope towards the building. The smell was intense, a heavy stink of sweet, burnt, flesh and rotting blood that wrapped itself around me and clung to my clothes and hair. The chapel consisted of two buildings, backing onto a slight rise. There was a clump of eucalyptus trees at the bottom and a stand of banana groves and some scrub lying at the back. The soles of my suede boots scrunched slightly on the gravel as I walked up the slope towards the epicentre of the stink. The first thing I saw was the corpse of a woman lying in the doorway of the chapel, arms outstretched, dried skin pulling back from the frozen rictus of her rotten mouth. Clothes that were starting to rot stuck to her, a jagged hole was bashed in her skull. I stepped over her body, held my breath, and looked into the interior of the chapel.

Twenty rows of pews, each raised no more than a few inches off the ground, lay in front of a brick altar on which sat three skulls on a dirty sheet. As I walked forward into the chapel, I tried desperately not to breathe in. I knew that this was the only way to prevent myself from throwing up. The smell was like a solid entity that filled the inside of the building. I walked forward. The only way to get from one end of the room to the other was by walking on the pews. Which meant walking on the rotting, fly-covered, interwoven tangle of skulls, partially decomposed bodies, and swathes of old clothing covered in a sticky glue of rotten flesh and dried blood. It meant walking on the filthy mattresses, smothered in decomposed flesh and excrement. It meant stepping across the cooking pots and bundles of possessions, and over the chopped-up faces with the flesh falling off them. I had to put my foot on these things every time I took a step forward. The bluebottles and flies rose in a cloud as I moved in the direction of the altar. With every step my feet seemed to sink up to my shin in this crunching, glutinous mass of body-parts and personal effects. Four months and ten days before, this had been 1500 terrified Tutsis and all their worldly goods.

I made it to the door at the far end, and tried to leap from the closest pew into the sunlight without stepping on any more corpses. I nearly made the jump, but had not had any space for a run-up to give myself sufficient momentum. I only landed a foot or two from the grass and brickwork at the chapel's exit. But falling short, even by this small distance, meant that one foot thumped down into a rotting and stinking mattress, and the other crunched through the back of the browned, putrefying skeleton of a child, a sizeable hole smashed in the back of its grey skull.

On the road outside, Melchior was fiddling with the back door and conversing quietly with an old man who was leaning on a stick. I walked out of the red metal gate, still breathing in lungfuls of air, and stood at the side of the road. Everything on my person, from my clothes, to my hair, to the flight bag I had slung around my shoulder, seemed to smell of dead bodies. I asked Melchior to translate so that I could ask the old man some questions. There was a half-hearted to and fro in Kinyarwanda, most of it put on for my benefit, I suspected. Then Melchior translated for me, saying that the old man was not from this commune, or area, and had not been present when the killings had taken place in the middle of April. Was he, I asked Melchior, a Hutu or a Tutsi? Tutsi, the man replied. And his family, where were they? His wife, sister-in-law, three of his five children and his father had been killed just outside the town of Kibuye in

April, and he had fled with his other two children to a village just to the north of Ntarama.

Kibuye, I saw from my map, was in the far west of Rwanda, on the shore of Lake Kivu. Melchior had taken the wheel, and we were bumping back down the dirt track that led to the main route back to Kigali. Despite Melchior's protests, I had decided to sit in the back of the minibus to keep the smell of bodies away from him, and to try and allow some of the air flowing in through the windows to carry away the stink. Melchior seemed very nervous, and told me that only he should be allowed to open and close the sliding door on the minibus. I didn't pay any attention to him, as his complete lack of knowledge of Rwandan geography was almost certainly going to preclude him from driving our film crew up to Zaire. We swept down the red dirt track and, just before we crossed the Nyabarongo river, into which thousands of Tutsis had been thrown to drown in April and May, we hit a road-block. Across the road in front of the single-span ironwork bridge was stretched a length of string, attached to a wooden post. Three soldiers from the Rwandan Patriotic Front, the Tutsi rebels who had invaded Rwanda from Uganda in April, were sitting underneath a canopy of banana leaves on upturned beer crates. One of them stood as Melchior drew the minibus to a stop in front of them. He ambled over to the side window, holding his Kalashnikov upside down by its magazine, and scrutinized my press pass. Waving us forwards, he slipped the string from the top of the post and let it fall into the dusty road, as Melchior accelerated forward onto the clattering plates of the metal bridge. The road at the other side of the Nyabarongo was built up on an embankment that ran over marshy swampland on the far bank of the river. We were rolling forward in fourth gear when I decided to open the minibus' side door to let some more air in. I pulled hard on the handle, letting the door slide back on its runner, allowing the fast, warm breeze to blow over my sweating, stinking body. Melchior braked hard, changing down the gears, but not before the large white door had slid back without stopping, coasting whirringly off its guide, and fallen backwards into the van's slipstream. I watched it hit the side of the road, bounce on one corner, and then roll down hill, gathering speed, before it somersaulted with a splash into a large pool of green water at the bottom of the slope.

Two hours later, I filled the bath in my presidential suite with two inches of reddish water from the jerry-can provided each morning. Water supply to the city was still cut off, although I had come across a party of Texan civil engineers that morning. I knelt in the bath, washed first my hair and face, then sat down and lathered my torso and legs. Finally I rolled around in the soapy water to do my back. Rinsing meant standing up and pouring water from the yellow jerry-can over my head. I thought I'd leave the water in the tub in case there were no more jerry-cans forthcoming. For drinking and cleaning teeth, there were bottles of mineral water available from reception at ten dollars a litre. There had been little more than a minor argument with Melchior in the hotel car-park on our return. I'd given him his seventy-five dollars, and the bad news that he, his minibus and his sliding door would not be coming to Zaire. He was still angry about having to slide down the embankment and wade up to his knees in the swamp to retrieve his door. He had been wearing clean slacks and patent leather brogues which were now covered with mud and green slime. He demanded that I pay for the repairs and give him two hundred dollars, but I'd shrugged and left him under one of the eucalyptus trees in the car-park trying to reattach his door. The sun was getting low outside the windows of my suite. But it was still hot as I pulled on a t-shirt and clean jeans and went downstairs to the bar to have a drink and get my lift to the MSF party.

As the waiter uncapped my Primus lager with a warm hiss, I lit up and thought about everything I had yet to do. We could film at Kabgayi or at Ntarama. We could interview MSF at the King Faisal Hospital in Kigali, where there were still Hutu militia patients. We could try to film captured militiamen, arrested by the Tutsi RPF, inside Kigali prison. Assuming that I could find a driver to get us to Zaire, and assuming that once in Zaire it didn't take more than two days to find and interview our guilty Hutu ministers, then we would get back to England in time for the transmission of our programme. The problem was that I was trying to apply English deadlines and working methods to an African story. It didn't work. There were two journalists at the Diplomates Hotel who had been tracking down Ministers and army officers from the former Hutu administration for nearly a month. They had not only been in Rwanda, but also in Goma, and in Zaire's capital, Kinshasa. The more I thought about it, the more it seemed that I would have to be extremely lucky to find anybody, let alone a former minister guilty of inciting, organizing or perpetrating genocide who was prepared to stand up and admit all on camera.

I ordered a second Primus and stared through the trees in the hotel garden to where the sun was going down in a scarlet line on the horizon. I had my list of things to do in my notebook, and had worked my way down to the last item. It read: 'Carol – vegan.' The producer with whom I would be working was not only vegetarian, but vegan. It was up to me to find her the right kind of food. She wouldn't be able to eat eggs, so the hotel omelettes were off limits, chips fried in animal fat were a no-no, and stringy Rwandan chicken or goat was clearly out of the question. It looked increasingly likely that for a week she might have to starve.

The Médecins sans Frontières party had been given because all of their staff had been working non-stop since April. By the time I had arrived over a hundred people were gathered in one of the lorry garages of the old warehouse. There was a barbecue, food was laid out, and a Rwandan band was warming up. I grabbed a cold bottle of Primus and started to circulate. Not wanting to appear the absolute beginner in Rwanda that I was, I tried not to stress how little time I had spent in the country. I had a lengthy conversation with Anne-Marie in which I told her all about the French Foreign Legion, and described my experiences in Djibouti nearly a decade before. Her interest had a lot to do with the fact that MSF's legal directorate was trying to ascertain the extent of French government – and by extension French military – involvement with the former regime of the Rwandan Hutus in the years leading up to 1994.

I told her that when I had served in the Foreign Legion's Parachute Regiment in the 1980s, small teams of men were detached from the Regiment's reconnaissance platoon on training missions in

Rwanda. To the best of my knowledge these had continued as late as 1993. I also told her about what had grabbed my eye on my way out of the Diplomates Hotel for the party that evening. Alongside the stickers from CNN, the BBC, French radio and wildlife and conservation organizations on the hotel door, I had been surprised to see one bearing the distinctive emblem of my former unit in the Foreign Legion, the Amphibious Warfare company of the paras. On the same panel was a sticker bearing the logo of the Groupe Barril, a private French security company run by a certain Capitaine Barril who had previously served in the Groupement d'Intervention de la Gendarmerie Nationale, or GIGN, France's leading anti-terrorist police unit. My limited information seemed only to confirm further Anne-Marie's conviction that French military units had been intricately involved in training the Hutu militias – the interahamwe – as well as the army and gendarmerie, all of whom carried out the genocide.

The food on offer was rice and salad accompanying goat kebabs, but by the time I'd had a conversation with a British nurse who'd left the NHS to come and work in Rwanda, it had all been eaten. This meant that I hadn't had anything to eat since my omelette at breakfast. Coupled with the six large bottles of Primus I'd consumed, it meant that I was well on my way to getting drunk. One of the French nurses from MSF seemed to have foreseen this. As I walked towards the trestle table that had been laid out with all the food, she started breaking open cardboard boxes containing transparent sacs of oral rehydration fluid, designed to be administered to cholera patients. I picked up two of these sachets, read that the ingredients contained both potassium and glucose and took a gulp. The fluid tasted warm and bland. It needed perking up, so I added one sachet to half a bottle of cold Primus and tucked the other in the waistband of my jeans. The band was warming up. I lit up a duty-free Benson and Hedges and leant against a table as the bass player, heavily overcoated despite the warmth of the tropical night, thunked out a few chords to soundcheck the keyboard player. The lead guitarist, who was wearing a thick green woollen balaclava, threw in a brief dash on his imitation Fender Stratocaster. The drummer picked up the rhythm, and they launched into an electric version of 'Auld Lang Syne'.

Driving towards Gitarama the following day, I remembered that I had finished off the evening by drinking a couple of shots of gin and oral rehydration salts. After a lift back to the Diplomates Hotel, I had eaten half of one of my vacuum-packed sachets of sausage, beans and onions, before falling asleep half-way through a last cigarette.

Anne-Marie and I had emblazoned a blue and white Kigali taxi with MSF stickers and were now on the thirty-five-kilometre trip south from Kigali to the small mission station at Kabgayi. The road from the capital to the central Rwandan town of Gitarama was tarmacked and the driving was fast. Our route wound up and down hills terraced with small farming plots. Patches of avocado trees interspersed the ubiquitous clumps of banana and eucalyptus. Red dirt paths climbed and fell in between the small groups of grey mud houses. Grass had started to grow on the patches of land that lay uncultivated, their owners presumably either killed or fled into exile. We were waved through three different RPF road-blocks. The teenage soldiers with their customized Kalashnikovs and South African R-4 assault rifles sat on their upturned Primus crates in the dust and watched our taxi spin by.

I wound down the window and let the warm air blow in my face. The tight thumping of the previous night's hangover started to recede.

Our taxi turned in through the gates of the Kabgayi mission and hospital compound, and the driver curved his vehicle round to a halt. The moment Anne-Marie and I got out the same sickly, heavy smell that I had encountered at Ntarama church hit my nostrils. We walked down to a long, single-storey building which housed the hospital wards. Inside were about a hundred patients, all Tutsis, sitting on the floor of the corridor, and lying on the few available beds, desperately nervous. On the other side of the corridor from the patients' rooms were a series of interlinked shower and washrooms from which emanated the familiar smell. All over the floors lay the outlines of human bodies, the shapes etching in thick, dark red bloodstains the positions their corpses had lain in after they were killed. Up the walls of the shower rooms were tracked hundreds of dark smears, where the bloodied hands of those in their final death agonies had left their mark; reddish-brown handprints stamped on the sky-blue paintwork. Even the plasterwork seemed to exude a smell of rotten corpses.

Anne-Marie and the MSF doctor in charge told me a little of what had happened at Kabgayi. By mid-May 1994, an estimated 500,000 people had already been killed in Rwanda. The Hutu extremists were on the run, and the Tutsi RPF, which had invaded the country from Uganda as soon as the genocide had begun on 6 April, now controlled more than half the country. The RPF had taken the key western town of Kibuye, on 28 April, forcing 250,000 people, mainly Hutus, to flee towards Tanzania. Meanwhile, the interim government that the Hutu extremists had declared after the death of Habyarimana had been forced to flee the capital, and set up their headquarters at Murambi, three miles north of Kabgayi. The area they controlled consisted of the west and the centre of the country, an area that had become a free-for-all killing zone where Tutsis and moderate sympathizers were hunted down and slaughtered. Fighting for the capital, Kigali, continued while thousands of Tutsis and Hutus, displaced from other parts of Rwanda, fled southwards.

Thousands had taken refuge in and around the grounds of the former Roman Catholic seminary at Kabgayi, the largest of its kind in Rwanda. Over 1500 were crowded into a barbed-wire enclosure which lay in the seminary grounds, while hundreds more took refuge in three lecture halls. By mid May, Rwandan government troops and the interahamwe controlled all access to Kabgayi, manning road-blocks on the main road south from Murambi and guarding all access points to the compound. Hundreds more militiamen and soldiers were camped in the forests surrounding the seminary complex. The displaced people inside were trapped.

Throughout May, Tutsis and their sympathizers were plucked at random from inside the barbed-wire enclosure by soldiers and militiamen, mainly at night, and taken away to be killed. The soldiers threw hand-grenades at random over the barbed wire, while lists were compiled of all those inside the seminary grounds. There was little or no food, and the Red Cross, which had tried to set up a hospital at Kabgayi, could do nothing. The only people who could provide any kind of food or medical supplies to those trapped inside the wire were an order of Roman Catholic nuns who did what little they could. They too were under threat of death. On 22 May, the RPF seized Kigali airport and Kanombe barracks, the main strongholds of government forces in Kigali, and advanced southwards. On 3 June, they liberated an estimated 38,000 displaced people, mainly Tutsi, crowded around the mission station in Kabgayi. But for an estimated 1700 people behind the seminary barbed wire it was too late. Before the government forces and the militias retreated, they had slaughtered as many people in the camp as they could.

Anne-Marie and I walked out of the hospital and across to Kabgayi cathedral. In the cool gloom of the red brick building there was total silence. At the head of the aisle, in front of the altar, were two graves dug in the church floor. These belonged to two bishops who had been killed in the cathedral. The sacristy had been looted, and hymn books, vestments, candlesticks and altar cloths were strewn across the floor. Outside the cathedral a stony path led down between clumps of pine trees to the barbed-wire enclosure. Hundreds of large yellow sunflowers were growing in the long grass. The air smelt of death. It was very quiet.

We pushed through a gate into the area enclosed by the wire; to the left were three long lecture halls, and to the right, two groups of small whitewashed huts. Jumbles of broken cooking pots, scraps of clothing, half-burnt eucalyptus branches and piles of ash were almost the only traces that remained of all the terrified people who had sheltered there for over a month. Almost, but not quite. In the whitewashed huts, among torn sacks of maize meal whose contents were spread over the floor, were dozens of light-blue school exercise books. On the pages of these books, written in a neat copperplate hand, were lists of all the displaced people who had taken refuge at Kabgayi. It detailed their names and their communes of origin within Rwanda. Lines had been ruled across the pages, dividing the lists into blocks of around thirty names each. Dozens of these blocks were ticked neatly in blue marker-pen. These represented those who had been killed.

Outside on the grass lay a few more reminders of what had happened. There were dozens of tiny scraps of dense black hair attached to little stretches of skin, where children had been scalped with machetes. Thick eucalyptus logs lay in the earth, their surfaces scarred with machete and axe cuts, their bark dark with dried blood. They had been used as chopping blocks. Lying under a tuft of grass I saw an arm which had been hacked off at the elbow, the dried brown skin rotting off the bones, the fist clenched. The warm, meaty fug of death clung to our clothes as Anne-Marie and I climbed back up the path, past the sunflowers and the pine trees. The MSF doctor said that it was not safe to walk in the trees, as, in a last act of savagery, the militiamen and Hutu government troops had laid mines.

Two days later I left all my equipment in my presidential suite and told the hotel manager I would be returning in forty-eight hours. I took a Canadian airforce C-130 Hercules back to Nairobi to fetch my producer and the film crew. There were no commercial flights operating out of Kigali, and unless one chartered an aircraft at great expense, the only option was one of the United Nations flights run by the Canadian Air Force. The crew were wearing combat fatigues and tight black t-shirts marked with the name and number of their squadron. They gave us a short security briefing before we settled into the webbing seats running the lengths of the interior of the fuselage. The pilots accelerated down Kigali's runway, and climbed into the blue sky, heading west for Kenya. Inside the plane, the Canadian loadmaster relaxed. He had had his Beretta pistol cocked in his hand during the whole take-off procedure. Now he settled it back into his shoulder holster, and sat back on his jump seat to read a Tom Clancy novel.

Rudi Vogs was waiting for me on the Lord Delamere Terrace at the Norfolk four hours later. He was drinking coffee and eating Tilapia and chips. I sat down opposite him in one of the club chairs and asked for a menu.

'So, man,' he said, wiping tomato ketchup off the fringes of his beard. 'How was the Kig?'

I leant across to shake his spare hand and then lit a cigarette.

'It was . . . OK,' I said. 'Got lots done. But what a totally fucked-up place,' I added, staring off into the middle distance to where a group of tourists were boarding a safari minibus by the hotel entrance.

'Yeah, man, tell me about it. Does your head in what those people have done to each other. Unbelievable . . . that much hate.'

The Kenyan waiter, wearing a tartan waistcoat, came across and I ordered a pint of Tusker lager. The menu was divided into sections, each with a cheery heading like 'Cold, Snacky and Nice'. I hesitated between the steak-and-kidney pie and a well-done hamburger, finally choosing the latter. I'd checked back into the Norfolk and spent half an hour under the shower, trying to scrub out the smell of Rwanda. I'd packed my clothes, stewed with the smell of death, into a plastic bag and handed them to the Kenyan laundry boy.

Rudi plopped a spoonful of ketchup onto the crisply battered corner of his fish and scrunched it into his mouth. Around us, parties of American tourists dressed in brand-new khaki safari outfits were loudly debating which of the items on the menu were safe to eat.

'So, Christian. What next? When are you and the crew going back in? How long will you need the plane for? I can do you a good deal on a return trip, even come and pick you up in Zaire . . . Goma maybe, don't know if you're going there, or Kinshasa even. Yeah, Kinshasa. You've got to visit Kinshasa , man. That town. Whooeee. Groovy or what? That Kinshasa pussy just hits you in the face . . . it's fucking sensational.'

I explained our movements, telling him that Beverley, the producer, was arriving from London that evening, and the cameraman from Johannesburg the following day. The sound-recordist was already in Nairobi.

'So, the way I see it,' said Rudi, 'you need a Beechcraft into Kigali, and then one to come and pick you up from Goma, possibly going on to Kinshasa. Is that right? Let me see . . .' he took out a small calculator from the pocket of his jacket.

'I'll do you five thousand to Kigali, another seven and a half to come and get you from Goma, and if you need to go on to Kinshasa, that'll be another thirteen thousand five hundred. Twenty six thou in all for cash dollars.'

Taking a swig of my Tusker, I said we'd do the Kigali and Goma legs, and then wait and see on Kinshasa, depending on whether or not we found any of our guilty Hutus in and around the refugee camps.

Rudi lit up a Marlboro and leant forward conspiratorially, whispering despite the noise of conversation around us.

'So this lady producer . . . she's a vegan, yeah? Won't touch meat, no? So tell me, Christian,' he laughed, starting to guffaw through a cloud of cigarette smoke, 'if she won't touch meat, how does she get through the night?'

I went out to Jomo Kenyatta airport at four o'clock in the morning to fetch Beverley. She'd said she didn't feel safe arriving by herself. Five foot three with a blond pony-tail, she was wearing Marks and Spencer shorts and boots which, in keeping with her vegan status, she assured me were not leather. She was flustered because a box of video tapes for the camera had been stolen after she had checked them in. She was disorientated because she said she had been drinking red wine and champagne almost all the way from London.

We took a taxi back to the Norfolk, the Kikuyu driver huddled in his overcoat and balaclava against the night-time chill. On our arrival at the hotel Beverley insisted on coming over to my room with her clipboard and going through the details of my last five days in Kigali. I also reported that I had had a meeting with the office of World-wide Television News in Nairobi, from whom we were hiring our cameraman and sound-recordist, and that all seemed organized. However, I had watched Beverley since her arrival at the airport, and it had become glaringly obvious that her methods of working, so laboriously assimilated in the United Kingdom, did not travel. She was a television producer who believed in order and tidiness, who believed that things should happen the way in which she had planned them, who believed, most fundamentally, in the unassailable rectitude and importance of television. She had cut her teeth in

Britain making consumer programmes about the safety of airline seats, producing investigative programmes about minor skulduggeries in the medical profession, or the shortcomings of the Labour Party's employment manifesto. She came from a world where people returned her phone calls, kept appointments made weeks ahead, and trod in awe of the world of television. Ten hours into her first trip to Africa everything she knew would turn to sand.

Jonathan Cavender, the chief cameraman from Worldwide Television News' Nairobi bureau who I'd met the night before, was Beverley's diametric opposite. A flamboyant, six-foot tall, blond Englishman, whose grandfather, he claimed, was the notorious World War Two German tank ace, Hasso von Manteuffel, Jonathan was a veteran of thirty-six trips into the chaos of Somalia's civil war, where he had bought the Kalashnikov assault rifle and two 9mm handguns that he kept in his Nairobi apartment to deter burglars. Even his t-shirt was made by an outfit called 'Conflict Clothing' whose logo was a Heckler & Koch sub-machine gun. His second wife, Ruth, had accepted his proposal of marriage, made in a Kenyan taxi, and over our drink, after three glasses of white wine mixed with Diet Coke, had told me that she thought he was 'different' from most men she knew.

Jonathan's two local Kenyan employees at WTN, Idi and Josphat, had named him 'Lord Blah-Blah', for his tendency to shout and scream at them whenever he wanted anything done. Josphat acted as Jonathan's sound-recordist much of the time, a post that he preferred immeasurably to the alternative, which meant sitting in the office carrying out minor administrative tasks. He had managed to persuade Jonathan that he was considerably less intelligent than was the case, so as not to be consigned to an office-bound existence. To prove that he was short of intellectual capability, he had claimed that just after his birth demons had sucked his brain out with a straw. It was from Jonathan that we were hiring our camera-crew.

On the advice of a number of other TV crews who had encountered problems while filming in Zairean refugee camps, we had decided it was crucial we had a white film crew. The refugee camps around Bukavu and Goma, to where a large percentage of the former Rwandan government army and the Hutu interahamwe militias had fled, were dangerous places. The militias and the military controlled access into the camps and the distribution of food-aid delivered by international agencies, and had, to all extents and purposes, recreated in the sprawling settlements the same hierarchical structures that had existed in their Rwandan villages. In recent days a number of aid-agency vehicles had been stoned while trying to drive into Mugunga camp, outside Goma, and film crews getting out of cars or Land Cruisers had been attacked. An American documentary crew I had met at the Hotel Diplomates had had a particularly bad time. They had driven into Katale camp, north of Goma, stupidly, in a car bearing Ugandan numberplates. The thousands of Hutus at the entrance to the camp had assumed they were linked to the Tutsi RPF, which originated in Uganda. The moment the vehicle was spotted, it was surrounded by a shrieking crowd of Rwandan Hutus, spurred on by militiamen standing at the back of the crowd screaming for the blood of the Americans. The car had been rocked, and was on the verge of being turned over, its occupants dragged out and chopped to death, when the Rwandan Tutsi driver had managed to accelerate forward and make it out of the camp and back on to the road. At least three photographers had also had narrow escapes when crowds they were photographing turned nasty. I was all too keenly aware of my lack of experience, both in Rwanda and Zaire, and knew that I would be highly dependent on our cameraman to keep us out of trouble.

By the time we were airborne over the Rift Valley in Rudi's chartered Beechcraft, problems were already setting in. Feeding arrangements for Beverley had proved difficult even in Nairobi, with its huge variety of restaurants. A Chinese meal with Jonathan and Ruth had raised the issue of monosodium glutamate while, at the European-orientated Norfolk, the grated cheese had had to be carefully extracted from her sandwich. An Indian meal had seemed to provide a satisfactory compromise, until it transpired that melted butter had been used in one of the dishes. Rwanda and Zaire, with their economies and restaurant options devastated by civil war and humanitarian disaster, were going to be difficult. But Beverley's dietary idiosyncrasies were as nothing compared to the problems posed by our film crew. They had come to meet us at the Norfolk and, as we sat on the terrace sipping lime juice, we had assumed that it was a case of mistaken identity when Victor and his sound-recordist had introduced themselves. Victor, from South Africa, and Hassan, who came from Kenya, were coal black. Beverley was, to put it mildly, furious, especially as Jonathan could not be reached at the office, and she had no way of hiring anybody else. Victor had straight away made it clear, if only through the excessively slow way in which he carried out any task assigned to him, that he was not best pleased at being told what to do by a short, cross, blonde woman. Hassan was very quiet, but as it was he who would be carrying most of the heavier equipment, it didn't help us to learn that he was still recovering from being shot in the leg in the Somalian capital, Mogadishu.

On our arrival at Kigali airport, Victor was sulking after Beverley had criticized him for not reacting fast enough to her request that he film our landing in Rwanda from inside the aircraft. She told him to be first out onto the tarmac so he could film our arrival, but when he clambered down the flight steps, he – and I – were surprised to see a party of RPF soldiers, who smacked to attention as he stepped onto the tarmac. A threadbare, scarlet carpet stretched a few feet from the terminal entrance towards our aircraft, and when Beverley stepped down, the soldiers, all of whom were wearing East German camouflage and brand new black Wellington boots, presented arms. An officer with a sword saluted. A couple of government officials stiffened into a position of attention. Victor, for lack of anything else to film, rolled footage of the guard of honour, and a Land Rover marked with a Union Jack screeched to a halt and two British men jumped out. They were wearing multi-pocketed photographers' waistcoats and jeans, and had 'British Army' written all over them. Beverley, they urgently informed the Rwandans, was not Lynda Chalker, British Secretary of State for Overseas Development.

Two porters accepted ten dollars from Beverley to haul all the baggage out past the stuffed buffalo and the gorilla made of soap to where my newly hired driver and vehicle were waiting. David McBride was a six-foot-three Australian, who was the senior security officer in Rwanda for UNICEF, the UN children's fund. He had served in the Household Cavalry in the UK for five years before applying to join 22 Special Air Service Regiment in Hereford. Immensely strong and fit, he had boxed at university and in the army, but despite two almost-successful attempts at the Regiment's gruelling selection tests, he had not made it into the SAS as an officer. He had gone to work for Defence Systems Limited, a private security company run by a former SAS Squadron commander, and they had assigned him to work on the security detail of a diamond mine at Mbuji Mayi in central Zaire. When President Habyarimana's plane went down, David was moved to Rwanda. I had met him by chance at the bar of Diplomates three nights before, and given him a simple proposition: in return for two thousand dollars in cash, he was to make a trip to Goma, on supposed UN business, in a UN four-wheel-drive vehicle, and take us with him. Having driven us to Goma, he was to stay with us until we had left on our charter flight back to Nairobi. It was clear that he had reservations about the offer, but the fact that he had turned up to meet us at the airport meant that he had accepted.

That evening David, Beverley and I went over to the British army contingent, or 'Britcon' as it was known, at the Amahoro stadium. We picked up Major Mike Russell and another subaltern friend of David's, and drove off to try and find something to eat. The Rwandan capital was pitch dark, and as we turned out of the Amahoro stadium the night lay warm and black in front of us. A Scottish corporal on guard duty at the gate saluted Major Mike and we turned left and headed back to the centre of the city. David pushed the film soundtrack of *The Big Blue* into the Isuzu Trooper's CD player as we came to a temporary halt in front of a late-night supermarket, lit by hurricane lanterns, that had somehow remained open. David and his friend went inside in search of alcohol, just in case there was none to be had at the restaurant. Major Mike, meanwhile, started telling us how his unit had come to be in Rwanda, while I chipped in, giving Beverley as much background as possible from the notes I had been reading over the last week, and trying to get the complicated details straight in my own mind.

UN peace monitors had been based in Rwanda since 1 November, 1993. The Arusha Accords had been signed in August 1993, in the northern Tanzanian town of the same name, by the Rwandan government of President Juvenal Habyarimana, and by the Tutsi Rwandan Patriotic Front, largely based in neighbouring Uganda. The point about the RPF, I said, trying to remember a long conversation I'd had with a French journalist three nights before, was that they were largely made up of Tutsi refugees who had fled Rwanda in 1959, after ethnic fighting with the Hutus. The RPF had invaded Rwanda in 1990, demanding a power-sharing agreement and the right to resettle thousands of Tutsi refugees who were living in Uganda. Backed by French military support, part of which came from my former colleagues in the French Foreign Legion, Habyarimana's army had beaten off the RPF attack and the Tutsis' charismatic leader, Fred Rwigema, had been killed. A low-intensity civil war had continued until the Arusha Accords were signed in 1993.

However, Juvenal Habyarimana, the hardline Hutu President who had come to power in the 1973 coup, was loathe to give in to demands for power sharing in the government and for an increased Hutu–Tutsi ethnic mix in the army provided for by the Arusha Accords. The party he had founded following the 1973 coup, the Revolutionary Movement for National Democracy (MNRD), had become the country's sole party under a new constitution in 1978. Habyarimana had been reconfirmed as president in 1978, 1983 and 1988, winning more than 99 per cent of the vote. He saw no reason for power sharing. The UN peace monitors in Kigali were joined in late 1993 by Belgian paratroopers who formed part of the UN Assistance Mission in Rwanda (UNAMIR). They policed the ceasefire agreed under the Arusha Accords, but the RPF and the MNRD, who were supposed to have agreed to a transitional government, continued bickering, each side blaming the other for blocking its formation. Then, on 6 April, Habyarimana's jet was shot down, and the hardliners within his party went into action.

Beverley and Major Mike both asked the same question at the same time: why, if Habyarimana, a hardline Hutu, was keeping Rwanda a one-party Hutu state where the Tutsis didn't have any say in politics, was he killed by even more extremist Hutus? They were right. This seemed to be the most obvious question. I thought that on his return from Tanzania, the extremists within his own party had probably been scared that Habyarimana had compromised in Arusha, giving in to pressure from regional leaders to allow the RPF back into the political system. Better kill him, blame it on the RPF, and then incite the Hutu population into carrying out the mass slaughter of Tutsis, telling them that systematic massacres of their ethnic opposites was the only way to forestall a genocide of Hutus planned by the Tutsis. Jean-Phillippe Ceppi, the journalist from *Libération* in Paris, had explained to me how the population had been wound up to a fever pitch of anti-Tutsi suspicion during the preceding three years. Radio broadcasts on the now infamous Radio Mille Collines, exhorting Hutus to kill the Tutsi 'cockroaches', had only been part of the scheme.

David and his friend, a cavalry subaltern, came out of the makeshift supermarket having paid fifty dollars for two bottles of champagne. We turned back on to the main road and headed towards the commercial centre of town, set on the same hill as the Diplomates Hotel. David turned up the volume of the music, lit up a Marlboro and flicked his ash out into the African night.

'I do like the thought,' he said, pointing at the Isuzu's dashboard, 'that some granny in Walthamstow has given her savings to a United Nations charity, just so I can have a CD player in my car.'

Major Mike leant over from the back seat and I continued my makeshift political narrative. After Habyarimana's death, the immediate reaction of the international community had been to panic: within twenty-four hours, the Rwandan Prime Minister, Agathe Uwilingiwimana, and ten Belgian paratroopers were tortured and killed by the Rwandan Presidential Guard, and France, Belgium and the United States started to evacuate its foreign nationals from Kigali. By 21 April, the UN Security Council had passed a resolution reducing peace-keeping forces in Rwanda. It was only a month later, on 17 May, after an estimated 500,000 people had been massacred, that it approved a 5,500-strong force for Rwanda.

Major Mike Russell was the second-in-command of the British contingent in Rwanda. It was a composite unit of engineers, sappers, medics, infantry and signal specialists under the command of a Royal Marine colonel. It included part of Mike Russell's own unit from Aldershot, 63 Airborne Logistics Squadron, which in turn formed part of 5 Airborne Brigade, the UK's quick-reaction force comprised of parachute- and helicopter-trained troops. Major Mike's unit had been on exercise on Salisbury Plain, he said, when they had been put on alert to go to Rwanda. Not all of his men had welcomed this chance to see service abroad, he said. One corporal was particularly resentful at having to go and help what he called 'a load of fucking darkies'. While the men were being briefed on Salisbury Plain by the Squadron sergeant-major, this man could be heard muttering racist complaints at the back of the group. He was a member of a hard-right British movement, and within two days of their arrival in Rwanda, the corporal had excelled himself. The decomposing bodies of three Rwandans had been discovered in a ditch at the back of the stadium by a group of British soldiers. The corporal had run out to have a look, returning shortly afterwards to ask if he could keep one of the dead men's fingers as a souvenir. When Major Mike heard about this, he decided enough was enough. The corporal was ordered to report to him in full battle-order, with rifle, pack and ammunition, ready for a special mission. According to his colleagues, he was extremely excited. Secret mission? What could this mean? It might just be his chance to 'go and banjo some coons'.

Instead, he had been instructed to go and report himself to two Ghanaïan captains, large, overweight men for whom service with the United Nations was more about inflated salaries and duty-free shopping opportunities than soldiering or peace-keeping. The corporal, as he later recounted it, had gone into their office wondering if these two men were to be the first two targets of his own, personal mission of ethnic cleansing. As he stood in front of them, reluctantly putting his feet together in a semblance of the attention position, one of the captains had turned to the other, beaming across his wide, sweating face, and roared with laughter. 'Look,' he'd said. 'It's our new white batman.'

David and I were studying the menu in Kigali's Chinese restaurant while Beverley complained to Major Mike about the sad state of race relations within our team. Victor had not endeared himself to Beverley that afternoon when we had gone to film genocide victims at the King Faisal Hospital. She had asked Victor to film a self-explanatory sign on the outside of the building, a distinctive picture of a large black machine-gun with a thick red line across it. David and I had turned away and started walking back to the car; Beverley went over to Victor, looked into the camera's viewfinder, and started to swear at him. It transpired that he did not know how to focus the lens of a Betacam.

I'd thought for a moment that Beverley's antagonism was going to split the team down the middle, between blacks and whites. But it became clear that she wasn't satisfied with David either. It was obvious to me, after a week in Rwanda, that having a big, capable, French-speaking white driver, who was not intimidated by African soldiers, at the wheel of a UN-marked vehicle, was going to be a major advantage when we got to Zaire. Beverley said, dismissively, that she didn't trust David because he had 'the eyes of a rapist'. The third member of the team, Hassan the sound-recordist, was doing his best in a quiet sort of way, but the bullet wound in his leg didn't make for swift movement. We had a week ahead of us in two difficult, dangerous countries, trying to make a complicated film within impossible time constraints, and already the cameraman and pro-ducer were hardly talking to each other.

Things got worse the following day. In the morning David had had to return to UNICEF, to lay the plan which would allow him to take us to Zaire, while we had managed to secure an interview with Alison Des Forges, the greying woman I had spotted eating papaya on my first morning at the Diplomates Hotel. She was an author of several works on Rwanda, and had been visiting and working in the country for years. She was back in Rwanda trying to find out what had happened to a lot of friends of hers, most of whom had been killed, as well as carrying out an assessment mission for an American Human Rights organization. By the time she was sitting in a chair on the terrace, waiting to be interviewed, she had just returned from visiting the site of a mass grave south of Kigali, which she had been told contained the bodies of several friends of hers. She had been crying. I thanked her profusely for agreeing to do an interview with us. We needed her to explain on camera the different roles played in the planning and execution of the genocide by each of the former government ministers and army officers whom we were trying to track down. She'd given us half an hour of her time, and Beverley and Victor were just set to start the interview, when an argument developed between them. Victor went between the camera lens and Alison, and refused to move. Beverley started to shout, and then Victor walked away, standing on a corner of the terrace, swearing under his breath. In the end, Beverley asked the questions, while I kept the camera rolling, changing the focus every five minutes with her help. It was my first experience of using a television camera.

The Rwandan Ministry of Justice had given us permission to film in the Central Prison in Kigali, where an estimated 1600 prisoners were being held by the beginning of September. They were a mixture of former Hutu militiamen arrested by the RPF, known Hutu sympathizers, Rwandan former government soldiers, common criminals and a large number of Rwandan civilians who had been denounced by neighbours or acquaintances for having participated in the genocide. The prison was housed in a 1930s red-brick fort, which lay on a hillside just behind Kigali's central market. It had been built to house about 400 inmates in conditions of acceptable comfort and security, but by the time we arrived it was already grossly overcrowded. I had expected to be escorted inside the walls by armed RPF guards who, I'd thought, would look after us while we filmed. After introducing ourselves to the prison governor, showing our letter of authorization and signing his visitors book, we were led over to the main entrance. There were two sets of barred gates between us and the mob of prisoners inside. Three gaolers, dressed in orange boiler-suits, unlocked the outer gates, through which we passed, leaving the armed Rwandan soldiers outside. In front of us was the other barred gate, pressed against which were hundreds of half-naked inmates, staring flatly at the four of us.

Beverley had dressed suitably for an unescorted visit to an all-male prison full of suspected genocidal murderers. She'd put on white shorts, a sleeveless top in semi see-through silk and her non-leather vegan boots. As the only French speaker, I was going to be asking the questions, while Hassan, limping slightly, would do the sound, and the terrified-looking Victor would film. The moment the gaolers unlocked the inner gate, we were surrounded by young, muscular men, many of whose bare chests were covered with cuts and slashes that had become infected. There was no room to move, so I pushed forward against the crowd to give us two feet of space. There was much arguing as two tall, powerfully built men, both wearing sunglasses, and one sporting a waist-length pink fur coat, pushed their way forward. They identified themselves as in charge of '*liaison*' for the prisoners, and said they would be happy to help with any translations. Meaning to make things easier, I took out two packets of Winston cigarettes and started to offer them round. There was a mini-riot, as some fifty prisoners tried to get to my outstretched hand. We were flung back against the bars of the inner gate as the frantic, screaming gang surged at the cigarettes. After a lot of shouting, the prisoners moved back a foot or so, and I tossed the packet into the air. It was caught by a younger man, who was grabbed by another ten men, until the '*liaison*' man in the pink fur restored order with a series of violent slaps and blows. Calm reasserted itself. Victor and Hassan were now nowhere to be seen, hidden in a sea of aggressive, anxious black faces. Beverley was slapping her clipboard with her hand, demanding silence. Victor reappeared, looking startled, and filming began.

'Please ask this man,' said Beverley to our pink-furred '*liaison*' man and indicating another prisoner, 'why he is in this prison, and whether or not he killed anybody during the genocide, and if so, how many people and why?'

I translated the question from English into French, trying to take off some of the sharp, interrogative edges. I was a newcomer to interviewing these people, but I suspected that a roundabout subtle approach might work better.

Pink Fur Jacket took a drag on one of my Winstons, and translated into Kinyarwanda. The interviewee nodded several times, looked at Victor, said three words, then started to take off his shirt.

Pink Fur Jacket translated back into French, then I told Beverley that we ought to ask the question again. The man's answer had been four words, 'one month, cows,' and 'torture'.

We asked the question again, and this time the answer came back quickly. I suspected Pink Fur was feeding him answers.

'He says,' I told Beverley, 'that he was tending his cows on the hills outside his commune, which is in Bugesera, south of Kigali, in the month of June. He was arrested by the RPF, who then tortured him with machetes and wire. He asks you to look at his arms.'

The man had taken off his shirt and was showing us the skin on the inside of his elbows. There were two deep, swollen lacerations, one on the inside of each elbow, both of which had become heavily infected, and were now bursting with pus. This, the man then explained, had happened when he had been tied up with wire by Tutsi soldiers.

Beverley then asked him why he had been tied up. The translation of the question from French into Kinyarwanda prompted several of the prisoners around us to start removing articles of clothing.

'When the RPF invaded Rwanda,' translated Pink Fur, 'they started carrying out a genocide. They had shot down the plane of the president, and then they started on their plan of extermination. These men here are some of the innocent victims, the few left alive, that escaped the anti-Hutu pogroms that began when the Arusha Accords, designed to let us all live in peace . . .'

I suggested to Beverley that we try another tack. We finally got one of the men in front of us to admit that large-scale killing had been carried out by Hutus, but no, he had not killed anybody, and anyway, these killings were only carried out to prevent a genocide of Hutus being committed by Tutsis. Now, he said, if we didn't mind, could we film his back?

A dozen deep cuts, swollen with pus and heavily infected, crisscrossed his shoulder blades and the middle of his back. This was Tutsi torture, he said, inflicted with a machete. I had no doubt that it was true, but what, I wondered, had he done between April and May that might have merited it? Another man showed us the putrescent flap of skin where his left ear had been. A third, supported by two colleagues, showed us his ankles, ballooning as the skin strained under the pressure of the infected tissue underneath. Both his achilles tendons had been slashed with a machete to stop him escaping.

By now we were surrounded by prisoners removing their clothes. Behind Beverley a man gestured for us to look at a hideous wound on the inside of his upper leg, dropping his stained white shorts as he did so. Then I noticed another man standing directly behind her, eyes closed, face furrowed in concentration, grimy fist pumping furiously at his erect penis.

'Beverley,' I said, raising my arms so that I could push through the crowd back to the gate. 'I think it's time for us to go.'

With the soundtrack of *The Big Blue* playing, David took us the long way round to Zaire. We drove south-west to Gitarama, and then cut through the mountains of central Rwanda to reach Kibuye, set on the eastern shores of Lake Kivu. The lake forms the frontier between Rwanda and Zaire. At its northern extremity, on the border, lies the Zairean resort town of Goma, while at its southern end is the town of Bukavu. Lake Kivu then runs out into the Rusizi river, separating Burundi and Zaire before entering the northern end of Lake Tanganyika, which has Burundi and Tanzania on its eastern shore, and Zaire on its west. Both lakes are volcanic and deep, Kivu formed by the volcanic range of Virunga that lies along the borders of Zaire, Rwanda and Uganda. At least two of the volcanoes in the Virunga National Park are still active. Before the war in Rwanda the park was best known for its large colony of silver-backed mountain gorillas. Dian Fossey's conservation work was carried out in the Virungas, and it was here that she was murdered, almost certainly on the orders of the wife of the Rwandan president.

By early September 1994, the towns of Goma and Bukavu were the epicentres of enormous concentrations of Burundian as well as Rwandan refugees. After the abortive military coup in Burundi in 1993, in which the country's first democratically elected Hutu president, Melchior Ndadaye, was murdered by Tutsi paratroopers, hundreds of thousands of refugees fled, escaping ethnic violence between Hutu and Tutsi that claimed at least 150,000 lives. The majority of these refugees fled into western Tanzania, eastern Zaire and southern Rwanda. After the Rwandan genocide claimed the lives of an estimated 800,000 people in April and May 1994, two million Rwandans, mostly Hutu as we've seen, fled, first into western Tanzania in April, May and June. They established themselves in camps run by the United Nations High Commission for Refugees (UNHCR) on the fertile grass plains around Benaco and Ngara. After the RPF took Kigali on 4 July, one and a half million more Hutus fled south-west across the Zaire border into Bukavu, and north-west into the Zairean town of Goma. To further complicate matters, the Burundian Hutus who had fled north into Rwanda in 1993, now fled *back* into Burundi, establishing themselves in six camps on the Rwandan–Tanzanian borders. This huge dispersal of population could be divided into six effective areas (see map section):

Goma, Zaire: 700,000 Rwandan Hutu refugees in five camps who had fled Rwanda in July and August fearing RPF reprisals after the 1994 genocide. About 50,000 people had died in a cholera epidemic.

Bukavu, Zaire: 350,000 Rwandan Hutu refugees in eleven camps who had fled Rwanda in June and July 1994 to escape the RPF.

Uvira, Zaire (south of Bukavu): 210,000 Burundian Hutu refugees in nine camps who had fled their country in 1993 after ethnic violence following the coup in Burundi.

Rukuramigabo and Magara, northern Burundi: 200,000 mainly Rwandan Hutu refugees who had fled the advance of the RPF in mid 1994.

Ntamba, western Burundi: two camps containing 75,000 Rwandan Hutus.

Benaco and Ngara, western Tanzania: 750,000 predominantly Rwandan Hutu refugees in eight camps who had fled Rwanda in

April and May 1994, many of whom had committed genocide, who were fleeing the early advances of the RPF.

In twelve months, according to the UN report I had on my knees as we drove north now, along the shore of Lake Kivu, there had been 1,200,000 people macheted, shot, drowned, burned, strangled, raped and clubbed to death in Rwanda and Burundi. As a result 2,785,000 people had been made refugees, there had been two coups, two genocides – one of which, in Burundi, was continuing. Three presidents had been assassinated, two civil wars fought, 50,000 people had died in a cholera epidemic, and the international community had done little to try to stop it. This was what happened, I thought, looking at my map of the Great Lakes Region, when two tribes went to war. If anything could exceed the level of death and misery it was only the level of hatred between Hutu and Tutsi.

The last nine days seemed to have been the most dramatic I'd experienced for nearly ten years, since I'd walked across the Djiboutian desert while trying to desert from the French Foreign Legion. Apart from the corpse of an old man in London in the lead up to Lady Diana's wedding in 1981, the bodies at Ntarama church were the first I'd ever seen. A lot of the journalists who had arrived in Rwanda from April onwards had seen wars elsewhere. The civil war and famine in Somalia from 1992–1993 had immediately preceded the genocide in Rwanda, for instance. Yet I somehow doubted whether the events in Bosnia, Somalia, Afghanistan or Lebanon could equal what had taken place in Rwanda and Burundi. It was the vastness of the concept of genocide that was staggering. The more I read my notes and reports, the more I talked with more experienced journalists, and, most importantly, the more I listened to the accounts of the victims and perpetrators, the better I grasped the scale of it all. Nearly a million people killed in six weeks – the total estimate varied depending on whom you spoke to – with agricultural implements, automatic weapons and clubs. At that rate Hitler would have completed the Holocaust in nine months, not six years. Stalin would have exterminated his ninety-five million Russians in a fifth of the time it had taken him. Yes, I began to understand the process of it the more I saw the physical results of the killing – the corpses, the graves, the empty villages. But to understand how and why one part of an ethnically split population was motivated and organized to *exterminate* the other was going to take a lot longer to comprehend. I certainly wasn't going to manage it in twelve days with Beverley. But already, after seeing Ntarama and Kabgayi, the enormity of what had taken place among the eucalyptus trees, along the red dirt roads, and in the towns and villages of Rwanda was beginning to take a hold on me.

In the back seat of our car, however, dramas of their own were unfolding. Beverley was reading Victor the riot act. She was telling him that conditions were going to be a lot harder in Zaire and that she didn't want any repeat of the incidents that had taken place in Rwanda. Tapping her clipboard, she said that had it not been impossible to get another cameraman flown over in time, she would have sent Victor straight back to Nairobi. Even without Victor's look of sullen resentment, it was clear that things could only deteriorate in Goma. David and I grinned at each other as she spoke. It was apparent by now that Victor was an arrogant South African black male who had big problems – understandably – with white people giving him orders. Worldwide Television News in Johannesburg almost certainly employed him as a camera assistant to film in black townships like Tokoza and Soweto where white crews couldn't go. If Victor had been a slightly more accommodating individual and more technically proficient, things might have been better. Instead, Beverley's lack of experience and inflexibility were exacerbating the situation.

The closer we got to Zaire the more nervous I became: conversations with other correspondents in Kigali and Nairobi had done nothing to reassure me. These experienced journalists, most of who had at least one, full-scale, battle-heavy disaster behind them, talked off-handedly about filming Somali inter-clan firefights in the madness of South Mogadishu as 'doing the Mog', and referred to the mujahedeen in Afghanistan as 'the muj'. Conversation at the hotel tables of Kigali had been of narrow escapes in refugee camps, of interahamwe blood-madness in Rwandan churches. For one, getting arrested in Bukavu by drunken, drugged Zairean paratroopers, and being imprisoned for a day was 'a bore'. These foreign correspondents had shivered through Afghan winters together, borrowed each other's satellite phones on hotel roofs in Somalia, moaned about the so-and-so who hadn't returned the five hundred dollars loaned in Sarajevo. Since becoming a journalist in 1989, the furthest I'd gone from home was four days in Belfast. The approaching Zairean border filled me with terror.

We stopped a few miles short of Gisenyi so that we could get ourselves ready. I was assuming that the Zairean soldiers at the border held the power of life and death over anybody who passed through their domain. I was expecting to have all my dollars stolen, my entire collection of jungle survival items confiscated, and perhaps be beaten up. At the very least, I might get a Kalashnikov butt in the face for an out-of-place comment. Rwanda had shown me the extent that people could go to when threatened or when coerced into violence. The RPF soldiers whom we had met had been uniformly civil and helpful, but then, as David pointed out, they would be. They were a conquering force that had won the battle for their own country. They occupied the moral high ground. They had nothing to fear from the press. But there were apparently no rules in Zaire. Mobutu's corrupt government three thousand kilometres away in Kinshasa had bled the country dry. The military and police hadn't been paid. Nothing worked. Inside this crumbling regime was a further kernel of potential horror: the Zaireans, hating the Tutsi Rwandans, had welcomed the refugees with their caravanserai of genocide perpetrators, and were actively sheltering them. We had to get past the Zaireans to reach the violence and chaos of the refugee camps, and then infiltrate these to get to the genocidal Hutus. And this was long before we sat down and accused them of being mass-murderers. My palms were dry, my heart was beating fast, and I was close to panic. I was chain-smoking. We drew away from the banana grove at the side of the road where we had stopped to further conceal our valuables. I was rapidly assessing the worst thing, short of torture or death, that could happen to me. I hadn't ruled out rape. For this reason, I'd discounted the traditional last-resort hiding place, and had all my remaining money and half of Beverley's taped to the insides of my legs. I walked like a cowboy who had wet himself.

David, smoking a Marlboro, took the Isuzu Trooper down a gentle curve where banana trees grew close to the road. Then we were on the wide, tree-lined avenues of Gisenyi. Single-storey villas with red-tile roofs and intricately carved metal balustrades sat on the right hand side of the road. The gardens were full of banana, avocado, lemon and bougainvillea trees. On the left was a line of pine trees, a thin, sandy beach, and the calm ripple of Lake Kivu. A triangular road sign told us that the border post was coming up. I looked at Victor, and was shocked. He looked even more terrified than I felt. His eyes were huge and he was pouring sweat, breathing hard. He must really know something, I thought. Beverley, not interested in the view out of the windows, was ticking something off on her clipboard. David slowed the vehicle as we came around a curve in the road to where a red and white metal barrier stretched across the road. We had to get out of Rwanda first.

Twenty minutes later, passports courteously marked with Rwandan exit stamps, the barrier went up and we were through into a hundred metres of no man's land. Ahead was another barrier, and a single-storey customs building painted yellow and white. We accelerated forwards, and the first Zairean soldier I had ever seen came towards us. He saw the UN markings on the vehicle and lifted the barrier, waving us towards the side of the road. He was wearing the old US Army tiger-stripe uniform, German paratrooper boots and a dark green beret with a large shield-shaped insignia. Around his waist was knotted three turns of pink climbing rope and his sunglasses were white and horn-rimmed. On his Romanian assault-rifle were five magazines taped side-to-side with blue and white UNHCR tape. I got out of the car, my trousers sticking to the insides of my legs.

With David leading, we walked up three steps in to a small office with three desks. There was an up-to-date calendar, showing a giraffe, on the wall. I felt briefly reassured. Surely a group of people who would bother to put up a picture of a giraffe and who cared about what date it was were not going to make me drop my trousers? Victor had been told at the last moment by Beverley that she wanted him covertly to film the entire customs process. He was breathing in and out very fast like a runner. The three people in the office were all in civilian clothes. The man who seemed to be in charge took all our passports and opened a large log-book. In it, I noticed the names and passport numbers of dozens of other western journalists. Another tiny glimmer of hope took hold. Surely not all of these people could have been robbed or sodomized? Catherine Bond, I thought, reading a name sideways. What deprivations had she had to endure to get through? A night in a local hotel with a Zairean paratroop commander making hideous demands? And what had Chris McGreal had to do? Close his eyes against burning tears as half a platoon of Zairean mortarmen loosened their flies and shuffled into a terrible queue behind him?

A man in a white silk shirt with a ruby set on his signet ring took down our details. He handed four of the passports to his colleague who was sitting at another desk. Then he looked up at us and smiled, waiting for an instant that seemed to last hours.

'Have a nice time in Zaire.'

Then he picked up Victor's passport and his expression changed. He snapped his fingers and called him over.

At the other table, the smaller man opened all our passports.

'So, do you want visas?' he asked, without looking up. His stamp was readied.

'We got them before coming,' I explained in French. 'Look . . .' I showed the page with the multiple-entry Zairean visa. It had taken a frustrating day in London to obtain.

He nodded, piling David's, Beverley's, Hassan's and my passports in front of him.

'These four,' he said, 'are acceptable – you will, of course, have to pay fifty dollars . . . administration fee each.'

I was about to leap forward and offer him one trouser-leg's worth of dollars. Then Beverley intervened.

'Tell him please that we'll need an official receipt.'

The man furrowed his brow and looked at her as though she had just announced that she had recently arrived from Saturn. Then he leant forward and took down a green folder marked with a leopard's head. From this he extracted four pieces of carbon paper and four sheets of pink paper. Then he started to write out a laboriously worded request for the acceptance of an administration fee voluntarily given, the proceeds to be donated in total towards the moral upkeep of Goma Customs Post (Main Branch). As he started writing, I walked outside for a cigarette on the steps with David. Another man in civilian clothes came up to me.

'Smoking, you know? It's bad for you. Elvis Presley . . . James Dean? They both died of cigarettes. Now you give me one cigarette and five dollars.'

I did both, then relaxed into a slump on the steps, breathing with relief.

Our four passports were returned to us and we were free to drive into Zaire. Victor, however, wasn't. It transpired that he had visited Goma before and had not had his passport stamped on exit. The customs officers explained very politely to Beverley and myself, in exquisite French, that since Victor had not officially left the country, he must, therefore, still be in Zaire. Therefore the person attempting to get into Zaire on his passport must be a liar, an infiltrator, a spy. He snapped his fingers, called for the sentry, and pointed at Victor, explaining something in local dialect. The sentry called over three other soldiers who had been leaning against a scrubby pine tree at the other side of the road. They pushed into the small room and started shouting at Victor, who began to dig his own grave deeper. He offered the man with the signet ring five hundred dollars to confiscate his camera off him.

It took half an hour of wheedling, as well as a bribe of another hundred dollars, to get Victor into Zaire. He claimed that he had been filming with a German crew last time round and that he had left on a helicopter without getting his passport stamped.

'Victor,' said Beverley, pointing at him and wagging her finger. 'You're fucking lucky that I don't take your passport, your camera and all your money, leave you in no man's land, and get you pushed into the lake.'

'I'll do it for you,' offered David, climbing behind the wheel of the car.

David, Beverley and I were still discussing ways of killing Victor twenty minutes later when we drew up outside the Nyera Hotel, on one of the side streets off Goma's main avenue. After nine days of Rwanda, the menu in the Nyera was a dream. Meat, fresh vegetables, Belgian fish dishes, chips, avocados, prawns and steak. We took three rooms, unloaded the car, and went in to order. The restaurant was on an outside terrace, with pink table linen and maps of the National Park on the wall. The Primus lager was ice-cold and the bread was fresh. Only the flies reminded us of the proximity of the refugee camps. The only other residents of the hotel were two men from the Associated Press, a photographer and a reporter. The photographer was over six foot tall. He had swept-back blond hair, smart sunglasses, a baseball cap bearing the AP logo, worn backwards, and US Marine desert boots. Round his neck he wore two plastic-laminated press passes, and a set of army dog-tags. His Nikon cameras only half obscured the logo on his t-shirt. It was made by Conflict Clothing, like Jonathan's. Dominic Cunningham-Reid's t-shirt had a map of Somalia on the front, and the words MOGGED OUT written on the back.

He and David fell straight into a discussion about ways of getting into the refugee camps. While they talked, the Zairean proprietor of the hotel walked over, proffering his mobile telephone.

'How's Zaire, man?' came the crackling voice of Rudi, calling from Kenya.

He'd had a message from our office in London. They wanted us to go to Kinshasa, find two or three interviewees, and then fly back to Goma. Rudi said he'd do the round trip for thirteen and a half thousand. Cash. In advance, just in case we got robbed in Zaire.

'Rudi, tell them to wait. We might get lucky in Goma. Let's stick to the plan that you come and get us tomorrow afternoon. Ring back this evening if the office in London wants an answer.'

Leaving Victor and Hassan to themselves in the hotel, Beverley, David and I drove off to explore filming. Having a camera with us would have been a good idea. Without it, if we saw anything good, we would just have to return the following day with Victor. It was two o'clock in the afternoon, and the sun was hot. At three-thirty the following day, Rudi's pilot would be on the tarmac at Goma airport. We had a day to find our guilty men. My earlier fear of the Zaireans seemed to have vanished, although I was not looking forward to going into the refugee camps one bit. If I'd been with Dominic Cunningham-Reid, or Jean-Phillippe Ceppi, it would have been different. As it was, I couldn't see any way we were going to track down our men in time. That meant Kinshasa, which in turn meant another, different kind of chaos.

Back at the hotel, we were saved, temporarily, by the screech of brakes outside. Richard Dowden, the *Independent* correspondent, and a woman called Tamsin from the British Overseas Development Agency walked in to the hotel. Richard was after the same men that we were; he knew what he was doing, having covered Rwanda almost from the start. We agreed to follow him through Mugunga refugee camp towards Lac Vert, the hideout of the former government army, the gendarmerie and the interahamwe.

The volcanoes of the Virunga range stood to our right as we drove west out of Goma towards the camp of Mugunga. As soon as we left town, the road, the verges, the dark brown and purple volcanic rock plains, the banana plantations and the clumps of scrub were all full of people. There were people huddled under the ubiquitous blue plastic sheeting given out by the UNHCR, people squatting by fires, people standing in the road, and people lying on the ground. They were cooking on fires of eucalyptus branches, they were pounding maize, they were listening to the radio and they were sharpening machetes. They were arguing with each other, they were defecating on the ground, they were building houses out of branches, they were hammering tins into pots and pans and they were shivering with malaria under plastic shelters. They were dying of cholera, and they were staring at our car and waving their fists. They were drinking Primus and they were laughing. They were hiding weapons, flaunting hand-grenades, laying out stolen sacks of relief supplies, buying tomatoes, edging out of the way of our vehicle and lying dead, rolled up in rush matting. Out of our sight, inside their shelters, they were having sex with each other and conceiving more Hutus.

There were men, women and children. They were carrying yellow jerry-cans, balancing bundles of branches on their heads and holding radios on one shoulder next to their ears. They were pointing gun-like fingers at us, leaning on sticks, staring threateningly, or they were waving. They moved the corpses in the rush matting out of the way of our tyres, or they watched us drive over them. The noise of quarter of a million of them was like a clattering, muttering roar.

We rolled along in first gear, David's hand constantly on the horn. The wave of people parted for us at the very last moment, their bundles and clothing whispering against the sides of the car as we drove. We'd been to see the UN security officer and he had advised us against being out after five in the afternoon and against getting out of the car. We'd heard that people had run over refugees in the crush, and the last thing we wanted was an old woman under our tyres and an angry militia mob around us. We probably would have been fine had we got out of the car, and filmed, but we didn't want to try. Ahead of us Richard's white Land Rover pushed through the throng of people. He was looking for the turn-off on the left through the banana trees and down the track to Lac Vert. Richard had told us that many of the senior Rwandan government army officers along with senior administration officials had taken refuge down by the lake. It meant going off the road for five kilometres, away from any escape route, straight into the lair of the men we were hunting.

It was starting to get dark, earlier than it normally did here on the equator. The sky over the camp was black with volcanic ash and the smoke of 200,000 cooking fires. The air smelt of human excrement, eucalyptus smoke, sweat and fear. The terrifying apprehension I had felt coming across the border had resurfaced and I couldn't wait to be gone. I hoped that our guilty men would not be anywhere near the military camp, otherwise we would have to come back the following day with Victor.

Richard turned off past a scraggy tree bearing a wooden sign pointing to the left. 'Lac Vert', it said. We followed. The tarmac ended and the track became simple volcanic rock. We bounced after the Land Rover, swaying from side to side, winding down the hill, the road disappearing behind us. It was getting gloomier among the trees, and at the side of the road we were passing knots of truculent young men in sodden military fatigues and military boots, some clutching machetes. All of them just staring. They had a way of looking that was slab-faced and hostile, silently, unceasingly aggressive. Every five minutes, Richard or I would lean out of our windows and ask the way to the camp. The young men, all military or interahamwe, pointed further down the track and said nothing.

We drove on, and it started to rain. The sky went from grey to black, and the knots of young men by the road increased. The hard, rock track went through several hundred metres of banana plantation. There was no room both for the car and for those walking. The militiamen stared and hardly moved. Always they gestured us further onwards. Finally Richard braked, and David drew to a halt. I asked some more young men where the headquarters were. They said nothing. Beverley was getting agitated in the back of the car. She kept demanding to know the whereabouts of the camp. In the dark, black volcanic rainstorm of eastern Zaire, to a malnourished, psychotic, traumatized, violent Hutu thug who has been killing and killing and killing for five months, her words could have meant nothing. Her questions were meaningless. All they knew was that the men in charge were at the bottom of the hill somewhere among the banana trees. We stopped again and I got out to talk to Richard. He agreed we should turn round and return to Goma. It was almost dark and we still had forty minutes to drive. David agreed. So did I. So did Tamsin. Beverley thought we ought to continue, accusing us of being scared. She was right. I was. I told Richard to keep our headlights in his rear-view mirror, and as the two vehicles slowly turned round on the narrow path, I looked behind me down the track. A group of ragged men in soaking green army uniform had materialized like shadows from out of the banana trees and were walking towards me. Some had sticks or clubs, and the others were slapping dirty machetes against their palms. Richard had turned the Land Rover by now, and was waiting for David to follow. The militiamen were ten metres behind me as David reversed. They were walking slowly but deliberately, staring ahead at me. The soft, dry slapping sound of stick and machete against palm continued. David had turned round. I got into the vehicle, slammed the door, and shouted 'drive!' We roared off, the tyres throwing shards of volcanic rock backwards. I looked behind, to where a line of fifteen men stood motionless in the gloom, forming a wall across the track where I had been.

When we got back to Goma, David and I went straight to the bar at the Nyera, grabbed three large bottles of Primus, and retreated to our room. We were swearing and cursing at Beverley's stupidity. On the road back, she had gone on and on about how we should have continued, about how David and I were cowards, how we shouldn't call ourselves men. She was in charge, not us. If Richard wanted to turn round then we didn't have to follow him. David said nothing. Later, at the hotel, he said that if Beverley couldn't see the danger, then she was an even bigger fool that he thought she was. I was convinced we'd done the right thing. I had watched the faces of the young men at the sides of the track, and knew there was a point when we had just driven too far. Richard Dowden had known, too.

I ran the deepest bath I could and took off my filthy clothes, untying my money-belt from around my waist, letting everything drop to the floor. I got into the bath. It came up to my neck. It was my first hot water for four days. As the relief of being out of Lac Vert camp came into focus, I realized that we still did not have a second of TV footage of any guilty men. Staring at my toes poking out of the water at the end of the bath, I went over what we had. Kabgayi mission station, with an MSF doctor talking us through the moment he discovered all the bodies. A long walk through the King Faisal hospital with shots of child amputees and different genocide victims. An interview with a legal expert from MSF and lots of general views of Kigali. Us landing in Rwanda, crossing the border, and interviews with interahamwe amputees in Kigali who claimed the RPF had chopped off their legs. Plus, of course, Beverley in Kigali prison. I had no idea what we were going to do the following day. Both David and I were wholly against returning to Lac Vert. We wondered whether there might be a way of finding these men somewhere in town. Perhaps at the Hotel Karibu, where many of the former ministers were meant to be staying. We could worry about that tomorrow, I thought, rising from the bath to dress and move off to the bar for dinner.

The elbow-shaped bar of the Nyera Hotel was crowded when I got there, hair still wet, money-belt full of dollars. The bar was half open to the hot African night, and David was already drinking with Richard, Dominic Cunningham-Reid, and a chunky American who turned out to be Scott Peterson, from the *Daily Telegraph*. I was in good company. Victor and Hassan were having a quiet dinner on their own, Victor eating a steak and looking sullen. I went and told him how risky it had been that afternoon. He was uninterested and said nothing, turning away from me and chewing with solid, bovine concentration. He almost choked on a lump of meat when I told him he should get a good night's sleep because he was going back in to Lac Vert camp the following day by himself, on foot, disguised as a refugee.

David, the others and I took the large round table by the barbecue and ordered supper. Beverley had at last found something she could eat. Chips. This was a good thing because layers of skin were peeling off her face and I was concerned that she might have scurvy. Everybody ordered large steaks, but I wanted to be more adventurous, so ordered an avocado with freshwater prawns. I didn't stop to think where the prawns might have come from. We had South African red wine to go with our Primus, and the atmosphere at the table was good. Beverley, sitting next to Richard, claimed that he was trying to rub his hand up and down the inside of her leg. After the main course, half of which I couldn't eat, because my prawns tasted the same as Kabgayi had smelled, we had pudding and switched places at table. Richard said he knew which rooms at the Karibu hotel were occupied by Rwandan ministers and former army officers. He was staying there and had been watching them for three days, he said. Taking out a pencil, he wrote 'Bizimungu – 26,' and 'Bizimana – 13,' on a paper napkin. He allowed me twenty seconds to read it and memorize it before screwing it into a ball. Bizimungu and

Bizimana were the former Rwandan chief of staff and the former defence minister respectively. I nodded over at Beverley, who was resisting Dominic Cunningham-Reid's attempts to push a large forkful of pink steak into her mouth. She got up, we went over to the bar, and I told her the news. She smiled, and clapped me on the arm.

'We'll go over there first thing tomorrow and bump them at breakfast time. Great.'

We returned to the table, and shortly afterwards Beverley announced that she was going to bed. She would not be joining the rest of us at the Hotel Karibu, where Dominic said there was a party for 'loads of Dutch nurses'.

David, Dominic and myself climbed into the Isuzu and headed off into the night. We went through the dark streets of Goma, and to the Karibu Hotel, which was lit up, busy, and had a car-park full of expensive vehicles. Although it was less than a kilometre away from Mugunga refugee camp, it was a world away. The hotel was full of flashily dressed Zairean couples, and the dining room was crowded. The party for the Dutch nurses was, in fact, a private Zairean wedding. We drank Primus in the garden and watched a hundred couples swaying to the singing of a local man. He was wearing one white glove, a bowler hat, a red jumpsuit and pointed Chelsea boots with glitter on one of them.

'He's Goma's number one Michael Jackson', a pair of Zairean women informed us. They drifted over to our table by the swimming pool and tried to sit on our laps. They told us that the real action to be had in Goma that evening was in a club on the main street, so we boarded the Isuzu and set off.

The doorway to the Hole in the Wall Club was barricaded with a piece of corrugated iron and guarded by two Zairean bouncers, who let us in for ten dollars each. It was crammed with aid workers, Zaireans and soldiers. Bottles of Primus were passed over our heads by sweating drinkers, and I drank warm gin and tonics at five dollars each. A crowd of Dutch aid workers joined hands and swung round to a Bryan Adams song. I suspected that General Bizimungu or defence minister Bizimana could have been somewhere in the throng, jiving earnestly to Cher singing 'the Shoop-Shoop song', but if they were I wouldn't have recognized them. A man with a scar across his nose and wearing a shimmery silver suit with nothing underneath the jacket breakdanced furiously in front of the three armed Zaireans by the turntables. Finally he leant backwards and fell into the lap of an Irish aid worker. At four-thirty, David drove me back to the hotel, left me collapsing into bed, and returned to the dance floor.

Breakfast passed in the warm, disjointed fog of a hangover whose component parts were red wine, gin and Primus. I hadn't heard David come back in so was surprised to find his driving functional that morning. By the time we arrived at the Karibu Hotel, I was feeling sick. We crunched over the crushed volcanic rock that passed as gravel on the paths of the hotel garden, and stopped in front of room number thirteen. It was a bungalow overlooking the lake. Nobody answered our repeated knocking. The reception desk refused to tell us the name of the guests in each room, saying that they had a number of Rwandans staying, but that they had all left for Kinshasa. A knock at the door of number twenty-six proved more fruitful. We heard feet approaching, and then the door was opened. The man standing there was either Rwandan or Zairean, I supposed, and was wearing nothing but a tight, red thong, stained at the front. He asked us what we wanted.

'Good morning, sir,' said Beverley, as Victor filmed the man scratching his chest. 'Are you General Augustin Bizimungu, former chief of staff of the Rwandan Armed Forces?'

The man looked at us. He examined my press pass carefully, blinking in the warm Zairean sunlight. Behind him in the bedroom, I could see two slender African girls. One was sitting on the end of the bed putting on her bra.

'Sir, we would like to ask you about a number of events that took place in Rwanda between April and June this year. Events that led to the deaths of many people.'

Beverley turned to a page on her clipboard that listed various massacres.

The man pushed one hand down inside his thong, scratched vigorously, then wiped his nose with the same fingers.

'I'm a business man,' he said, beginning to close the door. 'I am here with my daughters. We are here for commerce. The Rwandan problem does not affect me,' he added, pushing the door shut in our faces.

A slow drive through Mugunga camp yielded nothing more than a lot of footage of the same refugees we had seen the afternoon before. They looked less threatening in the sunlight. We did not go down the track to Lac Vert. By the end of the morning we were sitting in a dusty café facing out over one of Goma's roundabouts. We had four hours until Rudi's plane arrived, when, it seemed, we would go home empty-handed. Next to us was an affluent-looking Zairean man with a gold identity bracelet and sky-blue silk shirt, talking loudly on a clumsy portable phone. He finished his conversation, put the phone down, and was about to pick up his coffee cup when the waiter approached him.

'Anything else, Mr Mayor?'

Beverley and I, sitting at the next table, looked at each other and raised our eyebrows.

An hour later, we were sitting in the red, furred upholstery of a large, white Mercedes driving towards an appointment with two men. They were men, the Mayor had assured us as I passed him three hundred dollars on the café terrace, who had been high up in the former Rwandan regime.

The car twisted and spun through Goma's back streets up to a house surrounded by a high, white wall, where it tooted at the gate. A muscular man with a bare chest, carrying a Kalashnikov, opened the gate. He looked over us, then waved us in. The Isuzu followed. We got out, and were lead towards two chairs in the shade.

'Here,' said a welcoming man in a dark suit and red tie, 'you can wait for the president.'

Neither Beverley nor I had any idea who was coming out of the house. Around the inside of the garden walls, three men carrying machetes walked along the edges of the flowerbeds. The engine blocks of our cars ticked as they cooled. The sun was directly overhead. Every ten minutes an aircraft, a Boeing 737, or Hercules or a Russian Ilyushin would scream into Goma airport, full of relief supplies. Finally, we sat on the lawn in the shade of an avocado tree, and were introduced to two men who seated themselves opposite us. We prepared to do the interview.

They introduced themselves as Joseph Nzirorera and Matthias Ngirumpatse respectively. Next to Beverley, I sighed with relief. Thank God, I thought. With only two hours to go, we had fallen on two of the original architects of the genocide. Nzirorera was the former secretary-general of the MRND, the hardline Hutu party created by President Habyarimana in 1973. Sitting in front of me in a pair of black slacks and a black silk shirt, he was a close friend of the late former president, and came from Gisenyi, the same part of Rwanda. He was widely credited with being behind the arming and training of the interahamwe. Matthias Ngirumpatse, a lawyer, had been minister of justice in 1992. He was the brains behind the militias, and chairman of the MRND.

We sat for an hour with the two men as the sun burned down overhead and I began to wonder if I was getting heatstroke. I was feeling disorientated. Around the garden walls the men with the machetes prowled and the relief flights screamed overhead.

Nzirorera blamed the international community for putting the population of Rwanda into such panic in April 1994 that a genocide was allowed to occur. Both men insisted that the RPF had carried out genocide since it tried to invade in 1990. Nzirorera insisted it was impossible that a million Tutsis had died as there had only been some 700,000 in Rwanda in early 1994. Both men said that there should be a tribunal established to discover who was really guilty, and both men blamed the United Nations for deserting Rwanda. But it was when Nzirorera, exasperated, said that even if he was imprisoned or condemned to death, his party would continue the fight, and would return to Rwanda to kill more Tutsis, that I knew we had got what we'd come for.

He then leant over, waited for the camera to stop rolling, and asked Beverley out to dinner with him the next time she was in Paris.

She was still tutting about the predictability of men an hour later when we loaded all our equipment onto one of Rudi's Beechcraft at Goma airport. David stood at the bottom of the aircraft steps with

Dominic as we closed the door. We taxied towards the end of the runway, past an encampment of Foreign Legion paratroopers, and to the take-off point. The pilot accelerated the engines, let off the brakes, and minutes later we were airborne.

'Two and a half hours flying time to Nairobi,' he said, as we climbed into the bright blue sky.

'We're clear of Zairean airspace, now,' he assured us, leaning back from the cockpit.

At that moment, there was a lurching, burping feeling in my stomach, as though a lift had suddenly descended. It seemed that a large, liquid weight was moving towards my colon, unstoppable, pressing. We were clear of Zairean airspace, but not of the effects of Zairean food. The reason the freshwater prawns had smelt of death, I realized, was because they could only have come from Lake Kivu, into which thousands of cholera victims had been thrown over the last six weeks.

Looking behind me, I saw there was no lavatory or enclosed space on the plane. We had two and a half hours to go.

'Beverley,' I said. 'I want you to talk to me and distract me. Just don't let me think of anything below my waist.'

Then I clenched.

Chapter 2

Where Were You on the 6th April?

Victor was shot in June the following year. He was driving in Burundi with a WTN producer, Vincent Francis, in a convoy that included the US Ambassador. They drove into an ambush north of the capital, Bujumbura. Their car was stopped, Francis was shot, and Victor was forced to kneel at the side of the road. The gunmen who had carried out the shooting – thought to be Hutu rebels fighting the Burundian Tutsi government – ransacked their vehicle. Victor was then shot with a Kalashnikov at point-blank range and left for dead. When he regained consciousness he was in hospital in Bujumbura, and Peter Smerdon, the deputy bureau chief from Reuters in Nairobi, was trying to prevent Tutsi militiamen from breaking into the room to finish him off. Victor was lucky. With head wounds and his camera hand mangled, he and Smerdon left Bujumbura on a charter flight. The body-bag containing the corpse of Vincent Francis was stowed at the back of the Beechcraft. Victor never filmed again.

Ten months after our charter aircraft left Goma, my bowels gurgling with the onset of amoebic dysentery, I went to live in Africa. I based myself in Nairobi as the East Africa correspondent for the *Sunday Telegraph*. By September 1995, I had made four more trips to Rwanda, and was beginning to understand some of the complex events that had surrounded me on my first journey the previous year. The more I tried to make sense of what had happened, the more it became evident that the mass killings of 1994 had been the culmination of political and socio-economic developments in Rwanda dating back years. Hatred, mistrust and paranoia between

Tutsi and Hutu had not developed overnight. The plane carrying the Presidents of Rwanda and Burundi had not been shot down by accident by some soldier fiddling with a missile. Hutu hardliners had been plotting the genocide. There had been mass killings in Rwanda over thirty years prior to 1994, and the corpses I had trodden on at Ntarama church were produced by a hundred years of politics and social history. Hutu and Tutsi had been deliberately stage-managed by the Belgians into a falsely balanced relationship of superiority and inferiority. But the tiny central African country that had found itself at the centre of international news from 6 April 1994 onwards, had once been a state where Hutus, Tutsis, and the Pygmy minority, the Twa, had coexisted comparatively peacefully.

The enormity of the events that took place in Rwanda after the start of the genocide meant that most journalists' stories were occupied by the vast death tolls, the epidemics of biblical proportions, the movements of millions of people. There was little space for background information, for any explanation as to why nearly a million people had been killed by their fellow citizens. There was lots of talk in the media of 'traditional ethnic animosities', and 'long-standing tribal rivalries', and the 'knock-on effect of ethnic slaughter'. But Rwanda was more complex than most journalists – myself included – had imagined.

The 1994 Rwandan genocide had, by late 1995, elevated the country's political and socio-economic importance to a level far beyond what would be expected of the world's nineteenth least-developed country. Over 150 aid organizations were based there. Rwanda, and its refugees in neighbouring Zaire, Tanzania and Burundi, had become a source of extremely lucrative contracts and projects for every kind of humanitarian and development aid organization. The continuation of crisis in the region was to suit the aid organizations very well: it raised their profile, raised their income from government, private and UN grants, and sustained their existence. The UN continued to spend a million dollars per day maintaining the refugee camps in Zaire alone. There were some 3500 UNAMIR troops in Rwanda, and the country was constantly on the agenda of the UN Security Council. Like Afghanistan, the former Yugoslavia and Cambodia, Rwanda had, by its internal political and social failings and the persistent inability of the outside world to resolve them, become a country that, in terms of international profile, was a whole lot greater than the sum of its parts.

It had not always been thus. Before the arrival of Europeans in the late nineteenth century, Rwanda had existed as a feudal state ruled by a king. It is a small country, comprising 26,400 square kilometres of highly fertile land set on a range of hills that averages 4000 feet above sea level. Not for nothing did the early European explorers call it 'the land of a thousand hills'. Deep valleys, steep slopes, rolling pasture and thickets of trees predominate. There are also two main forests, at Gishwati in the north-west and Nyungwe in the south-west. The rest of the country is as agricultural now as it was a hundred and twenty years ago when it was first visited by white men at the beginning of the 1890s. The climate is subtropical and yet temperate. The temperature remains a steady average of 20°c all year round, and there is abundant rainfall. In some parts of the country it has been possible to harvest four crops per year. In 1994, at the end of the genocide, the avocados, bananas, sweet potatoes, maize, cabbage and corn had grown in abundance, and not been picked. The harvests rotted on trees and in fields in eerie juxtaposition with the corpses rotting and buried all over the countryside.

By 1900, early explorers had discovered that Rwanda was also an extremely crowded country, even by African standards. Rwandan social and agricultural society was traditionally based on the politics of the hill, where every inch of available land was allocated and farmed. Under such circumstances, dense overpopulation by closely interlinked and hierarchical social groups all keen to exploit the soil, required a highly evolved social and political form of control if conflict was to be avoided.

Nineteenth-century Rwanda rose to this challenge. Resources were limited, the need for food was great, the geographical movement of the population was restricted, and the density of the population was twelve times the average of other sub-Saharan countries. Nevertheless, the three ethnic groupings of Hutu, Tutsi and Twa managed to live together, to intermarry, and exploit the land to their mutual benefit. Four-fifths of the population were Hutu, one fifth were Tutsi, and the Pygmies, or Twa, made up a tiny percentage. If anything, these Twa were the original inhabitants of the area that is now Rwanda, Burundi and eastern Zaire. They were forest-dwelling hunters who made excellent trackers and soldiers, and who fell between the two ethnic stools. They were used as agricultural labourers and mercenaries by Hutus and Tutsis alike, and mildly discriminated against on the basis of their size and physical differences.

Today, Pygmies continue to fulfil this role. In the massacres that followed the 1993 coup in Burundi, the Tutsi army and the Hutu rebels both employed the Twa to carry out massacres for them. A Methodist missionary who watched the Pygmies fighting in Burundi recalls them going into action – 'battle' would be an incorrect term for a massacre of mainly women and children – armed with Kalashnikovs, machetes, spears and blowpipes. A piece on Burundian television about the Twa featured an interview with an adolescent Pygmy, who was asked by a grinning Tutsi what he wanted to do when 'he was bigger, and had grown up'.

The three groups were not tribes, in the way that the South African Zulu or Zimbabwean Shona are tribes, but socially and politically differentiated ethnicities. They spoke the same language – Kinyarwanda – and were all part of the same Banyarwanda tribal grouping. Under their king, or mwami, they tilled the land, harvested it, sowed, reaped, grazed cattle, waged war on their enemies and consolidated their territory. Their life was little different to that lived by fifteenth-century Gaelic warriors, except there were more of them, on less land, and the weather was better.

The mwami was, to all intents and purposes, God. A separate vocabulary existed to denote his daily activities. His authority was embodied in a traditionally sacred drum, the *kalinga*, which was decorated with the testicles of his slaughtered enemies. Beneath the king, the court and the land were administered through a complicated system of hierarchical administrative structures comprising chiefs, tax collectors and soldiers. Different chiefs were in charge of the administration of different aspects of land management, from agricultural production to taxation. Most chiefs were Tutsi. Taxes, in the form of money, collective labour, beef, milk and agricultural produce, were paid collectively by each community. By the mid-nineteenth century, it was possible to generalize and say that Hutus tended towards growing and tilling, and Tutsis towards cattle ownership. As cattle were the central currency and asset, the balance of power favoured the Tutsi on the whole. This was, however, by no means absolute. Prior to the 1860s, many chiefs were Hutu, and some Tutsis farmed the land. The army was ethnically mixed, and intermarriage common. As society was patrilinear, a Hutu woman marrying into a Tutsi family assumed her husband's ethnicity, and vice versa. Ethnic equality was not an issue. The social structure that was in place had existed *per se* for over 400 years.

The mwami was at the centre of this universe, and beneath him, in an expanding pyramid structure, authority was devolved right down to the individuals who controlled each parcel of land on each hill. When I questioned people in Rwanda about the way their country was organized, each person, for whatever area, could trace a direct line of authority from him or herself directly to the government. The basic unit of administration was the sub-sector, comprising a group of ten houses with their attendant plots of land. This extended to the sector, then to the sub-commune, then the commune, then to deputy provincial level, then provincial and then governmental. Given that in many places in the country, a hill of one square kilometre would be inhabited and farmed by two to three hundred people, this meant that every square metre of land was part of a huge, multi-tiered chessboard, administered in a straight line from the king.

The harmony of the three different ethnicities changed at the end of the nineteenth century when white men arrived. In Kinyarwanda they were known as the *abazungu*, while in coastal Swahili they became known as *wazungu*. The phrase had come to mean white man or outsider. The first white men were German, and then Belgian. The famous explorer John Hanning Speke landed on the edges of what is now Lake Tanganyika in the mid 1860s, at the town of Nzanza-Lac in southern Burundi. He did not, however, enter the territory that is now Rwanda. He described Hutu, Tutsi and Twa as 'barbarous'.

Probably the first *mzungu* to arrive in Rwanda was the German Graf von Gotzen, in 1894. Africa had been carved up at the Berlin Conference in 1885, when the British, Germans, Belgians, French and Portuguese decided who would get which chunk of the continent to oversee. The Germans got Rwanda and Burundi, which was administered as a province of German East Africa, known as Ruanda–Urundi. After the First World War, with the Germans defeated, Belgium took over the colony under a League of Nations mandate. The mwami continued to rule. But while the Germans had been content to oversee the country almost at a distance – before the First World War there were fewer than a hundred Germans in Ruanda–Urundi – for the Belgians, running the country as they saw fit meant exacerbating the ethnic links between Hutu and Tutsi to suit their own ends. Ruanda–Urundi was nothing like the Congo, where, under Leopold II, they had fiercely exploited the country for its natural resources, mainly rubber. Still, they made dramatic changes to the culture and society of their little Rwandan colony. The ethnic differences and hatred between Hutu and Tutsi that exploded in the 1994 genocide began with the Belgians.

By the time they left Rwanda to elections and independence in 1959, the Belgians had made three vital changes to the pre-colonial order in the country. They had introduced Christianity, they had changed the ways in which the ordinary people were obliged to pay taxes and supply communal labour and, most importantly, they had changed the way that the Hutu and Tutsi in Rwanda saw themselves. Bolstered by the legacy of the early European explorers, obsessions with 'race-science' and their theories that the tall, fine-boned, thin-nosed, slender-fingered and aristocratic-looking Tutsi were of superior racial and geographic origin to the Hutu, the Belgians introduced the concept of ethnic difference and inequality.

John Hanning Speke, who claimed to have discovered the source of the Nile in Lake Victoria, thought the Tutsi were descended from an Ethiopian tribe, the Gallo, who were Nilotic. Other Germans, Italians and Belgians variously credited the Tutsi with descent from

Egypt, Melanesia, Asia, India and Tibet, while more extreme theories claimed that they had come from the Garden of Eden, Iceland and the lost city of Atlantis. The Hutu, with their flatter faces, earthen fingers, and thick lips, farmers and cultivators of the land, came from the 'negro breed' whom Speke described as wanting nothing more than a life of 'drinking, singing and dancing like a baboon', when not occupied with farming and the conquest of neighbouring land. The Tutsi, these Europeans decided, were the ones who could be entrusted with power. By 1959, 95 per cent of chiefs in Rwanda were Tutsi, although they made up only 14 per cent of the population.

Under this system of Tutsi domination, the Belgians implemented a second form of social change and control, again based on the idea that the cattle-owning Tutsi were intrinsically superior to the field-digging Hutu. The collective system of taxes and communal village labour that had existed in pre-colonial times was abolished. Now the Tutsis oversaw a system whereby every member of every agricultural family provided communal labour such as digging ditches, felling trees, clearing land, re-foresting and building roads, at the same time as paying exorbitant taxes, via the Tutsi chiefly hierarchy, to the Belgian government. When crop-growing and herding for their patrons was taken into account, a Hutu family could easily spend up to two weeks every month forced, under the threat of violence, to perform tasks that provided nothing for their own benefit. In 1931 and 1932, the three different ethnicities of Hutu, Twa and Tutsi were all issued with identity cards by the Belgians, further dividing the population along ethnic lines.

In 1932 the Belgians found a king they could deal with, Mwami Mutara Rudahigwa. He was sympathetic to their western ideals, converted himself and the whole country to Christianity, and allowed the Belgians to run the country as they wanted to. This split the pro-Belgian Tutsi elite from their compatriots still further. As Christians and chief, they were given priority in education, and a head start in the crowded Rwandan employment sector. The struggle for privilege, for education and for jobs, was the same as the struggle for land and power in the rural communities. The Tutsi also realized faster than the Hutus – because they were closer to their colonial masters – that if they sided with the Belgian colonial concept of administrative and political reform, they would benefit. By 1959 the number of Tutsis in university education was almost double that of Hutus. This, combined with the different policies of labour, taxation and religion meant that by 1959 Hutus felt inferior and exploited. They began to accept the concept of Tutsi hatred as central to their ethnic identity. It was the Tutsis, their former ethnic brothers, who they had come to believe, through subtle manipulation, were responsible for their oppression. In seventy years, the Europeans had created a new Rwanda that suited them. But the centre could not hold for long.

Political parties were formed at the end of the 1950s into pro-Belgian Tutsi, anti-Belgian Tutsi, and Hutu. But as the Tutsis' political arrogance increased, the Belgians were now starting to come round to sympathizing with the Hutus. When violence between the political parties erupted in 1959, as if they could not make the situation any worse, the Belgians backed the Hutu. Their support for the Hutu led to an ethnic shift in power. In early 1960, they replaced most of the Tutsi chiefs with Hutus, who in turn immediately led anti-Tutsi rampages all across Rwanda. This provoked a mass exodus of Tutsis to Uganda and Congo.

The Belgians organized communal elections in 1960, and nearly 65 per cent of the votes were won by the newly formed Hutu party PARMEHUTU. Under the leadership of Gregoire Kayibanda, this party, which drew most of its support from the north-west of the country, oversaw the creation of a new administration in Rwanda. Chiefs were abolished, and replaced by 229 new 'communal' leaders, called 'bourgmestres'. Ninety per cent of these were Hutu, 70 per cent of which were hardline PARMEHUTU. As violence continued between Hutu and Tutsi, and as the latter fled the country in ever increasing numbers, the Belgians and the largely Hutu government administrators met in January 1961 and declared the Republic of Rwanda to be independent. Twelve years of ethnic violence was to follow.

The influences of one hundred years of involvement by the

Catholic church, Germany, Belgium and France in the lives, administrations and social structures of the Rwandan people can be seen simply by looking at the Christian names they chose for their children. At the font, priests suggested suitable names to their parishioners. But when left to choose for themselves, Rwandans, coming from a society where the individual had little control over the running of his or her daily life, seemed to vie with each other for the most florid, historically complex and religious names.

They began with simple, god-fearing ones, such as Dieu-Donne (God-Given), Archange (Archangel), and Marie-Vièrge (Virgin Mary). Next came inspiration from the religious calendar: Fête National, and Fête de Roi (the Feast of Kings), which was the same as Epiphane. On the Zairean–Rwandan border in 1995 I met a Hutu refugee woman from Butare called Jean d'Arc.

From the Old Testament came Melchior, Balthazar and Evariste, from the New, Xavier and Innocent. Dismas was the name of the good thief next to Jesus at the crucifixion, who asked for his forgiveness. The German Protestant tradition was evident in names such as Froduald and Landwald; Greek and Roman mythology with Venuste, Aphrodite, Juvenal and Apollinaire, while from Middle Europe came Protais, Ponthien, Eustache and Sixbert. Classical Latin provided the name Dative, but the most bizarre and imaginative names Rwandans simply made up to coincide with activities going on around them. If Fête National was a name given to a baby born on one of Rwanda's public holidays, then Monoprix must have been chosen by a member of the elite while wandering around a French supermarket. Roi-Louis (King Louis) is a wonderfully inventive name for a child that was probably born somewhere on a muddy Rwandan hillside. And one can only deduce that a father, somewhere in Rwanda, had been dreaming of public service and watching football when he named his son John Pele Fireman.

By the time of independence, Rwandans were predominantly Catholic; in some communes, church-going was practically compulsory, and names of those who did not attend were listed and reported to the local mayor. Although the country was flooded with aid workers – its orderly, non-political society making it almost a darling of foreign donors – and despite the over-population, there was no birth control. More Hutu babies simply meant, after all, less space for any Tutsis, whose numbers were now subjugated officially to 9 per cent of the population. Each commune had its school and its hospital. Chapels and small churches abounded on the hundreds of hills: little red-brick buildings looking over the terraced farm plots, the dirt tracks, the banana trees, and the lines of digging, hoeing, cultivating peasants. If the Rwandans gave their souls and their prayers to God, then they gave their time and their energy to their social and administrative superiors. Those at the top took, and those at the bottom gave. Increasingly, they gave their time and their physical labour. The results were everywhere to be seen: roadside ditches were dug, irrigation systems plotted, and forestry controlled. The European Union had provided a number of Paved Road Grants to Rwanda – and Burundi – and the results were evident by the time I came to be driving across the region from 1994 onwards. From Kigali northwards to Ruhengeri and Gisenyi, south-west towards Gitarama, Butare and Cyangugu, and east towards Kibungo and Tanzania, the roads were surfaced to an almost European standard.

The first outbreak of ethnic violence in an independent Rwanda was in December 1963, by which time nearly 150,000 Tutsis had left. In that month, a group of Tutsi exiles tried to invade Rwanda from Burundi. Using this invasion as an excuse, President Gregoire Kayibanda's government slaughtered 10,000 Tutsis in eight weeks, including every remaining Tutsi politician. Hutu hardline politics were now firmly in place. Kayibanda effortlessly reproduced the authoritarian political tactics of the Belgians, and of the mwamis before them. Hutus were given priority in education, in the military and in the civil service. The official percentage of Tutsis in schools, university and the civil service could not be more than 9 in concordance with the official percentage of Tutsis in Rwanda. As a result of the former Belgian favouritism for the Tutsis, they often held key jobs, particularly in the civil service, the largest public employers in the country. Hutu extremists did their best to have them ousted from these positions. At the same time, Rwanda's economy plunged, the predominantly peasant population suffered famine on three different occasions, political splits worsened between PARMEHUTU and its 'softer' southern Hutu colleagues, and the army seemed on the edge of rebellion. Tutsis were still fleeing the country, and were building up a diaspora, living mainly in Uganda, estimated to be over 500,000 strong. Without the country they continued to be indiscriminately hunted down.

Hutu paranoia of Tutsi intentions was strengthened in 1972 when the ruling Tutsi minority in Burundi massacred some 200,000 Hutu to secure their hold on power. When the Rwandan army chief of staff, Major-General Juvenal Habyarimana, carried out a bloodless coup in July, 1973, everybody heaved a sigh of relief. One of the first things he did on assuming power was to promise Tutsis that their safety was assured.

President Gregoire Kayibanda starved to death in his prison cell in 1976. Habyarimana, a hardline Hutu from Gisenyi in the north-west, outlawed political parties in favour of his own, the National Revolutionary Movement for Development (MRND). Every single Rwandan had to be a member of the party and, along with a commitment to communal agriculture, communal labour, almost compulsory attendance at church and the carrying of identity cards declaring both ethnicity and commune of origin, the state verged on the totalitarian.

President Juvenal Habyarimana was not, among the Rwandan Hutu elite, considered to be an aristocrat. He didn't come from a family with any long pre-colonial history that could trace its lineage back to the time before the Europeans arrived. He came from the commune of Giciyi, a deep valley in Gisenyi. It was arch-hardline Hutu territory, prime PARMEHUTU land, and a strange, ghostly place. Down on the valley floor there is a river, with clusters of villages strung along the road. But the hills flare up to two thousand feet the moment you turn off the track. Among the windblown pine trees and eucalyptus forests at the top you feel you could be in Montana, rather than on the equator. To the north-west lies the hideout of the Gishwati forest, and then Lake Kivu and Zaire. It was even said that Habyarimana was descended from

Ugandans or Zaireans. His wife, Agathe Kanzinga, was also from Gisenyi province, but she had a well-established lineage, a chiefly background, and a family-backed, rural power base to support her.

Rwandans were afraid of Agathe. She was reputed to be a witch. A Rwandan woman I had questioned about the president's wife told me that it was clear that she was a sorceress. She had been seen dressed in the skin of snakes and wearing glasses that stopped the daylight from touching her eyes, a sure sign that she was in league with the devil.

There was a simple explanation for this, one that says much about Agathe Habyarimana. After the RPF took Kigali in July 1994, two journalists I knew were among those who looked round her looted, destroyed palace, fishing for souvenirs. The alleged sorceress liked shopping in France, a country which by the late 1980s was increasingly backing the Rwandan government. She was happy in Paris, and on the streets of Geneva, as many other dictators' wives had been before her. There is something about the high fashion, the explosive prices, the bowing shop assistants on the Faubourg St Honore and on Geneva's rue de Lyons that puts African dictators and their wives at their ease. It is, presumably, a feeling of being attended to, of being deferred to by the white man. When you are Agathe Habyarimana buying white leather cocktail dresses and red acrylic hot pants with dollars that you have stolen from your country's international aid budget, it feels doubly right. You are, after all, only returning the money to the country from which it came.

In her ruined Kigali residence, among the serried ranks of French cosmetics, the trashed wardrobes full of ballgowns, and the white plush carpets on which the teenagers from the conquering RPF had left their diarrhoea, there were a couple of snakeskin cocktail dresses. They were made for a large woman. Corinne Dufka, the Reuters photographer, kept one of them for a while, but then threw it away. It was almost twice as big as she was, she said, and anyway, it had bad associations. But for a Rwandan peasant woman from Gisenyi who had never been to the capital, let alone to Paris, stories of the president's wife wearing a cocktail dress of snakeskin and a pair of horn-rimmed sunglasses was clear proof that here indeed was a mistress of Lucifer.

And Agathe, like any good witch, was plotting. She had her own little cabal of cronies, fixers, sympathizers and henchmen. They came from the same family, the same commune, the same complex Hutu lineage as she, which traced its links, and loyalty, back to the mwamis of old. Since Rwanda was without a multiparty political process, power devolved to those who were closest to it, but without a strong Hutu lineage of his own, Habyarimana increasingly relied on that of his wife. Agathe's henchmen came to be known as the 'akazu', from the Kinyarwanda word for 'little house', referring to her private, personal court. There were seven or eight men directly allied to her, either from her immediate family or related. These included four hardline army colonels, one of whom, Theoneste Bagosora, was to play a leading part in the implementation of the genocide. Anybody who crossed the akazu or who tried to interfere with their hold on power was making a mistake. In April 1988, Colonel Stanislas Mayuya, a friend and close associate of President Habyarimana, was murdered. He was thought to be setting himself up for the position of vice-president. He was killed by Colonel Laurent Serubuga, one of the insiders of *le clan de Madame*, as the akazu was also known. The sergeant who actually carried out the killing, and the attorney who organized an investigation, were also murdered by Agathe's henchmen. The President's private aide, Colonel Elie Segatwa, was also inside Agathe's group. He later switched his allegiance to Habyarimana, and was in the president's plane when it crashed on 6 April 1994.

With nearly eight million inhabitants Rwanda was vastly overpopulated, and land was more scarce than ever. The illiterate peasants had no choices in their lives: everybody voted for the MRND (Habyarimana had gained 99.98 per cent of the votes in 1988) and everybody did as they were told. The country was organized as it had been under the mwamis except that now power ascended in a straight line to the president, and his wife. The unit of land and social management was still the *colline*, or hill, with the lowest unit of people management being the *sous-secteur*, or sub-sector made up of ten houses and families, run by a chief who reported to a head of sector and so on.

There were eleven *prefectures*, or provinces. In the west, in Byumba and Kibungo, the landscape was rolling hills, parkland and swamps. On the border with Tanzania was the Kagera National Park, from which the animals, apart from some gazelle, had long since been driven away by hunting and poaching. Journalists visited the hotel in the park after the genocide, and discovered that it had been taken over by animals: cows were grazing the gardens and baboons were sitting on the sun-loungers by the pool.

Kigali province was in the middle of the country, divided into two: Kigali, and Rural Kigali, which stretched all the way down to the Burundian border in the south. Ruhengeri and Gisenyi, where the hardliners came from, were in the north-west, Kibuye and Cyangugu in the west and south-west, on the edge of Lake Kivu, and Gikongoro and Butare in the south, on the Burundian frontier. Gitarama was bang in the middle. Each province had a capital, from which it drew its name.

Rwandan society under Habyarimana was extremely ordered. When I had visited the grounds of the Kabgayi seminary in 1994, where 1,800 people had been massacred, I had picked up several identity cards of people who had been killed. That of a woman born in 1938, surnamed Kabasinde, was typical. She came from the prefecture of Gitarama, where her number was 311,703. She lived in the commune of Mugina, but had been born in Nyamabuye and, in 1994, when she fled to Kabgayi, she had been living on the hill called Kiyonera. She'd had four children, one boy and three girls, and the eldest girl – and second child – had died in 1966, less than a year old. Kabasinde's father's surname was Mubeuka, her mother's Kibanje. She couldn't drive, had no bank account, had never been to a state-registered hospital, and her occupation, like millions of others was *nzi*, farmer. Her identity card was stained with mud, earth and water, and had been taped back together. She was clearly one of several wives, as there was no name of a husband. Before fleeing to Kabgayi she had never travelled out of her home commune, and in place of a signature there was an inky thumb-print. She could not read or write. She was a Hutu.

A black-and-white photo of her showed a young woman in a striped, scallop-necked top, a skirt wrapped around her as far up as her chest, wearing a white headband. That she had abandoned her identity card – her most vital possession after her money – showed that she had been killed, even though she was a Hutu. Her Christian name was not recorded.

The peasant populations grew different crops, depending on the height above sea level of their particular province. Cattle were everywhere, while in the higher lands of Ruhengeri and Gisenyi, in the foothills of the Virunga volcanoes, cabbages and sweet potatoes were staple crops, along with beans. The soil was darker, contained more potash, and was very fertile. Maize and corn were grown in Gikongoro and Butare, which were slightly flatter and better irrigated provinces, while Kibuye, Byumba and Cyangugu were the staple areas for coffee and tea, the country's two main cash crops. Avocados and bananas grew everywhere.

Rwandan peasants, like poor Africans everywhere, lived on a staple diet of ground maize meal, oil, beans, salt and tea. In Kenya this maize- and corn-meal cross between porridge and cake is called *ugali*, in Uganda *posho*, in South Africa *pap* and in Zimbabwe *tsadze*, all varieties of a high-starch meal that is low in proteins and vitamins, and which, if taken as the main source of nutrients from birth, as it often is, can lead to severe deficiencies. Rwandans supplemented it with oil, avocados, beans and eggs, and when possible, beef or meat from a goat. Banana beer was brewed and, for the more affluent, there was Primus, bottled in Burundi, Rwanda and Zaire. An Englishman who worked for the Primus breweries told me in September 1995 that the amount of formaldehyde put into Primus varied from country to country. It depended on how long the beer was expected to be kept before being drunk, and the number of impurities that crept in during the bottling process. In Zaire, he said, the supply of currency was unpredictable, and thus so was the predicted shelf-life of the beer. More importantly, as rats, snakes, rodents and other impurities were alleged to get into the vats in

Bakavu, the amount of formaldehyde tended to be higher. Rwandans were cagey, he said, about formaldehyde. With their paranoia about being poisoned, they liked to know what was going into their beer, so less went in to Rwandan Primus than Zairean. Burundi put the least preservative in the tall, three-quarter litre, brown bottles. The biggest single client of the brewery in Bujumbura was the military, who consumed their beer almost as soon as it was issued. Keeping the troops in a state of permanent semi-drunkenness was reckoned to be one way to make them more malleable to the idea of killing civilians.

In 1996, when I lived in Burundi, no military road-block in any of the more violent and combat-heavy provinces was complete after midday without its crate of Primus and its half-drunken patrol of soldiers. In the barrack-room where the bodyguards of the Burundian president slept when off-shift, only two images featured in the pictures and magazine photos stuck up on the walls: the Princess of Wales, and tall, golden bottles of Primus.

Under Habyarimana the country pulled itself up from qualifying in World Bank statistics as the seventh least-developed country in the world in 1976, to the nineteenth in 1990. This was partly because Rwanda was not at war, and therefore qualified for enormous amounts of foreign development aid. To western politicians in Europe, Canada and North America, Rwanda was the only country in the region that did not have some form of armed conflict or political disintegration going on within its borders. There was the MRND party, and that was the state. Uganda had undergone its own massacres under Amin, followed by invasion from Tanzania and a decade of civil war. Tanzania, at the end of the Cold War was for the West that most feared of bogeymen: a socialist state. Even worse, she was supported by China. Zaire, under Mobutu, had ceased to function as an economic entity. In Burundi, the Tutsi elite were so desperate to retain power that their record for ethnic violence far surpassed anything Rwanda had come up with in the preceding thirty years. In 1972 nearly 200,000 Hutus had been killed in the tiny country, whose ethnic make-up, agricultural economy and power structure were remarkably similar to neighbouring Rwanda's. Belgium, France, Switzerland, Scandinavia, America and Canada queued up to donate money to Rwanda. And social indicators in the 1980s appeared to show that this aid was having some effect on standards of health, education and financial development. Donor aid, being the self-perpetuating financial phenomenon that it is, continued to flow. The hundreds of aid workers based in Rwanda could argue that it was worth continuing to fund the country, because the more money they pumped in, the more standards continued to improve. By 1990 they were pushing more than US$150,000,000 per annum through the diminutive state. Switzerland in particular found that Rwanda conformed to its ideal of tidiness and industry, and gave more money to it than any other: it is for this reason, as well as for its physical geography, that Rwanda was given the nickname 'Switzerland of Africa'.

Madame Habyarimana was more than happy with this. Not only did it mean more snakeskin cocktail dresses and sunglasses, but it meant that her akazu had to rely less and less on skimming the country's regular cash exports – coffee, tea and tin – for their financial subsistence. Then, in the mid eighties, coffee prices fell and tin ceased to be a viable form of income after the world market prices dropped so low that it was not worth trying to produce it. This translated into a gross shortage of foreign capital and less money to run the government and the enormous bureaucracy and civil service that it supported. Less money, too, for the Hutu elite to cream off. The administration became increasingly dependent on foreign aid as a source of supplementary income, and the people far more reliant on agriculture. By 1988, Habyarimana, his wife, and all the other clans, families and inter-married associated Hutu political groups were struggling to hang on to money and power. When the government budget was cut by 40 per cent in 1989, it was the peasants that bore the brunt of it. Increased corruption followed at government level, as competition for decreasing resources *increased*, and the already tightly stretched, over-worked peasant population was asked to produce more food, dig more roads, graze more of their superiors' cattle on less and less land. The population went on growing and the supporting social back-up systems weakened. In 1990, Habyarimana attended a Franco–African summit, and heard from President Mitterand that he wanted to make Rwandan eligibility for US$38,000,000 worth of annual French bilateral aid dependent on democracy. He saw change in the wind. So did Madame Agathe Habyarimana, and her supporters. If multi-party politics were introduced, then even more parties would be pushing for a slice of a steadily shrinking cake and her power would diminish. And all of this was before anybody in the Rwandan Hutu government took into account the armed and increasingly aggressive and vociferous Tutsi exiles massing in Uganda. Madame Agathe needed new allies, more powerful than those she found around her. And she needed them fast. They came to her rescue just as her increasingly beleaguered husband announced, that summer, that he was in favour of multi-party politics.

A military training and technical cooperation agreement had existed between Rwanda and France since 1975, two years after Juvenal Habyarimana came to power. Under this agreement, France was permitted to train and give technical advice to the Rwandan army and air force, but was not to intervene militarily. However, the agreement was signed between Habyarimana and Mitterand's Ministry of Cooperation – nobody else. If France overstepped the original rules of her agreement no other country was going to be in a position to complain. By 1989 there were over 400 French civil and military personnel inside Rwanda, part of France's annual thirty-eight-million-dollar aid package. These 400 personnel included a number of military training officers and senior paratroop non-commissioned officers (NCOs). France also exported some military equipment to Rwanda. By the late 1980s this material support consisted of ten Panhard-90 armoured cars, four Gazelle helicopters, some anti-aircraft weapons and, most crucially, a number of MILAN anti-tank missile systems. The French military training and assistance team was known as the DAMI, or Detachment d'Assistance et de l'Instruction. It was almost permanently based in Rwanda from 1986 onwards, according to French special forces personnel who served with it. The military assistance was predomi-nantly based on training given by special forces teams. In addition to these instructors, there were a few regular army men teaching the Rwandan government forces in the use of artillery, signalling equipment and the use of the Panhard armoured cars, as well as the flying and maintenance of the Gazelle helicopters.

As far as the French government was concerned, Habyarimana's MRND party was the democratically elected power in Rwanda, and in supporting him, financially and militarily, they were supporting French interests. Rwanda was no different from every other African country in which they then had influence. In 1985, these included Gabon, Senegal, Ivory Coast, Zaire, the Central African Republic (CAR), Chad, Burkina Faso, Djibouti and the Comoros Island of Mayotte. Troops were permanently based in Mayotte, Djibouti, the CAR, Gabon, and on the Indian Ocean island of Réunion. These 9,500 troops were split between personnel from the French regular army, the navy, the Marine Commandos and the French Foreign Legion. The benefits for France were obvious. In Djibouti, Senegal, the Ivory Coast and Mayotte, France could take advantage of a deep-water port. Combined with a network of troops stationed across the continent, with ready access to airstrips, this meant that French troops could react at very short notice anywhere in Africa or the Middle East. They could carry out operations to rescue French expatriates at risk from civil unrest or military disturbance, or they could counter threats to French interests.

Economically speaking, France was keen to capitalize on reciprocally advantageous deals, such as the mutual military intervention policy it had signed with Gabon. French troops were based in Gabon as part of a security and training force; they also provided the executive security for the Gabon government's economic policy, which included supplying France with uranium at advantageous prices. Elf-Aquitaine, drilling for oil off the coast of Congo, owed its presence there to a defence agreement France signed with the Brazzaville government. Preferential treatment was also accorded to French companies in the awarding of contracts in Djibouti, Senegal and the CAR. The mutual intervention treaties signed by all these states were simple. If Gabon, or Djibouti or Mayotte, for example, were externally threatened, they could ask France to intervene militarily. Most importantly, France could intervene without being asked.

Habyarimana enjoyed French military and economic support because his country was Francophone, and because he was seen to support French interests in the region. The point was not that the French particularly objected to countries such as Rwanda *not* speaking French, but they were aware that a change in the language could only come with a government that was not necessarily committed to beneficial relations with France. Much has been made of France's desire to keep large parts of Africa French-speaking. Many people have argued that for France, cultural and linguistic domination of their former colonies were ends in themselves, to protect which they were prepared to go to any lengths, even as far as backing a regime as murderous as that of the Rwandan Hutu interim government in 1994. But the political extremism and lack of political hope that was to lead to the 1994 genocide in Rwanda were some years in the future at this point. It is unlikely that between 1985 and 1992 the French military personnel based in Rwanda were aware of any plans connected with mass-killings, politically affiliated slaughter, or genocide. They were simply keen to maintain their African sphere of influence. Language was no more than the most obvious signifier of the sympathies of a country whose economic, strategic and political ends were of interest to the French.

France's policy in the Elysée presidential palace in Paris was formulated by a separate department, the Africa Office, or *cellule d'Afrique*. This was run, up until 1992, by François Mitterand's son Jean Christophe, known popularly as *Papa m'a dit*, or 'Daddy told me to'. His role was to oversee the administration of the commercial, military and economic links between the French government and its African satellites. This was a fluid mandate, and could include such tasks as arranging the supply of French prostitutes to the Gabonese president and expensive gifts for African leaders, like the Mystere Falcon-50 executive jet and crew he gave to President Habyarimana in 1990. It also included briefing domestic and foreign intelligence on which European arms traders were currently in vogue with the

French government. Decisions about France's African interests were also coordinated by the Ministry for Cooperation, which, after 1990, contained a department that dealt with the military aspects of their alliance with Rwanda, including the coordination of arms supplies. Assistance in setting up and maintaining recruitment, surveillance and trafficking operations fell to the French domestic intelligence services, the Direction de Surveillance de Territoire (DST), and the external intelligence services, the Direction Generale de Service de l'Extérieur (DGSE). As French army officers often provided information for the DGSE, and as DGSE agents were often former army personnel, the lines could become blurred. Personnel involved in African operations were sometimes on secondment from the French Foreign Legion, regular army parachute regiments, the Marine Commandos, or the French gendarmes' anti-terrorist squad, the GIGN, or Groupment d'Intervention de la Gendarmerie Nationale. These men from two government departments, two different intelligence services, one police unit and three competing army special forces units all met at the centre of a Venn diagram over central Africa. The ambiguous lines between the departments, agencies and units assured a level of unaccountability should any of these operations go wrong. All these things were eventually to transpire in Rwanda.

How did the French army and intelligence services feel about Rwanda? Rwanda was not like Algeria, or Indo-China, former colonies which the French had felt were almost part of metropolitan France. All the same, the small central African state formed part of the French *pre carre*, or backyard, in Africa, and as such had to be looked after and protected. This translated into keeping it economically, politically and strategically onside, as well as shielding it from non-Francophone influences. French soldiers of the former colonial army, including the French Foreign Legion, had felt so strongly about the decision of de Gaulle to give independence to Algeria in 1962 that they had mutinied. Many senior French officers felt similarly sentimental about France's protectorates in black Africa, although it is doubtful they would have mutinied to protect them.

The tendency within the elite of the French armed forces to

mythologize and romanticize its past is very strong. The 11th Parachute Division, and especially the Legion's 2e Régiment Étranger de Parachutistes, believed strongly in a proud military tradition of battle-honours won on the fields of Indo-China and Algeria. Both were former colonies where the salt of the French army had fought, and won battles, only to be betrayed by politicians back home. There was a whimsical belief that the colonial lands rightly belonged to France, but that history had always seemed to snatch them away. If one adds to this self-belief of the military elites an ideological conviction, endorsed from the president downwards, that it was of paramount importance to keep France's African lands French-speaking and French-thinking, then one can begin to understand why a country as small and insignificant as Rwanda mattered so much.

For the French, the only visible alternative to a Franco-sympathetic Rwanda, run by a French-supported Habyarimana, was the anathema of an Anglophone Rwanda controlled by Ugandan-backed Tutsis. The French were much further sighted than their African friends: they were watching the developing power of the Rwandan refugees in Uganda, who were close to and allied with the soon-to-be Ugandan president, Yoweri Museveni. They predicted an attempt on Rwanda by 1991 – in which they were proved correct – and they felt strongly that a loss of Hutu power in Rwanda could only lead to a destabilization of Mobutu in Zaire, and an extended threat to French-sympathetic governments in central and west Africa.

It was with this mindset that French military instructors were serving in Rwanda in the late 1980s. There were personnel from the French regular army and from the 11th Parachute Division's regiments. This division was made up of all the regular army parachute regiments, including the 1er, 2e, 3e, 5e and 8e Régiments Parachutistes d'Infanterie Marine d'Assaut, or RPIMAs. It also included the 35e Régiment Parachutiste d'Artillerie, based at Tarbes in the Pyrenees, as well as the Régiment Hussards Parachutistes. Most importantly, it contained the French Foreign Legion's 2e Régiment Étranger de Parachutistes, based at Calvi in Corsica. Each of these regiments included one reconnaissance platoon which acted as a form of special forces unit. The platoons were trained in a variety of disciplines, including counter-terrorist warfare, amphibious warfare and high-altitude military free-fall parachuting. They were also trained to act as instructors for other military units. Within their regiments, they were normally known either as the Chuteurs Operationnels, after their parachuting techniques, or, more commonly, as the Commandos de Recherche et de l'Action dans le Profundeur, or CRAPs. This was an acronym whose irony was not lost on its many English-speaking members.

Small numbers of men from the CRAP special forces platoons of the 11th Parachute Division arrived in Rwanda from 1987 and 1988 onwards as part of the Detachment d'Assistance Militaire et de l'Instruction. For the Foreign Legionnaires at least, it was a choice assignment, second only to being posted to the island of Mayotte. After training in mainland France and Corsica, and postings to the jungles of French Guyana and the deserts of Djibouti, Rwanda was a rest. The French aimed initially at improving the skills of the Rwandan regular army and the Presidential Guard. These included such disciplines as artillery fire-control, basic tactics, use of mortars and small arms, signalling and strategic command of units in the field. They set up a commando school and a number of assault courses based on their system back home. The Rwandan gendarmerie were given instruction in drill, discipline, use of firearms and crowd-control techniques. In 1988, the thought of genocide in Rwanda was far away; the concern for the Rwandan government was a possible Tutsi invasion from Uganda.

This worry became reality on 1 October, 1990. The political situation in Rwanda had become increasingly tense, and Habyarimana found himself threatened from both inside and outside his country. The Tutsi guerrilla forces in exile, calling themselves the Rwandan Patriotic Front, finally invaded from Uganda. Both President Museveni of Uganda and President Habyarimana were abroad, away from their respective countries. On 4 October, France intervened, at Habyarimana's request, and a personal visit to the French minister for cooperation in Paris was made by Rwandan Foreign Minister Casimir Bizimungu. Paratroopers were flown in. In fact, on hearing of the invasion from Uganda, Mitterand had already told his minister of defence, Louis Joxe, that intervention was necessary. In turn the commanding officer of the 2e REP deployed 150 men from the Central African Republic's capital of Bangui to Kigali, three hours flying time to the south-west. *Opération Noroit* was underway.

Several hundred troops from President Mobutu's Presidential Guard Division also deployed to Rwanda, as did half a battalion of Belgian paratroopers. The Rwandan government was successful in repulsing the RPF in fighting during which the Tutsi commander, Fred Rwigyema, was killed. Some allege that he was killed by his own men, but it was more likely that it was an accidental shot fired by a retreating member of the Rwandan government forces known as the Forces Armées Rwandaises, or FAR.

French and Rwandan concerns focused immediately on the possibility of a repeat invasion, and they started formulating plans that might prevent it. Certainly, for Habyarimana, the Tutsi invasion confirmed his fears of a menacing Tutsi diaspora, intent on resettling Rwanda. And if the initial offensive by the RPF had been repulsed, by 1991 the fighting in the north of the country was continuing. The commander of the RPF was now one Paul Kagame, a capable and popular officer who had been on a military training course at Fort Leavenworth in the United States when his fellow Tutsis first invaded Rwanda. In January 1991, Paul Kagame attacked the north-western town of Ruhengeri, the heartland of the Hutus, and ten miles north of where Habyarimana himself came from. As the counter-insurgency war in the north continued, so the involvement of the French deepened. The troops serving on *Opération Noroit* were no longer the single company of the 2e REP coupled with a few teams of their special forces colleagues from *les CRAP*s. Their strength had grown to over 600, and by mid 1992 there were some 850 French troops based in Kigali. Their proximity to, and control over the military aspects of the regime of President Habyarimana was increasing.

Their tasks had now devolved into several separate areas of operation. French troops were actively in charge of coordinating and leading the Rwandan government army, the FAR, in action on the ground. They also ran parts of the intelligence services for the government and controlled Kigali airport, into which increasingly large amounts of arms were flowing. They controlled training of the Rwandan armed forces and, in May 1992, a Lieutenant-Colonel Chollet was given command of all operations involving the FAR. In Paris, they were backed up at governmental level at the Africa office of the Elysée, the Ministry for Cooperation and at the Ministry for Defence.

If the French were later behind the shipments of weapons for a large-scale re-arming of the FAR and the Hutu militias in 1994 and 1995, it was nothing in comparison to their programme to arm them the first time round in 1992. France supplied the Rwandans with arms directly, as well as through Egypt and South Africa. Other countries that delivered weapons to the Rwandan Hutus were Russia, the Czech Republic and Slovakia. The French state-controlled bank, Credit Lyonnais, insured for six million dollars in 1992 a huge delivery from Egypt, and in the same year, the South African government company, Armscor, made a deal with Habyarimana worth another six million. A good idea of what the FAR and the Presidential Guard were receiving can be gained by looking at detailed lists of each shipment.

The Egyptian deal comprised the following:

450 Egyptian copies of Chinese AK-56 or Russian AKMS
   Kalashnikovs
2000 land-mines
200 kilos of high-explosives
6000 high-explosive mortar-rounds for 120mm mortars
70 × 60mm and 82mm mortars
10,000 mortar rounds
6 × 122mm D-30 artillery howitzers
3000 artillery shells
2000 rifle grenades and RPG-7 grenades
3 million rounds of 7.62mm, 9mm, 5.56mm and 12.7mm
   ammunition

The South Africans then supplied more:

250 7.62mm SS-77 belt-fed machine-guns

3000 × 5.56mm R-4 assault rifles, as supplied to the South African army

10,000 × M-26 fragmentation grenades

30,000 × 40mm grenades

70 × 40mm grenade launchers

100 × M-1 60mm mortars

1.5 million rounds of .50 calibre heavy machine-gun ammunition

25 × .50 calibre Browning machine-guns

These large shipments of small arms were just what was needed for the low-intensity bush war that the FAR and the Presidential Guard were fighting against the Tutsi RPF. The high concentration of mortars was perfectly suited for short-range offensive war, while the Egyptian copies of Kalashnikov and the South African R-4 assault rifles were ideal for use at ranges up to 400 metres in the bush. As they arrived, all of these weapons would have been distributed by the French military personnel, who would also have carried out all training in their use.

The Rwandan army had grown from a strength of about 5000 in 1988 to some 45,000 men by 1993. A number of the CRAP corporals, sergeants and sergeant-majors were soldiers who had attended so-called *Commando Moniteur*, or Commando Instructor courses at the French regular army training school at Mont St Louis in the Pyrenees. Along with French weapons training and tactical expertise, commando techniques formed part of the infantry training being given to the FAR and the Presidential Guard.

While it is impossible to pretend that the French troops in Rwanda were ignorant of the existence of the increasingly violent militias attached to the Hutu political apparatus, it is a moot point as to whether they actually trained them. They didn't need to. Their military role in Rwanda was intended to provide their Hutu allies with the necessary logistical wherewithal and military expertise to defeat the RPA in classic and guerrilla warfare. They trained, led and operated with the FAR and the Presidential Guard. These were the men who formed the vanguard of the killers, the shock troops of the genocide. In the first twenty-four hours of the massacres, the Presidential Guard was responsible for a large percentage of the killings in Kigali.

It is almost impossible to conceive that the French would have been officially allocated to train the youth militias. However, the French military was fully aware that weapons from its supplies were being used to carry out civilian killings before 1994. And Rwanda was not Europe; the selection procedures for French military training courses would have allowed militiamen through their vetting process. The interahamwe were essentially trained and organized by civilian extremists, but the Presidential Guard and the FAR were involved in their training and they were armed with weapons provided by the French. Many of the recruits to the FAR came from the militias, and recruits to the Presidential Guard from the FAR. By 1993, when the majority of the men deployed on *Opération Noroit* went home, there would have existed a cadre of several thousand soldiers who had been trained, directly or indirectly, by the French military. It is inevitable that as the European troops relinquished command of the Rwandan army's operations, discipline would have plummeted. Members of the FAR who either deserted the army, or who left, would have attached themselves to the militias.

When, in 1994, I interviewed the former MRND officials Nzirorera and Ngirumpatse in Goma, they said, off-camera, 'the French made and kept the interahamwe'. This is not strictly accurate. The French special forces instructors instructed Rwandan army soldiers. In the social collapse of 1994, these men went on to massacre Tutsis or trained men who did. The French trained men *who carried* out a genocide, not *to carry* out a genocide. But when the killings started, the thousands of men they had trained were at the forefront of the action.

If the French military teams and their Rwandan army counterparts had been busily engaged in fighting and organizing a counter-insurgency war against the RPF, then similarly dramatic developments had been taking place within the political arena. Madame

Habyarimana, her band of followers and her husband's government were, by 1992, under more pressure than ever before. In April 1992 a new cabinet was sworn in; the MRND and its sub-division the MRND(D), the National Revolutionary Movement for Development *and Democracy*, had to share power. However, they kept half the cabinet ministries. Habyarimana had been forced to accept power sharing with the largest opposition party, the MDR, and there were even to be peace talks with the Tutsi RPF. The akazu was not taking this well. Prior to the advent of political power sharing, there had been a spate of violence in 1991 and 1992. Political hardline militias, coerced by local authorities and aided by the peasant population, had claimed the lives of hundreds of Tutsis. These killings were normally presented either as self-defence against the RPF, or aimed at pre-empting attacks by Tutsi on Hutu.

The hardliners were getting nervous. As if power sharing wasn't enough, the new constitution demanded that the president step down as head of the armed forces. It said that the Service Centrale de Renseignement, the SCR Secret Service, in the running of which the French were deeply involved, should have its powers curtailed. For its part, the SCR cadres that supported the continuation of a single-party state run by the MRND(D) simply moved closer to the akazu. Killings continued in the countryside, justified by the RPF threat and the constantly reiterated whispers that the ultimate aim of the Tutsis was to rise up and slaughter all Hutus. MRND(D) cadres and hardline Hutu politicians oversaw the planning and implementation of the killings. An element of collective guilt was introduced among the peasant population who were coerced into carrying out the actual slaughter. It was ten Tutsis here, nine there, fifty on this hill, twenty-two on that. The orders for the killings were given in the same manner as for the *umuganda* or communal labour. Killing Tutsis was for the 'communal' good. The physical actions of slaughter were represented in the same vocabulary used to denote key tasks of agricultural labour: 'bush-clearing', 'weeding', 'cleaning', 'sorting out the good from the bad'. The RPF continued to carry out guerrilla actions in the north-west. There were violent demonstrations for and against political power sharing, minor army mutinies, more ethnic violence camouflaged as work for the 'communal good', and an economy on the verge of collapse.

The war against the Tutsi, even with French support, was costing Rwanda twenty million dollars a year. In two and a half years, half of the country's hard-currency reserves had been spent; the Rwandan franc had halved in value and foreign debt had reached almost a billion dollars. A grudging peace was signed with the RPF in July 1992. Habyarimana was obliged to enter into regional discussions at Arusha in Tanzania to work out the modalities of power sharing, both political and military, with the RPF. It should be stressed that the antipathy, aggression and coerced violence against the Tutsi ethnicity was the work of the MRND(D) hardliners, rather than Habyarimana himself. He had announced on his accession to power that violence against the Tutsi should cease, and he had tried to keep to his word. But by the end of 1992, power was slipping away from him in a direction that could only spell disaster. Anti-Tutsi violence flared up again in response to the news of the peace process: Hutu hardliners, from the MRND(D) and the almost more extreme Council for the Defence of the Republic (CDR), attacked Tutsis in the Kibuye region. Nearly 100 were killed and some 500 wounded. Once again, the local peasants had been briefed that there was 'communal work' to be carried out. 'Important bush-clearing work' had to be finished. So out came the machetes, and then it was time for the night-time patrol up into the hills to the houses where everybody knew the Tutsis lived.

CDR demonstrations in Kigali and Ruhengeri came out openly on the side of the French, whom the Hutus saw as their last hope to block any Tutsi involvement in the political and military process. The French training of the FAR, the Presidential Guard and the gendarmerie continued: an estimated 1400 French combat troops were in Rwanda at the end of 1992. The FAR and France's other trainees were instructed in all sorts of disciplines: laying mines and preparation of explosives, hand-to-hand fighting, house-clearing, signals, artillery techniques, anti-aircraft and anti-tank warfare, shooting, small arms drills and first aid. And the arms continued to flow along with the training personnel. From June 1992, the man at the helm of the French Presidential Palace, *cellule d'Afrique*, was Bruno Delhaye. He provided firm support from Paris for the French officers fighting their bush war two thousand miles further south near the equator.

Madame Habyarimana, too, had been busy. Allegations were that the akazu were behind the creation of the so-called 'Zero Network' death squad, which had been implicated in some of the massacres in 1991 and 1992. The *Reseau de Zero* was meant to be made up of soldiers, former members of the Presidential Guard, and SCR intelligence agents who had refused to dilute their power by accepting any political opposition. It also included members of the MRND(D) and CDR youth militias. The primary instinct of this organization was to resolve any political and military impasse by the implementation of selective, anti-Tutsi, anti-liberal-Hutu violence. Behind it was Madame Agathe's akazu, containing her three brothers, the president's personal aide, Colonel Elie Segatwa, Colonel Theoneste Bagosora, the cabinet director of the Defence Ministry, and the heads of military intelligence and the Presidential Guard.

French involvement in the background of this organization was by now complicit: they had trained the Presidential Guard, they assisted in the running both of the SCR and the military intelligence services, and they had armed the army. They knew by early 1993 that both the MRND(D) and the CDR had created militia youth-wings. These were known respectively, in Kinyarwanda, as the 'interahamwe' and the 'impuzamugambi', 'those who work together', or 'those who work together for a common aim'. These groups were armed by various factions of the army, and a number of their members had in fact been trained by the French, both when they wore the uniform of the FAR or the Presidential Guard, or when they had managed to infiltrate French training programs in the preceding three years.

The RPF attacked Rwanda again in January 1993, advancing south from Byumba in the north-east. They had attacked in response to the killings of up to 300 people by interahamwe and impuzamugambi militiamen in the north-west of the country. They nearly marched as far as Kigali, but halted by mid-February. The DGSE, or French external intelligence services, blamed the 'Ugandan' RPF for a massacre of Hutu civilians they claimed had been 'found' by FAR troops inside RPF territory. In other words, the French were now overtly backing the interahamwe actions. Three hundred extra French troops had been sent to Kigali on the news of the RPF attack, along with additional supplies of ammunition. It was probably their presence in the capital that prevented the Tutsis from attacking it. Violence was accompanying every political development: every move by the RPF, every concession made by Habyarimana at Arusha during the peace talks, every proclamation made by liberal Hutu politicians was answered by MRND(D) and CDR killings. And these killings were carried out by the interahamwe and the FAR, in an intelligence operation run by the French army.

Increasingly armed and, if not directly and personally physically trained by the French, then tangentially approved by them, the militias were encouraged in their work still further by the broadcasts on Radio Mille Collines. This station, a subsidiary of Radio Télévision Libre des Mille Collines, or RTLMC, was based in Kigali. It had started broadcasting in August 1993, and was owned and financed by Felicien Kabuga, a businessman who had bankrolled the interahamwe. It was a populist broadcaster full of catchy music, the perfect listening antidote for the Hutu peasantry when engaged in some mindless, collectively authoritarian task such as ditch-digging, road-clearing or tree-felling. The music and political exhortations were interspersed with endless anti-Tutsi proclamations, calling on the Hutu 'faithful' to act against the Tutsi *inyenzi*, or cockroaches, as the RPF were known.

The paranoia of the Rwandan Hutus was rigorously reinforced in October 1993. Melchior Ndadaye, Burundi's first democratically elected president, was kidnapped at gunpoint in Bujumbura by a small unit of Tutsi paratroopers, then taken to a military barracks where he was beaten to death with machetes and a hoe. The reaction of the Hutus in the Burundian countryside was immediate: some 45,000 Tutsis were slaughtered in under a week in a systematic reprisal action coordinated by Hutu communal leaders and politicians. One hundred and sixty thousand Tutsis fled to army-controlled 'safe areas' while the Tutsi military are estimated to have killed 30,000 Hutus and sent another 300,000 fleeing as refugees into Rwanda, Zaire and Tanzania. For the increasingly desperate and marginalized hardline Hutus in Rwanda – now coming to be known as '*les power*', or 'Hutu Power' – this was the final proof they needed that there was a deliberate Tutsi plot afoot to wipe out Hutus. Radio Mille Collines picked up the ball and ran with it. Their message, repeated again, and again, and again, like a dreadful, repetitive dirge, was simple: the Tutsis are going to kill you. The Arusha Accords are just a bluff. Now is the time to arm yourselves and do the work that has to be done. Send the *inyenzi* back where they came from.

On my first visit to Kigali, I had interviewed a Tutsi nurse at the King Faisal hospital who told me that through the second half of 1993 there were almost daily appeals on the radio for an increase in anti-Tutsi violence. While Beverley, the luckless Victor and I had been tracking down our Hutu ministers in Goma, another team from our programme had flown to Montreal. They'd gone to find Leon Mugesera, until 1994, the vice-president of the Gisenyi branch of the MRND(D), whose speeches to the Hutu party faithful were often broadcast on Radio Mille Collines. Armed with a tape-recording of one of his speeches made in 1992, our camera crew tracked him down to a supermarket in Montreal. The bespectacled man cornered by the dairy produce fridges in a Canadian delicatessen seemed a long way from the man who had given the famous speech whose message was that one of the Hutu's main mistakes had been to allow Tutsi exiles to escape Rwanda unharmed in the 1959 pogroms. All Tutsis, he had said, should be thrown into the Nyabarongo river – which flows towards Lake Victoria – it was time to 'wipe them out'. Confronted on camera, Mugesera was unapologetic.

In the last days of 1993, with militia violence on the increase, the first UN peacekeepers started arriving in the capital and the French officially departed. The peace talks in Arusha, signed in August, had stipulated that a peace-monitoring force should be deployed from the United Nations to allay the fears of both sides. UN Resolution 872 created the United Nations Assistance Mission in Rwanda (UNAMIR), mainly composed of Indian, Bangladeshi, Belgian and

Senegalese troops. The force went some way towards settling Tutsi fears about the increase in militia-organized violence. The Arusha Accords allowed, principally, for political power sharing and an ethnically united army. The MRND(D) and the CDR, the interahamwe, the akazu and the Hutu hardline elements saw their power-base disappearing. They were convinced that the RPF was rearming in Uganda – it was – and was intent on reinvading the country. It was. They saw their allies, the French, deserting them, and their formerly sympathetic President Habyarimana compromised. It was the beginning of the end. An essentially political process interspersed with occasional violence had not worked. The hated RPA *inyenzi* had even been allowed to station 600 men in Kigali as part of the Arusha Accords. Hutu Power's supply of military support was flying back to Paris – only seventy French soldiers remained in Kigali by New Year 1994 – and RPF delegates were starting to demand to know why the Arusha conditions were not being met. Perhaps, thought Hutu hardliners, now was the time for the 'final solution' long mooted as the only answer.

Radio Mille Collines continued to churn out its propaganda. The RPF Radio Muhabura replied by denouncing the distribution of arms to Hutu militiamen. UNAMIR sent another 1000 men to Kigali. The RPF demanded to know when they could start implementing the power-sharing schemes of Arusha and threatened to break the ceasefire if Habyarimana didn't act; even President Mobutu of Zaire stuck his oar in and encouraged Habyarimana to get on with the process. The akazu drew up lists of those whom they had decided must die if they were to reclaim the situation. The radio never stopped. Arms distribution continued furiously despite weak protestations by the European Union and UNAMIR. The Rwandex Chillington company had a metal-works factory in Kigali, owned by a Briton, which produced agricultural implements including hoes, scythes and simple lawnmowers. It produced and sold more machetes in February 1994 than in the whole of 1993. And still Habyarimana dithered about implementing the terms agreed in Arusha.

Violence broke out in Kigali and Butare at the same time. Fifty people were killed before and after the assassination of an opposition politician in Kigali. UNAMIR informed the UN Security Council that it could do nothing to stop the distribution of arms to the militias: the UN refugee agency warned of a bloodbath. Still the radio repeated its messages, breakfast time, lunch time, in the afternoon and in the evening. Kill the Tutsis. The work has to be done. If the work is not done you will be killed yourselves. The *inyenzi* are preparing for their own version of the slaughter in Burundi. President Habyarimana will sell you out. Now is the time to prepare your weapons. Put the Tutsis in the Nyabarongo river where they belong. Think of the work that has to be done. It is only to prevent the cockroaches from killing our president and taking over the country. Our friends the French cannot help us any more. Prepare yourselves. And so it continued, four times a day, every day, week in week out. We will not, said the radio, allow ourselves to be killed. We will kill you.

And through these weeks of chaos, as Kigali descended into a free-fall of political violence, as exhortations to ethnic violence were read out over the radio four times a day, every day, as the main cities of the country turned into weapons distribution points, as Habyarimana dithered and the RPA threatened, UNAMIR and the United Nations did nothing.

Their force commander, a Canadian major-general called Romeo Dallaire, had received a warning in January 1994 from a top-level interahamwe informant, a security adviser to Habyarimana. This man had said that 1600 militiamen were trained and ready in Kigali with access to arms caches, and were preparing plans for mass killings of Tutsis; they could, they reckoned, kill 1000 in twenty minutes. Lists had been drawn up; the informant himself, along with other men, had prepared plans to attack government officials and UNAMIR soldiers. He would accompany Dallaire to the site of the arms caches, in return for a promise of UN protection for him and his family. Dallaire decided to act immediately. But first he checked with Kofi Annan, then Head of UN peacekeeping, at UN head-quarters in New York. Annan, now UN Secretary-General, said no. Adamantly. Dallaire must report the matter to Habyarimana, as per

UNAMIR's mandate. So he did. And the one chance of rooting out the genocidal plotters, and possibly preventing the events of April 1994, was missed.

The UN in Rwanda was headed by a Cameroonian Special Envoy, Jacques-Roger Booh-Booh, a man who lacked decision-making capabilities, vacillated, made weak threats, and didn't understand the situation. He was, in short, unsuited to the job, and out of his depth. He was a gift to the Hutu hardliners. It is hard to imagine anything weaker than the threat from Booh-Booh issued on 4 April, two days before the genocide began. The message to the inter-ahamwe and CDR militias was that the UNAMIR budget might not be renewed unless they stopped arms distributions, pulled themselves into line and accepted the terms of the Arusha Accords.

Two days later, President Juvenal Habyarimana was returning in his Mystere Falcon-50 jet from Dar es Salaam. He had just had immense pressure put on him by the presidents of Tanzania, Uganda and Burundi, and the vice-president of Kenya, as well as by the Organization of African Unity and regional European diplomats, to honour the terms of the Arusha Accords. He was accompanied by his private aide Colonel Elie Segatwa, his chief of staff and three other aides. The plane was flown by a three-man French crew, and Cyprien Ntaryamira, the Burundian President, was on board having asked for a lift. As the aircraft came in over the centre-line at Kigali airport, at 8.17 p.m., there were two loud explosions. The jet burst into flames, and crashed into the garden of the president's residence killing everybody on board. Rwanda's hundred days of killing, the world's swiftest genocide, had begun.

Chapter 3

A White Man's Playground

It was unlikely that anyone would ever know who shot down the plane of President Juvenal Habyarimana, I thought, standing on the balcony of Kigali airport in November 1995. It was a bright, sunny day and Rwanda was stretched out before me, all green fields, red earth and blue sky. I was eating a cheese-and-ham sandwich and drinking Primus, looking over at Masaka hill, from where Rwandan witnesses claim to have seen missiles fired at the plane as it came in. All that is known for sure is that there were two explosions, one on an inlet manifold and one on part of the fuselage.

Nothing but rumour exists as to who might have carried out the attack. In any case, the genocide that started immediately after it rather eclipsed the plane crash. All that really mattered was that Habyarimana had died, and the killings had begun. Nevertheless, it is interesting to look at the plane crash, as it forms the lynch-pin moment between one part of history in the Great Lakes Region, and another. Almost everything of importance that has happened in Rwanda, Zaire and Burundi since 1994 began with the moment when the Mystere Falcon-50 went down; the resulting wars, civil conflicts, movements of refugees, massacres and humanitarian disasters that, at the time of writing, rock Democratic Congo, Angola, Rwanda, Burundi, the Central African Republic and parts of Uganda began at that moment. At 8.17 p.m. on 6 April 1994, two degrees south of the equator, at Gregoire Kayibanda airport in Kigali.

The Tutsi Rwandan Patriotic Front said it was the hardline Hutus from the akazu who shot the plane down. Hutu hardliners blamed the RPF. The RPF also said it could have been the French, while the

Hutus also blamed the Belgian military, before the RPF blamed Belgian mercenaries dressed as Rwandan Hutu extremists. Somebody started a rumour that missiles had been fired at the plane by aid workers from the Belgian Red Cross. Almost every possible party that could have been involved has blamed the other for the incident. But the list of possible culprits narrows considerably if one examines who would have even been capable of carrying out the attack.

The theory that ground-to-air missiles were used is based upon eye-witness reports from Rwandans on the ground and an examination of the aircraft structure after the crash. Independent western security analysts have suggested that rather than two missile strikes, the aircraft could have been blown up from within by an explosive device. For the missile theory to be workable, it is first necessary to examine the kinds of missiles that could have been used. Bernard Debre, a French minister, alleged that SAM-7 or SAM-16 ground-to-air missiles, manufactured by the former Soviet bloc, were confiscated from Iraq during the Gulf War by the Americans. These were then supplied to the Ugandans, who in turn supplied them to either extremist Hutus or to the RPA. The Pentagon have denied this.

The Belgian prime minister, Jean-Luc Dehaene, announced that a governmental commission of enquiry had found no evidence to link French participants to the action. The plane was shot down from the area of Masaka Hill, at least 400 metres from the beginning of the runway centre-line. This was an area controlled by the Presidential Guard, patrolled by UNAMIR soldiers, to which the RPF would have not been able to gain access on that day except by heavy fighting. The RPF battalion, even assuming that it had wanted to shoot down the plane, was nowhere to be seen, as it did not leave its barracks in the Kigali Parliament building until the following day.

The missile theory persisted sufficiently for the RPF to be blamed by hardline MRND(D) and CDR Hutus from Agathe Habyarimana's akazu. On 6 May 1994, she signed a contract with the private French security official, Paul Barril whose sticker I'd seen on the door of the Diplomates Hotel. Barril undertook to investigate the incident, and appeared on French television on 28 June, saying that the RPF had shot down the plane. He claimed to have various pieces of evidence, including the plane's voice-recorder and the missile launchers, but was unable to supply either. One theory is that he knew the identities of the (possibly) western hitmen who fired the missiles, and was blaming the RPF as a smokescreen.

Who could have fired the missiles? It would have to have been somebody with the necessary training and experience. The FAR and the Presidential Guard had only been trained by the French in the use of the MILAN. This is a tube-operated, wire-guided anti-tank missile designed to hit tanks at ranges of 2500 metres at speeds of around twenty miles per hour. The operator fires the missile, which then arms itself at a range of 200 metres, and is guided onto target by the operator through an optic sight. It would have been next to impossible to shoot down a fast-moving jet at close range with a MILAN in broad daylight, and totally impossible at 8.17 p.m., when Kigali is in darkness.

The missiles that could have been used are American Stingers, or their technical predecessor, the Redeye. Other possible culprits are SAM-7s or SAM-16s, shoulder-to-air missiles. But these require a lot of practice to use, are slow to reload, and, more importantly, are heat-seeking, which means that to achieve two direct hits on a jet aircraft landing at night, they would have to have been fired simultaneously, as the aircraft would have rocked violently off-course on first missile impact, causing the second to miss target. The missiles, being heat-seeking, would have 'locked-on' to the heat signature of the engines before firing, and then, once very close to the aircraft, exploded as they would have been proximity fused. Missile experts and those who have experience of using anti-tank and ground-to-air missiles know that being able to guarantee a direct hit with such a missile requires an operator to have fired at least twenty live missiles in practice. The absence of anything approaching this kind of number of SAM, Stinger or Redeye missiles in arms being delivered to Rwanda at this time, suggests that there would not have been any Hutu extremist, French-trained member of the Presidential Guard or not, who could have shot down the aircraft.

A couple of people with extensive missile experience could have been hired to do the job. Ukrainians or South Africans would have been the natural choice. But to buy the missile launchers, hire the men and buy the necessary missiles for them to practise on in a third country would have cost the network of Agathe Habyarimana at least half a million US dollars, which it would have been extremely difficult to obtain without alerting her husband, or the French. Even if she were to obtain this kind of funding, she would have had to have obtained the missiles on the illegal weapons market. Enter Paul Barril and his colleague, former French DST intelligence agent, Pierre-Yves Gilleron, another friend from GIGN days. The president's wife would have approached him to make any weapons purchases for her. Barril had been involved with the Habyarimana family from the early 1990s, and in 1993, was employed to protect the Burundian president, Melchior Ndadaye. Despite his GIGN background though, he couldn't protect Ndadaye from his violent death in October 1993.

Stinger missiles were first used outside the territorial United States by the British SAS in the Falklands, in 1982. Even those with which the mujahedeen shot down Russian Mi-24 helicopters in Afghanistan were used only under close supervision by US and British special forces. They are very, very hard to get hold of, even on the open market. The Provisional IRA, with all its weapons-purchasing experience, has never managed to buy a Stinger, and only ten-odd SAM-7s. It would be surprising if Barril's network of contacts could do any better. (And this before he had to ship the equipment to Rwanda without alerting the French military personnel who controlled Kigali airport.) Even if all these hoops were jumped through, the two operators would have had to guarantee two hits on a fast-moving jet aircraft as it landed in the dark. It is just possible that the plane was shot down by white missile operators whom the French troops allowed to enter Rwanda. France would be the first to deny that it so treasured its Rwandan connections it was prepared to initiate the deaths of up to a million people, but it is conceivable that they were nervous enough of increased Tutsi influence in Rwanda, and had been assured by Agathe Habyarimana's hardliners that the shooting down of the aircraft would only be followed by extremely limited killings. To this end they might just have allowed a team of foreign triggermen in to do the job, because there was no way they would do it themselves and risk getting caught. It would have to have been a particularly hard and professional team though, because it also involved killing three French pilots, personally chosen by President Mitterand's son.

The theory that an explosive device was placed on the aircraft by Hutu extremists before leaving Dar es Salaam is much the most likely. In a pressurized cabin of a jet aircraft, two explosive charges no bigger than a hand-grenade would have been sufficient. They would also have been easier to plant on the aircraft, possibly in luggage. The alleged missile strikes in Kigali would probably have been from back-up members of the team who managed to get in two shots with ground-to-air missiles, fired as a last resort because they thought that the explosives on board had not detonated. However, nobody has ever confessed to the bombing, nobody has ever been caught, nobody has been tracked down by journalists. Nobody has surfaced with claims of responsibility. The guilty parties are probably all now dead, and the final truth might never be known.

I was on my sixth trip to Rwanda since Beverley and I had taken off from Goma a year before. Arriving in Africa in July, I had based myself in Nairobi. For two months I had lived with Samantha Bolton, the press officer from MSF, at her beautiful house off Riverside Drive on the western edge of the city. There were goats in the garden, and the bathroom taps electrocuted you in the mornings if you turned them on when the kettle was boiling in the kitchen. After two months I moved into a large ground-floor flat off the Ngong road which I shared with an English businessman and an American news photographer, David Guttenfelder. There was a communal swimming pool and bougainvillea grew over the vine by the gate. The gardener used to lay his maize out to dry on the lawn. I used the flat as the base from which to cover east and central Africa, when I had enough expenses funding from the newspaper to travel the huge distances required.

So I was on a limited budget that November in Kigali. I was

staying at the Hotel Kiyovu, a single-storey building set on the slopes of the same hill as the Diplomates and the Mille Collines, the capital's most expensive hotel. There had been some killing in and around the garden of the Kiyovu, and bodies had been buried somewhere nearby. When I opened the doors of my room in the morning, the hot wind outside brought a drift of the smell that was all too familiar from 1994. Most of the other occupants were military officers with UNAMIR. The previous night, there had been the tick-tack of stiletto heels in my corridor, and an orderly knocking at the door of each of the rooms. When I opened mine there stood in front of me a Tutsi prostitute. She had long, red fingernails, hair-braids and tired eyes. She asked simply: 'Do you want it?'

Three doors down, at the room of a Ghanaian major, she found a welcome.

The next morning I got up, brushed the scuttering cockroaches from my floor out on to the verandah, where they were swooped up by the hovering kites, and went in to do my teeth. Inside my sponge-bag, waving its antennae at me, was a large ginger cockroach that had spent the night sleeping on the bristles of my toothbrush. When I recounted this story to an American woman working for the United States Agency for International Development, she, like so many other people gathered in Rwanda that year, seemed to have an even worse anecdote than my own. In a hotel room in Zagreb, she said, she had returned to her room during a power-cut. She fumbled for her toothbrush and toothpaste, and started cleaning her teeth. She didn't realize there was a cockroach on her brush. She brushed away, squashing its head and antennae between her two front teeth.

Kigali was full, that autumn, of all the different white tribes that make up the world of development, humanitarian aid, journalism, international diplomacy and military intervention. And like the American woman, every member had their story to tell. But the tales they recounted each night, over cold beer and barbecued meat, served under the warm tropical sky bright with stars, were stories of how they came to be in the country, and what they thought should be done about it. There were more than one hundred and fifty aid agencies working in Rwanda. There was every kind of organization from Médecins sans Frontières with its ninety expatriate staff to the tiny, two-man band, bargain basement outfits that every international disaster attracts. There were UNAMIR soldiers on attachment from the armies and police forces of Australia, India, Canada, Ghana, Russia, Uruguay, Jordan, Pakistan and the United States. There were five United Nations Agencies. There were expatriates who had never left Kigali.

An American diplomat serving at the United States Embassy had told me that he had been called in to see a Rwandan government minister. The official had pointed to a list on the wall behind him, on which were written the names of each of the organizations represented in his capital.

'So, tell me,' the minister had said, pointing at the names, 'what do all these organizations actually do? All I see is traffic jams of Toyota and Nissan four-wheel-drives every morning, stopping Rwandans getting to work. Give me one good reason why we shouldn't expel nearly all of them from the country?'

The American diplomat could say little. The Rwandans had a point. After the genocide had begun, the United Nations had done nothing but reduce the number of UNAMIR peace-keepers to a handful – 270 – as around them hundreds of thousands of Rwandans were butchered. Major-General Romeo Dallaire, the Canadian General in charge of UNAMIR, had estimated that it would have taken no more than 5,000 armed and trained troops physically to stop the killings. But the United States, deeply reluctant to commit troops to UN peace-keeping operations after the debacle in Somalia in 1993, had not backed any plan of intervention. Ten Belgian paratroopers who formed part of the UNAMIR detachment in Kigali in April 1994, had been tortured and killed by the Rwandan Presidential Guard. On the night of 7 April, a UNAMIR detachment had driven to the house of Agathe Uwilingiyimana, the Rwandan prime minister, to rescue her. On arriving at her house, set in the centre of Kigali, they realized that it was a trap. Interahamwe elements were already in the prime minister's courtyard and opened fire on their vehicles. Madame Uwilingiyimana was killed. Her husband and five children escaped. The ten Belgians were told by soldiers of the Presidential Guard to lay down their weapons. This they did, in keeping with their mandate. They were then taken to the Guard barracks, where they were tortured. One of the soldiers had a tattoo cut off his shoulder with a machete. Another had his ear slashed off with a bayonet; a third lost his nose. They were in radio contact with their superiors, who were in turn, in contact with Dallaire who, under UNAMIR restrictions could not intervene. On their return to Brussels, the Belgians' colleagues cut up their blue UN berets with bayonets to show their disgust with the United Nations mandate that had made it impossible to take action to save their fellow paratroopers. Thereafter the Belgians and the French intervened only to save their own nationals.

The French, of course, took a rather more pragmatic approach than the Belgians as the killings erupted. Although there were 2500 UNAMIR troops in Kigali, France wanted to carry out its own operations. A large company group of nearly 200 French regular army paratroopers from Bangui, in the Central African Republic, landed at Kigali airport on 9 April, in an operation code-named 'Amaryllis'. The French were saving their own. They had orders not to become engaged in firefights with the interahamwe, FAR, or Presidential Guard but only to rescue their nationals and their Rwandan 'allies'. These allies included Agathe Habyarimana and half of the akazu, who were flown to Nairobi. It did not include a Rwandan Tutsi called Charles, the librarian at the French Cultural Centre in the capital.

Charles lived several hundred metres from his place of work, and when the killings swung into full pace, on the morning of 7 April, he watched from the window of his flat as groups of men, women and children were forced to lie on the pavement by the interahamwe, before being machine-gunned and hacked to death. Charles rang his office six times to ask for help. He was told by the French staff to 'make do'. Finally, on the morning of the eleventh, he climbed out of his flat over the roof. At the entrance to the apartment block, fifty of his neighbours were lying in a pool of blood. He managed to make it to the cultural centre, only to be told by French paratroopers on the morning of the twelfth that they were leaving, 'because we've got all the French people out'. Charles and the other Rwandan employees at the centre were left to fend for themselves. The French paratroopers had gone as far as to smash a hole in the false ceiling of the library, in which they told the Rwandans they could hide. Outside, on the streets of Kigali, there were militia road-blocks every 200 metres: hundreds of drunk, drugged, screaming Hutu gang members were slaughtering every Tutsi they could find, and any Hutu suspected of sympathizing with them.

Charles was saved by Belgian soldiers, who arrived at the centre intending to use it as a base. They hid the Rwandans under a tarpaulin in the back of a lorry and took them to the airport, where they were evacuated, along with Madame Habyarimana and others, to Nairobi.

One man surnamed Gakumba said that when he managed to reach the French Embassy, seeking protection, he was amazed to see who was being evacuated by the French paratroopers.

'Imagine my incredulity to see the people who were gathered in the French Embassy! All the high-ups from the former regime, and their families, the ministers from the president's [Habyarimana's] party, his in-laws. There was the director of Radio Mille Collines and his assistants, well known for their exhortations to commit massacres . . . On the way to the Embassy, at dozens of road-blocks, I saw people sitting on the ground, arms tied behind their backs, in the process of being killed, who cried out for help when they saw the UN troops go by without doing anything.'

He goes on:

'I don't know what these powerful people from the [Hutu hardline] regime had to fear, since I saw them going in and out of the embassy with their FAR escorts to go round the parts of the city where the massacres were taking place. In due course, they would have meetings in the French Embassy to discuss how the situation [the killings] was developing; they took pleasure in totting up the total number of the victims, or complaining that such-and-such a person had not been killed, or that such-and-such a part of the city had not been cleaned. They were boasting about the results of their plans and the exploits of the militias. The night I spent there was one of the most agonizing of my life. The following day the French ambassador [Jean-Phillippe Marlaud] began the evacuations of all these people to the airport. First on the list of people earmarked for evacuation were certain people well known as heads of militia gangs.'

If, at a very generous stretch, it could be claimed that the French had not known about the preparations for the genocide, or about how their arms and their military training were being used, then the situation was clearly different now. The Tutsi RPF had attacked from Uganda on Saturday the ninth, and the Hutu interim government, declared on the night of the sixth, had evacuated to Gitarama on the twelfth. The Belgian government wanted the UN Security Council to modify the UNAMIR mandate to allow troops to intervene, but France, whose troops were under threat of attack by the RPF if they got involved, blocked this. Both Belgians and French rescued their nationals and their respective Rwandan 'friends', and flew out of Kigali. Operation Amaryllis ended on Tuesday the twelfth. On 21 April, UN Secretary-General Boutros-Boutros Ghali and the Security Council approved the reduction of the UNAMIR peace-keepers from 2,500 to 270. By this stage, more than 200,000 Tutsis and moderate Hutus had been slaughtered.

Eighteen months later, I could see why the Rwandan government was infuriated by the overload of expatriate humanitarian staff in their country. It was too much, too late, and misguided. Only Médecins sans Frontières (who lost over two hundred local Tutsi staff in the genocide) and the International Committee of the Red Cross (ICRC) had stayed in Rwanda after April. But now, Kigali and the countryside of the Land of a Thousand Hills had become a white man's playground. There were American evangelical groups preaching forgiveness, there were non-governmental organizations running drama groups for traumatized Tutsi rape victims. The United Nations organized a drawing competition for orphans of the genocide, but most of the pencils and paper were stolen, and then the children produced naive pictures of UNAMIR troops raping Tutsi women. Down at Ntarama the caretaker was incensed that some Australian soldiers had been caught trying to steal skulls from the massacre site in the church. The whole tiny land was once again in the grip of international aid, as it had been in the 1980s, and once again most of those concerned had little idea of what was going on. The work of the good – MSF, Oxfam, the ICRC – was being obscured by the irrelevancies of those for whom Rwanda was just another profile-boosting aid project. Rwanda was feel-good, kudos-making stuff, which qualified them for governmental grants back at base in the UK, America, Scandanavia and the EC.

The Texan company, Brown and Root, sent American construction experts to repair the drainage system in Kigali. Two of their men were lodged in the Hotel Diplomates, next door to Julian Bedford. That year he was the Reuters News Agency correspondent, and also the boyfriend of Samantha Bolton. Julian described their daily after-work routine of Primus, heavy rap music and sex. Occasionally one of the boys would knock on Jules' door of an evening. He'd be resplendent in camouflage, net baseball cap with the logo of the National Rifle Association, shorts, construction boots and thrash-metal t-shirt.

'Hey Jules,' he'd say. 'Fancy coming whoring?'

I stood next to a Brown and Root boy one evening in the toilet queue at the Sierra Indian restaurant, opposite the American Embassy. He and a colleague were sitting with two Tutsi prostitutes. The Texan complained that his girl kept rubbing his leg under the table.

'When it comes to it, boy,' he said to me, waiting for the men's toilet to come available, 'you've got to choose. Which comes first? Your curry or your piece of ass?'

In the evenings, the international crowd moved to the American Club, a small compound set just down the hill from the Mille Collines. Here the American Embassy had set up a bar and club, complete with swimming pool, snooker tables, kitchen and restaurants, where expatriates could relax in the evenings. American paratroop colonels in singlets and expensive trainers leant at the bar, chugging Budweisers and forking ketchup over their chicken Maryland. Beretta pistols poked from the backs of their shorts. Female staff from the humanitarian world flirted with Canadian and Australian soldiers. Bodyguards from the German and Belgian Embassies elbowed through the throng of United Nations refugee protection officers on a weekend off from the chaos of Goma. Plates of hamburgers, chips, steaks and salads were handed across the bar. On the tables under the Heineken and Kronenbourg umbrellas, there waited the sets of Heinz ketchup, Belgian mayonnaise and English HP sauce, reminders of a faraway home.

Such was the frustration and resentment felt by many RPF soldiers at all this misguided international charity that had arrived too late, that they expressed their bitterness in a very direct way. They robbed the aid workers' offices, they burgled their houses at gunpoint, they expelled some of them from the country, and they stole their expensive white four-wheel-drive vehicles. Much of this crime wave, they explained, was carried out by deserters or common criminals. But in the car-park of the Mille Collines at weekends, when the Tutsi elite attended weddings or went to lounge by the hotel pool, there would always be several powerful vehicles that had originally belonged elsewhere.

If there was one common point of agreement between Paul Kagame's government, the United Nations and all the disparate aid organizations in Rwanda by late 1995, it was on the need to repatriate the Rwandan refugees living outside the country. There were some two million of them living in Zaire, Tanzania and Burundi. The RPA was particularly worried about the refugee camps in Goma, from where it was feared that the Hutu militias and former government army were planning a reinvasion. Arms had been flowing to the ex-FAR and the interahamwe almost from the moment their interim government had quit Kigali the previous year. The hand of the French could be seen in many of these arms deals, and the American government was convinced that a French intelligence operation aimed at destabilizing Rwanda was being run from their embassy in Nairobi. Word in London and Paris was that a few ex-GIGN gendarmes and ex-CRAP paras who'd worked in Rwanda before were looking for volunteers. There were two training camps being operated west of Bukavu and rumour had it that DGSE money was behind them. The Hutu hardliners were openly training in the camps around Goma and Bukavu.

After our return from Africa in September 1994, Beverley had gone to make a film about the American invasion of Haiti while I became even further involved in the Rwandan story. In October 1994, very few journalists had any details of the French rearming of the Hutus in Zaire, nor about the European air cargo companies that were shipping the weapons. I probably knew less than anybody. Our programme's break into it originated through luck.

Peak Aviation was a two-aircraft cargo outfit based in West Sussex. They'd ship pretty much anything. Flowers from Nairobi to Amsterdam, live calves from Nigeria, day-old chicks to the Yemen. The crew members were close to the edge with the owner, Alan Moffatt, because he consistently failed to pay them. Finally they approached our television programme. Everything they gave us, including aircraft flight logs and bills of lading for arms shipments, showed that not only Peak Aviation but at least three other companies had been involved in flying cargoes of weapons into Goma between May and November 1994. A United Nations arms embargo prohibiting the delivery and sales of weapons to the interim Rwandan government had been in place since May 1994. Everybody suspected the French but nobody had yet been able to prove it.

Peak Aviation and the other companies were using their two Boeing 707s, each with a cargo capacity of 41 tons. They were flying in automatic weapons, hand-grenades and ammunition from Chile, via Recife in Brazil and then to Goma after refuelling at Sal in the Cape Verde Islands. The suppliers in Chile included Carlos Cardoen, a major Chilean arms dealer who had been involved in supplying Iraq with South African G-5 howitzers in the Iran–Iraq war. Moffatt was also picking up weapons in Tirana, Albania, where, our crews informed us, Israeli officials had on one occasion loaded thirty-nine tons of Egyptian hand-grenades destined for Goma. Flights had also been secretly diverted while en route for Yemen. We followed Moffatt's trail and discovered that he was being sub-contracted as an arms shipper by a middleman living in Norwich, one Willem Ouwendjwik. Ouwendjwik, in turn, was liaising with

Moffat on behalf of an Ostend-based cargo company, Air Transvaal, which had been paid three different sums of money by a front company operating for a private French security company. There our trail went cold, and efforts to investigate Air Transvaal's bank accounts and find out which private French security company was contracting aircraft to fly weapons into Zaire, was blocked. Had we succeeded, I suspect that we would have found the footprints of Madame Habyarimana, Jean-Christophe Mitterand and probably Paul Barril along the way. We knew that the Rwandan who was arranging at least some of the arms shipments was a former bourgmestre from Kibungo called Remy Gatete, known to the British National Criminal Intelligence Service as Jean-Marie Gatete. Both the American Central Intelligence Agency and, strangely, Saudi Arabian Intelligence were following the progress of these arms flights.

Aside from the pick-ups from the Israelis in Tirana, the crews, and their colleagues in the air cargo industry had picked up weapons from Burgas airport in Sofia, Bulgaria, from a company called Kintex. There had also been shipments from a French company called DYL-Invest from an airstrip outside Lyons. Other names implicated were given variously as Liberian World Airlines, DAS Aviation and Transami. By far the largest sums of money, they said, had come through DYL-Invest from a company called Sofremas. From May to June 1994, between eleven and fourteen arms flights were believed to have carried arms from Europe to Goma, not only for Sofremas but also from Israel and the former Soviet Bloc. After the flood of Hutu refugees moved into Bakavu and Goma in July 1994, many of the aircraft, including Peak's Boeings, camouflaged themselves with stickers bearing the logo of Médecins sans Frontières. DYL-Invest was involved in the shipping and sub-contracting for the shipping of at least six of these flights.

Sofremas, in 1994 and 5, was a French state-owned company that exported and through-imported weapons. These were manufactured in France and in South Africa, Israel and the former Soviet Union. DYL-Invest was a shipping company based in the foothills of the French Alps that simply took on air cargo transit deliveries. If Sofremas was involved in shipping weapons to Goma in contravention of the United Nations arms embargo imposed in May, then it meant that the weapons would almost certainly have been sold by the company to a dealer or buyer who had a fake 'end-user certificate'. This would have covered the French links by declaring that the weapons were destined for a country other than Zaire or Rwanda. But the evidence that Sofremas was involved as a French parastatal meant that there was no way that the government could deny involvement.

So, after a large amount of legwork, we established that arms were being supplied to the former Rwandan government and military, as well as to the interahamwe militias. These arms shipments were either going directly from a French parastatal, and being shipped by a French company, or were being sub-contracted by a series of French middlemen and front companies. All were going to the regime that had carried out a genocide that had left such legacies as the mountain of corpses in the church at Ntarama. The FAR and the interahamwe were being re-supplied.

There was nothing surprising to me about the worldwide arms industry supplying weapons to the former Hutu regime. An arms industry exists, legally or illegally, to supply weapons to areas of conflict at a profit for the proprietors, regardless of the nature of the conflict itself. But what I found more complex was why the French could still want to support, covertly or otherwise, a regime that was as uncompromising in its barbarity as that of the Hutu militias and former Rwandan government. By the end of 1994, we had spent nearly two months tracking the arms links across Rwanda, Zaire, France, the United Kingdom, South America and Europe. There was no question but that the French government had rearmed a regime responsible for the massacres of nearly one million civilians. At this stage, we had nothing as concrete as an admission of involvement from Paris. Nor did we have all the links of proof, all the paperwork needed for our jigsaw. But we were getting close.

There was little reaction in the British media to our film, *The Gunrunners*, when it came out in November 1994. A couple of French newspapers showed interest in the details we had, but that was it. The United Nations had already covered their backs: on 7

September 1994, in a meeting in New York on the Great Lakes Region, the United Nations Security Council approved Resolution 1013, which asked for the setting up of an independent commission of enquiry to investigate the supply of weapons to Rwanda and the former Rwandan Hutu regime in contravention of the UN arms embargo. This followed concern, they said, being voiced by many member states that the refugees were being rearmed and retrained in Zaire. I waited to see whether anything would be done.

In August 1995, I'd made a trip to Goma, and in Kibumba camp had spoken to a number of former militiamen who claimed that they were preparing to attack Rwanda. By autumn, I'd collected enough information about RPA heists of cars, and stories of army deserters holding up the offices of NGO. I needed to send a story to the *Sunday Telegraph* on my return to Nairobi, and hoped that up in Rwanda's north-west, around Ruhengeri and Gisenyi, I could pick up more information about the increasing cross-border raids that were now taking place. Coupled with another trip to Goma to nose around the airport, I thought, it would make a good start on a story about continuing French involvement. I toyed semi-seriously with my first paragraph as I got my belongings together for the first leg of my trip.

A year after the genocide which killed nearly a million people in Rwanda the perpetrators are being rearmed and retrained in Zairean refugee camps in preparation for a reinvasion of their country. This time, however, they intend to finish the job. Western diplomats in the tiny central African country told the *Sunday Telegraph* this week that they fear France, ally to the former government, is behind the plan . . .

It sounded good, I smiled, making a small stack of my remaining hundred dollar bills and folding them into my pocket. Not for the first time, I yearned for the thick wedges of cash I had transported around the Great Lakes Region in 1994. I could have used it much better now. Covering East Africa was cripplingly expensive. What with flights, telephone charges, hotel accommodation, car-hire and food, I would end up spending nearly fifteen hundred dollars on my week in Rwanda and Zaire. I suspected I would soon have to find another outlet for my talent. The *Sunday Telegraph* paid me expenses, but only for stories they accepted. From Rwanda they might take two, and the one they wanted did involve the Rwandan army stealing cars and holding up aid workers, but it also involved something more.

'What we really want,' I was told a couple of days before, 'is something like this. Hang on . . . let me give you a couple of lines.'

He recited his idea down the phone.

'"Natasha lives in the heart of darkness. Her job is saving Rwandan refugees. But today the twenty-three-year-old nurse from Hampshire is heart-broken. Marc, her hunking boyfriend from the Canadian army, has chucked her. He's run off with Charlotte from MSF . . ." Something like that. Reckon you can find it? Give it bags of colour, we'll get the subs to bang it to the top of the page.'

'Ummm . . . yes. I dunno, people here are a bit . . .'

'Yes?' said the voice from Canary Wharf.

'A bit serious. I was thinking . . . I don't know.' I let it all out in a rush. 'There's a really good story about French involvement, an intelligence operation, arming the interahamwe . . . arms to refugee camps. They're going to finish off the genocide.'

'Yes?'

'Mmm.'

'Got any documents?'

'Not quite, but good quotes.'

'I think we'll stick with the aid-babes. "What's a nice girl like you doing in a place like this?" That kind of thing. Clubbing on the equator. My Rwanda love hell – by Tamara.'

'I'll do my best, but if I get anything on the French . . .'

'Sex. Bags of local colour.'

'I'll try, but I'm not promising . . .'

'"UN Peacekeeper love-rat humped and dumped me."'

I had already made three trips to Rwanda since July, one to Zaire, one to the Comoros Islands, one to Somalia and three within Kenya. As I walked out of the Kiyovu Hotel, pocketing rather less change than I had anticipated after paying the bill, I made up my mind to move once I got back to Nairobi. It was a pity that stories like the Comoros Islands and Somalia didn't come along very often.

The coup d'état that had taken place in October 1995 in the Comoros Islands had been the perfect Sunday newspaper story. Veteran French mercenary Bob Denard had got together a crowd of his old gunmen and deposed the government of the tiny Indian Ocean islands. It had everything Canary Wharf liked. It was whities with guns going mad in paradise. It had mercenaries, the Foreign Legion, palm trees, machine-gun fire under the tropical stars. The coup story that every Africa correspondent has to cover once. The sacked presidential palace, the rebel takeover. Hardened veterans of five African wars coming off the sea by night. And then the new government announced at dawn from the burning radio station.

It had been remarkably like that. One of my favourite books was *The Dogs of War*, by Fredrick Forsyth, which featured Bob Denard in the plot. The arms shipments loaded aboard the old freighter bought in Rotterdam, the trip round the Cape, the teams of mercenaries recruited in Paris and Brussels. It was all there.

Reuters had chartered a Beechcraft and I'd taken a seat. The *Sunday Telegraph* had cleared their lead foreign page for me; all I had to do was get into the capital of Grand Comore. We just managed. At one point a fourteen-hour pirogue journey across open sea had seemed our only option. It ended up with Reuters, *Le Monde* and myself being the only journalists there for three days. On day five the French re-took the island by force. It was a cloudy night with no moon when a GIGN team abseiled onto the roof of the French Embassy. At the same time Commando Marines hit the port. The French special forces fanned out into the town, set up roadblocks in the dark. We were woken in the hotel by a Puma helicopter flying overhead and by a telephone call from Bob Denard saying the French had hit the island. I had pulled a flak-jacket over my head and forgotten to shave as 20mm anti-aircraft shells thwacked into the port.

My first firefight was a messy affair. In that grey warmth and half-light of a tropical dawn, I had found myself taking cover on a tree-lined boulevard down by the port. High-velocity rounds from a group of French commandos whacked off the corner of the harbour-wall. In the confusion and the noise and the dust, four people were hit in front of us. Two were French journalists. One took a 5.56mm round through his thigh after his own countrymen opened fire on a taxi full of the French press. A Comorian soldier had his chest blown out with a GIGN burst of automatic fire.

The story moved quickly, and four days later we were boarding an Air France 747 that had come in from Reunion to rescue trapped French civilians. It had quickly transpired that the coup was a put-up job. Denard and his lacklustre band of men had toppled the government simply so the French would have a chance to intervene and impose a regime of their own choosing. The mercenaries had turned out to be rather less the dogs of war they wished they were. Fewer than five had been in action before. But the islands had been beautiful. Blue, blue sea and tiny beaches. A people whose idea of crime was vanilla smuggling. White and pink frangipani flowers on branches bowed in the warm, tropical wind. It was a long way from Hutus and Tutsis.

After checking out of the Kiyovu, I headed into the car-park to look for a car to hire. I found Innocent sitting on the red-plush front seat of a white Toyota Corolla, reading a newspaper. He was wearing carefully ironed lime-green slacks, and tasselled loafers in two shades of brown. The bodywork of the car dripped from where he had washed it. He folded his newspaper as I approached. We leant against the bonnet, side by side in the warm morning sun and bargained. Innocent went in at $250 a day, but within ten minutes we'd agreed on seventy-five. He'd realized I wasn't from a cash-rich American TV crew, and that I had visited Rwanda before.

We threaded our way through to the Gitarama road. The car seemed to go well, and Innocent appeared to know how to drive. It was not always so. Negotiating rates with drivers could be one of the more frustrating parts of working in Zaire and Rwanda. Most of the drivers were Ugandan Tutsis who had bought or hired their Toyota

Corollas, their Nissan Sunnys or their Datsuns in Kampala. If they were the owners of the vehicles, it meant that they would have spent every dollar they had, and probably many that they had borrowed, to buy the car. It was in their interest to charge as much per day as possible to recoup their costs. The daily hire rate was set by the clientele who used them, predominantly journalists. All the aid workers and UN staff had their own four-wheel-drives, heavily branded with logos and stickers, weighed down with Codan radios and other communications equipment.

First you found your driver. Your Innocent, your Protais, or your Balthazar would normally be sitting in the shade outside the entrance of the Mille Collines, chatting with the other 'taximen'. You took him out of their hearing and negotiated the daily rate. First you explained that you knew Kigali well, and were not part of a visiting American TV crew. Second, you assured him that you were not going to be driving anywhere dangerous; if you were, you simply waited till you got there to tell him. Third, you made it clear that the price negotiated in advance was the price you were going to pay. Retrospective negotiation was a frequent tactic. Fourth, you explained that he was driving on your time. While he waited for you outside a government ministry, hotel or an office building, it was not permitted to drive off to Kampala, pick up his children from school, sub-contract the car to a cousin for moving building equipment, or use it to transport goats.

Vehicle-hire horror stories were legion. My house-mate in Nairobi remembered a Toyota Land Cruiser pick-up that in Rwanda in 1994 had been passed from journalist to journalist. The original hire had been made some time in late May, when the country was in chaos, the genocide at its height. As each successive photographer and writer from the Associated Press had rolled through Kigali, the vehicle had been handed on to them by their departing predecessor. Everyone in turn had thought that somebody else had paid for it, until, by October, it was assumed the original owner was dead. It was in this vehicle that I had ridden on my first night in Kigali. By the time the battered pick-up, its windscreen cracked and one door refusing to close, had rolled into

Zaire, everybody had forgotten it had ever had an owner. Until he turned up at the Nyera hotel in Goma one night, accompanied by three drunken Zairean paratroopers, demanding $16,000 in cash.

The money had been paid. But if journalists sometimes made for nightmarish clients, it worked the other way too. The sleek, nearly new saloon hired late at night in the Mille Collines car-park for an early departure would not be the car that materialized in the heavy darkness at four a.m. the following morning. The driver would have sent his 'cousin' with his 'reserve' car. But he would still try to stick to the negotiated price for a driver who couldn't drive, had probably never been outside Kigali, in a car whose engine seemed almost routinely to be on fire. Like anywhere in the world, you had to be firm, and to know how to bargain. For the Rwandan, Ugandan and Burundian drivers sitting on the concrete balustrade surrounding the Mille Collines flower beds, any day could herald the arrival of their fantasy, their dream-ticket; an American film-crew, or inexperienced group of European journalists, who would pay what was asked. Innocent had asked me for $250 a day not because he thought he and his car were worth the money, but because there was a 2 per cent chance he might get it.

Their other fantasy, that myth that they talked about in their quiet moments, was the white man who thought that by overpaying black taxi drivers he was atoning for the sins of his colonial past. Ten months later, I was to stand in the lobby of a hotel in Burundi and watch this in action. An American working for a liberal, East-Coast human rights group had been fleeced by a Burundian. She had requested a driver who spoke French, accompanied by an anglo-phone translator, in a four-wheel-drive vehicle that could go any-where. What she got was a creaking blue-and-white taxi, with a French-speaking Burundian driver who said he was studying English at university – he spoke some five words – and who told her that they would not need four-wheel-drive capability outside the capital. The woman made the fatal mistake of not haggling and settling the deal in advance. When the time came to pay several days later, the driver stood four-square in the lobby of the hotel, surrounded by his colleagues, and demanded nearly three hundred dollars a day. She backed down. He got the money.

Innocent and I filled up with petrol and cleared the road-blocks on the outskirts of town. As we crossed the heavy, red Nyabarongo river and pulled uphill, the dashboard emitted a discreet chime to indicate we were topping a hundred kilometres an hour. Red carpeting covered the dashboard. A gilt decoration hung from the rear-view mirror. We sped on.

All the time I drove around Rwanda that autumn, the whole of the international humanitarian community dealing with Rwanda seemed to be on their way to, from, or in the process of attending or reporting on one, great, endless meeting. Across every hotel bar of the Great Lakes Region, in the United Nations conference rooms of New York, Kigali and Washington, on the NGO radio networks of Zaire, Rwanda and Burundi, as well as in the international media, there was a lot of concern being voiced as 1995 drew to a close. In Kigali, the UNHCR's elaborately titled special envoy for Rwanda, Burundi and the Great Lakes Region, Carrol Faubert, was talking about the 'absorption capacity' of refugee reception centres within Rwanda. He said that the UNHCR could handle up to 20,000 returnees per day. The mood in the Zairean camps for a return to Rwanda was 'favourable'. This was directly contrary to what some fifty journalists had witnessed in August, when the only way refugees could be forced to return from Goma was at Zairean gunpoint.

Butare was the second city of Rwanda, lying two hours south of Kigali.

It was here that many of the worst massacres had taken place in April and May 1994. MSF had a meeting about returning refugees and decided that it had two years' worth of drugs ready, should the people in Zaire make a move. The 120-bed hospital at Kabutare was the only hospital in the district that still functioned. The medical coordinator, a red-haired French woman called Françoise, told me that most of the medically trained personnel in the area had either been killed or had fled to Burundi or Zaire.

Meanwhile, a regional conference on the Great Lakes had been announced by the presidents of Uganda and Zaire. Under the auspices of former American president Jimmy Carter, Rwanda, Burundi, Tanzania, Uganda and Zaire would all meet to discuss the situation.

A day later, Innocent and I drove to the north-western town of Gisenyi, on the Rwandan side of the border from Goma. Lieutenant-Colonel Vladimir Belski, a United Nations military observer on attachment from the Russian army, was holding a security meeting. This involved all the UNAMIR detachments, UN sections and the various aid agencies based in the north-west of the country. His prognosis was not good. Hutu militiamen were infiltrating the region from the refugee camps around Goma. They would move into the dense Gishwati forest, lie up for a couple of days, and then move out of the forests to lay mines.

'It's unpredictable,' said Belski, standing in front of me in his Russian uniform.

'The problem is that nobody knows where these mines are going to be laid next. They are becoming more and more numerous and there is no discernible pattern to them. The other day, the RPA captured a man and he confessed under questioning . . .'

Belski looked at me and smiled.

'Questioning means torture up here. The RPA have got a new technique they've been trying out recently. They nail the prisoner's feet to the floor with large nails. Then they make him do sit-ups till he talks.'

He helped himself to one of my Winstons and lit up, walking over towards the wall. A huge map showed all the communes of north-western Rwanda. His cigarette finger traced a path from the shore of Lake Kivu in towards the Gishwati forest.

'Anyway, after they had questioned this man, he said that he was from the interahamwe, on an infiltration mission. Look,' he said, pointing at a number of villages on the map.

'All in one week: Basasamana. On the seventeenth, two warnings of mines, the RPA open fire on somebody. The eighteenth, five interahamwe captured here.'

He stubbed the village of Rubavu with his finger.

'These guys were questioned as well and admitted they were on their way back from a mission. Later in the day, the RPA were attacked with grenades in Bizizi; they gave chase and contacted them at Kinyamzovu. Killed two of them. Another captured on the nineteenth. On the twentieth, the villagers in Matura are claiming the interahamwe are somewhere in the area after they find mines on the road. Then a killing in Shyira – same day.'

He paused, then dropped his cigarette end into a carved wooden ashtray on his desk.

'Twenty-first – a group of thirty of them comes over from Lac Vert and Mugunga. Another one of them gets questioned. One of the girls who cooks in our house, her father works at the *cachot*, the lock-up. Says this one took a long time to die. He said before he died that a party of sixty or seventy infiltrators were due to arrive in Rwanda in the next two to four days.'

He walked over from the map and sat on the corner of his desk, facing me.

'You want to know how all these killings of civilians are going on in this area? The local people – they don't have a choice. Look, on the twenty-second, the RPA go into Matura village. They tell the local people that if they don't start reporting more interahamwe incidents, they'll get the same as what happened at Kanama. You remember? Hundred and ten civilians killed in one night by the army? Then you have the other side – we've had the Mayor, the bourgmestre of Kanama in here saying that the interahamwe have turned up there threatening the people, telling them they'll die if they don't support them.'

He lit one of his own cigarettes, and blew the first drag of smoke out of the window.

'These people are completely trapped.'

I met Melissa Sargaison from the British medical aid agency MERLIN, as she was coming out of Gisenyi hospital. She'd just had a meeting with local officials from the Rwandan Ministry of Health. On the hospital door, the bullet holes had been filled but not yet painted over.

'Disasters hit without warning – don't bother to knock,' said a sign.

Melissa looked as though she was enjoying herself. We rode in the white MERLIN Land Rover over to the house, set on the road leading out of Gisenyi, where the rest of the six-strong team lived. The garden was full of bougainvillea, there were avocado trees, and a view led straight across to the plains outside Goma, five kilometres away. Behind us, Renamo the cat and Bob the dog were sleeping.

'You make the choice to come and be in a place like this,' said Melissa. 'Apart from indiscriminate things like mines, most of the danger is targeted towards local people. I was working in the intensive therapy unit at Guy's Hospital before I came here. I thought, why am I here haemodialysing eighty-nine-year-old men, spending two thousand pounds per person per day on drugs. It wasn't me.'

Like the MSF teams in Butare, the MERLIN group was waiting for refugees to come back home across the border. They had enough equipment both at the base and at their health centre at Gacuba, in the foothills of the mountains outside Gisenyi, to treat 10,000 people per day for three months. They also ran four health centres where, as well as treating the local population, they provided technical and financial help for the local Ministry of Health officials.

Unfortunately for my article, Melissa had not just been chucked by her boyfriend. He was sitting next to her in the garden. I'd thought for a moment that there might have been a grisly contretemps with Vladimir Belski. A Doctor Zhivago scenario on the edge of Lake Kivu. But no.

'London got cold feet about us helping the perpetrators of the genocide in Lac Vert,' added Melissa's boyfriend, who also worked for MERLIN, along with another Englishman who broadcast on Radio UNAMIR in Kigali under his DJ's pseudonym of Doctor Freddy Lovecraft.

'That was why they pulled us out of Goma.'

I stayed with the MERLIN team for a night, and drove back to Kigali the following day. In the forests and mountains around Gisenyi, the army was fighting its own counter-insurgency war against the ex-FAR and the militias, where no quarter was asked for, nor given. As we drove through the outskirts of the town of

Ruyengeri, we slowed to let an RPA patrol cross the road in front of us. The men trooped across in single file, dusty, tired, and looking very different from the clean soldiers in the capital. There must have been forty of them, tramping along with 60mm mortars and tripods on their backs, cases of 7.62mm machine-gun ammunition in their hands and mattresses rolled on their heads. Some had rucksacks on their backs, some had their equipment in fibre suitcases balanced on their heads. Some held their Kalashnikovs or Heckler & Kochs or Belgian FN-FALs in one hand, while in the other was half a sack of beans or maize or a dirty jerry-can of water. I wondered what it must have been like, patrolling off into the hills above Ruhengeri that day. Most of the soldiers had either battered army boots on their feet, or gymshoes or Wellington boots. A few wore flip-flops. I wondered whether they came from the Gisenyi–Ruhengeri region, or whether they had been born in Uganda. A Rwandan army captain, Frank Ndore, known as 'four-fingered Frank', after a missing digit on one hand, had told me that the RPA tried to send soldiers from one particular region back to their home area to fight. This made it much easier to track down and identify the militias and former government soldiers.

I don't know what the French had managed to teach the former Rwandan government army, but whatever it was, it had not been sufficient to beat Paul Kagame's RPA. The FLA and Hutu militias had been effectively routed all the way across Rwanda. Successful mass killers they might be, but the Rwandan Hutus had no military prowess that had ever resulted in any kind of victory on a battlefield. The French had provided the backbone, the technical expertise and the fighting ability when the RPF were driven out of Rwanda after the invasion in 1990. And the RPF had not forgotten this defeat, nor had they forgotten the French involvement in it. Meanwhile, the whole expatriate population of Rwanda was waiting for the refugees to come home, the weight of their efforts concentrated on helping those who had killed, as well as their wives and children.

It was lunch time, when I got back to Kigali, and the bars and restaurants of the capital were crammed with white aid workers, diplomats, soldiers and Rwandan government officials. I headed for the American Club to look for Lieutenant Kent Page, a Canadian military officer who was the official UNAMIR spokesman.

While away, I had missed the fiftieth anniversary celebrations of the United Nations, which had been commemorated in Kigali with a programme of sporting events between UNAMIR troops and the local Rwandan teams. The highlights had been a ten-kilometre track event, in which the Rwandans, running barefoot, easily beat the UN, and a football match. The score in the football had been 3–1 to the Rwandan team, against their opponents, a squad from the Ghanaian peace-keeping battalion. At one point it looked as though the Ghanaians were going to put a goal in, when the ball was handled outside the Rwandan area. The referee, a Rwandan, didn't blow the whistle for a penalty but did just afterwards when a Rwandan player was obstructed from behind by a Ghanaian. A fight erupted on the pitch between the two teams, whereupon a number of the Rwandan supporters in the crowd decided to rush the pitch. One of them grabbed a Kalashnikov from an RPA soldier on the touchline, and mayhem broke out.

Luckily, Rwandan officials managed to calm the fracas after a minute and a half of chaos, and order was restored. Rwandan officials protested, their minister of sport described it as a 'diplomatic incident,' and the party for the fiftieth anniversary was cancelled.

'It's a tragedy,' Kent Page said, sitting under a beer umbrella in the American Club, 'when underlying resentments boil up over something that is meant to be a competitive sport. But it happens a lot in football, not just in politics.'

Returning to Nairobi from a trip away was always a depressing experience. Coming back to the dusty Kenyan capital after the firefights and energy of Mogadishu or the labyrinthine politics and genocidal excesses of Rwanda always smacked of anticlimax. It was like coming back to boarding school at the start of a new autumn term. There were stories to be written, expenses to be filed. Kenya never seemed to want to open itself and show interest in the affairs of other countries. I dumped my possessions on the carpet of the flat and fell into the swimming pool. It was the end of November and

Nairobi was hitting the peak of the hot season. At four in the afternoon the dry air was brown where it hung over the plains, soaring to a fierce, crackling blue overhead. Chugged with exhaust fumes and heavy with the dust and sweat of overcrowding, the city seemed to be panting.

Esther, our maid, scooped up my dirty clothes and took them out to her yard to soak. My face in the bathroom mirror as I shaved was tanned, and I had a v-shape of tanned skin on my chest. It was a Wednesday evening, and I felt that I had been away from Nairobi for weeks rather than just eight days. I pulled on fresh clothes, rolling the sleeves of my shirt, then headed up the drive to the taxi rank on the Ngong road. Five minutes later, I rattled down Valley Road in an old black London-Look. All the traffic was heading out of town. A sticker on the sliding glass panel separating me from the driver announced 'this taxi is fuelled by the blood of Jesus Christ'. I got out at Chester House, the city-centre tower block that housed the Press Centre.

The corridor was lined with dark-brown wooden doors, each bearing the sticker of a different news organization. At the far end was the office of the *Financial Times*. There I found their correspondent, Michela Wrong, leaning back in her chair, suede court shoes perched on her desk, talking on the phone. When she saw me, she leaned over the desk, not halting her flow of conversation, and passed me a one-page fax from the swirl of papers in front of her. It was headed with the logo of Oxfam, and was from their office in England.

'Dear Michela,' it began. 'We were given your name by your office in London, and are contacting you in reference to a proposed economic survey of Burundi we would like to carry out.'

I stopped reading and looked at Michela. She put her palm over the receiver of the phone.

'Can I borrow this to read?' I asked.

'I was going to pass it to you to have a look at.'

'I'll leave you to it,' I said, standing up. 'Drink at the Norfolk afterwards?'

She nodded.

I bustled up the crowded sidewalks of central Nairobi, heading for the Norfolk Hotel. Like Rwanda and Somalia, there was direction and pulse here, I thought, but the people looked more tired and cowed. The pavements were cracked and pot-holed from lack of maintenance; everything seemed broken. But everybody was busy. If you didn't have money in Africa, there never seemed to be an opportunity to slow down, to stop thinking about hussling a living. Everything in that square of roads and alleys of uptown Nairobi happened on the street, fifteen little dramas touching each other on ten metres of dusty pavement. A gang of street children in greasy rags stood at a taxi rank, soft-drink cans filled with cobblers glue hanging from their lips. Two old women sat on the pavement knotting carnations and roses into a wreath. A shoe-shine boy leant against a broken-headed parking meter eating chips from a bag marked 'Farmers Choice sausages'. Leaning inside the glass of a chemist's shop, there was a large display sign showing a wriggling, smiling worm wearing a top hat and carrying a cane. 'Worms go back to school too', said the caption on the sign, which advertised anti-ringworm treatments. At the entrance to the New Florida nightclub a bouncer was brushing dust from his dinner-jacket; in the dirt beneath his feet, a child laid five packets of Sportsman cigarettes out on the money page of the *Daily Nation*. His leg triangled out sideways, crippled with polio. Five cobble-stone widths away, an old woman made a pyramid of individual shortbread biscuits and a packing crate. The crumbly towers leant against a line of twenty green and red boiled sweets, sold singly. A night-watchman, the ubiquitous Kenyan *askari*, arrived for work; his job to guard the cars that would park outside an arcade full of restaurants. He reached into a doorway behind one of the women twisting the wreaths, and pulled out a grubby white carrier bag marked with the logo of the Uchumi supermarket chain. Inside was the uniform of his night job. He pulled on crumpled blue trousers with a red stripe up each leg, and a jacket with grubby epaulettes. From a ring on his belt he hung a black, wooden side-handled truncheon. On his head he set a peaked cap, the vinyl on the crown cracked and bent. He would be on duty till dawn, and then would sleep on the ground. Running through this hum of activity and livelihood that spanned both edges of the pavement, was the constant flow of feet. The city's commuters hurried for their bus, bustled along to their matatu stage, or prepared to walk home. From ground level all the eye saw was a mass of footwear scuffing and clicking past. There were cracked vinyl loafers, their seams ingrained with dirt from days of walking through the dust of shanty-town paths, there were broken, worn-down brogues, holes gaping, heels scuffed, there were shoes whose owner could afford a twenty-shilling shine, and there were the broken flip-flops and blistered cracked feet of the urban destitutes.

Up past the entrance to the Safari Club Hotel, I crossed the road and walked carefully through the flickering, hooting mass of matutu minibuses, past Nairobi's Central Police Station. Three shiny, khaki police Land Rovers were loading officers at the entrance for night duty somewhere in town. At the back of the building were the cells, and from the glassless, barred windows came a smell of rotting humanity and tired sweat, accompanied by a low, rumbling moan. Next, on the right, was the Engineering Faculty of Nairobi University, the pavement separated from the grass frontage by a low, thorn hedge. Up ahead was the Norfolk Hotel. Taxis and minibuses turned in front of it.

I sat at an empty table on the Lord Delamere terrace. A Kenyan waiter in tartan waistcoat appeared at my side.

'You have ordered for your Tusker Keg, sir?'

As my pint was poured up at the bar, I pulled out Michela's fax. Oxfam was looking for somebody to go to Burundi and carry out an economic survey. This, they explained in the letter, would enable them to assess the viability of future programmes there. Burundi, I thought. The Oxfam survey, if I could get it, would mean money. Charge fifteen hundred dollars for a fortnight, plus expenses. Get to know the country – write some articles as well. I had resolved to make some changes on my return to Nairobi anyway. Although I had only been in the region for five months, and was the new boy of the press corps, two things were immediately apparent. The first was that the Rwandan genocide and the Somalia story had been the biggest stories of the last four years. Rwanda would become big again, but not until the refugees came home. Nobody in Kigali thought this imminent, despite a New Year deadline imposed by Zaire. The Sudanese civil war would trickle on until the next famine, the best Uganda had to offer was two low-key guerilla conflicts, and the Somalis' refusal to play ball with the west over the last three years had consigned them to a decade of obscurity. As for Tanzania, well, it was a beautiful country. Everybody who had just returned from covering the elections had said how laid-back and nice the Tanzanians were, but nothing ever happened. Worse, from our point of view, it was a country at peace.

It was a ruthless and cynical train of thought, but I didn't have the luxury of thinking otherwise. I didn't have the corporate expenses, or staff job, or secure posting that so many of my colleagues enjoyed. Unless I could find a story that I could make my own, perhaps cover for a wire agency like Reuters or the Associated Press, as well as the BBC, or Voice of America, I would be stuck in Nairobi too much of the time, unable to afford interesting trips, writing two articles a month for the *Sunday Telegraph*. In other words, I'd be broke. Perhaps Burundi was the answer. It sounded different. The agencies were using descriptions like 'slow-trickle genocide', and 'boiler-plate ethnic conflict'. Word was that several thousand people a month were being massacred, mostly at the hands of the Tutsi army. It was politically complex and dangerous. Nobody wanted to go there. The last western journalist to be based there permanently had been William Wallis from Reuters. He'd been scrambled out of the country in a hurry eight weeks earlier after one death-threat too many from the military. One final thought made up my mind: the risk. Rather like the French Foreign Legion, I'd regret it if I never tried it out. Who knows, I thought. The story's complicated, I don't know much about it, and I'll probably be useless. But I had to try. Watching the approach of the small, svelte form of Michela, I was suddenly reminded how, by comparison with most of my colleagues, I didn't really cut the mustard as a foreign correspondent.

My pint of Keg Tusker arrived at the same time as she did.

'Gin and tonic?' I offered.

She settled and held out a hand.

'Fag.'

I handed her a Benson and Hedges and took out the Oxfam fax.

'What do you think?' I asked.

'I was going to give it to you before you went to Somalia. Wondered what you'd think.'

'Why don't you do it?' I asked.

'I can't afford to take the time off. And frankly,' she added, laughing, 'who wants to spend three weeks in Burundi?'

'But . . .' I said, 'I don't know Oxfam, I've never been to Burundi, and as for economics . . .'

'Exactly. That's what I thought. They can't find anybody. You'll be perfect.'

I met with Oxfam three days later. Their outgoing country director interviewed me. I explained that I wasn't exactly a Burundi specialist, but I did have a background in investigative journalism. I cited my time working for *World in Action* in the UK. She in turn introduced me to a senior official from the organization, who was visiting Nairobi from England.

'So,' asked this senior, rather grand woman, bustling furiously off to dinner with several members of her Nairobi staff, 'Where were you? London School of Economics? The Economist Intelligence Unit? You're an economist by training, I take it?'

The following day I went to Finance House, next door to the Press Centre. I had a brief chat with Peter Smerdon, the deputy bureau chief of Reuters. They would take anything I could send, he explained. They'd had precious little good coverage from the country since William Wallis had left.

Crossing the street after my visit to Reuters, I bumped into the *Newsweek* correspondent, Joshua Hammer. He was a veteran of Somalia, a journalist who'd arrived in Kigali just days after the genocide had started. Excited, and more than a little eager to impress, I told him what I was going to do.

'You're fucking mad,' he said, and crossed the road.

Later that day, I packed my body armour into my canvas Gap bag, and telephoned the World Food Programme in Nairobi to ask about UN flights to Bujumbura.

Part II

Chapter 4

Red Dust, Machetes and Eucalyptus Trees

If there was a full-scale civil war being fought in Burundi, then it was going on somewhere else completely. If there was industrial-level ethnic cleansing being carried out, then it wasn't anywhere near me. The afternoon was silent. I had disembarked from the UN aircraft expecting to arrive in a city that looked the same as Kigali in April 1994. I had stood alone on the tarmac of Bujumbura airport and cocked an ear, half expecting to hear the sound of artillery, the crack of small-arms fire, the rushing bustle of a hundred thousand refugees in flight. Where were the palls of smoke from the burning buildings? Where were the rows of injured civilians awaiting the promised evacuation that everybody knew secretly would never come? Why hadn't the glass of the airport windows been blown out? Two Burundian policemen were checking passports. I was through in minutes, my bags unchecked. The terminal was very clean, very tidy, and almost deserted. Could this be a country where a genocide was being committed?

My imagination had, as ever, been working overtime. Spurred on by descriptions of civil war and genocide, I had anticipated militia road-blocks manned by drunken youths on the road from the airport, piles of Hutu and Tutsi corpses lying in ditches, a heavy military presence, an occupied presidency and choked hospitals. I had half-envisaged fleeing queues of refugees blocking the highways, and armoured cars surrounding a TV and radio station that was in flames. On the flight in I'd wondered whether I should put on my flak-jacket before we touched down. I had imagined myself grabbing the first available car, thrusting a hundred dollars at the driver, shouting 'take me to the hotel'. Despite my African travels and working experience of the last year, I had somehow formed a picture more like the riots in the Congo in the 1960s, spiced up with images of the French Foreign Legion parachuting into Zaire in 1978 to save white hostages trapped by drunken, raping, rampaging mobs. I had really thought that the taxi might swerve giddily to a stop in front of a besieged hotel, perhaps defended by terrified UN troops from a plucky faraway country like Bangladesh or Nepal. In my mind they'd be down to their last dozen mortar bombs, their officers long-dead, and the shrinking perimeter under the command of a thrice-wounded sergeant-major. Selfless nurses would have been co-opted into filling sandbags. Bare-chested MSF surgeons who hadn't slept for a week would be carrying out amputations in the cellar by the light of hurricane lanterns. I'd imagined hideously injured troops fighting a terrible rearguard action from the lawn, of slit-trenches dug where once flowers had grown. Hundreds of frightened international staff would have taken refuge in the kitchen. They would have eked out weeks of siege on a diet of tinned pineapple chunks and swimming pool water, itself polluted by corpses and excrement. I was thinking Arnhem, of Monte Cassino, of nightmare artillery duels across the mountains, of streets rolling with spent cartridge cases, and dead bodies being eaten by three-legged stray dogs.

I shook my head as the taxi driver turned to me for directions.

'*M'sieur?*'

'The Novotel, please.'

It was with more than a little surprise, and perhaps some sense of bathos, therefore, that I enjoyed a calm drive into the centre of the capital. The driver charged a perfectly reasonable ten dollars. Once at the hotel, I saw lots of soldiers – well, ten, and one of them was reading a newspaper – but was amazed to check in to an already reserved room, the smiling Tutsi receptionist handing me my key. The lift purred upwards. The bellboy welcomed me to Burundi, asking after the weather in Nairobi. He looked curiously at the shell dressing and morphine syrettes taped to the shoulder of my flak-jacket. We got to the fifth floor, a long, quiet corridor lined with scarlet carpeting, and found my room. There were no sandbags in sight. Five minutes later I was alone in my room, trying to undo the window which had no handle. Outside in the hotel garden, palm trees swayed. There was a splash from the swimming pool, the low mutter of voices. It was a Sunday afternoon in an African capital. The city lay calm, quiet and dusty. Palm, eucalyptus, avocado and mango trees grew everywhere, the avenues were wide and clean, the houses white with red roofs. Bujumbura lay in a natural amphitheatre, surrounded on three sides by mountains, and one side by the blue lake. Of course, I reasoned rather lamely, the rebels would have observation posts in those hills. Come nightfall there would be the whistle of incoming fire, the scramble for the bunkers. I laid out my toothbrush and razor, hung my clothes in the wardrobe, and wondered what to do next. The phone rang.

'Not been shot yet?'

It was Corinne Dufka, giggling from Nairobi. I assured her that there was a heavy military presence on the streets and that I thought things could well be tense.

'It's always like that. Be careful. Enjoy the pool. Ring me.'

Downstairs I walked onto the terrace bar and sat down. Two crowned cranes strutted around the flagstones, picking at crumbs thrown down by Belgian aid workers having a late lunch. The sun-loungers by the pool were all taken; the frangipani trees with their yellow and pink flowers dropped blossoms into the deep end. Children played as the shadows grew longer. I ordered a passion-fruit juice.

'Burundi is now situated as Rwanda was between the signature of the Arusha Accords in August 1993 and the start of the genocide in April 1994,' I read in my notes. 'The legal government is paralysed, extremist groups hold the country virtually hostage, violence is rampant and the media publish incitement to murder. Failing international intervention . . . catastrophe looks inevitable . . . number of victims could still reach 150,000.'

Oh God. I read on. 'First democratically elected Hutu president, Melchior Ndadaye, killed in coup in October 1993.' (That would be the incident with the gardening instruments and the Tutsi paratroopers that Paul Barril had failed to prevent, I remembered.) 'Estimated deaths 50–100,000 as Hutus take revenge on Tutsis and Tutsi army then retaliates. An estimated 50,000 killed since then. Cycle of massacres. Spiral of violence. Demonstrations. Youth militias.'

It didn't look good. It seemed that I had arrived in Burundi as the story was about to happen, rather than after it was over. I was the only journalist there. The warm, balmy afternoon by the swimming pool went cold and I felt as though several feet were marching over my grave. What was my responsibility for Reuters? Finding out what was going on and warning the outside world? I thought that sounded rather self-important. Certainly beyond me. Keeping track of events on a daily basis? Setting myself up as a kind of independent arbitrator? (The hotel door open day and night; Hutu and Tutsi equally welcome. The Chivas Regal being passed from hand to hand as enmities forged over decades dissolved. And then the trill of the phone with that midnight call from Madeleine Albright?) No. I suspected that for the time being the best thing to do was to try and meet the twenty most influential people in the capital, from both sides, and keep a sort of daily check on them. Then I'd send Nairobi what I thought was important. That, and the normal round of news events that in Burundi would surely make themselves apparent.

The benefits of having worked in Rwanda were paying off. I could see the framework of politics and events around me, even if I couldn't establish the component parts. Reuters was going to be a different bag than the *Sunday Telegraph*. It wasn't weekly stories any more, laden with colour, about wacky expatriates having a tough time on the equator. In Burundi I was responsible for all aspects of its reporting. News, features, urgents, analyses. And if something really, really important happened – like yet another head of government being killed – I could send a bulletin, the fastest-moving, most urgent piece of news you could put on the Reuters wire. I'd only been in the country for two hours, but I suspected that if we were ever to send a bulletin, it would contain a selection of the words coup, president, assassination, genocide and dead.

I was also supposed to supply economics information on coffee prices, tea exports, banking, and trade. I knew that Reuters would want something more fact-rich than a piece saying that the country exported 'loads of coffee' or that its tea prices were 'rocketing'. The Nairobi bureau had a stringer in Somalia, Mohamed Guled, who, like myself, was new to Reuters and hadn't benefited from the two-year London training scheme, the graduate selection, the executive choice.

When Somalia's leading warlord General Mohamed Farah Aidid, the man who had faced down the might of the US Army, died in Mogadishu, it was the biggest bit of news that Mohamed Guled would probably ever handle for Reuters from his country. I was to be in the bureau in Nairobi when his fax came in.

It had been written in pencil, diagonally across a page of A4 paper.

General Mohamed Farah Aidid was died yesterday late in South Mogadishu, according to all of his vice-presidents after made him an operation at his upper right chest which was hit a bullet last week during the fighting at Medina district of South Mogadishu.

Today, after the pray of Friday will burying at SOS hospital area of South Mogadishu. I will explain later. (End.)

Later on, the statement released on his radio confirmed 'the diedness of the General Aideed. Signed Mohamed Guled, Reuters, Mogadishu.' It was to be one of my favourite pieces of reporting.

I wasn't sure how my economics reporting was to go, not only for Reuters, but also for Oxfam. I thought that what I'd do was to ask a few pertinent economic questions to everybody on my list of the twenty most important people, and then, sort of, collate it. I had a meeting that evening at the hotel with the Oxfam country coordinator, and I needed some background. I signed for my passion-fruit juice with a flourish and walked to the lifts. As I waited for it to descend, I looked at the 'employees of the month' photographs that were hung by the elevator doors. Set against a background of Yukka plants in the garden, the photos showed two men. One was a waiter, named Fulgence, and the other, a manager, called Dieu-Donne. A world where there was the continuity and time to make lists of achieving hotel employees was not a world perched on the edge, I thought, rather puzzled. But I was still half convinced that two kilometres away in the hills was a Hutu mortar crew, Festus and Clovis. They'd be silently measuring the range to the Novotel car-park from a dugout scraped out of the bright red earth.

My room, being on the fifth-floor, accumulated much of the heat that rose through the concrete of the clumsily designed hotel. I still couldn't get the window to open, so took my documents back downstairs and found a table.

Burundi had roughly the same ethnic makeup as Rwanda, being 85 per cent Hutu, 14 per cent Tutsi, and 1 per cent Twa. Like Rwanda, it subsisted on the same system of small-scale agriculture, on a highly socially controlled network of hills. Flying in that afternoon, I'd found it if anything greener than Rwanda. It was even more fertile, the earth even redder. Prior to the arrival of the Germans in 1893, and the imposition of a Belgian mandate in 1916, there had been no record of ethnic massacres. There was a king, from the Baganwa lineage, and the Belgians administered Burundi and Rwanda from Bujumbura. In Burundi too, the administration had favoured the Tutsis.

The first multi-ethnic political party had been the National Unity and Progress Party, or UPRONA. It had been founded before independence by the king's eldest son, Prince Louis Rwagasore, along the lines of a liberation movement. The Belgians had countered this by backing the Christian Democratic Party, or PDC, which lost the pre-independence elections to UPRONA. A Tutsi prime minister led the first independent government, although Prince Rwagasore was assassinated by PDC leaders. This was why the Avenue outside the hotel was called Boulevard UPRONA. Parliamentary elections in 1965 gave the Hutus almost 70 per cent of the majority, but the king listened to the Tutsis, refused to introduce a Hutu prime minister and put in a member of his own family instead. Hutu army officers attempted a coup and Hutu militiamen massacred 500 Tutsis in the central province of Muramvya.

I got out my map and found Muramvya, bang in the middle of the hills. I also marked an asterisk next to 1965 in my notes, adding the note 'first massacre'. I'd already found in Rwanda that when talking to politicians and army officers I needed to have my wits about me. They could be talking about Rwanda in 1959 (20,000 dead, mostly Tutsis), and I could be thinking about Burundi in 1965 (3,500 slaughtered, mostly Hutus).

Tutsi militiamen backing Captain Michel Micombero, a Tutsi officer from the Hima clan in Bururi, took revenge. I found Bururi on the map, in southern Burundi. Several thousand Hutus were killed and most removed from positions of power and influence in the civil service, in the army and in universities. Micombero, helped by white mercenaries recruited from the Congo, overthrew the monarchy and assumed total power. He purged the army, and replaced the officer corps with soldiers from his own clan.

'*M'sieur?*'

It was the waiter. I shifted in my plastic beach chair, reached for my cigarettes, and ordered an Amstel lager.

'And some peanuts, as well please.'

I had only been one afternoon in Burundi, and so had never visited Bururi. But that was where Micombero's Hima clan came from, and lots of them seemed to join the army. I thought hard and made a bet with myself. In countries like Rwanda and Burundi, where social class and wealth was all about land and cows, why did one whole clan group veer towards the armed forces? I wagered that the land in Bururi was like mid-Wales. High, windy, barren and difficult to cultivate. Possibly full of people who wanted to escape, and separated from the capital by mountains. People from Bururi would be looked down on, would have a strong feeling of inverted snobbery, and probably dismiss education. Many people would join the army to improve themselves in their own estimation, to become part of an elite. In doing so, they cut themselves off sub-consciously from civilians and believed themselves superior thanks to the nature of their military calling. Then I read on. The Hima clan, it transpired, were considered inferior to the bourgeois Tutsis from the centre of the country, both in terms of class and education and according to the cattle and land-ownership criteria.

To gain authority over the land-owning Tutsi middle classes, Micombero had to make them believe that there was an external – i.e.

Hutu – threat. This he was clever enough to do. Next, he saw that he had to wipe out two kinds of opposition: the rich, high class Tutsis, which also included the monarchy, and the Hutus, who might pre-empt his strike or prove, at some later point, to be intellectually and socially superior to his small band of rough-hewn, Bururi army boys. It was at this point that Burundi became irretrievably divided along ethnic lines. Micombero was a small-minded alcoholic officer with social pretensions, but no social or material assets to support them, who'd been passed over for promotion twice in his early career. He was a poor soldier and an uninspiring leader. Like many soldiers, he probably felt most comfortable in purely military company. As this military company would all have come from three very small social sub-groups from the same fifteen kilometre radius, it cannot have been difficult to communicate fears of social and professional repression among them. Micombero's hardline regime also made sure that UPRONA, although supposed to be a party of dual ethnicity, was simply a tool of the army.

In April 1972, the biggest killings to date took place in Burundi. Hutu militiamen trained in Zaire decided to put an end to the regime of Micombero. They saw a future under his dictatorship where they would eventually have no rights at all. They crossed Lake Tanganyika on pirogue canoes and landed near the town of Nyanza-Lac, where John Hanning Speke had made his landfall over a hundred years earlier. At the same time, Hutus attacked the capital and the central town of Gitega, targeting Tutsi men, women and children. About 5,000 were killed. The revenge of Micombero was to be absolute.

The Tutsi army had been further trained by French, Belgian, Rhodesian and German mercenaries who had found themselves unemployed at the collapse of the civil war in Biafra. Micombero said that the Hutus were going to kill the Tutsis if the army didn't get there first. He inspired enough anti-Hutu paranoia in the ranks below him to instigate a mass ethnic killing of some 110,000 Hutus. His interior minister shot the king. Three hundred thousand Hutus fled into exile in Zaire, Rwanda and Tanzania. Micombero's state security apparatus then hunted down and systematically exterminated every single Hutu in the country who had an educational qualification higher than any western ten-year-old. Thus did Micombero purge his intellectual and class paranoia, and thus began the ethnic deadlock between the Burundian Tutsi army and the Hutu majority that continued unchecked as I sat in my chair at the Novotel on my first afternoon in Burundi.

The 1972 killings went on for three months. Hutus were removed from every level of power in the country, right down to junior administrators in local government. One of the side effects of this quasi-genocide was that in neighbouring Rwanda, Tutsis were persecuted further and Juvenal Habyarimana took power to bring a halt to the violence. Micombero remained in power until 1976, when he was toppled by one of his insiders, Jean-Baptiste Bagaza, also from Bururi, and also a Hima Tutsi.

'Amstel?'

The waiter put my beer down on the table, and slipped a saucer of peanuts alongside them. The swimming pool had emptied, parents and children were drifting towards the terrace tables. The light began to thicken over the gardens. I wondered what was happening out in the hills; how many Hutu rebels were sitting in the banana plantations getting their weapons out; how many Tutsi soldiers were preparing to go out on patrol.

Bagaza's regime, if anything, only served to make the control of the paranoid Bururi army clique more totalitarian. Hutus had been almost totally squeezed out of the educational system: only 20 per cent of students at the National University were Hutu, and 90 per cent of the teachers were Tutsi. The Tutsi students, studying agriculture, economics, philosophy, were allowed to keep weapons in the dormitories. Even Burundian students abroad were spied on. Bagaza's state security apparatus made Burundi one of the most tightly controlled countries outside the Communist block. Press freedom was almost non-existent: state spies were on every hill, reporting to the government. The Catholic Church was targeted as a last resort of free speech; any member of any religious order who spoke out was detained and tortured. Bujumbura had become a sort of tropical Kremlin.

Finally, Bagaza went too far. He tried to clamp down on the one institution which guaranteed his power: the army. He tried to exclude officers and NCOs who were not from the Bururi hardline clique, and found himself imprisoning members of the Tutsi social and political elite. The army turned on him in 1987, and a group of senior non-commissioned officers replaced him in a bloodless coup. He was replaced by yet another military officer from Bururi, Major Pierre Buyoya. Buyoya was far more liberal than Bagaza. He cut back on discrimination against the Church, released all political prisoners, and was astute enough to realize that unless the Hutu and liberal Tutsi were given some form of political expression, the country would become interminably wracked by round after round of massacre. But Buyoya did not go far enough, fast enough. Only a quarter of his first cabinet were Hutu. No Hutus were allowed anywhere near the judiciary or the civil service, and certainly nowhere near the army. University education was still almost closed to them, and among Tutsis, the demonization of the Hutu continued. They were presented to the non-educated, illiterate majority of rural Tutsis as those who would rise up again and kill them. Buyoya saw this spectre looming in the fog, waving its machete, and tried desperately to do something about it.

The Hutus beat him to it. An extremist Hutu organization, PALIPEHUTU, or Party for the Liberation of the Hutu People, had been created in 1980 by Remy Gahutu, a Burundian exile living in Rwanda. In May 1988, it put out a particularly aggressive message propagating the idea that ethnic discrimination would be solved only by use of violence. In August that year, they took action in northern Burundi. Parties of Hutu peasants, led by PALIPEHUTU activists, attacked groups of Tutsis. Two days later, the army arrived, and started massacring groups of Hutu indiscriminately: the government said 5000 people were killed, foreign observers said between 15 and 20,000. Sixty-thousand people fled to Rwanda. The attack had been organized by the Hutus to pre-empt Tutsi violence; the Tutsis were happy to respond to such provocation, as they feared the liberalizing moves being made by Buyoya, which by then included the appointment of a Hutu Prime Minister. Sporadic ethnic violence continued, but by 1993 the multi-party electoral system under Buyoya had culminated in free elections. Melchior Ndadaye, a Hutu from the FRODEBU party, the Front for Burundian Democracy won the elections with 65 per cent of the votes.

And then in October 1993, hardline elements of the army rose up, murdered Ndadaye, and declared a coup. After unilateral condemnation from international donors, the coup collapsed, but an estimated 100,000 people were slaughtered in the ethnic violence that followed. Burundi was like a to and fro on a chequerboard, I thought. Massacre, army reprisals, political change, calm, political paranoia, clampdowns, massacre. Then reprisals, political change, calls from the international community, withdrawal of donor funding, repression, massacre, reprisals, coup, new president, democracy, massacre . . . and so it seemed to go on.

Shortly after President Cyprien Ntaryamira was killed in Habyarimana's plane, the Hutu Sylvestre Ntibantunganya was elected president. He did not have the backing of the army. Former interior minister and hardline Hutu Leonard Nyangoma, elected out of the cabinet in October 1994, took the armed struggle into the hills after his hardline Hutu faction had been driven out of the Bujumbura suburb of Kamenge by the army.

By September 1994, a year before I arrived in Burundi, both parties, both ethnicities, had come together to sign an agreement called the 'Convention of Government'. This provided for power-sharing between the two main parties, the Hutu FRODEBU and the Tutsi UPRONA, for the rest of President Ntibantunganya's term. But of course, hardliners on both sides refused to have anything to do with it.

On one hardline side were Bagaza's Tutsis, who had formed a party called PARENA. Allied to them was Tutsi militia, called SOJEDEM, or the Society for Democratic Youth. They recruited street gangs – rather like the Rwandan interahamwe – who called themselves by such names as the Sans Échec (those who never fail), and the Sans Défaite (the undefeated). These militias provided the muscle and the anarchic element necessary for urban violence and large-scale ethnic killings, often after being paid by their political sponsors. All of these gangs were armed by the army, with weapons bought by Bagaza on the open international market (through Dar es Salaam from China and Singapore), and by private drug-smuggling and gold-dealing enterprises run by various Tutsi army officers.

Facing the Tutsis from the other corner of the ring was Hutu former interior minister Leonard Nyangoma's breakaway FRO-DEBU faction. This was known as the National Council for the Defence of Democracy, or CNDD. The armed wing of the CNDD was called the FDD, or Front for the Development of Democracy. They had their own street militias, mainly Hutus who had been driven out of Bujumbura by the army. These were called the JEDEBU, or Democratic Youth of Burundi. From the ethnically cleansed suburb of Kamenge, from where Nyangoma came, there was also the Chicago Bulls militia, so-called because they all sported red baseball shirts bearing the team's logo. There were also the Jeunes '72, or the Youth of 1972.

Since the killings in 1993, much of the Tutsi population had been gathered into displaced persons camps, or moved to various centres in towns, markets, schools or communal buildings, where they were under the protection of the army. Bujumbura had become completely mono-ethnic. The only Hutus who now entered it did so during the day, leaving at night to return to the hills. The agricultural framework and structure of the country had collapsed; many Hutus hid from the army during the day in wooded and swampy areas, only emerging at night to cultivate their crops. The Tutsi were unable to herd or breed their cattle, and food was a major problem. The towns were essentially controlled by the army, Tutsi militias and Tutsi displaced people, while the hills were the land of the Hutu. The FDD, helped by displaced Hutu, were fighting a full-scale civil war against the army and the Tutsi militias. Hundreds, sometimes thousands of people were dying every month. Things were going to get worse.

I finished my glass of Amstel and raised my arm for the waiter. I wondered, this time without irony, whether my fertile imaginings of earlier that afternoon – the embattled capital, a besieged hotel, life under fire – would become a reality.

*

What were my predictions going to be for the Burundian economy, I considered, as I sat upstairs and tried to get the window open with the handle they had given me at reception. Perhaps I could just write the words 'terminally buggered' on one piece of A4 paper and leave it at that. I couldn't see how the economy was going to continue to work, given the prognosis of the country which I had just read at length. I had a shower and felt better, then went downstairs to meet the man from Oxfam.

The terrace bar was crowded. At the white plastic tables crowds of white aid workers drank Amstels and Mutzigs, the bottles jostling for space with the radio handsets and mobile telephones which were standing up in a forest of aerials. I didn't recognize anybody. The waiters dashed from the bar to the tables and back again. At the far end of the bar was the restaurant, half full at six o'clock. The swimming pool glistened, lit from under water. A thin screen of pot plants divided it from the bar. A man with glasses waved at me from the far end of the curved counter.

'So, Christian, get in safely?' asked John Myers, Oxfam's country coordinator, filling a glass with beer and taking a handful of peanuts.

'Yes, fine,' I said ordering my own beer. 'To be honest, I didn't expect it to be like this.'

'No?'

'No. I thought it would be more . . . chaotic.'

'What? Road-blocks, Kalashnikovs, that sort of thing?'

'Sort of,' I said. 'More, I dunno, at war.'

'It's all rather invisible, you'll find.'

John Myers had wet hair from the shower and was wearing a pair of expensive-looking sandals with cross-country soles. There was a lot of tracking and velcro on his feet.

'And the economy,' he asked. 'Where do you start?'

I breathed in. Sound authoritative. Don't assume anything. Be straight. He's probably an aid expert, a hotshot who's just got in from two years in the field in Afghanistan, or something. Remember the bullshit factor? Simple – don't.

'Tomorrow. First thing. I've got a coffee expert in the morning, then structural adjustment policy in the afternoon; World Bank just before lunch. Squeeze in the army end of the afternoon. I've already started a few basic notes. General outline, background, questions on fiscal policy. That sort of thing. Open mind – very important.'

'What is their fiscal policy, do you think? In aid terms, anyway?'

'Burundi? Well, coffee and tea form the backbone. Fluid financial indicators. Steady though. Exports – bit like the spine of their economy. That's how I've always seen it. Everything else, cotton, gold, tin, that's the skeleton.'

John looked at me strangely. We ordered another drink. I asked him about his background.

'Afghanistan. Two years, then they sent me here, to oversee the projects. Part of what you're going to be doing will help us assess how we should continue.'

I nodded. 'So who are all these people?' I gestured behind us at the tables.

He pointed out people.

'UNHCR. Tricky. Lots of refugees the Burundian army are trying to force back to Rwanda; they're trying to make sure it happens in a semi-civilized way. The others – MSF, the usual crowd.'

A Burundian army officer wearing the tabs of a lieutenant-colonel shouldered his way to the bar and stood next to us.

'Ministry of Defence spokesman,' said John quietly. 'Nutter. Has the ear of the Tutsi militias.'

The man turned towards me. I smiled. He introduced himself.

'They say you're the new correspondent for the BBC,' he said. 'We must speak. Ring me tomorrow.'

He gave me his card. Lieutenant-Colonel Longin Minani. Spokesman for the Burundian army.

'Watch them,' said John. 'They're trying to get the aid workers in the north of the country to pull out. Not keen to have too many people around up there. Too much to see.'

'Now,' he said. 'It's eight. Curfew time. We all turn into pumpkins by nine.'

In the next half hour the bar almost emptied as the aid workers made a dash for their vehicles. I was left by myself. I wandered over to the restaurant section and, for forty minutes, ate a meal in total silence. The moment my plate was cleared of each course, the waiter materialized and removed it. By nine-fifteen I was alone with my coffee and red wine.

That night was very long and very hot. I discovered that if I left my window open, the room filled with mosquitoes. If I closed it, the temperature rocketed, the air-conditioning didn't work. The night was silent. Enough mosquitoes had infiltrated the room for rest to be impossible. Four in the morning found me wide awake, furious, pouring with sweat, standing naked on the pillow trying to swat mosquitoes with a paperback. When the light crawled in through the windows at six-thirty, I estimated I had slept for two hours, smoked five cigarettes, and been bitten twenty-seven times. It was not a good start.

My first task the following day was to find a car. Unlike the Mille Collines Hotel in Kigali, there was no gathering of taxi drivers sitting out in the car-park with a range of variably trusty Toyotas and Datsuns. I was approached only by drivers whose vehicles turned out to be rattling blue-and-white taxis, all with an important component part – a windscreen, a silencer, an ignition system – missing. So it was with a sigh of relief that I accompanied a man called Zephyr out to where his low-slung but intact Datsun was standing in the shade. The passenger seat was soaking wet – he explained that he had just washed it – so by the time I arrived outside the Ministry of Defence, the back of my trousers were soaking and I was in a foul mood. Zephyr said he would be back in twenty minutes after he had gone to fetch some medicine from his doctor.

Lieutenant-Colonel Longin Minani was reading a maths book at his desk when I walked in. Bespectacled, in full dress uniform, he shook my hand, and gestured to a seat in front of him.

'So, Jennings,' he said, writing down my name on a piece of paper with a pencil on whose side were inscribed the words CRAZY PUSSYCAT. 'English: Jennings – a strange name. Jennings Christian.'

'Christian Jennings, the first name is my Christian name, the second is my surname . . . like Longin Minani. Minani isn't your Christian name.'

'No. Very much not. Longin is my name. Lieutenant-Colonel. Your predecessor Wallis, he had difficulty with this. He had difficulty with many things, Wallis. BBC William. Wallis of the lies.'

I looked at the Colonel's card. Massachusetts Institute of Technology. That explained the maths textbook he'd been reading. Clearly an intelligent man.

'So. You are working for Oxfam? Or Reuters? I thought you said the BBC?'

'For a few days, Colonel, I have to write a paper for Oxfam. Then the BBC and Reuters.'

'You have our trust here, Jennings Christian. We know you will write the truth. The Hutus here, they told Wallis of the BBC stories, and he believed them. He was my friend, I helped him. But Reuters paid him to write lies, William of the BBC. We had to escort him from the country, for his own protection.'

Oh God, I thought. Is it all going to be like this? Do I have a year of this ahead of me? I know now why nobody wanted to come to this awful country. I have to make this work, I thought. I'll be talking to this man almost every day.

'Tell me, Colonel. How is the military situation? How is the interior of the country?'

'Gradually, Christian, the people are coming around to our way of thinking; they are coming to understand that violence is not the only way, that the Convention of Government can help our country. The local populations are also realizing how they can help, that the presence of destabilizing elements must be reported to the military, that we are there to protect them.'

My felt-tip scuttled over the page.

'The events of this country are misunderstood by the international community. Would they have welcomed Burundian intervention in the United States after President Kennedy was killed? Did the people rise up? We are saying to the people – come to us. Let us protect you, tell us where the armed bands, the assailants, those that kill Tutsis, where they hide.'

I turned my page, sharply, taking it all down.

'Can I ask you, Colonel, what was the position at Gasarara on the—'

I consulted my notes.

'The fourteenth of November, last month. Villagers said that the army killed many people on the hills outside the city.'

'Gasarara. Yes. The rebels.' He moved his maths book to one side, and shuffled his glasses. 'At Gasarara, there are many rebels. The night before, they had attacked one of our positions. We had to move in to take control; many of the rebels were killed. Others were scattered. Our men could not take prisoners in the dark.'

'So would you say, Colonel, reports that four hundred civilians were killed is untrue, is the figure invented?'

'Our men were forced to defend themselves, the assailants were taking cover behind the women, the children.'

I rose to my feet.

'Colonel. A pleasure. Can I ring you when I have questions? We will be speaking a lot, I feel.'

'Jennings.'

He stood and shook my hand.

'Let us have supper. Now – I must look to my work,' he added, picking up the Crazy Pussycat pencil. 'But remember: William of the BBC. Wallis of Reuters. He had to leave because we could not help him. William of Wallis. Hah! If he had listened. His voice was hijacked at the end, the armed bands took it away. Jennings Christian. Wallis of Reuters. The truth must be remembered.'

I walked past the sentry at the gate of the complex. He had stuck a Russian Makarov pistol into the waistband of his combat trousers, but had left his flies undone. The muzzle pointed out like an oiled, steel penis.

'The United Nations High Commission for Refugees,' I announced grandly to Zephyr, sinking into his damp upholstery. For some reason the car smelled of Scotch.

We rattled and bumped along the rutted sand and earth roads down towards Lake Tanganyika. The leaves of the mango trees had a fine coating of dust on them. I reread my notes about Gasarara.

14.11.95: The army kills over 400 villagers in Gasarara, Bujumbura Rural, in response to a Hutu attack on any army position. This is the largest number of Hutu killed in a single reprisal since 1993.

This had been compiled by the UN, local human-rights groups, and international aid organizations, as well as the local clergy. As for William of Wallis, Wallis of the BBC, my predecessor, he was the one who had been escorted to the airport by armed UN guards before the army had a chance to kill him. I felt I knew where I stood with Minani.

The office door of Hitoshi Mise, the UNHCR head of office for Burundi, was open. He rose to greet me, a small, intensely neat, Japanese man.

'Jennings. Take a seat.'

There were fears, he said, tapping a map with his glasses, that the army were going to try forcibly to repatriate some of the 150,000-plus refugees he had in six camps in the north of the country. At the moment – for this he meant that day – he was not too concerned. Conditions were satisfactory. There was not too high a presence of former Rwandan government soldiers or interahamwe militiamen in the camps, men he referred to by their French name, of 'intimidators'. He promised to let me know if the situation developed, to keep me abreast of events. He was extremely polite, in a fussing, assiduous way, but seemed anxious to get me out of his office. I told him that since we were both staying at the Novotel, we would see each other again. He nodded. As I walked down the corridor towards the stairs, I could see all of Mise's staff in their offices, working their way through the huge budget allocated to the UNHCR to keep their office running. The air-conditioning alone consumed $20,000-worth of fuel, generator time and power in their Burundi offices. Some of their staff, with their daily allowances, were earning nearly $2000 a week to sit in the office, compile reports about the movements of the refugees, their health, their literacy rates, their education, their morale, their daily levels of militancy, their housing, their schooling, their political views, their intentions to return to Rwanda.

I just had time for a quick trip to one of my economics

interviewees. Zephyr pushed his foot down and the saloon moved fast up towards the centre of town. Zephyr cackled furiously and swerved the wheel round to avoid an oncoming lorry full of cabbages. I asked after his medicine.

'I found it this morning. The doctor tells me I have to take it morning and afternoon. I have a stomach ulcer, you see.'

If I couldn't stay long with my economics interviewee, it was because I couldn't sustain a long conversation about the International Monetary Fund's structural adjustment policy in Burundi. I accepted a cup of tea off him, despite the scorching heat of the morning, and leant back in an armchair as he gave me an armful of the collated IMF and World Bank reports on Burundi.

'You must read them,' he said, 'because if you don't, nobody else will.'

Lunch at the Novotel was in the restaurant, set under an awning sandwiched between the bar and the swimming pool. The menu was on laminated plastic, and decorated in jaunty colours. I felt that I was going to get to know it well. I chose a tuna salad. Afterwards I sat in the scorching heat, thinking that a siesta was in order. The food had a soporific effect, the sun made one sweat as you ate. I bumped into John Myers from Oxfam on the way out into the lobby.

'Going well?'

'Structural Adjustment.' I nodded at the pile of books in my arms. 'Saw Minani this morning.'

'And?'

I raised my eyes.

John laughed. 'Keep in touch. We need to discuss a finishing date for the report.'

Oh no, I thought. The idea of actually writing it was something I wasn't yet thinking about. Behind John Myers were two UNHCR staff whom I had seen in Hitoshi Mise's corridor. One of them smiled at me in recognition, so I introduced myself and handed over a business card.

'Pirjo Dupuy,' said a gravelly voiced woman with sleek dark-red hair. 'I'm Mise's deputy. You met him this morning. And this is Betsy Greve, Protection Officer.'

She had long, dark blonde hair, was wearing a multi-pocketed waistcoat with the UNHCR logo on the chest, and had eyes that seemed, or so I thought then, to entrance and take hold of you. I smiled, shuffled my feet and shook hands. The conversation that the three of us proceeded to have lasted no more than thirty seconds, yet it joined an echo that I felt, that year, must be repeating itself a thousand times round the crisis-hit Great Lakes Region. It combined professional assessment, declaration of principle, flirtation, and statement of intent.

'Betsy. You were in Goma?'

'Weren't we all? Still got the cough.'

'Black Goma cough. Volcanoes, cholera and refugees.'

'I've just got in from there,' she said. 'I was head of protection for Kibumba.'

'You must have known Paul?'

'Who used to live with Anne-Sophie in Kigali?'

'No, who went out with Tina in Burundi. 1994. Field officer.'

'Who nearly got chopped up in Cyangugu?'

'Just after the French arrived in ninety-four.'

'When the Hutus started crossing over?'

'Hundred thousand over the Rusizi River.'

'Yeah. When the Ethiopians panicked.'

'And the Zaireans opened fire.'

'Yeah. Paul. So – Burundi now.'

'Oh yes,' she said. 'So, Reuters. How's that?'

'You know. How's UNHCR? How many refugees have got you here? I need to get up to speed – find out more figures.'

'Come by the office.'

'Have you got coffee?'

'Yup. Real Zairean. WFP [World Food Programme] flight brings it in from Goma.'

Pirjo Dupuy stood watching us.

'Say hi to Paul if you speak to him.'

'What's your call-sign?' She gestured at my radio-handset.

'Oh, it's an Oxfam one. I'm going to try and get my own. What's yours?'

'Bravo Hotel Four.'

'I'll call you. Enjoy your lunch.'

They walked off, and I stopped at the newsagent's shop in the lobby to buy Silk Cut. Hmm, I thought, smiling to myself. Ding-dong. I wondered naively whether these people were all too busy working, and thinking about refugees, to socialize. I took the lift to my room. My siesta was easier than my night's non-sleep, as the air-conditioning seemed to be working. I must be getting used to the Great Lakes Region, I thought. Throughout the entire crisis-interchange with Betsy, of mutual leg-cocking on humanitarian disasters, of professional scent-swapping, there was one thing I hadn't mentioned. For almost the whole period of which we'd been talking I'd been living in the UK, working on a TV chat-show in Manchester.

Four days later, I took a break from trying to write about a process I didn't understand – coffee production and its effects on the Burundian balance of payments, which I couldn't really grasp either – and attended the weekly UN security meeting. Christophe Boutonnier was a French paratroop officer who had served in one of the Régiments Parachutiste d'Infanterie Marine d'Assaut, and then in a specialist French police unit. Now he was the United Nations security coordinator. A small, powerfully built man, he carried a .357 Magnum in a bumbag around his waist, and was known to all and sundry by his UN radio call-sign, 'Whisky'. Every Wednesday noon he gathered representatives from all the UN agencies and aid organizations at his office to share the latest security details. Zephyr drew the groaning Datsun to a halt under the frangipani trees by the office, and asked permission to go and find some medicine from the stall on the corner. Inside Christophe's office about twenty people sat in a semi-circle underneath a map. Radio handsets squawked and stuttered: it was approaching lunch time. Every single aid worker and UN official was on the net, checking midday transport, arranging rendezvous, and coordinating arrival times at shared houses. Bujumbura was a crackle of radio traffic. Everybody communicated but nobody said anything. Each of fifty-five aid organizations and six UN organizations would give a short-wave radio handset to every one of its expatriate staff; many diplomats had them as well. They were meant to improve security and provide emergency communication in the event of car hijack by Tutsi street gangs (a common occurrence), open attack on the capital (rare), medical crisis (again rare, as there were so many doctors), or general security alert.

Each person had their individual call-sign, prefixed by that of their organization, which meant that there were up to 530 people jostling for radio-space. Once people had contacted each other on one open channel – channel five – they switched to channel six to continue their conversation. Some of the larger NGOs and organizations took up residence on more arcane channels – MSF on nine, for instance – but five and six were the meeting places, the crossroads of Burundi's radio traffic. Of course, they sharply decreased security and secrecy because all the different call-signs announced their locations and movements every five minutes. To further complicate matters, each organization had code words for the different bars, buildings, hotels, meeting places and government offices in the capital. So Bravo Hotel Six telling Bravo Hotel Four that she had just left location Yankee to take Four-Six to November Eight and would be with her in five, simply meant that two UNHCR officers were meeting at the Novotel for lunch and BH Six would be arriving in five minutes. Four-Six was probably a vehicle number.

Christophe started the meeting by reading out all the security incidents that had taken place in Burundi's fifteen provinces the preceding week. He gave an update on which roads were safe to travel, how many vehicles had been stolen, and how many attacks by 'assailants', or *bandes armées* – as the CNDD, the FDD, PALIPE-HUTU and the other Hutu militias were known – there had been. He also listed all the incidents of alleged violence by the army and the gendarmerie. Each aid agency representative was then asked if they had anything to add. I sat and listened to the litany of burnt houses, displaced populations, emptied villages, attacks, both criminal and ethnic, with machete and machine-gun, of Hutu attack and army response, of police raids and Hutu retaliations. But, Christophe said, it hadn't been too bad this week, or too busy. After the 400 deaths at Gasarara the army had taken a step back; the Hutus seemed to have pressed the 'pause' button. There were a few vehicles stolen from aid agencies, a few thousand people displaced, some small incidents, but the week's death-toll was probably no more than a hundred. I'd been told that in some months the estimated total for the entire country – Whisky reckoned he got to hear of 25 per cent of incidents – had been in the thousands.

The meeting was winding down when the attack started. From less than a kilometre away, there was the rapid, tearing crack of automatic fire. Kalashnikovs ripped and loosed off long bursts, then were joined by short, clattering bursts from belt-fed machine-guns. Grenades blasted. RPG anti-tank rockets whooshed and exploded with massive blasts. Then there was silence. Then a single thwacking, loud shot from an AK. Then the long, ripping crack-crack-crack-crack of another burst. Then shouting. Then silence.

'Ah-hah,' laughed Whisky. 'I spoke too soon.'

The meeting broke up. Handsets crackled into life. The squawk and squelch of static filled the room as several dozen humanitarian workers tried to discover from another dozen, all on a crowded network, what was going on. The result was a radio log-jam.

'What's happening?' asked one American woman desperately, her sandalled feet slapping the floor as she stood and ran to the door. 'Is that shooting? Are we being attacked? I must warn our staff. Is it an attack, anyone? Please?'

I looked at Christophe and smirked. A man from the UN looked at the American woman.

'No, sweetheart, that's not shooting. That's Hutus playing the grand fucking piano, you dozy cow.'

I grabbed a lift with Barbara Kierstens, a Belgian woman from MSF. I knew from Rwanda that she was no stranger to sang-froid. We went to her house, where MSF immediately convened a meeting. I telephoned the Novotel reception. They sent somebody to find Zephyr. Less than ten minutes later the Datsun rolled to a stop in front of the white MSF gates, Zephyr grinning at the wheel, his eyes yellow and wild.

'They're attacking Mutanga,' he said, reversing fast out of the gate, turning, and driving straight into a frangipani tree which promptly collapsed.

'We're off,' he laughed, reversing over the tree's smashed trunk, pulling the car round in a spray of dust and grit, hitting third gear before we got the hundred metres to the end of the road.

The town had suddenly emptied. Nobody was on the streets at all. We saw four women running furiously along, yelling, flip-flops splattering as they smacked against the hot tarmac. We headed for Mutanga, one of the smarter residential suburbs that lay at the foot of the hills surrounding the north, south and east of the town. Zephyr was cruising, I had my arm on his shoulder, reining him in. I was loading film into my Olympus. We drove straight down Boulevard 28 November, the hills rising to our right. A high bank protected our vehicle from the view of the gunmen in the hills above us and to our right.

I saw the crowd before I saw the body. Fifteen tall, thin youths, in a mixture of sports kits, jeans and t-shirts, and the tattered clothing of street urchins. They were gathered round a spot on the ground where a gap in the grass central reservation allowed drivers to turn from one direction of the dual carriageway to the other. On the ground a man was stretched out, arms half covering his head, blood streaming all over his torso, neck and the back of his skull. His clothes were twisted and contorted by the force of hitting the ground. The youths were jumping up and down around him as he tried to move. Eight of them had large rocks and chunks of breeze-block in their hands. They raised these above their heads, then hurled them down onto his smashed face. As they stoned him to death, more gunfire erupted from the right. The man on the ground tried to turn his face up towards the gang above him. He tried to say something. He tried to open his mouth. A large chunk of concrete was hurled hard onto his lower face. He rolled over. The youths stood there. Another burst of machine-gun fire sent them ducking for cover.

'How can they just kill him like an animal?' said Zephyr, his face contorted with anger and disgust.

I had just stared as we'd slowed down, almost stopped, then driven slowly past and accelerated.

'Zephyr. Turn round. Drive past again.'

It began to rain. Two soldiers had stretched large concertinas of barbed-wire across the road in front of us. We waved then turned back towards the man lying on the tarmac. The youths had gathered under the awning of a wrecked petrol station, watching us drive past with stony-faced aggression. We'd only have one go, I thought. As we stopped further up the road, turned round and drove back towards them, one or two stooped to pick up stones. Zephyr fired the engine. As we came in sight of the body, I aimed my Olympus, focused, and kept my finger on the motor-drive button as we passed. Blood ran from the body and mixed in with the rain water. Then we were past, and the soldiers were opening the barbed wire for us.

A hundred metres up the road, Zephyr pulled into the cover of the red earth of the bank and asked if he could go for some medicine.

'Don't be a twat,' I said in French.

He laughed. I got out. Zephyr turned the car around so that it was ready for a quick escape. I walked up the rain-slicked tarmac. The shooting continued. Cracking bursts dashed overhead. Grenades boomed and shook somewhere very close. Fifty Burundian soldiers in brown-and-green camouflage crouched in the cover of the bank; they readied magazines, and loosened the pins of hand-grenades. Several automatic rifles opened fire at once from a hill some four hundred metres away, sending bursts of fire thwacking overhead. The rounds whizzed and whistled through the rain-soaked air, which seemed to hum from their passing. I ran up to a group of three officers who were standing unconcernedly in the middle of the road, one of them pushing a Kalashnikov magazine into his leg pocket.

'Christian Jennings. BBC; Reuters. What's going on?'

The officers laughed.

'Why don't you go up there and ask them,' said one, nodding at the hills, from where another burst of firing erupted.

On the top of the bank, a row of soldiers was walking through the grass in an even line, firing in the direction of the hills. They were throwing hand-grenades towards the houses and huts that they passed. A heavier machine-gun thumped out a dozen rounds. They all fell face-first into the wet grass. I dashed under the cover of a mango tree, and crouched down, lighting a cigarette under the cover of my hand. I watched the hills, listening as the rounds whooshed overhead. I watched the mango leaves and small ends of branches float down onto my shoulders from the tree above me, and wondered why a tree had chosen that moment to shed its leaves. My mind seemed to move extremely slowly. Then another burst ripped overhead, and the leaves from two or three feet above fell onto me, along with a large chunk of smashed, yellow branch. I dropped to the ground. I watched the soldiers regain their feet, and move at a run towards the hills. One of the officers shouted out that Hutu rebels had managed to get in among the houses. Two hand-grenades were thrown towards a white house, exploding in the hot air, misty in the rain. I ran at a crouch back towards the car; Zephyr was leaning against it. We pulled away, through the barbed-wire, past the battered corpse. Rain water and blood flowed away in a little red stream.

The roads were deserted. The main avenue – Boulevard UPRONA – that led towards the Novotel was empty. But away from the firing all was calm. It seemed the military was already pushing back into the hills, despite the heavy firing. We were in the hotel car-park in four minutes, and in the lobby in six. It was crammed with panicking people. Radio handsets were crackling. People had bought emergency bags. One aid agency had already evacuated their office and house and moved into the hotel, crowding round the reception desk, demanding seven adjoining rooms.

On the terrace, waiters were trying to deal with the volume of food being ordered, the cries for drinks from white UN staff who thought their order was the most urgent. A pile of bags and a medical emergency kit sat by the corner of the bar. Somebody had bought a combat helmet. Mobile phones rang. A heavily moustached Belgian was on the line to Europe.

'No, bad. Probably going to get worse; heavy, heavy fighting – I mean, heavy, for fuck's sake. They're coming into town. We're all ready for an evacuation. I'll leave the line clear. OK. OK. Understood. Over and out.'

I spotted Betsy standing over by the restaurant with a knot of

Major-General Paul Kagame, Chairman of the Rwandan Patriotic Front and later Vice-President of Rwanda, April 1994

Left President Juvenal Habyarimana of Rwanda on a visit to France, April 1990

RPF soldiers inspect the wreckage of President Habyarimana's plane, shot down while landing at Kigali Airport, Rwanda, April 1994

Tutsi civilians shelter from the killing, Ste Famille church, Kigali, Rwanda, May 1994

A Tutsi woman, one of more than 1,500 massacred in Ntarama church, Rwanda, lies decaying where she fell, May 1994

Tutsi houses stand deserted in the village of Kibungo, eastern Rwanda, May 1994

Hutu militiamen at a roadblock in downtown
Kigali, May 1994

Tutsi civilians in a Hutu death camp, Kabgayi,
near Gitarama, Rwanda, May 1994

Tutsis killed on the road by Hutu militiamen, Kibungo, Rwanda, May 1994

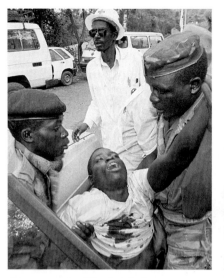

A government soldier shot during a gun battle with the RPF is delivered to a Red Cross hospital in Kigali, June 1994

Hutu refugees walk past the bodies of other Hutus killed by the RPF, Goma, Zaire, July 1994

Hutu refugees queue for water past the bodies of cholera victims, Goma, Zaire, July 1994

Frightened Rwandan refugees flee from their camps after repeated attacks by the Burundian army, Ngozi, Burundi, March 1995

Kaduha, Rwanda, March 1995: RPF soldiers gaze at Tutsi skulls placed as part of a memorial to some 12,000 people massacred here in 1994

Hutu children, orphaned, lost or abandoned, lie sick in a makeshift orphanage, Goma, Zaire, July 1996

The author, left, takes cover with other journalists from Zairean mortar shells, Gisenyi, Rwanda, November 1996

Opposite Prisoners accused of participation in the Tutsi genocide crowd into the prison courtyard, Gitarama, Rwanda, April 1996

The identity card of a dead Hutu woman, picked up by the author at a massacre site at Kabgayi mission station, Rwanda

President Sylvestre Ntibantunganya of Burundi pleads for international aid at a press conference in Brussels, March 1995

UNHCR staff and caught her eye. I moved over. But first I turned to Zephyr and clapped him on the arm. He smiled.

'Zephyr?' I grinned.

'Yes,' he answered, brow furrowing in anticipation.

'How about a large medicine?'

My reports to Reuters were not textbook stuff. I wrote fifteen lines about the attack and added three quotes. One was from Minani, who, from his office, confirmed the action. He added that the army was 'repulsing those whose aim it was to bring a genocide back to Burundi'. The other person I contacted was a British expatriate called Patrick Towers-Picton, a curious, sixty-year-old coffee trader who was also the honorary consul for the European Union. He had been in his bath, he said, when it happened, but added that as far as he could ascertain, it had been 'pretty damn heavy', and he couldn't remember the last time something like this had happened. The third quote was from one of the army officers on the scene. As I was sure happened regularly, I was the best placed witness to report on what was actually occurring. But in my piece I could only refer to myself in the third person as a 'Reuters correspondent who witnessed the incident'. I ran my fax downstairs and stood over the machine as it clicked through to Nairobi. Then I left the milling throng in the bar, and went back to my room. I lit a Silk Cut and stared out of the window, wondering what to do with my film of the man being stoned to death. Send it to Nairobi as quickly as possible, I thought. As I stood there, I remembered the moment that the man had turned his face towards his killers and tried to speak, before the last slab of concrete had probably killed him. What had he been trying to say? Did he think that there was still hope? Who was he? Some poor Hutu farmer who had been walking past a street gang, onlookers, as the firing began? How many people had been killed in his family? How many family members had his killers lost in 1993? Or 1989? Or 1972? Or 1988? Nobody would ever know.

One half of me, the journalist, was pleased to have been sufficiently swift-thinking and calm to get pictures of him being killed. Another part knew that there was no way I could have stopped the incident. I had arrived too late, would no doubt have endangered my own life, and would almost certainly have got Zephyr killed. A third part of me wished that instead of an Olympus OM-10 camera, I had had an AKMS assault-rifle in my hands and could simply have shot all fifteen of his killers for being cowardly, pointlessly cruel fuckers. It was one man, one death, one afternoon, one incident. I wondered how many people would die on both sides as a result of this day's attack. And how many more days there would be like this, and worse, before I was through with Burundi. A hell of a lot, I feared.

By mid afternoon, the firing was getting heavier, as the army bought up an armoured car mounted with a 57mm canon. Zephyr had got medicined-up in the bar for half an hour, and then seemed to calm down, eating two goat kebabs, with rice. He burped furiously in the car as we drove back to the north of town. His ulcer was in disagreement with the brochettes, he said. We turned onto Boulevard 28 November, the windows rolled down, the tyres swishing through the light film of rain that covered the road. The sun had come out and the hills looked greener than ever. The streets were still almost deserted. We stopped half way along the road, trying to find out where the firing was centred. It seemed to be coming from the university, set right up on top of the hill. We drove up. An armoured car was in the car-park firing rounds into the hills, while soldiers leaning on the parapet fired bursts of machine-gun fire at random into clumps of banana trees five hundred metres up the slope. Groups of students stood around cheering whenever the armoured car fired. These, Zephyr told me, were those hardline university students who kept assault-rifles in their bedside lockers and tortured the few Hutu students left in the colleges, especially those who did well in examinations. He told me of one Hutu student who had done particularly well in an engineering exam; for each ten points that he got above the pass-mark, Tutsi students linked to the Sans Échec militia had cut off a finger with wire-cutters.

Zephyr and I stood watching the action for ten minutes, chatting with the students. Then they realized I was a journalist and started crowding round, shouting, pushing, swearing at Zephyr. He didn't help things by telling them that they were scum for murdering innocent Hutus – he was still furious about the man being stoned to death that morning, even though he too was a Tutsi. The situation got worse. Two soldiers grabbed him, and started shouting at me. The students demanded to know how I had managed to infiltrate the university security system.

'I drove through the gate,' I said.

'Then you must be a spy.'

I told him to piss off and grow up. Then I decided I'd had enough.

'SILENCE!' I roared in a voice that owed every bit of volume and authority to non-commissioned officers' courses with the British Parachute Regiment, from sergeant-majors in Aldershot teaching us to shout orders from one end of a football field to the other.

'We're not spies, we haven't infiltrated your university, we've just come here to report for the international media. Please. Now, is anybody going to tell what's happening here?'

One of the legacies of the Legion's Parachute Regiment was not only an ability to speak fast, idiomatic French, but that whenever I spoke it, the ghost of my parade-ground past would wash over me. The students calmed down. Zephyr was let go. Two of the students pointed at the armoured car and said very seriously:

'We're pushing back firmly at the positions of the genocidal raiders.'

One of the university officials pointed up at the hills, showing me their positions. The only firing seemed to be coming from the military. Then the mood changed again, as one of the soldiers pointed at us, accusing both Zephyr and myself of being spies for Leonard Nyangoma, the head of the hardline Hutu CNDD. I stood there and explained as slowly as I could that I had been invited to stay in their country by their government, and that I had no more affection for Nyangoma than they did. But this time Zephyr had got back at the wheel of the Datsun, pulling it round so that I could back towards the open passenger seat and the damp, spongey upholstery.

As we rolled down the hill, I explained to Zephyr about being antagonistic. He said that his ulcer was hurting because of the man being stoned to death that morning. Medicine was needed. Rain was coming in off the lake, and the sky was getting dark. The pair of us were humming along in two different languages to an acoustic version of Tammy Wynette's 'Stand by Your Man'. It was recorded in Kinyarwanda.

The church at Sororwezo stands about four kilometres from Bujumbura, in the foothills of the mountains around the capital. It's a small building, surrounded by a number of mud and earth houses with corrugated iron roofs. There's a small communal centre and lots of banana and eucalyptus trees, and the villagers make their living through farming. Avocado trees climb back up the hill. The village of Gasarara, where the army had killed 400 Hutus in November, is not far away. Memories are long in Burundi, and when the army started their counter-attack against the Hutu rebels on 6 December, many of the population in the hills behind Mutanga fled to Sororwezo. They took refuge in the church, and in one of the communal buildings. When the army had finished blasting off large amounts of ammunition into the hills, the people started thinking about returning to their homes, their land, and their plots of runner-beans.

Word got through to the capital fast that something was going to go wrong at Sororwezo. Perhaps one of the Hutu domestic staff working for an aid agency asked their white employers to do something. Perhaps the message was passed by one of the hundreds of Hutus who poured out of the hills every morning into the capital, carrying their cabbages, their bananas, their avocados and chickens to the central market. By whatever means, word reached us, and forty-eight hours after the attack, we were pulling north. The Datsun smelled heavily of upholstery detergent and Johnny Walker.

About a kilometre short of Sororwezo, the tarmac turned to red earth ruts for a brief stretch, and then our path was blocked by soldiers. One soldier had linked approximately 600 rounds of machine-gun ammunition together into a single belt, fed one end into his weapon, then draped the rest around him like a bronze python. He explained firmly but politely to Zephyr that we couldn't proceed.

'Sororwezo is closed,' he said to me, accepting a Benson and Hedges. 'Administration is being done this morning.'

I got out of the car. Zephyr stayed inside, silent. I'd told him that if he didn't lose his cool by my birthday, I'd give him a prescription for some serious medicine.

'But I have business to do this morning there,' I explained in French. 'I have meetings to keep to.'

'No. Not allowed.'

'When will it be allowed?'

'When what has to be done is done.'

We reversed, thanking the soldiers for their helpfulness and drove back to town. We skirted down to the lake, through the centre, then back out towards the turning for Sororwezo. The soldiers had disappeared by now and we managed to get further forward until another patrol stopped us. They were not friendly at all. The car was forced to turn round at gunpoint, I was pushed back inside when I tried to get out.

The killing started late that afternoon at Sororwezo. Most of the families of the local population that had taken refuge there were women and children. The men older than fourteen and younger than eighty had disappeared. They knew, the moment the first army patrol sealed off the road leading down towards the outskirts of the capital, that something was going to happen. The women and children sat with their bundles of possessions, their manioc, their beans, their sticks and their mattresses, in the church. The Tutsi youths arrived in two lorries, singing. They were wearing basketball boots, tracksuit-tops, t-shirts and jeans, or simply the rags of the urban dispossessed. Most of them were carrying knives, machetes and small axes, while some had bought claw-hammers. They disembarked and, stood around for ten minutes. Then an army officer and a local administrative official from Bujumbura, accompanied by two SOJEDEM youth leaders, argued about money for another ten. The SOJEDEM leaders said that the men had to be paid. He wanted the equivalent of five pounds per man to do the work in the church. A bundle of Burundian francs changed hands. Many of the youths had been smoking marijuana or heroin.

The killing started, I was told by one eye-witness who escaped by hiding in a banana grove, 'before the sun went down over Zaire'. Lake Tanganyika is immediately below the Bujumburan hills: across it is the Luberizi plateau, behind which the sun disappears at about five-thirty each evening. The young men put down their Primus bottles, stopped singing and moved forward. The first woman to die had a small hatchet smashed into her skull before her left breast was cut off with a kitchen knife.

The following morning was bright and sunny, as ever. When I rose from another night of too little sleep, too many mosquitoes and heat that had exceeded a hundred degrees, there was a light mist over towards Sororwezo. The sun was still burning the moisture off the hills. I spoke to Minani.

'Jennings. Reuters. How are you? You see, the army has triumphed. The rebels have been driven back to the hills. We are in control.'

'Are there many people who have taken refuge, who have fled?'

'Jennings of the BBC. Oxfam by day, Reuters by night. Remember William and his voice. The only people who take refuge when the army arrives are those who are guilty already, and have something to hide.'

'What is happening at Sororwezo? I'm told the army has arrived.'

'Jennings – do not concern yourself with what has happened there; we have pushed back those with genocide on their minds. The hills are ours.'

Nobody knew for sure how many people died in that small village just outside Bujumbura, where Hutus took refuge from the army reprisal they knew was coming. The lowest estimate was forty-eight; a local priest said sixty-three. Four days later, after talking to witnesses, the figure went up. Comparison with communal lists showed ninety-three people missing, a third of whom were later to be found chopped up and drowned in two pit latrines. I reported this figure some days later when it came out. But for the people around Sororwezo, nobody did anything. Hitoshi Mise, rising early at the Novotel, could have seen the village if he'd looked out of his fifth-floor window. Marc Faguy, the United Nations special representative, could have driven there had he wanted to, or been well informed enough to know it was going on. The army knew they could get away with it, even with some 500 humanitarian staff sitting less than two and a half miles away.

I spoke to Minani again that afternoon.

'I'm going up to Sororwezo in the morning. I've heard that there were some events there yesterday.'

'Jennings, if you go up to Sororwezo, I will not be responsible for the actions of my men.'

'I'll be fine, Colonel, I just want to take a look around, ask some people what is going on. Why should there be problems? The rebels, as you've said, have fled.'

'Jennings, if you go to Sororwezo, you will have problems.'

'Come, Colonel. What's the problem with the village? It's just outside town.'

'Jennings Christian, listen to me. If you go to Sororwezo, I'll tell my men that it is possible they should not be responsible for their actions.'

I gave Zephyr twenty dollars extra that afternoon to go and drink himself senseless. I went to a birthday party on the beach, where two drunken soldiers opened fire on two hippopotamuses surfacing in the lake. While we were standing on the sand with our cold beers, a Tutsi militiaman threw a hand-grenade into a hospital ward. Both hand-grenade and hippos made it on to the BBC Africa Service that night. Afterwards I went out for a pre-curfew dinner with seven people from Oxfam, and Betsy. It was 9 December 1995, and I was thirty-three.

Chapter 5

Slow-Trickle Genocide

Wherever President Sylvestre Ntibantunganya chose to sit in his state drawing room, there were only three things that he could look at. The most appealing was probably the ornate, tropical fish tank, over four feet long and six feet high, that stretched along one wall. It was full of small golden and black fish. He had added several tank accessories; a little arch, a rubber mermaid, and a boat (which had sunk). If he chose to look the other way, he'd find himself looking at a portrait of himself by a local artist. It showed the president standing in a ceremonial robe, wearing his trademark spectacles, holding in his hand a bleeding human heart shaped like Burundi. Behind him flashes of red and yellow light, that looked surprisingly like mortar-fire, lit up the background. The third choice was an overdone, glossy photo portrait of him and his second wife on their wedding day. She was a young Tutsi in full marriage finery, with long, red fingernails and hair braids. She had slightly implausible breasts that seemed to point upwards, then half-left and half-right. His first wife had been killed in the October 1993 coup and, just prior to his accession to power, he had been taken aside and told that although he was a Hutu, he was still going to be president, and as such was privileged enough to be 'given' a Tutsi wife, to show the due respect of the Tutsi elite. His state drawing room was decorated in lime and yellow, calm enough colours for a man overseeing a country that had long ago fallen off a cliff. When I had told people that I was going to interview him, their unanimous wish had been to know how long he thought he would last.

*

The first week or so of the new year 1996 had not been a good one for Burundi. Hutu rebels from the FDD and PALIPEHUTU were clashing with the army in the hills around the capital. The main roads into Bujumbura were all being ambushed by Hutu rebels – there had been over twenty incidents in one week – and both Burundians and expatriates were under attack. Military and civilian positions in the six main towns had also been hit. Hutu rebels and Tutsi militias had attacked three of the six refugee camps in the north of the country, two of which had emptied, pouring 40,000 refugees back into Rwanda, Tanzania and the hills on the Burundian border. Aid agencies and the UN World Food Programme (WFP) had suspended activities in Ngozi leaving an estimated half a million people without food aid, after Tutsi militias had organized sixteen grenade attacks on their houses in forty-eight hours. Some fifteen aid vehicles had been hijacked at gunpoint in one week. The United Nations had upped their security rating to Phase Three, where all non-essential staff were to be evacuated from the country. Hundreds of houses were reported burned. Columns of refugees, many women and children, were being attacked, both by the army firing from helicopters in some places, and by displaced Tutsis coerced into killing Hutus as they poured across the Rusizi river from the northern Cibitoke and Bubanza provinces into Zaire. Nearly 30,000 had fled; deaths from crocodile attack in the river were rising.

Bujumbura had been under fire for the last three nights. Five power pylons supplying all electricity to the capital had been cut by Hutu rebels to the south, near the Rwegura Hydro-electric plant. Without electricity, no water could be pumped to the city purifying plants from Lake Tanganyika. Without water the health situation had quickly deteriorated. Médecins sans Frontières had already reported sixty-one cases of cholera at their isolation camp on the outskirts of the city. At night, the city was completely dark apart from the electric light provided by generators and the green, yellow and red flashings of trace rounds that cut the night sky. SOJEDEM leaders and other Tutsi militias had demanded strikes and closures of businesses in the capital until the army brought the matter in hand.

I could hardly get out of the capital. My Reuters reports, or file, as it was technically called, had been upped from felt-pen and paper to word-processor, urgent phone call and Burundian fax operator. I seemed to be spending my life between the phone and the lift, the lobby and the car, meetings and fast drives to the outskirts of town. Whisky and I thought it perfectly possible that 2,500 people had died in two weeks.

To cap it all, my heart was bruised. Betsy, the Dutch lawyer from the UNHCR, had fallen into bed at Christmas with a lantern-jawed Frenchman called Jacques who looked like an actor. Worse, he was some form of human rights investigator. They were on holiday in France as I sat in the car heading up the hill towards the Presidency to interview Sylvestre. I was listening as my new driver, Gaston, sung along to 'Tequila Sunrise'.

'I shiver whenever I see a Hutu, a Tutsi, or a Twa die,' said President Ntibantunganya, looking at his fish tank.

'I feel, with the Burundian army, that it is a mirror image of Burundian society. There are a majority of people who say that many parts of the army are committing atrocities. As their commander-in-chief, can I say that is true?'

I bit the end of my pen and said nothing.

'The answer lies with the people themselves – Burundi has a big heart, and this can't be destroyed.' He turned to look at the picture of himself carrying a heart.

'You see? Me? Burundi? Heart?'

I smiled. Please, he's got to say something important, something worth reporting. This is my first sizeable interview since I got here.

'Everybody must work together on our campaign of pacification – there's reconciliation for all, there's a dynamic of security, lies and truths, dreams and reality, they all get confused sometimes. But we're taking our pacification campaign out onto the road, into the provinces.'

Christ. Who elected this person? Perhaps he's afraid of saying anything controversial in case somebody takes offence and blows up his car?

'Negotiations with Leonard Nyangoma? The Burundian people must negotiate with themselves – the answer lies with the people themselves. The Convention of Government is clear. The war that swallows Burundi is brutal, selfish and barbaric at all levels. The rest of the country – apart from Karuzi – is slowly coming round to the idea that there might be other ways of doing things than violence.'

I sat with him for another hour, a man so scared of confrontation or action because he knew that whatever he did or said was going to offend somebody. He only laughed once, when I asked him whether he was scared of being president, given what had happened to his predecessors.

'When one has died in an air crash that started a genocide, and one has been assassinated in a coup that started another genocide, you smile and laugh when God gives you each day.'

I suspected he was trying to keep a low profile. I would have done.

Gaston was waiting in the car outside. What area should I cover next: should I head up to Cibitoke and Bubanza, and check out the military operations there? Or go right across the country to the Tanzanian border where 100,000 refugees were on the receiving end of a war of claim and counter claim, denial and assertion between Hitoshi Mise, the UNHCR, the Burundian army and the Rwandan government about who shot at who to make which refugees move back to which country on which date. Then there was straight security reporting. Every week I tried to estimate how many people had died. I based my estimates on Christophe's security reports, local radio, UN and aid workers' notes of incidents, and information received from the army. Finally there was great question of whether or not there ought to be some form of foreign intervention in Burundi: perhaps United Nations guards to escort humanitarian aid, or full-scale troop deployments in case the level of violence and killing got any worse. How much worse did it have to get? Was there a point at which a genocide swingometer in Washington hit a buzzer and Madeleine Albright suddenly took down her map of Burundi? The international community, that homogenous grouping of aid agencies, the United Nations, military consultants, governments and political advisors were up in arms. So were the swirling ranks of contact groups, human rights agencies and democratic institutes. Press releases, statements, declarations of concern, outraged sound-bites, definitive plans of action were all thick in the air in Washington, Geneva, Paris, Brussels, and Nairobi. By the time they had crystallized into decisions and action that would have a bearing on Burundi, they amounted to very little. Five UN human rights monitors were to be deployed within the next two months to assess the situation. A United Nations 'special rapporteur' would arrive shortly in Bujumbura to provide a preliminary assessment of the situation that was going to be further assessed by the human rights monitors when they arrived.

The deployment of UN human rights monitors had become a useful, face-saving tool in the UN armoury. It showed that they were concerned, it showed that they were willing to send somebody – anybody – onto the ground, and, most importantly, it meant that they could stall their detractors in the press and elsewhere. It had become a favourite response to international crisis in countries like Rwanda and Burundi. Even at the height of the Rwandan genocide, the UN thought that human rights monitors could affect the situation. On 24 May 1994, José Ayala Lasso, UN High Commissioner for Human Rights, wrote a piece in the *International Herald Tribune*. As he sat in front of his UN computer, a Rwandan was being macheted, burned, raped, drowned, shot or hacked to death every six seconds. Even if Mr Lasso was an exceptionally fast writer, and wrote his polemic in three hours (which he wouldn't have done – it would have taken him at least forty-eight), an absolute minimum of 1800 Rwandans would have been killed in the time it took him to write his piece.

Lasso said in his article that he took office on 5 April, the day before the Rwandan genocide started. He said that an emergency session of the UN Commission on Human Rights would open on 30 May. He added that this was only the third such special session to be called since 1946, reflecting the gravity of the situation. I wondered how long it would take to arrange a 'normal' session, for some minor case of international human rights violations such as Burundi, or East Timor.

In between the beginning of the Rwandan genocide, and his organization's emergency session Lasso had made a visit to Kigali and had a frightening experience with a militiaman at a road-block: 'He searched our armoured car with a live grenade in his hand. Knowing how I felt then, it is almost impossible to describe how those who cannot flee Rwanda must feel.'

Lasso acknowledged that 'peace and security are the responsibility of the Security Council', but added that 'the scale of human rights violations in Rwanda was such that there was a need for action even before peace and security could be fully guaranteed.' He alleged that his 'emergency session' could help stop 'the incessant rattle of death'. He viewed Rwanda as 'a litmus test of the international community's willingness to act against massive human rights violations'. The UN Commission on Human Rights, of which he was the head, was 'the principal UN body entrusted with the protection of human rights . . . but this crisis transcends anything we have seen'. His answer? 'The commission . . . should consider appointing a special rapporteur to examine all human rights aspects of the situation, including causes and responsibilities . . . such a rapporteur should be assisted by a team of human rights field officers.'

This piece in the *Herald Tribune* provided an enlightening insight into the thought processes and speed of movement of senior UN officials when confronted with a crisis as enormous as the Rwandan genocide. What Ayala Lasso was saying was that his response to the swiftest genocide in the history of the planet was to dispatch one man to 'examine' the situation. In the seven weeks it took Mr Lasso to come to this conclusion, 750,000 Rwandans were killed.

So what had the UN done about Burundi, where at least 60,000 people had been killed after the October 1993 coup?

In March 1994, four months after the Burundi coup, UN Secretary-General Boutros Ghali sent a 'preparatory fact-finding mission', to Bujumbura consisting of two men. Their report was made public on 24 February 1995, exactly one year and four months after the killings in question. In between, of course, another president had died, and perhaps another 30,000 people been slaughtered. On 26 June 1995, Boutros Ghali sent one more person to Burundi to look into setting up an international commission of enquiry.

On 28 August 1995, Security Council Resolution 1012 requested the secretary-general to 'establish, as a matter of urgency, an international commission of enquiry'. It asked for a mandate in which it would be possible to 'establish the facts relating to the assassination of the president of Burundi on 21 October 1993, the massacres and other related serious acts of violence'. Most importantly, it asked for a mandate that would recommend 'measures with regard to the bringing to justice of persons responsible for those acts, to prevent any repetition of deeds similar to those investigated by the commission'.

An estimated 100,000 people had died in ethnic violence in Burundi in the interim between November 1993 and the end of October 1995 when the commission had its first meetings. Reuters, Agence France Presse, the BBC, CNN and Radio France International were among the leading international news organizations which had documented the daily occurrences. The UN could not say it was ignorant of the facts. Moreover, this was a year after the Rwandan genocide, when the UN was desperate not to be seen to be dragging its feet in Africa's Great Lakes Region.

As the commission met in Geneva, the three Burundian military officers who took control of the crisis committee running the coup in 1993 were running the country's armed forces, security intelligence network and gendarmerie respectively. The commission arrived, set itself up in a hotel, and started work. Problems surfaced immediately. The government of Burundi had requested a judicial commission of inquiry, but the commission itself, 'a fact-finding mission with . . . wide discretion to make recommendations', had no judicial muscle, no powers of arrest or detention, no troops on call. It was, however, authorized to present a report on its findings to be given to the secretary-general. It said, though, that it would make its investigations as thorough as possible, to judicial standard, just on the off-chance that there might be a prosecution in the future.

Meanwhile, having failed to prevent the Rwandan genocide, the UN was in the process of serving the first indictments of the International Criminal Tribunal for Rwanda (ICTR), which had just been set up to run from Arusha in Tanzania. Dozens of journalists operating on their own, with low budgets, had been tracking down and interviewing the guilty Rwandan army officers, ministers and local officials for nearly two years. But it was to be another four years before the ICTR passed its first sentence, and long before then, an independent UN commission of inquiry had to sack a large number of its staff for corruption and inefficiency.

Back in Burundi, only five commissioners started on the non-judicial investigation into the 1993 coup and killings. That was towards the end of 1995. Two field investigators were to arrive the next March, five others by 19 April. The commission was to leave on 31 May, and, for reasons of security and personnel, able to examine incidences of massacres and ethnic violence in only three provinces; Ngozi, Gitega and Muramvya. It started work in Kirundo but did not have enough staff to continue. It could not carry out any investigations in the other eleven provinces for the same reason and because it was not allowed to visit any provinces considered by the UN to be a security risk. These included the provinces of Bubanza, Karuzi and Cibitoke, to which journalists such as myself and the more capable humanitarian agencies such as MSF and the ICRC were travelling on a weekly basis without any armed security. In December, the offices of the commission were based in the Bujumbura suburb Mutanga North, and some of the commissioners were present in the office when there took place the firefight between the army and the rebels that I witnessed. The commission was, of course, incapable even of considering the events at Sororwezo, two kilometres from their office, because it was not in their mandate. Nor, it transpired, was any directive to investigate the events of the 1993 coup itself. Eleven officers and other ranks from the army, summoned to appear and provide testimony, refused to turn up. The commission did not go and look for them, citing 'security concerns'. One of those summoned was Lieutenant-Colonel Lucien Rufyiru who, in January, was the senior military officer in the province of Bubanza. Hundreds of Hutus were being massacred by the army under his command, with the aid of Tutsi militiamen. Rufyiru was one of the officers who arranged the coup. It took me two and a half hours to find him.

The commission did not come cheap: the United Kingdom gave $31,250; Ireland $150,000; the United States half a million dollars, and Holland quarter of a million. Norway, Spain, Belgium, Sweden and Denmark gave another million dollars in total. It cost less than a dollar to jump in a taxi in central Bujumbura and ride down to the Hotel Source du Nile to see how the UN commission was spending this money. It had taken a whole floor of the hotel for security purposes, there were six bodyguards, a security co-ordinator and administration staff. There were parties, there was a lot of ostentatious travelling around in their white armoured vehicle, and, judging by their personal telephone bills, a lot of talking about it internationally. One commissioner left a seven-thousand-dollar personal telephone bill behind him, according to the hotel staff. Another left the country swiftly after a financial and emotional disagreement with a young Tutsi male prostitute. On some days both bodyguards and commissioners would complain that it was impossible to travel outside town because of the dangers, and that the lack of electricity and water made it impossible to work at their hotel. They'd pass the time by the Novotel pool, or in the bar instead.

Their investigation, such as it was, was the United Nations' and the international community's answer and final reaction to the ethnic violence and political upheaval of 1993. It was the UN's alternative to sending troops. Regardless of the fact that it stood by and did *nothing* in 1994 and 1995 as another 100,000 died, it could pride itself on the achievement of taking over two years and more than two million dollars to send fifteen people half way round the globe hesitantly to investigate – for factual reference only – a fraction of what had happened. That dozens of journalists had investigated the situation, and reported it, to far greater effect and at less than a hundredth of the cost, almost as it had happened, did not seem to register.

This, then, was the atmosphere into which the United Nations were going to send their human rights monitors. By UN standards, the country should have counted itself lucky. The Mayor of Bujumbura, Pie Ntiyankundiye, said to me one night in the candle-lit hotel bar at the Source du Nile that if it took one dead president, one coup d'état and a hundred thousand dead people to get fifteen UN Human commissioners to Burundi with no effective mandate, then at the present rate, in January 1995, the level of killing would not merit a phone call from the secretary-general. He then said the one thing that united Hutu, Tutsi and white expatriates in the country was that they all wanted to shoot Marc Faguy, the UN Special Representative. The human rights monitors, if they arrived, would almost certainly only be allowed to leave the capital under military escort. The UN delegate for the United Nations Development Fund in Burundi, a man named Khan, claimed not to have time to see me when I rang to set an appointment for us to talk about the human rights monitors. I returned to the Novotel and sent a few, short paragraphs from my interview with the president.

My musings on the UN had tired and depressed me, so after lunch I went to find Christophe to have some coffee, thumb through his collection of gun magazines and get hold of the latest security figures. I found him sitting in his office, while his assistant, who had the worst mosquito bites on her ankles I'd ever seen, kept watch on the radio transmitter. As this was made by a company called Higgins, radio duty was known by Christophe as '*le Higgins watch*'. Whisky and I stood over the list which showed all the security developments for the last seven days. Things were getting worse.

16 January: Army patrol burns seventy houses in Karuzi province in search operations for rebels who are suspected of attacking military position. Unknown number of civilian dead. [Whisky and I estimated that probably a hundred people had been killed, but as the information came from the army it was impossible to know. If seventy houses had been burnt, then approximately 400 people had been chased out, and the army might have killed a hundred of them.] Refugees continue to cross into Zaire from Cibitoke and Bubanza as military operations continue. Unknown number of civilian dead.

17 January: Two ambushes reported. One white priest reported injured. Six expatriates in three vehicles ambushed outside Ngozi by

suspected Tutsi militias. Nobody hit. Military reprisal operation begins in northern Bujumbura Rurale Province. Two Toyota Land Cruisers hijacked in Bujumbura. Reported large-scale killing of civilians in Bubanza province. Unknown number of civilian dead.

18 January: Shooting during the night in hills above capital. One expatriate vehicle stolen in Bujumbura. Total loss of water supply and electrical supply continues in capital. Aid workers delivering water in outlying Hutu areas threatened with violence by Tutsi militias. Eight Hutu inmates at Central Market Police Station tortured to death. Army and/or Hutu rebels attack Mugano military camp outside Mugano refugee camp in Muyinga province. 15,000 refugees break camp and flee as outbreak of shooting occurs. UN vehicle stolen late afternoon in centre of Bujumbura. Refugees wounded by gunfire after firefight on outskirts of Ntamba refugee camp, Muyinga province. Military operation continues in Karuzi province. Civilian death-toll unverifiable; aid workers warned to vacate four communes 'for their own safety' as search-and-destroy mission progresses. Ten houses burned in Tutsi suburb of capital.

19 January: Hutu politician shot dead in Bujumbura.

20 January: Toyota Land Cruiser stolen in capital. Hutu rebels attack suburb of Bujumbura.

21 January: Grenade explosion in Gitega. Military operations continue in provinces of Ngozi, Bubanza, Cibitoke and Muyinga. Refugees continue to flee area of Ntamba and Mugano camps. 15,000 gather on Tanzanian border. Student demonstrations organized by SOJEDEM Tutsi militia in Bujumbura, protesting against attacks by Hutus. Army reacts violently. No power or water.

22 January: Students attempt another demonstration.

23 January: Two attacks on military positions in Bujumbura and in Makamba in the south. Two soldiers are wounded, while the number of dead in the capital, on both sides, is unknown. Province of Bubanza reported 'almost deserted' after population flees army operations. Area inaccessible, number of civilian deaths not known. WFP and ICRC estimate that 100,000 civilians need food, water and shelter in insecure provinces of Bubanza and Cibitoke. Expatriate Land Cruiser hijacked with $7,500 in cash on board. This

takes the total of Land Cruisers stolen from aid agencies in Bujumbura in one month to sixteen. Honorary EU consul Patrick Towers-Picton assaulted in house robbery: said intruders were 'black ruffians'.

Christophe and I estimated that this list might represent a third of all incidents reported in the country, and that perhaps 500 people had died in one week as a result of them. It was impossible to say how many others had been killed; an unwitnessed killing at an army barracks, a slaughter on a lost, windy hillside where word didn't get to the capital in time, a murder by Hutu and Tutsi of two here, three there, one here. Ninety-three people had died at Sororwezo church six weeks before as a result of one army reprisal for one small attack. The vast operations in Bubanza, Cibitoke, Karuzi and Ngozi would be claiming much more than that. The roads to many of these areas had been shut off; no eye-witness reports could get out.

The lack of water and electricity continued. Supper every night at the Novotel was by candlelight. The staff were using the swimming pool water for the washing-up. In the mornings the coffee tasted of chlorine. I washed from jerry-cans of slightly murky lake water and then sweltered through the hot, long nights without air-conditioning, smoking and watching the tracer bullets over the hills. The roads into the capital were often cut; the items available on the menu decreased day by day. The Novotel Hotel was nearly full. There were aid workers who had evacuated their projects in the face of ongoing military operations in the interior, there were diplomats who came for dinner and stayed the night. There were UN staff who thought the security was better, and the floating population of journalists from the Nairobi press-corps who had come to cover the attacks on the refugee camps. One day I took a clattering taxi with a driver who spoke no French or English, and travelled north to the isolated province of Cibitoke. I sat on a rain-washed hilltop, behind the wire of a far-flung Burundian army fire base from where patrols were going out into the banana trees and forests of the valley below us. The captain who had led the trip explained that almost every night his men ran into rebels. These were the Hutu 'assailants' and '*bandes armées*' who were coming in from Zaire across the Rusizi river. The rain trapped us. For three hours we sat under a corrugated-iron awning as waves of thundering water fell out of the sky. His men bought kidney beans and boiled potatoes cooked in oil and salt. We drank several bottles of warm Primus. When I stood up to go and lose some of the lager, I stumbled into a deserted shed behind their huts, set on the edge of the back slope of the hill. It was dark in the wet, warm shed. I leaned against the wall, pissing on the earth floor. The light coming in through some broken slats on the wall settled on the tangled forms of three corpses in muddy brown and green uniforms, piled on the floor in a jumbled rigor mortis of blood, mud and wet camouflage. This was where the unit kept their dead until they could take them down the mountain. Later the rain clouds parted, and on the way back to the capital I stopped in one of several displaced persons camps. The communal leader, standing in a pile of cow dung, told how every night the army and rebels would hit each other. He had fled from his home several times before he came here, each flight leading him further northwards. He and a hundred others had come to a stop in this disused complex of cattle sheds on the banks of the Rusizi river, a kilometre from Zaire. He drew pictures every day, he said, to keep himself occupied, and showed me an elaborately planned pencil drawing of his ideal building: it was a cattle-rearing unit, which, he said, he would one day build. The early equatorial dusk was settling over the mud and eucalyptus trees. In the light of the first lantern I could see the bloated black abscess on his lower cheek, where a cattle tick clung to his face.

The lobby of the Novotel Hotel was full of middle-aged and elderly Japanese tourists at breakfast time the following day. Wearing soft blue denim hats, clutching Japanese Airlines flight-bags, and sporting soft shoes of no determinate style, they stood in a frightened gaggle in the middle of the lobby. I asked Victoria, the amiable Tutsi receptionist on duty, what was happening.

'Good morning, Mr Christian. How is the day?' she asked in French.

'Fine, Vicky, but who are these people?'

'They are the Japanese, Mr Christian. They arrived this morning. They have never been here before.'

'I can see that – where are they from? What does it say on the register?'

'O-S-A-K-A. Where is that?'

'Japan, Vicky.'

'Photographers Club of Osaka:' she read to me, 'Historic Cities Tour of Burundi, 1996.'

Lieutenant-Colonel Minani strode through the lobby at that point, waving a copy of *Time* magazine above his head, and patting his pistol holster.

'Lies, it's all Hutu lies! The man Purvis must go – he has told lies. I spoke to him; it is not in here.'

'Morning, Colonel Minani,' I said hesitantly.

'Where is Purvis of *Time*, Jennings? Is he in hiding? I did not say these things. He is a Hutu, it is clear. Purvis of *Time*, come out!'

He showed me the article he was waving above his head. It had been written by Andrew Purvis, the *Time* Magazine correspondent for East Africa, who had been in Bujumbura and in Muyinga over the last two weeks. The piece included a fairly innocuous line; something like 'increasing ethnic violence has led to a spate of reprisal actions by the Burundian army. Hundreds of innocent civilians are dying every month. Defence spokesmen in the capital said it was possible that elements of the military were responsible . . .' In terms of condemning the military, it was mild compared to some French and Belgian journalism, or the sheer weight of my reporting that Reuters was running.

'I think he has left, Colonel,' I said. 'I think he has gone back to Nairobi.'

'Running to his home, saying that I said lies I did not! I know you told him these lies too. Jennings and Purvis. Where is Tunbridge of the BBC, she is lying too.'

There must have been sixty people milling in the lobby and the bar area by now.

'*Excusez-moi, M'sieur, Cibitoke, Gitega, aujourd'hui?* Yes?'

An elderly Japanese man was tugging at Minani's pistol hand.

'What do you want now?' he said as the man bowed. 'Go away, I'm busy.'

'Urr . . . brochure say now . . . for us . . . Historic cities, us? Cib-e-to-kay? Ha! Today! For us, now say, Burundi historic city of Gee-tay-gaaH!! Ha!'

Minani looked baffled, his face screwing up under his glasses. The man stood in front of him, tapping a forefinger onto the brochure, showing Minani a photograph of Cibitoke town, and some tea fields in Gitega that had been taken a good fifteen years before.

'We go?' asked the Japanese man.

Minani slapped shut the copy of *Time*, said he'd talk to me later, and strode off muttering. The Japanese tourists were gathering around a selection of stands mounted with a display of first-day-cover stamps. I had been planning to do a day's coverage of these. The artwork was excellent, I would get two free sets, one of the country's different animals, and one of the six major Burundian cities. I couldn't wait to spend the day looking at nice stamps in the hotel lobby, doing a small piece for Reuters, and then swimming at lunch time. My trip to Cibitoke had been more frightening than I had anticipated. Not only had we finished the day off by visiting a military cemetery on the way back, but we had missed a rebel ambush by fifteen minutes, ten kilometres north of Bujumbura.

The confusion increased. I spoke to Vicky behind the desk but she wasn't sure whether the Japanese were coming or going. This was not unusual. The hotel reception was a model of bad organization. The crew of the Air France 747 that came into Bujumbura each week had left without paying their restaurant and bar bill the previous week. For a crew of fourteen the total was over five hundred dollars. Seeing a potential administration problem, Vicky had simply tacked the bills under those for a three-man TV crew who were leaving the following day. She was genuinely surprised when they refused to pay it.

The tour guide attached to the Japanese group explained what was going on. Her charges meanwhile had shuffled off to the restaurant which was serving breakfast, and were baffling the waiters by ordering salmon. They were a group of retired people from Osaka, all members of a photographic club. A shark of a travel agent had sold them an outdated package to Africa called Historic Cities of Burundi. It guaranteed that the group would visit Gitega, Cibitoke and Bururi, three of the more violent cities in Burundi, which that spring was rated the second most violent country on earth. The woman from the Tourism Board did not know what to do. She had instructions to keep them within the city limits; the authorities knew the kind of adverse PR they would get if a bus-load of tourists was hit by rebel or army fire. I suggested that she pack them up into the bus, and take them out on the road towards the Zairean border, to the north end of Lake Tanganyika. There they would be able to spend a day in the wildlife sanctuary. They would certainly see crocodiles, hippopotamuses, and perhaps various horned beasts, as well as lots of different birds. If they were particularly unlucky – it had happened to two aid workers – they would run into Hutu rebels crossing over the Rusizi river from Zaire. Anyway. It would keep them occupied. She should then bring them back to the hotel, put them up overnight, and hope that there was a sufficiently heavy firefight to scare them into going home the next day. She sighed. It was not, she said, going to be easy. Feeling that I had to get at least one quote from a Japanese tourist, I asked one man what he thought of the country so far. He grinned, took my proffered Reuters business card, and bowed.

'Very, very nice. Tomorrow historic cities! Tomorrow, Cibitoke!'

Under cover of the confusion, Hitoshi Mise hurried out of the lobby, trying to avoid my eye. The refugee exodus from the camps in the north of the country was turning into a minor scandal for him.

'Mr Mise? Can I have a word?'

He rushed out to his car. He hadn't been returning my mobile phone calls and was refusing to have a meeting. Things were being made harder for him by the fact that one of the Tutsi prostitutes who frequented the Novotel Bar had got hold of his mobile number. She was bombarding him with calls, asking to be his 'special friend'.

I found two of Mise's senior UNHCR staff out on the terrace and sat down to talk. I wanted to be sure of my facts before I drove to his office and confronted him. The situation regarding the refugees was complicated and Mise was trying to cover up what was actually going on. What had started out as a fairly minor movement of refugees away from their camps seemed to be turning into an attempt by the Burundian army to repatriate them forcibly to Rwanda. Allegedly this was being done with the cooperation of the UNHCR, in clear contravention of their humanitarian mandate.

There were six refugee camps in Burundi, housing a very approximate total of 150,000 mainly Rwandan Hutu refugees who had fled Rwanda in the spring and summer of 1994. Unlike in the camps in Zaire and Tanzania, the percentage of these refugees who had participated in the Rwandan genocide was low. There were some concentrations of former members of the Rwandan government army, the FAR, and the Hutu interahamwe militias, but there were far larger numbers of innocent Rwandan families. The Burundian army were keen to repatriate these refugees because they alleged that Hutu rebels based themselves inside the camps from where they carried out attacks on the Tutsi military. The UNHCR was keen to repatriate the refugees for two reasons. First, the UNHCR budget in Burundi was running out. Second, they wanted to try to repatriate these refugees before attempting to crack the hold that the Hutu militias and the FAR still had on the camps in Zaire and Tanzania.

The refugees in Burundi were divided into two main areas. In the north of the country, around Ngozi, 100,000 were gathered in the four camps of Ruvumu, Kibezi, Magara and Rukuramigabo. In the north-east, another 40 to 60,000 were concentrated in Magara and Ntamba, near the town of Muyinga.

On 5 January, the affable and competent Paul Stromberg, press officer for the UNHCR had given me the official line about the organization's intentions towards the refugees.

'The closure of these camps is the logical consequence of what we hope will be a massive return of refugees which the UNHCR intends to bring about by a stepped-up effort of voluntary re-patriation. Any operation to close the camps will be the result of humanitarian operations: the UNHCR is a humanitarian organization and does not indulge in anything other than voluntary repatriation.'

To give Stromberg the benefit of the doubt, one had to ignore the situation in the refugee camps around Goma and Bukavu in Zaire. It was hard to forget that there, the UNHCR and its 'implementing partners' were spending a million dollars a day to house, feed, shelter and provide medical facilities to over a million Rwandan Hutus, huge numbers of whom were responsible for carrying out killings in 1994; that in the camps of Goma and Bukavu former FAR soldiers and interahamwe militias were openly carrying out military training, buying and receiving shipments of arms, using the sprawling miles of refugee shacks as bases from which to launch cross-border raids, and preparing for a reinvasion of Rwanda, intending to complete the genocide. The situation regarding the refugees was getting complicated, and Mise was keen not to let it appear that it was getting out of control. In August 1995, Zairean soldiers had started forcibly to repatriate these refugees, and had pushed some 20,000 back over the border from Goma and Bukavu. Two UNHCR officials, one senior Zairean army officer, and at least one western diplomat based in Kinshasa alleged that the UN High Commissioner for Refugees herself, Sadako Ogata, had requested Mobutu to stop this repatriation. This was regardless of the fact that hundreds of thousands of the refugees in Zaire did not qualify for refugee status under the two conventions to which the UNHCR was signatory. So many of them could, at best, be regarded as illegal immigrants, at worse war criminals. The UNHCR had housed them in the wrong place, too. One of the paragraphs of their mandate required them to house refugees no less than seventy-five kilometres away from the border of their country of origin. In Goma and Bukavu they were sometimes less than five kilometres from Rwanda.

Hitoshi Mise was under intense pressure from Sadako Ogata to effect a repatriation of the Rwandan refugees in Burundi. It would save money, and it would enable her to answer the criticisms of her numerous detractors – most notably the United States – that she was dragging her feet on the refugee issue. The Rwandan army, the RPA, was starting to become impatient in Kigali, and was making noises about repatriating the refugees itself. Mise was also under huge pressure from the Burundian government, namely the army, to return the refugees to Rwanda. Ogata had materialized briefly in Burundi in January, not in her official capacity as head of the UNHCR, but as the 'personal envoy' of Boutros Ghali. This enabled her to avoid difficult, potentially compromising questions about the refugee situation. In the end all she said to journalists was that she had come to Burundi 'looking for all possible ways of improving the situation for Burundians and other people'.

Senior UNHCR officials told me that she had, in fact, had a series of meetings with Hitoshi Mise and the Burundian army in which they had discussed ways of forcibly repatriating the refugees in Burundi. An air of conspiracy began to appear around the December events that led up to that catastrophic first week in January when I had gone to interview President Ntibantunganya. The situation for the UN and aid agencies working in the four refugee camps in the north of Burundi had been exacerbated by a series of incidents around the town of Ngozi in December. All of the UNHCR and other humanitarian staff who worked in the four camps lived in houses in Ngozi. It was a quiet, hill settlement, set at a high altitude, surrounded by the eucalyptus forests and banana plantations of the mountains that crept north towards the Rwandan border. There was a small airstrip, where a Twin Otter aircraft chartered by the World Food Programme landed every few days. There was a tennis court, a few local bars, and several times a week the surrounding hills would echo with gunfire as the army, Tutsi displaced people and Hutu rebels continued their endless cycle of attack and slaughter.

Shortly before Christmas, a Toyota Land Cruiser belonging to the Belgian Red Cross had been stopped by three Burundian soldiers on a road leading to Bujumbura. The men demanded a lift. Following their strict instructions, the expatriate from the Belgian Red Cross told the soldiers that they would have to leave their weapons behind before boarding the vehicle, which they did. Shortly afterwards, the vehicle ran into a Hutu rebel road-block, where two of the three soldiers were killed, unable to defend themselves. The third, conveniently, made it to Bujumbura, where from a hospital bed he gave interviews to the local radio and TV stations about the incident. Lieutenant-Colonel Minani was at his bedside, and encouraged me to come and do an interview with the man. The gist of it was that the Belgian Red Cross was responsible for the deaths of the two soldiers, their driver had been in league with the Hutu ambushers, and that they were aiding the rebels. This sort of accusation was natural in a whole region where every side saw 'neutral' NGOs feeding or providing support to an opposing faction. Minani spun the story to his satisfaction, and Tutsi Sans Échec militiamen were briefed. The message was clear: the white men are on the side of the rebels. Within three days, the sixteen hand-grenade and rocket attacks on NGO and UN houses in Ngozi had followed, and in their turn, the suspension of all aid activities in the area. Much of the blame for this could be laid at the door of Colonel Minani, a man whose extremist views and unquestioning ethnic hatred overrode his innate intelligence. The new year saw the aid agencies and the UN in a tortuous series of meetings and discussions with the government, the army and their bases in Europe and the United States before they could resume their activities. There was talk of the UN armed guards being deployed to protect humanitarian convoys; the military were offering protection. Sadako Ogata had said that the Security Council were prepared to listen to her recommendations. In the middle of this confusion, as the security situation in the country worsened, and as Whisky and I kept our rapidly climbing weekly death-tolls, the UN special rapporteur for human rights arrived in the country.

On the night of the 17 and 18 January a military position on the outskirts of Mugano refugee camp was attacked. Three wounded were taken to hospital. Hitoshi Mise was in bed at the Novotel at the time but was able to assure me that the attack had been carried out by Hutu rebels. Minani, first thing the following morning, told me with complete assuredness that Hutu Rwandan militiamen had carried out the attack. It was not clear why members of the ex-FAR would want to precipitate any movement of the refugees back to Rwanda – it was entirely in their interest to keep their Hutu refugee population in exile in Burundi, Zaire and Tanzania alike. It is possible that they wanted the refugees to flee into Tanzania, away from the control of the Burundian army. However, the refugees claimed they were attacked by Burundian Tutsi militiamen, 15,000 refugees immediately moved seventeen kilometres to the Tanzanian border and tried to cross.

Within twenty-four hours this figure had grown to 17,000. Four hundred succeeded in crossing the frontier, despite the presence of the Burundian army, which shot at them. The refugees in Ntamba camp prepared to follow suit. UNHCR personnel were prevented by the army from reaching the refugees in their care. Once again, I found myself using the phrase 'number of civilian casualties unknown', in a report. The chief of staff of the Burundian army, Colonel Jean Bikomagu, one of the three coordinators of the 1993 coup, visited the area. A day later Mise reported that Ntamba camp had been burned to the ground. A few hundred refugees were still left in Mugano, some 20,000 were milling around the area of the Tanzanian border, others were voluntarily heading back to Rwanda. The UNHCR made a series of cosmetic protests against heavy-handed military behaviour, but for Hitoshi Mise, everything was going to plan.

Lieutenant-Colonel Firmin Sinzoyiheba, the defence minister, was another Tutsi army officer from Bururi, albeit a moderate one. I found him at the Novotel in the middle of the crisis, but he would not talk to me. On the telephone later, he told me his version of events.

'It's a naked lie that the refugees were attacked by the army; our position was attacked by rebels and there was an exchange of fire. The following day the unit went for assistance in a UNHCR car and when they returned they were fired on.'

He finished his statement with the cover-all military opt-out clause: 'There is no beautiful war, people die in crossfires, it is a fact of war and I regret it.'

Across the Great Lakes Region, according to Burundian and Rwandan military spokesmen that month, hundreds of women and children of both ethnicities were walking into 'crossfires'.

Mise got his facts twisted at this point. He claimed that Sinzoyiheba had to be lying as there were no UNHCR vehicles to be stolen, so the army could not have borrowed one. It was a convoluted and technically complex argument, and to most international observers at the time it must have seemed almost incomprehensible. But from the inside it gave a very important insight into how authorities in the United Nations were prepared to spin systematically to achieve their ends. As I was badgering Mise about Ntamba and Mugano camps, another colleague, Chris Tomlinson from the Associated Press, had discovered that Mise had been issuing inaccurate figures for the number of refugees in Uvira, Zaire. Mise had caved in with a clumsy u-turn when confronted by Tomlinson, an astute, aggressive Texan journalist, but only after digging himself in with still more lies.

In Mugano and Ntamba, refugees who had not got to Tanzania or Rwanda started to return to the sites of their former camps. Like refugees all over the Great Lakes Region, they sat down in the mud, waiting for free food and instructions from above. The Burundian and Rwandan governments organized a meeting with the UNHCR on 25 January at the Novotel, the so-called 'Fourth Tripartite Meeting' to discuss regional problems concerning Rwandan refugees. Doctor Ephrem Kabaija from the Kigali government assured observers and journalists that the authorities from Burundi, Rwanda and the UNHCR were doing everything they could to promote and plan the repatriation of Rwandan refugees. He, at least, was telling his version of the truth. Some 3,000 mainly starving women, children and old men had by now returned to the Ntamba site. This figure continued to grow, and by 1 February, there were 5 to 6,000 refugees around the former camp areas. UNHCR delegates told me that the Burundian military were moving 'in masses' towards the camp. All the men apart from the old had fled, there was little food, the UNHCR staff had left the area. The army were moving in.

Almost all of this information, concerning Mise and UNHCR movements, statements and plans was being given to me by Mise's senior staff. He had forbidden any of them to talk to the press, but they universally disapproved of his policies. He was, simply, an obedient bureaucrat, doing what he was told by a senior member of staff who happened to be Japanese, like him, and a woman to boot.

His staff loathed him. He wouldn't pass on any information to them about his activities or his intentions, and any staff member that openly disagreed with him found themselves seeking another posting. Sometimes three times a day his six most senior staff in the country would inform me, on the record, but unattributably, of what he was doing.

In the mud and rain of the burnt-out wreckage of Ntamba, the estimated 6,000 refugees were given three options by the army and the UN. Stay here, with no back-up or feeding facilities from the UN, despite their mandatory obligations, accept to be moved by the Burundian army to an army-supervised camp in the interior of the country, or return to Rwanda immediately. Those choosing to return were told that they would have to sign a voluntary repatriation form. The old women, children and old men were exhausted, hungry and frightened. Their own leaders who normally gave them instructions about what to do had fled. They knew that going back to Rwanda was hazardous, but staying in Burundi at the behest of the army would be even worse. They did not know what to do. So the army, with Mise's full knowledge, made their mind up for them.

I went to see him when the operation was over.

'We did not have time at Ntamba to explain to the refugees what were the recommendations. Were the refugees coerced? It is a question of interpretation. All the families [who chose to go back to Rwanda] signed voluntary repatriation forms. I had no contact with Sadako Ogata throughout, Geneva [the UNHCR's headquarters] was unconcerned, and there was no external pressure on me.'

Of these statements, only the last one is true. There was no external pressure on Mise because he was perfectly happy to let the army behave as they wished. As for the other statements, the three most senior staff under Mise in the Bujumbura office said that Geneva, and Sadako Ogata, were fully informed of the operation as it unfolded. About five of Mise's staff protested to him in writing about his actions. And the refugees who signed voluntary repatriation forms to go back to Rwanda? 'I saw two families standing by a lorry, trying to read these forms, wondering what to do, whether to go back to Rwanda or stay put,' a senior member of UNHCR staff told me.

'Two Burundian soldiers approached them and said that if they did not sign, they would be shot. They signed at gunpoint and were pushed onto the lorries. Other refugees were beaten with sticks and rifle butts.'

'I saw refugees beaten with sticks, clubs and rifle butts, being made to sign their forms and being forced onto the lorries,' said another member of staff. 'Ephrem Kabaija, whom Mise had made agreements with, was there watching it happen.'

'It will never happen,' Mise told me afterwards, 'that the military try and intimidate refugee camps.'

While I was arguing with him about the intricacies of his betrayal of the UN mandate concerning refugees, events in the country at large had been careering along towards a worsening of the crisis. The United Nations agencies and the forty-nine humanitarian agencies operating in Burundi, most of whom had technically suspended operations after the events in Ngozi, went back to work. For many, the improvement in the security situation outside the capital was academic, as they wouldn't work outside Bujumbura anyway. One British woman who worked for a minor humanitarian organization with Christian links couldn't bring herself to admit to what the Burundian army were really doing to the civilian population beyond what she'd seen for herself: she insisted on describing military atrocities as 'impoliteness'.

Mise tried to take his revenge, in a characteristically spiteful way. He insisted that I should not be allowed to use any radio handset that operated on the United Nations net, and he tried to ban me from attending any of the UN–NGO security meetings, despite Christophe telling him that sometimes half of any available security information was emanating from me anyway. It was one of Mise's colleagues, Mr Khan, the head of the UN Development Programme, who told Christophe to keep me away from the security meetings. Christophe laughed when he related the incident to me, saying that this man was 'afraid of his own shadow', so we went on supplying each other with information.

I had made other, more dangerous enemies by this point, anyway, almost without realizing it. One day my chunky mobile phone rang just as I was stepping out of Gaston's car. It was Colonel Minani, and he was incandescent with rage.

'Jennings! You are an enemy of the people! You are here on a mission to destroy the morale of the army! I will never talk to you again.'

I wasn't sure which of my articles was causing him so much offence. I tried to ring him back to ask him but he refused to talk to me. I felt that it wasn't the end of the world: I had the mobile telephone numbers of a number of other military officers, and could always ring them. One officer who commanded a battalion based in Bujumbura said that Minani was a 'mathematician, not a soldier'.

Just to be on the safe side though, I decided to pack my bags, shoulder my flak-jacket, still covered with Cibitoke mud, and change sleeping locations yet again. Madeleine Albright, the American ambassador to the UN, was on her way to Burundi and I didn't want to be looking over my shoulder while she was in town. Since I arrived, I had moved from the Novotel to a brief stay at Betsy's – waiting nightly for the call to the bedroom that would never come – and then back to the Novotel. I had then shifted my luggage up the hill to another friend's house while they were away, before taking a quick week at the Hotel Source du Nile. I was now back in the Novotel. Vicky told me that the day after I had left, the Japanese tourists had returned from their wildlife safari, enthusiastic but exhausted, and had sat down to dinner. There had been a misunderstanding when they insisted on trying to go for a walk after curfew, but everybody's worries had been resolved in one go when the Hutu rebels obliged by opening fire in the hills. It was a dramatic display; they had clearly got hold of a heavy machine-gun. Yellow and green Chinese-made tracer ricocheted across the hills. The tourists were speechless. They flew out of Bujumbura the following day.

Madeleine Albright arrived in United States Airforce Three. It was clear she had come to deliver a tough message to the Burundian government. Six diplomatic protection officers from the US Secret Service accompanied her. An Air Force surgeon in a flying-suit liberally splattered with insignia and unit patches shadowed her, a full medical kit in his bag including several pints of cross-matched blood. One of the secret servicemen had a belt-fed machine gun in his bag. They were prepared for a major attempt on her life, and the Burundian military were suitably impressed. At the end of a long day, throughout which all the journalists had spent chasing her around various locations, she gave a press conference at the airport.

'The prime minister read my message clearly,' she said, standing in the heat of the VIP departure lounge at the airport. 'I told him about the United States' and the international community's concern about a potential increase in violence. We are watching this country carefully and do not want it to fall into a hopeless abyss of violence.'

I got another mystery telephone call the following day.

'Jennings. We are watching you. If you are not careful it will be time for you to go back to where you came.'

What – South London? I thought, amused, pushing the 'Clear' button on my phone.

The following morning I was thinking about breakfast choices at the Novotel buffet when the phone rang again. It was the bureau in Nairobi. They had received information from the American Embassy in Nairobi, via Bujumbura, that there was a serious security threat against me. Minani and his Sans Échec militia friends, I thought. The office thought it best if I returned to Nairobi for a few days.

Chapter 6

Under Siege, Under Fire

The days in Burundi seemed to segue into a series of increasing body-counts, interviews with intractable politicians and discussions with hardline army officers. The nights, however, were dominated by the culture of the curfew. We all tried desperately to have a normal social life. From nine in the evening to five in the morning, everybody in Burundi stayed indoors. The only people abroad were those for whom the night was killing time. Where you were at half past eight in the evening was where you were going to spend the night. It was forbidden to drive outside after nine o'clock: those that did were stopped, either by the military, the police, or prowling Tutsi militiamen. Next door to the Novotel was the Meridien Hotel. To go from one to the other after curfew you either climbed through a hole in the hedge, or you walked out of the Novotel car-park, down ten metres of pavement, and in through the garden gate. Even to be seen on that ten metres of pavement was considered an arrestable offence.

By the beginning of March I had moved, finally, into a house which was semi secure, inside a UN compound in the centre of town. Nowhere in Burundi was really safe, however. Unless you were in a French military helicopter-gunship at the firing controls of a multi-barrelled Gatling gun, hovering over the city centre. But the house was less unsafe than many other places. There was electricity, sometimes, and a house maid who turned up, occasionally, and a gardener who slashed the grass with a sickle and pruned the lemon tree. Then he disappeared, taking all the gardening machetes with him. He had gone to sell them to his Hutu brothers in the hills,

Gaston joked one morning. I shared with Stacey White, who came from the Californian valleys and worked for the UN. She managed to work all day, improve her tennis game and run a full-time boyfriend, despite the curfew, the war, the endless security worries and the unceasing violence.

I think the situation made us all a little mad that spring and summer. The extraordinary claustrophobia of Bujumbura did not help. It was a tiny town. I was lucky that I could make my own rules. I could drive to Cibitoke any day of the week. I could sit up in the mountains on a rain-soaked firebase with traumatized, terrified Burundian soldiers, men ambushed every night on patrol, men who kept their dead comrades in a woodshed. If I so chose I could drive up to Muramvya through Bugerama junction on the Route Nationale One, which by mid spring that year was the most heavily ambushed road in the world. I could, if I chose, even drive right down to the southern provinces of Makamba and Bururi, where the war and the killings had worsened along the wind-blown ridges and in the forests full of pine trees. But for people like Stacey, the downside of taking a UN salary was having to abide by their rules. Bujumbura was a confined city, and the UN rules for their security were simple: be home by nine; don't leave the city; stay out of any risky areas; and don't leave home in the morning until UN security says it is safe to do so. There were United Nations security checks on the radio morning and evening. For many UN staff, the interior of Burundi was something they would never see during the whole of their six month stint. Some of the embassies were even more draconian. I often found myself being given security advice by diplomatic staff who had never, ever left the capital. I also frequently met Belgian, French and Greek businessmen who hadn't left Bujumbura for two years, who knew nothing of what was happening in the country in which they lived. For most expatriates, were they UN staff, diplomatic workers, or European families who chose to live in Burundi, the interior of the country had become demonized.

There were forty-nine non-governmental organizations, or NGOs, as aid agencies were officially called, working in Burundi by March 1996. More than three-quarters of these operated only within the capital. It was easy to blame security for the appalling working conditions outside, but Burundi was a country at war, as was Afghanistan, as was Chechnya, as was Sierra Leone. It seemed to me that many of the agencies liked the kudos on their manifestos that working in Burundi gave them. But they couldn't quite deal with the reality of it. If there were ever people who did understand the meaning of the phrase Big Boys' Games – Big Boys' Rules, it was the three people I considered the unsung heroes of Burundi's humanitarian community: Patrick Berner of the ICRC, Jean-Luc from WFP and Anique Hamel from MSF. Their organizations operated in the countryside, while most others sat in the capital, gossiping on their radio handsets, complaining about security.

I can't remember who it was who first coined the phrase 'Good For Burundi' to describe eligible members of the opposite sex. But I do remember that I was thinking more about GFBs than work the day I fell asleep in an interview. I'd gone to see Charles Mukasi, the head of the hardline Tutsi UPRONA party. He was, oddly, a Hutu. There were a limited number of very hardline Hutus who gave their allegiance to UPRONA, and Mukasi was one. There were hardline Hutus who had joined the army in the 1980s, and then seen their relatives massacred by Hutus in 1993, accused of being collaborators. Anyway, Gaston and I had driven round to the UPRONA headquarters and I had sat in a deep armchair to talk to Mukasi. The day was hot, it was just after lunch. Charles Mukasi was long-winded. I think we had been talking for an hour, and he had only got to the beginning of the twentieth century in his monologue. I was making notes about the development of the Burundian royal family, when I felt my eyes begin to close like a passenger in a car driving along a straight motorway. He was sitting opposite me, talking, when my head dropped, my eyes closed and I fell fast asleep. I don't know for how long I was out, but I remember coming to, jolting my head upright, and seeing that I had dribbled on my shirt. My biro had described a long, straight line down across the page of my notebook. Mukasi seemed not to have noticed. So deep had my instantaneous sleep been that when I woke I couldn't remember which country I was in. I sucked in my saliva and hastily looked on the walls behind him for clues. There was no map, nothing. He suddenly asked what I thought of the situation. For an instant I thought I was in Somalia. I threw out some random comment about disarming militiamen, and the need for political dialogue, and he was off again.

'By the 1930s,' he said, 'the situation between the royal family, the Ba-Hutu, and the Ba-Tutsi . . .'

I couldn't be bothered to take any more notes. I had, anyway, only come to see him to ask for his opinion on the forthcoming peace talks promised for April. I reckoned that as we had most of the twentieth century to get through I was fine for a bit. So I started making a mental list of Good For Burundis, or GFBs.

GFB was a term applicable to people of either sex: Stacey was forever asking my opinion of men in the international community in Bujumbura whom I thought it would be fun for her to go out with. Conversely, she thought my long-running crush on Betsy was a waste of time.

'Don't call her,' she'd say, as we shared our morning coffee in her UN bungalow. 'She treats you like shit! And she ran off with Jacques. In front of you as well. How dare she?'

I could only agree. I'd been staying in Betsy's house from mid December to the beginning of January, waiting, as I said, for the call to the bedroom that never came. That was nearly two months ago. There had to be others. So as Mukasi droned on, the hot sun lit up the rolling dust in the air, and I thought of other options. The war was intensifying, I was getting busier, security was becoming tougher, I'd had my first two death-threats, and like all of us I needed a distraction. The rules of the GFBs were straightforward. You could have an affair with them in Burundi – which, thanks to the radio net if nothing else, everybody would know about immediately. You could go for a week's holiday with them to Zanzibar. You could even catch the UN flight to Nairobi and stay at the Norfolk Hotel, enjoy drinks on the Lord Delamere terrace, meet your friends. But it almost went without saying that GFBs of either sex would not cut the mustard back home in Europe or the United States. I left Mukasi with a cheery handshake, a promise to see him soon. Remarkably, for a Burundian politician, he had a sense of humour.

Sitting in the red Nissan with Gaston, I made a mental list of my priorities:

   i. Try not to annoy the army too much. Find something else to write about apart from massacres.

  ii. Muster up courage to go and report on the fighting in Bururi. Find four-wheel-drive car to get there.

 iii. Don't drink gin at Novotel – too pricy.

 iv. Propose piece to Reuters about food shortages in north-west; use as excuse to invite Anne-Sophie on date disguised as fact-finding mission.

  v. If Anne-Sophie not returned to capital by Friday ring Médecins du Monde and say yes to party invitation for Saturday – borrow sleeping-bag to stay over after curfew.

 vi. Stall piece on army heroin dealing and gold smuggling in keeping with (i).

 vi. (a) Buy two hundred cigarettes from boy in Novotel car-park.

 vii. Burundi versus Algeria football match Saturday; find local sports reporters who can supply details for BBC.

viii. Borrow tennis racquet for Sunday tennis with Nicolette from MDM if interested.

 ix. Tell Reuters to send \$1,800 expenses and \$2,000 pay on next flight.

  x. Haircut before party.

 xi. Think about buying gun in case death threats continue.

I'd returned from Nairobi two days before after a three-day break. It turned out that the piece of journalism that had so irritated Colonel Minani, and consequently the Sans Échec militias, was a feature I had written about the Burundian army. Using quotes from various sources, including Whisky, I had put together what I thought was a rather fair piece. It had included, however, a line from Whisky, cited as 'a UN security officer', which said, 'the Burundian army are fighting a war they know they can't win, against a Hutu rebel army who know they can't lose.' It was militarily correct, but had driven the army spare. They accused me of undermining morale of the rank-and-file. It was important, therefore, that I found something else to write about. I had a feature on Tutsis and their cattle in mind. But this was going to present problems, as heavy fighting had erupted in the military heartland of Bururi, and it was inevitable the army would have exceeded themselves. Perhaps I could find a huge massacre committed by Hutus.

I also had to tell Charlotte that just because her Red Cross boyfriend was coming back after having been evacuated in December, it didn't mean she could see if he wanted to get back together, then pick me up if he didn't. Charlotte worked for a Canadian NGO and rated above GFB status, in that I would have been happy to go out with her in the UK. We'd had what she called *'un petit fling'* for two weeks. She'd moved into my room at the Novotel one night when the capital was in the middle of a firefight. She'd brought along four hundred cigarettes and a litre of vodka. For morale, she'd said.

Feeling rather jauntier than I had been before seeking Mukasi – interviewing him was like a lengthy, painless trip to the dentist – I thought I'd go swimming. Gaston seemed to notice my pick-up in mood because he turned up the volume on his live version of 'Girl from Yesterday'. He was singing along wildly as we swung around the main square, slapping out the bass-line on the outside of the car door. Our tapes now stood at three, including *Hell Freezes Over* – the live Eagles reunion concert. Gaston – a neat, sharply dressed Bujumbura Tutsi – particularly liked this. He could push the clutch in, change to neutral, bang out the drum solo in 'Tequila Sunrise' on his steering-wheel, then shift into gear and de-clutch in a matter of seconds. He particularly liked doing this on the road to the airport, where he could pick up speed. Then we had a compilation I had borrowed off Zephyr when I had sacked him, after his Johnny Walker consumption had rendered him semi-permanently paralytic. This contained the famous cover version of 'Stand by your Man' sung in Kinyarwanda. The rest of the tape was mostly Zairean music sung in the Lingala dialect. A mix of fast electric guitar, keyboards and drum, this music was known colloquially as *Kwasa Kwasa* music, from the French words *c'est quoi ca? c'est quoi ca?* It also had an irritating smoochy rap song, with a chorus that went: 'when I hit your G-spot, I wanna hear you moan.' Gaston had twice asked me to translate this, but I needed Nicolette or Anne-Sophie to help me get the right word. Then, like every other bar, airport lounge, car and club in the Great Lakes Region that year, we had *D'eux*, the French album by Celine Dion.

On the way back to the hotel we dropped in on the Prince Regent hospital. This was the only public hospital in Bujumbura, and many of the casualties from Cibitoke and Bubanza provinces were brought here. Interviewing the survivors of attack by army or Hutu rebels, especially in the comparative safety of a hospital, was a very good way of finding out what was going on in the parts of the country I couldn't reach through lack of time, or lack of adequate security.

African hospitals in war zones seemed to have a very particular smell. It was a combination of disinfectant, the earthy sweat of people who spend their lives outside, and a mixture of stale blood, urine and diarrhoea, overlaid with fear. I walked down the outside corridors of the Prince Regent Hospital, past the wards, looking for Nicolette, who worked as a nurse for Médecins du Monde, which ran the medical and surgical side of the operations at the Prince Regent. I found her changing the dressings on an old woman who had been shot by the army while fleeing Bubanza a week before.

'Christian. How are you?'

'Very well. And you? Much happening?'

'Quite a number of wounded.' She showed me the brownish-yellow hole in the woman's back. 'Cibitoke, Bubanza. I don't know if you want to talk to them.'

'I do, but I can't use it at the moment. Trying to keep a low profile with the army at the moment.'

'Ah. I get. Then you ought to go to Bururi. Lots of Hutu attacks there.'

'Mmm. Looking forward to Saturday?'

Nicolette smiled at me. 'Are you coming? Sandrine has said that everybody who's coming has to ring and say if they're staying the night.'

'I'm staying.' I closed my notebook.

'See you there, then,' she said.

I walked down the corridor, past a man with what looked like a smashed face, mumbling into a bedsheet he'd wrapped around himself. On closer inspection his teeth seemed to be protruding and he appeared to have lost his mouth. He held out a hand. I smiled and walked off. Gaston was sitting on his bonnet, watching the comings and goings of patients at the hospital. Nicolette reappeared, on her way back to her little office behind the Casualty Department.

I walked after her.

'Nicolette – I was thinking . . . on Sunday, after the party. Do you want to play tennis? I mean, if you don't have too much of a hangover?'

'Why not? But I'll be feeling awful. And I'm very bad at tennis.'

'Don't worry. So am I. Oh, just one thing—'

She turned round.

'That man in the bedsheet in the corridor. What's the story there?'

'He's the local schizophrenic; shouts all night long. Some Tutsi kids cut his lips off with a machete to shut him up.'

Gaston reversed out of the car-park, turning up the volume on 'New Kid in Town'.

Mukasi and his hopes for the peace talks in Mwanza, Tanzania, to be held the next month, added an extra paragraph onto my Reuters piece that afternoon. Most of it was concerned with the increase in fighting in the southern provinces of Bururi and Makamba, and I added in some information about the huge number of displaced people in the centre and north-east of Burundi. The previous afternoon, I'd taken a free seat in the WFP aircraft, and flown over the central town of Gitega and the province of Karuzi. The army was carrying out what they called a *ratissage*, which translated as a 'search-and-destroy mission'. I saw about eighty houses burning. Sixty-seven thousand people had been 'displaced' from their homes, pouring north-eastwards towards the Tanzanian border. For the WFP, this meant additional mouths to feed. Forty-five tons of maize was duly on its way.

The responsibility for feeding Burundi's Internally Displaced People (IDPs) fell on WFP and its head of delegation, Jean-Luc Siblot. Every time the army or Hutu rebels attacked, the local populations were forcibly evacuated, and they just hit the road, walking until they reached a point where they felt marginally secure. For the Tutsis, this would be in or around a town or military post. For the Hutus, this would be the mountains, low-lying swamp areas, or, if they were accessible, the borders of Zaire or Tanzania. Not only did the constant movement of people disrupt any form of agricultural production, it threw hundreds of thousands of people onto the humanitarian mercy of the ICRC, WFP, and MSF. The movements of the IDPs also upset the local social structures of the areas where they temporarily settled. In the remote rural communities of central Burundi, in the highlands of southern Karuzi, on the windswept mountain slopes of Bururi, or the grass and eucalyptus forest plateaux of northern Gitega province, the populations were even more isolated and insular than they were in Rwanda. If 9,000 strangers arrived from a commune thirty kilometres away and set up camp on the edge of the village, or outside the communal buildings, or by the small, local river, suspicion immediately fell upon them. I'd stood in central Burundi in an IDP camp and listened to an old woman with a black chicken squatting on her head tell me that there had been 'an arrival of strangers in the area, from across the river'. She could have been describing a troupe of caravans containing marauding Mongol hordes; but these 'strangers' came from a hill two and a-half kilometres away. Imagine, then, that 9,000 people arrive in the village from thirty kilometres away. But actually, they have been twice displaced already, and so have come from thirty kilometres away, and three months before that from twenty-five kilometres away, and a year before that from fifty kilometres away. In the massive flights of IDPs that took place after the failed coup in 1993, they came from even further, from Rutana, three provinces away. They have arrived in an area where the land ownership structures can be traced back to 1820. When there's gunfire at night, when cattle are found missing, when a mine is laid at the junction of three dirt roads, and the army turns up, who does the blame fall on? If the IDPs are Hutu, the army won't give them the benefit of the doubt. Depending on the mood of the soldiers, the character of their commander, when they were last paid, how drunk they are, and when they last lost men from their unit, the Hutus will be killed . . . If the

IDPs are Tutsi, and the local Tutsis are complaining about them, then the army could well turn a blind eye, or kill a few just to keep things calm.

From his office near the football stadium in Bujumbura, with his maps, his handset and his mobile phone, it was Jean-Luc's job to keep abreast of all these movements. The moment a village was attacked, an IDP camp fired on, a group of Hutus on the move, Jean-Luc was called upon to feed them. By the beginning of April 1996 the numbers of people depending on him in each province looked like this:

Bururi: 8,000 people displaced after Hutu rebel raids and subsequent army reprisals and fighting.

Makamba: 45,000 people displaced by Hutu rebel attacks from Tanzania and by Sans Échec forcing Hutus out of the province.

Muramvya: 20,000 displaced by rebel attacks and ambushes, especially in Kibimba valley.

Karuzi: 15–20,000 mainly Hutu civilians fled from their homes after heavy army reprisals for Hutu rebel actions.

Gitega: 39,000 IDPs.

Cibitoke: 70,000 IDPs.

This was just a rough estimate for the five central provinces, which, with Cibitoke, formed the centre of the war in April. Nobody could access most areas of Bubanza and Ngozi provinces, for instance, to find out about IDPs there. If the map of Burundi was shaped like a heart, then the fighting was concentrated in a central t-shaped area. Hutu rebels on the cross-bar of the 't' moved west to east and vice versa, from Zaire to Tanzania and back again. On the downstroke of the 't' they moved north to south from Tanzania, and came in from Zaire across Lake Tanganyika.

Lieutenant-Colonel Celestin Ndayisaba was waiting for me that evening at the Novotel bar, trying to look anonymous in a vivid blue and pink tracksuit. He'd pulled a baseball cap low over his forehead, but looked exactly like what he was: a senior Burundian military officer trying to look like a civilian. I'd sat with him for two hours a fortnight before in Cibitoke along with an American human rights investigator, discussing the state of the war, wondering what hopes there were for peace. Cibitoke had been warm and dusty, the rebels never far away. We'd drunk several Primus together; we'd eaten goat brochettes, bloody and rare off the grill at the officers' mess. I'd felt that he was an ally of sorts. He looked very shifty and uncomfortable this evening in the Novotel bar where we ordered beer. He came, he said, with a warning.

'I have been told, Christian, that you are trying to undermine the morale of the men. That you have been telling the army they cannot win the war.'

Colonel Minani had been at it again. That, or somehow Colonel Celestin had a way of accessing the Reuters news wire up in Cibitoke.

'Who tells you this, Colonel?

'I am a soldier, Christian. I have my intelligence. I know that you are trying to destabilize the army.'

'Colonel. Please. I have no interest in lowering the morale of your fighting men. I write about Hutus and Tutsis. And anyhow – it was somebody from the UN who said that you could not win the war.'

'But you wrote it. Tell me who this UN man was and I will feed him to my men.'

I bet Christophe had much more powerful allies than Minani could counter; Ndayisaba would have been told that I was personally responsible.

'Tomorrow, Colonel, I travel south to where the Hutus are killing in Gitega.' I didn't tell him I was going to Bururi.

'You must take care on the roads. Sometimes our men will take matters into their own hands, and we will not be there to stop them.'

'Colonel. Moderation – please. I cover both sides; I am a journalist.'

'Yes, but moderation . . . moderation in itself can be a form of extremism.'

He stood, and shook my hand. Death threat duly delivered, he could now go back to the officers' mess and tell Minani and his clique that he, Lieutenant-Colonel Celestin, fighting man, defender of

Cibitoke, had done what had to be done. But first he had one more thing to ask. He pinged one fat fingernail off his empty Primus bottle.

'You have money to pay?'

Christ! These people, I raged, as he skulked off. They ask you to buy their drinks even when they're threatening to kill you. I had found so far, with my three death threats and warnings, that I got so cross about them I wasn't scared at the time. It was only because people like myself were prepared to go to their bloody awful little country, I thought furiously, which they'd done such a good job of destroying, that anybody north of Cibitoke, or Rwanda, at best, knew what was going on here. Did they think that Madeleine Albright came to Burundi, wasting money on all that petrol for Airforce Three and sweating in a hot two-piece suit, for fun? Did they think that she felt that the well-being of Maryland and Illinois, the economy of Texas were threatened by their pissy, senseless genocide?

I stomped over to the bar and bought a bottle of Amstel lager. It was quarter to seven and people were moving off from the Novotel to have supper. At a table behind me the crowd from Médecins du Monde were gathered round a table and one of the women was speaking on her handset to Nicolette, who was at the MDM house. It sounded urgent.

'Mike Hotel Six to Mike Hotel Three, come in?'

'OK, Mike Hotel Three. This is what you need to do. Do you copy?'

'*Oui, je suis on standby*. To you.'

'OK, right, you've got the chocolate, right?'

'Mike Hotel Three to Mike Hotel Six. Affirmative. I've got the chocolate. I'm by the fridge door.'

'OK. Mike Hotel Three. Take six eggs from inside the fridge, and separate the yolks from the whites. Then boil some water in a bain-marie. Copy?'

'Affirmative. Visual with eggs.'

'Beat the whites, and fold in slowly – make sure it's slowly, Mike Hotel Three – we don't want the chocolate to stick.'

'Copy chocolate, Hotel Six.'

'Then take a metal spoon from the jar on your right, and beat the yolks. OK?'

'On standby, finding spoon. Putting water on to boil now. To you.'

'Copied Mike Hotel Three. Egg whites beaten?'

'Affirmative, Hotel Six. Chocolate mousse moving forward.'

'GET OFF THE SECURITY CHANNEL!!'

It was Whisky.

'Mike Hotel Three and Mike Hotel: channel five repeat for security use only, repeat security use only.'

I moved out to the car, and Gaston, who'd been leaning on the bar sipping a beer, followed me. It was now five to seven. We had five minutes to get to the Kasuku restaurant, I had an hour and a quarter to order, drink and eat, then Gaston would return at eight twenty, I'd be home by eight thirty, and he'd be back up the hill by eight forty-five. He thumbed a cassette into the machine and pulled fast out of the car-park, singing wildly in French.

> *Cherche encore, tant que brulera ta flamme,*
> *Le paradis qui dort,*
> *Dans le secret de ton áme.*
> *Cherche encore, suis ta lumière et tes lois,*
> *Si tu peux cherche encore plus fort,*
> *Et si jamais tu te perds, je serai là, je serai là.*

Gaston and I knew almost all the words to every song on our three tapes. Gaston had a slightly worrying habit of closing his eyes, and shaking his head from side to side as he tried to match Celine Dion moving up the octaves.

We pulled to a halt outside the Kasuku restaurant, I jumped out, and Gaston sped off. Through the garden with its straw thatch and gravel path I moved inside. The restaurant – its name meant 'parrot' in Swahili – was covered by a roof but open at the sides. It served the best food in Bujumbura. The bar was set on two levels and was crowded. As it was a Friday night, many of the GFBs were out to play. I ordered a large gin and tonic – despite my mental note earlier that day – and looked around. James Shepherd-Barron, former

British army cavalry officer and helicopter pilot, now the European Union humanitarian coordinator, was at the bar, jangling change in the pocket of his chinos. Beside him was Jean-Jacques, a Francophone man of indeterminate European nationality. It was he who flew the WFP Twin Otter, which had taken me up over Karuzi province the day before. He was, as always, in full pilot's uniform, his ironed white shirt open four buttons, a froth of chest mat sprouting forth. He had an arm loosely draped around a Belgian aid worker, who was fiddling with her Amaretto and Coke. His eyes scanned and quartered the room for new female talent. The Belgian owner was chatting semi discreetly to one of the bodyguards from the Belgian embassy, a paratrooper wearing forest-green sports shorts, slashed high up each thigh.

'So you reckon you can get it, yuh?'

'*Mais oui*. I'll be in Brussels next week. Go along to the shop on the Tuesday.'

'OK, super. I need the black nylon one, the underarm. With the back-strap.'

'For a Glock? Nine millimetre?'

'For a Glock. I'll give you the money tomorrow.'

'OK. Tell me? How much does a shoulder-holster come in at nowadays?'

Gordon Duguid from the US Embassy was there. He was the ebullient, euphemistically named head of the American Culture Centre. In fact, of course, he was linked to some American intelligence gathering organization or other. He was ordering Scotch. John Myers from Oxfam, who only three weeks before had received my extremely late and unauthoritative economics survey, was looking at the optics behind the bar as the waiter prepared his gin and tonic.

'OK, yeah, make it a treble.'

Whisky crunched in along the gravel path in a fluster of radio crackle and concealed firearms. He was accompanied by the head of security for the UN commission of inquiry, a Tunisian police colonel. This man, Mohammed Lejmi, known as 'Dali', looked like a matinée idol, and was wearing immaculate, perfectly faded tight jeans, whose belt was slung with the accoutrements of security: mobile phone batteries, Maglite torch, Leatherman multi-tool, pistol magazines. There was a gun somewhere. He had – reputedly – been spending a lot of time at Betsy's house since she had received a death threat from some Rwandan refugees. Dali had posted two Burundian policemen to guard her. These men passed out blind drunk every night on her lawn, and were checked on at regular intervals throughout the night by Dali himself.

Dali was still extricating himself from an affair with another friend of mine, a press-officer who had had a short, ill-advised fling with him just after she had stepped off the flight in. (Dali was rumoured to wait out at the airport as the weekly UN flight arrived, scanning the new female arrivals from the terrace.) He had made his move at Christophe's UN Security meeting, staring at her across the room and approaching her afterwards, to tell her she was beautiful and suggest an immediate lunch. He was also just getting himself out of a simultaneous love affair with a woman from the UN. Betsy herself had told us all that when he had taken her out to supper at Burundi's over-opulent, flashiest restaurant, his opening line had been: 'It's extraordinary. We've both been here for months, and I've only just noticed how beautiful you really are.'

She fell for it. There had to be something to it, though, I'd thought. Perhaps it was the assurance of security; the feeling of being looked after; that warm hand. I really ought to buy that gun this weekend, I thought. Then they'll be queuing up under the mango tree outside Stacey's house. Get Gaston to go to the market with me: Russian Makarov pistol; fifty rounds; hundred and fifty dollars. Have something ready for when Minani's bluster pushes some heroin-crazed Sans Échec gang over the edge. In reality, though, the problem was that if 'they' ever came over the garden gate, I'd have to be able to hit 'them' and not the gate-boy, or Stacey. After four or five glasses of wine, or three large gin and fresh pineapples, I fantasized about having an AK-74MS. This was the latest addition to the Kalashnikov range, with shortened barrel, fifty-round magazine, and a small Maglite torch taped to the fore-grip, zeroed in so the beam and the bullet followed the same path. When I caught myself thinking about that, I knew secretly that I was better off with mobile phone, notebook and biro. For all my knowledge about the interior, of massacres, about politics, of being on the inside track of what the prime minister had said that particular afternoon, I think people in general, and GFB women in particular, felt I was just a howling security risk. Being seen with me too often was akin to asking for a bullet in your windscreen or a Chinese hand-grenade over the garden-wall at one a.m.

'Christian. Your table's ready.'

I picked up my beer and moved to a table with James Shepherd-Barron, John Myers and Stacey. Red wine was ordered; the menus inspected.

'So, James,' I said. 'Big day Monday?'

'Oh yes,' added John. 'Brian Attwood and Emma Bonino. You'll be busy.'

'Don't,' laughed James. 'It's all I need. And I'll be the one getting the stick when they cut off EU and US aid to Burundi.'

'Think they'll do that?' asked John, passing the menu back to the waiter, ordering vegetable stir-fry. I asked for chicken satay.

'They could, theoretically, cut off all humanitarian aid to this country. Think about it: they cut off all the development aid last November. We're now supplying a quarter of the country's GDP. We cut off that – the elite start to suffer, and things, if they can, get worse.'

'There'll simply be no money,' said John. 'Ask our economist here,' he said grinning at me.

'If all the humanitarian aid supplied by us disappears, all of the NGOs pull out, apart from a few,' said James, asking for another Scotch.

I thought about it. The United States Agency for International Development (USAID) and the European Community Humanitarian Office (ECHO), of which James was the Burundi head, supplied almost three-quarters of the international aid. Faced with the rising level of violence, the intractable nature of the conflict, and the point blank refusal of either side to talk to the other, the head of

USAID, Brian Attwood, and EU Commissioner, Emma Bonino, were arriving in Bujumbura on Monday.

'They'll be seeing everybody,' said James. 'The PM, president, minister of defence, UNHCR . . .'

'Cocktails with Mise,' I said. 'You know one of the girls that cleans the rooms at the Novotel found some dried noodles in his suitcase? Thought they were drugs?'

'God. Imagine: Mise arrested.'

'Can I join you?'

It was Jean-Luc from WFP. He helped himself to a large glass of red wine from the carafe. I ordered another.

'So, James. To Monday.'

He raised his glass.

'Poor James,' said Stacey. 'Everybody's going to blame him if the aid gets cut off.'

'And I think it will be,' he said. 'And if it is, this place is going to get a whole lot nastier, very fast.'

'Oh bloody great,' I said, waving at the waiter. 'And I'll get blamed by both sides.'

'No more than you deserve, Christian, let's face it.'

Jean-Luc shuffled his moustache and pushed his spectacles back onto his nose, swilling his red wine round in his glass. James lit up; John looked serious for a moment, and Stacey kicked my leg under the table, laughing. What with Gordon from the US Embassy, Patrick from the ICRC, Anique from MSF and a dozen others, these are all the people I need in Burundi, I thought. Everybody else was just a waste of space. I raised my glass.

'James, a toast. To people like us. A new category: BTBs. Better than Burundis.'

'TGFBs. Too Good for Burundis.'

'Now, Stacey,' said Jean-Luc as we were finishing our meal, trying to look mysterious and seductive. 'I've got this bottle of sweet Sauternes, very cold, at the house, that's begging to be drunk. What do you say?'

'Yes,' I said.

'No Christian. It would be wasted on you.'

'In that case,' I said, 'I'm taking up that invitation to go to Paul's house, drink his champagne, and watch *The Italian Job* on video.'

'I'll give you a lift,' said James. 'I'll come too. I think I'll leave my housemate to it this evening. He's entertaining tonight.'

'Right. It's ten past eight. Let's get the bill. Quick one at the bar. Then home. Coming Stacey?'

'I'm coming to Paul's,' she said. Jean-Luc pretended to look put out, then noticed a very beautiful Scandinavian journalist who had arrived that afternoon from Johannesburg. She had rather demurely asked me to 'look after her, and show her around'. She was now having dinner with some of the bodyguards from the UN commission of inquiry. Dali was almost humping her leg.

Gaston had reclined on his seat outside, and was listening to some Zairean music.

'See you at the hotel tomorrow at twelve,' I said. Part of my elaborate security arrangement was that I assumed Gaston, being a good Tutsi and very scared of the military – they'd shot his brother for a reason he wouldn't divulge – was letting the army, the cops or one of the Tutsi militias know where I was staying every night. It improved my chances a bit if he didn't know where I was. James pulled up in his Mitsubishi Pajero. Then we were off, driving fast through the market, across Boulevard 28 November, and up the hill. We pulled into the gate of a UNHCR house where Mise had given his Christmas party, and parked. The dogs barked. The lights of the city were below us, behind us the dark, silent hills, and in the distance a glimmer on the lake.

'So,' said Paul and James. 'We've got a bottle of chardonnay, a bottle of champagne, some red, and vodka. Where shall we start?'

The following morning was cold and hungover. I woke in a spare bedroom at Paul's house, and went through to the kitchen, looking for coffee. On the sitting-room table were the empty champagne bottle, another wine bottle, and half an inch left in a bottle of Stolichnya. For some reason that had made perfect sense the night before, Paul had taken the cork and the neck off the champagne bottle with a carving knife. James, I remembered, had said that in the cavalry all champagne was uncorked with a sabre. Stacey emerged shortly afterwards, groaning, saying that she had tennis that morning.

We drove back down the hill towards her house. I remembered that I had a Land Cruiser and driver waiting at the Novotel to take me to Bururi. It was eight thirty, and a grey mist hung over the lake. We made a quick stop at the house and swept out of the gate, only to get stuck in the mud right outside. I was just getting worried – Bururi was three hours each way – when help appeared. It was Stacey's neighbour, a UN security officer at the wheel of his Land Cruiser.

'Are you familiar with your winch?' was his first question as he got out of his vehicle.

Few people in Central Africa could have been more suited to the task of pulling a vehicle out of a quagmire than this man.

And few people could have been less familiar with the workings of an electric winch on a Pajero than Stacey White. For all her intellectual acuity, she was not a mechanic. I don't think winches had been on the syllabus at school in the San Fernando valley. However, they clearly had been on the syllabus at the US Army Special Forces training centre, at Fort Bragg, South Beverleyina, where Jean-Phillippe claimed to have completed part of his military life. He was the quintessential Great Lakes Man, a genre I had privately identified.

Great Lakes Man was everywhere in central and east Africa in 1995 and 1996. You would find him attached in a civilian capacity to UNAMIR in Kigali, as head of Premises Security, exerting an authority and vigilance far exceeding his post. He would wear his plastic identity pass at all times, introduce ranks among his civilian staff and make frequent requests to be armed. You would find him lying underneath a Beechcraft at Entebbe airport in Uganda talking knowledgeably about the brake-fluid options on a light aircraft, or wearing a UNHCR baseball cap in a Goma refugee camp, radioing authoritative messages to base about water-pumping requirements, and tanker manifests. The secret dream of Great Lakes Man was to be made head of security for an outfit like the International Order of

Migrations, or UNICEF. Something not too taxing or frightening, but requiring a lot of talking on the radio. Wearing a t-shirt stitched with the logo of some long-defunct UN peace-keeping operation, he was the man who talked loudly throughout the UN flight from Nairobi to Zaire about how he, and four of his former friends – strangely absent – from the US Special Forces could solve the Burundian situation in ten days with four helicopter gunships. Great Lakes Man knew the hand-signals required to clear a C-130 Hercules to take-off position on a desert airstrip. He kept a Global Positioning Satellite system in his Land Cruiser. Great Lakes Man surrounded himself with a tangible aura of privileged, more confidential knowledge than everybody else; he liked to think he knew things. The functioning of ports and the tarmac density of small runways in central Bosnia were meat and drink to him. He always said he got the best deals at hotels. Every situation in which he found himself was tinged with the vocabulary of crisis; he was a man whose home number might, in his imagination, be on a CIA file. The criteria for Great Lakes Man had become so well defined in my mind by April 1996 that I had written them down one day.

i. Given any opportunity, GLM speaks in radio-code, if possible using the phonetic alphabet. His home in Kigali, Bujumbura, Goma or Ngara is called by a name: Charlie Hotel Six, or Mike Whisky Nine. Never is it called Number Eighty-Six, second on the left past the blue gate, just past the petrol station on the way to the airport.

ii. GLM abbreviates everything, especially city names. Bujumbura is 'Buj'; Kinshasa is 'Kin'; Nairobi 'Nai'. Driving from the Rwandan border town of Gisenyi to Kigali is called 're-basing to the Kig'. Mogadishu, of course, will forever be known as 'the Mog'. This stems from those halcyon days when he was seconded to run some unit like the Tracked Vehicle Lubrication and Oiling Point (always thereafter known on t-shirts and embroidered leisure garments as TRIVLOP SOMALIA) for the Pakistani,

Italian and Canadian UN peace-keeping forces. He did the Mog big time. For a year afterwards he was 'Mogged-out'. As he used to say to the second-in-command of the unit from which he was seconded, the Mog was 'one crazy bitch'. This unit, the 189th US National Guard Special Logistics Regiment, took casualties in Somalia, and GLM toasts them each time he uncaps a beer. He won't say, of course, that these men died in the following ways: one had his throat slit by a Somali gunman after he had made the man's teenage sister pregnant when she came begging for used cooking-oil at the barracks. The second was asleep under an armoured personnel carrier when it drove over him. The third died in a chip-fat fire in Baidoa. The fourth, a young, overweight lieutenant from the little town of Bigot, Kentucky, was hung by his own men with a length of washing line in Beled-Weyne, after being found taking polaroid photographs of a twelve-year-old Somali virgin with a marine distress flare stuffed in her back passage.

iii. GLM is very likely to be HIV-positive. This is partly because once he has had more than four bottles of Primus, or Tusker, or Amstel, he can't really stop. After downing a third of a bottle of Captain Morgan mixed with Fanta, those horny little black foxes just look so becoming. GLM doesn't help matters by eschewing the use of condoms.

iv. GLM wears his own form of civilian uniform: UN multi-pocketed waistcoat, TRIVLOP SOMALIA maroon polo-shirt, jeans, designer climbing boots, and the baseball cap of whichever UN organization has taken him on this time. He finds, curiously, that his contracts seem to be getting shorter. Attached to his belt are a Leatherman in brown case, his Maglite torch, his radio handset with all call signs listed, and a small leather case for his Zippo lighter. He smokes red Marlboro.

v. GLM thinks white Kenyans are a misunderstood species. He thinks that President Moi is treated unfairly by the international press, and that the US could have won the battle of Mogadishu with the right political backing. He is convinced that any white woman sunbathing alone by a hotel swimming pool in sub-Saharan Africa wants to have sex with him.

An hour after the struggle with the winch, I was heading south-west towards the province of Bururi. We climbed out through the hills surrounding Bujumbura. Army patrols at the sides of the roads and on the hills increased. Red-bereted paratroopers stood in the dust in groups of three and four, leaning their belt-fed machine guns on piles of wood. They made small stacks of rifle-grenades on the windowsills of ruined mud-brick houses, destroyed in 1993. They tramped in lines along the verge, wrapped round and weighed down with belts of ammunition. Around each corner we turned there was another hill-top in front of us. Huge piles of red earth slithered in places down on to the road. Under the occasional bridge dark-grey water ran deep between banks grown thick with bullrushes, elephant grass and saplings. Thin muddy paths led through the fields. Then the road climbed, the air thinned, and we were in tea country.

The flat, lawn-like curves of tea estates stretched right and left. In the middle, at occasional intervals, there were small, thatch-roofed shelters where the crop was gathered. It didn't look as though it had been harvested recently. Towards the horizon there were ridges lined with pine trees, expanses of flat, windblown land and mountains of grey rock. This was Bururi, the homeland of the elite of the military, the land I had bet with myself was no place to raise animals. It was as I had imagined it. Along a stretch of dusty road we turned right, and eventually across a heavy, metal bridge that shuddered as we passed over. In the foothills to the right, hot and still in the late-morning sun, we found the seminary and the hospital of Rumeza.

'It was five o'clock in the morning,' wheezed eighty-three-year-old Michel Hamteya, an old Tutsi lying under a greasy grey blanket in one dark concrete-floored hospital ward. The air smelt of fear and blood.

'I woke up with my wife; the children ran away, shouting "Help!

Help! Help!" They were people originally from here who were attacking; they were looking for money, but I tried to defend myself. There was a woman with them.'

Despite his efforts, Michel was bayonetted by the Hutus three times in the stomach and left for dead. A man two beds away from his, Antoine Baramhitia, took up the story.

'They came back ten days ago. They were young, numerous and barefoot, and only six out of them had weapons: the rest had machetes and knives. They said they were looking for the military.'

Michel and Antoine both came from the sectors of Musenyi and Songa, six kilometres from Bururi, where there was a large army detachment. Their hill and village of thirty-five houses had already been attacked twice by 19 March, many of their cattle had been stolen, and there was an unknown number of wounded. The Hutu rebels were described by the men as a mixture of local men, young stragglers speaking Kinyarwanda in old military uniforms who were ex-FAR from Rwanda, and Hutu civilians they did not know. The army surrounded a number of hills with armoured cars, and took up positions on the tracks running through the forests. Most of them would withdraw to the safety of Bururi at night. In the hills, Michel and Antoine could hear the Hutu militiamen singing every night. Then on the night of 21 and 22 March, they attacked. They slid through the military lines, split into several groups, and attacked three hills at Songa and Musenyi. The killing went on all night.

In the large, airy bungalows at Bururi hospital, the beds and corridors were all full of the survivors. Pierre Nahibandi had survived the attack. A Hutu, he had lain on the ground in the mud and pretended to be dead as the killers went from hut to hut, stabbing the children and mutilating many of them with machetes. Hands and legs were cut off and placed in piles. The young girls and the women were held down. They were raped first by the Hutu attackers, and then with sharpened branches and bayonets. Then they were hacked to death. All of them. The army could hear everything going on but did not intervene. The people on the hill were half Hutu. Some were pushed into one of two communal latrines to drown. The Hutu attackers then started a huge fire in the centre of the village out of straw and thatch, and threw the remaining wounded onto it along with the corpses. The military arrived at nine the following morning. The death-toll from that night on the three hills of Musenyi alone was 643 people.

But Pierre Nahibadi had an even worse story to tell. The Tutsi children from Rumeza school and seminary were sent out to carry out a revenge mission against Hutus. The teenagers, aged from fourteen to twenty, tracked down those Hutus who had survived the attacks at Songa and Musenyi, and attacked them afresh. They said that they must have collaborated in the attack if they had survived. Seven of Nahibandi's children were killed. The attack by the schoolchildren was followed up by the reprisals of the military. It isn't known how many they killed, but an investigator from the American group Human Rights Watch stood on the hill with the army some days later, as it started to pour with rain. Whoever, she said, had dug the mass graves should not have done it on a steep slope. As the rain took away the first lumps of topsoil, the outstretched hands, the muddied dead faces began to appear. She didn't know who had killed these people.

We turned off left towards Musenyi, and climbed along a track, turning, after a kilometre, down another one that led across a small stream. Around a hill in front of me were the hills of Songa and Musenyi. We drove on. The air smelt, once again, of death. I walked up towards the sodden, still smoking collection of thatched mud huts at the top. There was nobody around, nothing to be seen, except here and there in the ground the great red-dirt scars of mass graves. We drove back towards Bujumbura over the clanking iron bridge, driving fast. The road-blocks surrounding the capital closed at five thirty. I had only driven to Bururi to visit the hospital and carry out a general investigation into the process of the fighting. A look through the hospital admissions book told me the communes of origin of those with machete and gunshot wounds, so I knew now where some of the killings had taken place. The ratio of dead to wounded was over twenty-to-one, and the incidents at Songa and Musenyi were just two in a spate of fighting that, for seven days, had been sweeping across Bururi. The figure I had verified – 643 – could be one fifth of the week's total, or it could be more. It certainly was not less. How many hundreds or thousands who would never be counted were lying out there in pit-latrines, in mass graves, or just rotting in the forests?

What would stop this mad level of slaughter in Burundi? The answer was the old cliché about a strong, central government with balanced ethnic representation. Every wrong perpetrated over the last thirty-five years needed to be righted. Hutus needed to be re-empowered under a strong democratic leadership, like that during the four months leading up to President Melchior Ndadaye's assassination in 1993, which had been universally popular. Extremist militias had to be disarmed, disbanded and criminalized, the army disbanded completely, and only then reinstated as an absolutely ethnically balanced entity. The same with the police and the gendarmerie. The system of justice needed to be overhauled, and massive investment made in primary health care and education. The rural economic mainstays of coffee, tea, agriculture and livestock-rearing had to be brought back into production, the ethnic divide between cattle-owning Tutsis and land-tilling Hutu abolished. The three different ports that functioned on Lake Tanganyika needed to be overhauled. This dream state of affairs, which would never occur in Burundi until somebody invented magic, would have to be overseen by a minimum of 25,000 competent, patient, well-trained, diplomatic, low-key western troops, funded by the Organization of African Unity (OAU) from African government budgets. If any of the member states refused to donate the requisite funds, every single unit of international aid would be removed from that country. These troops would have to be stationed in every village, near every hill, on every bridge and outside – and inside – every government building in the capital.

The whole country would be put to work, five days a week, rebuilding the communal structures, the roads, the ditches and rescuing the farm land. The community projects and the rebuilding of educational and health structures would be carried out by no more than a dozen internationally recognized groups – MSF, the ICRC, Oxfam. No international organizations with any religious links would be allowed in the country. There would be no foreign loans to the country. The international troops would remain until it was self-sustaining, the government governing, and the army keeping the peace. There was a possibility that this might happen spontaneously, but the people of Burundi – and Rwanda – were so conditioned to do as they were told that this was unlikely.

Does this project seem draconian, I asked myself. We sat in the Nissan Patrol, swinging through the late afternoon back to Bujumbura and an aid party. It was no more than a hybrid of all the plans being put forward by the international community. Everything seemed to be under consideration at once: UN guards for international aid convoys; direct military intervention; an intervention force stationed in Zaire; an intervention force comprised of African states; a United Nations protectorate policed by troops with orders to quash any ethnic violence. And what about the suggestion to recruit freelance UN peace-keepers and station them in Burundi?

Failing this, it did appear that everybody would be forced to revert to a solution for Rwanda and Burundi suggested by Sam Kiley, the *Times* corespondent for Africa: 'Build a very high wall around both countries, and fill them with concrete.'

I don't know which transgression it was that earned me my fourth death threat: arguing with the prime minister on Burundian television or misreporting the results of the Burundi–Algeria football final. I came back from Bururi depressed by the senseless slaughter that had taken place in the south. A local reporter who had attended the football game, the final of an African international, gave me the results. I telephoned them through to Reuters, leaving the BBC to pick them up from there. It was just as the Algerian team had been leaving the airport that they were surprised to hear that they had won a match in which they had conceded the only goal ten minutes before the end. The Algerians had been reluctant to come to Burundi in the first place. It was, they said, a murderous country full of extremists, where they could easily get killed. The Burundians for their part had been unwilling to stage the game in Algeria. That too, was a murderous country full of extremists, where they could easily get killed. But the final meeting between both sides had been peaceful.

Eighty minutes of play had left no score, until the Burundian winger put one in at the eleventh hour. There had been shirt-swapping and back-slapping, and the Burundian fans were jubilant. For a moment ethnic difference could be forgotten as a rare moment of national unity occurred. They'd beaten the silver-footed visitors from the north, the turf-gods of the Sahara. The reporting in Kirundi on the local radio had been ecstatic. Radios were clutched to ears in the bar of the Novotel as the BBC Kirundi service came on and listeners awaited a repeat of the cherished result from the ultimate world authority on news. There had been a terrible silence as the score was announced. Mystification turned to anger, anger to rage. The international community, once again, had let Burundi down. And the one person in Burundi connected with the BBC was Jennings of Reuters. Lieutenant-Colonel Longin Minani was informed immediately.

On Monday I'd appeared on local television with the prime minister, at a press conference he gave after his meeting with Attwood and Bonino. He'd had his knuckles severely rapped and been told he couldn't have any more pocket money to divert from aid to buy weapons. He was feeling embattled and his back was against the wall when he emerged from his office to meet the press. I got the second question in, asking him if he would ever negotiate with the CNDD, implying that it was his only recourse. It transpired that the night before, Hutu militias had raided his home town of Ryansoro in the southern extremity of Gitega province, and the rebels had killed seventy-four people and burned lots of houses.

A true Tutsi, the prime minister added the worst news with a shake of his head.

'They even killed the cows.'

By Tuesday evening Brian Attwood and Emma Bonino had gone: their message had been harsh. They could not continue to support the economy of the country while there was an internal conflict. The money they were giving to Burundi was being used to prop up the economy; an elite was profiting. This was their last chance.

'The international community's initiative is a life-preserver being thrown to the people of Burundi,' said Brian Attwood. 'If they don't grab it this time they might end up like Rwanda, and the inter-national community might not be so interested.'

Burundi was left with a small pledge of funds, for emergency food assistance, and for a six-month bail-out for the UNHCR. There was a cocktail party at the Novotel in the evening, to which every expatriate of note was invited. By the time speeches were finished, thank-you handshakes completed, there was little left for drinking before the curfew expired. I found myself in the hotel garden watching fifty aid officials try to get through a groaning table of alcohol in forty-five minutes.

'Quadruples all round, I think,' said a white-suited James Shepherd-Barron.

The following morning I was on the road south again. The town of Makamba had been attacked. I had to drive almost to the Tanzanian border to reach the site, and when I did, it was terribly familiar. The burnt-out ambulances at the hospital; the local population of Tutsis clustered around the town hall. A furious and aggressive population baying for blood almost turned on our vehicle as we drove to the hospital. The patients had been turfed out at dawn when the rebels arrived. A man with both legs in plaster hobbled on crutches towards the safety of the hills. The local anaesthetist working for MSF had been executed in front of his family. On the tiled floor of the hospital mortuary I counted the tangled body parts of six children and seven adults, their eyes frozen in the terror of death. A baby's corpse, eviscerated with a machete, lay in the khaki knot of its intestines. We had little time. I saw the blood-stained hospital wards, the looted pharmacy where the desperate rebels had stolen every box of paracetamol for use as anaesthetic, and noted down the reactions of the local army commander. His men were still counting the carbonized remains of a family burnt to death in a house near the main square. At two o'clock the rain swept in from the mountains overlooking the town and we took a different road back, fearful that the rebels who had attacked would ambush us on our return. As always in Burundi, there was a doubt as to who had killed who, and why. The expatriate team from MSF had pulled out the day before the attack; it turned out that under cover of the Hutu raid, the local Tutsi militias had taken their chance for revenge. The MSF anaesthetist, a local man who preached unity and dialogue, had been shot for operating on Hutus in the hospital.

It took us four hours to get back to Bujumbura this time. On the way we listened to Marc Faguy from the UN being interviewed on the radio about violence and dialogue. Thirteen more unarmed monitors from the Organisation for African Unity were to be sent to Burundi. I could only imagine that thirteen more rooms at the Hotel Source du Nile were being booked, another thirteen international lines cleared at the switchboard. The teenage hookers would be even busier. Faguy finished on a note of desperation: for the violence to stop there would have to be some attempt at dialogue. He added, however, that it was very difficult to imagine both sides engaging in proper debate while at the same time killing each other. The country was stuck. We stopped briefly outside the town of Rutana, where an army lorry had taken a turn too fast in the rain. The soldiers who had been standing up in the back had been thrown onto the tarmac as the lorry turned on its side. A dead soldier with half his face gone was lying on the verge. The wounded were stumbling across the road in the rain. We took two men to hospital and left them as it started to grow dark. We made the capital just in time to slip through the last road-blocks before they closed.

The following day, with little ceremony, half of the politicians in the country seemed to have left for Tanzania. Marc Faguy was nowhere to be found. Charles Mukasi was not in his office; the US Embassy seemed empty. Had there been a coup that nobody had noticed? This was a repetitive fear of mine. Given that everybody in the country expected there to be another army takeover at any moment, I often wondered how it would come when it did. Perhaps it happened that morning? I rang the new Ministry of Defence spokesman, Lieutenant-Colonel Isaie Nibizi, a moderate officer who had tried to play a calming hand in the 1993 coup. What was going on?

'Oh, they've all gone to the peace talks in Mwanza.'

In the rush of Bururi and the weekend I had completely forgotten about this. Julius Nyerere, the former President of Tanzania, had managed to persuade both the UPRONA and FRODEBU parties to gather round a conference table in the Tanzanian town of Mwanza to discuss the possibility of peace. It gave some idea of how total was the military's control over the country that very little had been said about these peace talks. I caught Charles Mukasi on his mobile phone, at the airport.

'If Leonard Nyangoma is there I'll be coming straight back. There's going to be a delegation from UPRONA, which is why I'm going. But any initiative that doesn't lead to the destruction or disintegration of the CNDD is for me useless. Nyerere said that it would be a matter for FRODEBU and UPRONA only.'

I stood in the garden of the Novotel, hastily ringing everybody I could think of, so that I could put a report together. Both Colonels Bikomagu and Simbanduku from the gendarmerie and the army respectively said they had nothing to do with it, the Ministry of Defence said they were 'undecided', while Marc Faguy at the UN was crowing about it as though it had been his idea. He hoped, he said, that this was the beginning of dialogue. But everything militated against the idea of peace. The centre of the country was disintegrating. Gitega province was in a situation of total war. The number of IDPs was climbing, the refugees in the north of the country showed no signs of wanting to go home. Politically, the deadlock was as total as ever, despite the initiatives of Julius Nyerere, which I suspected were cosmetic. Everybody expected an army coup d'état at any moment.

I was moving house or hotel every two weeks now. It seemed to have become accepted wisdom among expatriates that I was a serious security risk, and that sharing a house with me was not a good idea. I'd moved out of Stacey's UN house because of the security problem. I suspected that her boss, Mr Khan from the UN, had had a word. Following the incidents with the refugee camps, Hitoshi Mise was still trying to avoid me, while Colonel Minani bristled and cut me dead whenever he saw me. Security was on everybody's mind, and as I saw it, the expatriate community had split into two, very predictable categories in the face of the worsening war.

On one side were those who considered security to be paramount, who would suspend their operations outside the capital and sit it out at the Novotel, doing anything they could to avoid confrontation and danger from the army or the militias of both sides. These organizations included all of the United Nations agencies, except UNHCR, and forty out of the forty-nine aid agencies working in the capital, as well as most of the embassies. People in this category either had nothing to report of interest, as they rarely ventured out of their hotels or compounds, or were reluctant to talk to me publicly as they thought doing so constituted a security risk.

On the other side were the handful of organizations that insisted on continuing to work outside the capital, or who were willing to exchange information with me. Nobody wanted to be quoted though. By late April, almost none of my reports on matters relating to security or the war carried anybody's names but my own. Everybody was a 'humanitarian source', a 'western diplomatic observer', or an 'aid worker'. Everybody was frightened. The python of paranoia was tightening its coils around the country.

My main sources of information were Christophe Boutonnier and his UN security reports, Patrick Berner at the ICRC, and MSF. Two or three times a day Gaston and I would speed by their respective offices, trading information about the latest attacks, IDPs, and the inside track on political developments in the crisis. John Myers from Oxfam had brought his team in from the field, but continued to supply me with what information he could. Jean-Luc at WFP kept his office door open, while the staff from CARE were always welcoming. Over in the UN building, Marc Faguy was almost hostile, and seemed to become more terrified and cautious by the day. His Egyptian deputy, Abdul Hani Aziz, was by contrast calmly reassuring. As an African, and a military intelligence colonel to boot, he understood what was going on, and could make sense of the tortured political and military machinations around him. On the floor below his office were the rooms occupied by Studio Ijambo, an independent radio station run by an American NGO, Search for Common Ground. They employed both Hutu and Tutsi journalists, and were probably the only non-biased media organization in the whole country. I spent more and more time in their offices, mostly with Alexei Sindahije, a half-Tutsi, half-Hutu journalist who was always willing to take their white Land Rover and drive out into the countryside to investigate the war.

I filed my copy to Nairobi and sat down by the swimming pool for a coffee. With the peace talks progressing in Tanzania, the army would probably launch some new offensive against the rebels with a huge body-count. I'd be duty-bound to report it, the army would get pissed off, I'd get another death threat. At some point I would also have to start reporting on the army's drug and gold smuggling operations in Cibitoke, and the incoming flights supplying weapons to the beleagured military. The peace process, however fruitless, was only going to make the army feel more insecure as it chipped away at their power-base. Sooner or later, they'd go for another coup. Anybody who got in the way of their gold, arms and drugs deals would be pushed out of the way in the manner they best understood: through violence. The hardline military knew very well that there would come a point when the Americans and the UN would not publicly be able to stand by and watch any more killing take place. The army also knew the only way it would hold onto power was through more violence. As I was the one person who showed the ability to investigate and report on many of its killings, I had become a major impediment to the army's policy of keeping its war as covert as possible. The problem was compounded by the fact that I worked for Reuters and the BBC, the two most influential English-language news organizations in the world. It didn't take too much intelligence to see that I had a limited shelf-life in Burundi.

I believed, however, that it was best to behave with hindsight in mind, to see yourself as others later might. 'Jennings had a good war,' I saw them saying. 'It was his bitter rearguard action that was later to make people ask: where exactly *was* Burundi?' I thought that if I could make it to six months in-country, then that would be respectable. It would be two weeks longer than my predecessor had lasted. I'd had my fourth death threat the day before. I worked out that it must have taken Minani a bit of time to find somebody to pass on the message to me. I doubted it had much to do with the football and believed it to be a deliberate piece of occasional harassment designed to make me paranoid. As a technique it worked well. This latest threat seemed to come with a bit more exasperation, a bit more desperation behind it. I'd been standing in the UNHCR office when my phone rang. The caller found the courage to say who he was and where he was calling from: 'Jennings. This is the head of security at the prime minister's office. We can find no other explanation for your behaviour than to say that you must be the son of Leonard Nyangoma. And like him, we will crush you.'

The Colonel then started shouting uncontrollably. I just turned my phone off.

I decided to have the rest of the afternoon off, and went shopping. I had a date that evening with Anne-Sophie, freshly returned from up-country.

I spent the equivalent of sixty dollars on salad, cold meat, some fish, and three bottles of South African chardonnay. Anne-Sophie, bathed and brushed, turned up at the house at seven-thirty. I wasn't sure what my chances were. My friends Greg and Jane from the BBC had met her, and Greg told me with some authority that she was gay.

'Christian, she kept telling us about her women's football team, and her all-girl rock-climbing club. She definitely bats for the other side.'

By the end of bottle of chardonnay number two, I was beginning to think he was right. We had sat outside on the terrace and eaten. The night was warm and there were lots of stars. By the time she told me how she and a girlfriend had been thrown out of the football team, I thought that once again I was destined to fall asleep silent, unreflecting and alone. Her chum had been the goalkeeper for another all-girl team, and had been asked to leave after she kept letting in Anne-Sophie's goals. But it was now after nine o'clock, and Anne-Sophie had no choice but to spend the night. Dinner had hit the table at precisely nine-o-two. In response to Christophe's nightly UN radio-check, Anne-Sophie had said over her handset that all was fine, that she was not at her team's base, but that she was contactable in emergency at the Reuters mobile phone number. The moment radio-check was over, the whole team from Médecins du Monde chorused 'Good night, Christian, and good luck!' over their radio handset. That ruled out Nicolette if things didn't develop tonight, I thought.

After three bottles of wine and eleven cigarettes, I thought it was probably time for coffee. I was percolating the coffee when I turned to find Anne-Sophie standing behind me. I turned, she smiled, and in a second we were kissing. What a surprise, I thought. We left the coffee, grabbed each other, and minutes later our heads hit the pillow of my double mattress. We almost ripped each others' clothes off. I tried to light a candle but it seemed she preferred the room in darkness. Perhaps she had a terrible scar, I thought, giggling to myself as we kissed each other some more. Perhaps a stab-wound on the breast, the result of an armed lesbian showdown in a Parisian alley. Things, however, progressed as womens' magazines say they should, and in due course the star-fished Anne-Sophie stretched her arms over her head and whispered in French: 'Where are the condoms?'

Ha! I thought. Right here within arm's reach. My side of the double mattress was next to the cupboard, and I'd left the door ajar, the pack of three unwrapped, just where I could put my hand on them.

'Come on, Christian,' she whispered.

I sat bolt upright, very fast, reaching for the cupboard. Suddenly, with a flash of yellow light, the noise of a cabbage being hit with a baseball bat and a skull-jarring wallop, my face exploded. I bounced backwards onto the mattress, swearing.

'Shit! Shit! Shit!'

I could feel blood pouring down over my mouth. I had inadvertently sat up and head-butted the edge of the cupboard door, in a line from my forehead, down the centre of my nose, across my mouth and onto my chin.

'What's happened?' said Anne-Sophie through the darkness. 'What's wrong?'

The bathroom mirror showed a split lip, a bashed nose that was not, fortunately, broken, and two heavily bleeding nostrils. Pink loo paper shoved up both seemed to do the trick. I returned to the candle-lit bed and an Anne-Sophie still keen.

'Do you mind,' I said in polite French, through my bloodied boxer's face, 'if we leave it till morning?'

I woke two hours later to find her smoking by candlelight. Tears were on her face. My mouth was thick with clotted blood and the taste of wine and cigarettes. Both nostrils were blocked.

'I'm alright,' I said, rubbing her tanned, freckled back. 'I'll be fine by morning.'

'It's not that,' she sobbed, turning towards me, silhouetted in the candlelight. 'it's just that . . . I'm gay.'

We could have left it at that, gone to sleep, had coffee in the morning. But Anne-Sophie wanted to talk it through. The lemon tree outside was reflecting the dawn sun before we slept.

We went for brunch at the Novotel, and then for a walk on the small stretch of beach that was considered safe for expatriates. It lay north of Bujumbura, where the Rusizi river flowed into Lake Tanganyika. The water was clear and warm, and lapped onto the pebbles. We held hands as we walked along the shore, chatting away, and my hope was rekindling. We could be back at home in bed in twenty minutes if she changed her mind, which she seemed on the verge of doing. Underfoot were dried logs, bits of plastic, the occasional flip-flop washed down the crocodile-dense Rusizi from a refugee who had not made it to Zaire. The wind came in across the clear water; things felt open with Anne-Sophie. Then there was a light crunching underfoot, a slither of gravel. We looked down at where her Nike trainer had touched down.

'*Eh, putain,*' she swore.

Under the sole of her foot was the dried, windblown whiteness of a child's skull.

'Fuck this bloody country,' she shouted into the wind, waving her fist at the green hills behind us.

Chapter 7

Once Upon a Time in Mutoyi

Lieutenant-Colonel François Fyiritano was a good soldier. He was in charge of a battalion of commandos who, in late April, found themselves on operations south of Gitega. Fyiritano had no time for killing civilians or carrying out atrocities: he was one of the Burundian army's more compassionate, balanced soldiers. So when elements of his unit went into the marketplace of the small village of Bukirasazi and threatened to kill any Hutus they found, he put his foot down. There were to be no extra-judicial killings. The civilian population was to be left alone. Only armed Hutu militiamen were to be considered targets. The colonel was standing just outside the marketplace when the first bullet hit him. The second killed him. Hutu eyewitnesses – eleven of them – said he was shot by his own men. His own men said he was hit by a sniper operating from across the valley. Minutes after his death his men opened fire on the narrow, wooden stalls of the marketplace. Initial reports found twenty-two dead, although the total was, as always, believed to be much higher.

By chance, I was in Gitega hospital that day. It was a grim sight. The single-storey bungalow was divided into two wards, and every bed was full. Some had two or three patients in them. Most were survivors of a Huto attack that had taken place ten days before at Makebuko, south of Gitega. Fifty-two people had been hit on two hills. The Hutus had hit the Tutsi civilians first and then the military. The hospital had fifty-five beds, no antibiotics, very few bandages and disinfectants, and only one doctor, Doctor Caniseus Mbonyin-gingo.

'This man's sternum is smashed by a bullet. Happened a week ago

227

last Friday. When he was found three days later, his whole chest cavity seemed to be full of pus. He says four people were killed in his house and the military didn't arrive until the day after.'

We continued along the rows of beds, Dr Caniseus reading aloud from the notes at the bottom of each bed.

'Woman; amputated leg. Grenade killed five in her house. Military arrived the day after.'

We stopped at a bed where a nurse was tweezering patches of pus-soaked gauze off the side of a patient's skull.

'Woman, machete, head.'

Next to her in the same bed was a woman with a swollen arm. The skin was bursting with yellow pus.

'Gangrene. No surgery. It'll be amputated. Now, let's see . . .'

We stopped at the bed of a child with a bandaged face.

'Ah, yes. He's six. The rebels caught him as he was trying to run away. Shot him at point-blank range. Bullet went in through one side of his mouth and out through the other.'

We went outside and the doctor made sure that he was not within the hearing of any soldiers.

'You see, we don't have enough surgeons or doctors here. Quite often I catch the Tutsi nurses changing dressings without cleaning the wounds, letting the gangrene set in. And this morning we had this massacre in Bukirasazi. They killed their colonel, Fyiritano, or so the soldier outside told me. But be careful here. Everybody knows who you are and what you're doing, and the military are very nervous.' I thanked him.

A soldier was sitting on a wall in front of the hospital. I gave him a cigarette.

'We were standing together, me and the colonel. The soldiers came out of the market, saying they'd found Hutu rebels. The colonel asked where the weapons were. The soldiers said that they were hidden, but they knew the Hutus were all "assailants". The colonel said that they must be left alone.'

'And then?'

'And then the men put the Hutu peasants into a line. The colonel walked forward and said that no civilians were to be killed. The men armed their weapons . . .' the soldier made a swishing noise to indicate a Kalashnikov being cocked '. . . and the colonel walked forward. Then two shots were fired from behind and we were both hit.'

'A sniper?'

The soldier shook his head.

'The shots were fired from just behind us. It was a sergeant who did it.'

I left him, and walked over to another group of men leaning against a vehicle.

'Colonel Fyiritano? Well, it was like this. He was driving along by himself, and from the other side of the valley, a sniper hit him. The rebels have these new Russian weapons, paid for by President Mobutu . . .'

I went back into the hospital. In the main office three Tutsi girls were discussing how to use the two new computers which had arrived. I asked how many patients there were in the hospital.

'Patients?' said one. 'Don't ask me.'

Back on the ward the nurses had finished their rounds. A middle-aged Hutu man was brought in and laid on a blue plastic sheet. His left leg was snapped almost in half at the knee. The jagged bone stuck out through the flesh. Every muscle on his torso was rigid with pain as they set him down. A soldier walked in, and stood next to me looking down at the man. He smiled. Then he lifted up his left leg, and stamped down on the man's smashed knee joint with his heavy boot.

'*Ca va?*' he asked with a grin, as the wounded man doubled up with an agonised yell.

By mid April 1996, Gitega province was in a state of total war. The five United Nations human rights monitors recently arrived in the country estimated that 2,500 people were killed in Gitega in ten days. The ICRC suspended their operations there on the nineteenth after a hand-grenade exploded outside their house.

'Human rights are not particularly respected in this country,' Lieutenant-Colonel Nibizi told me in the capital the following day.

'If they were we wouldn't have these deaths every day,' he said, displaying an astonishing capacity for stating the obvious.

Nibizi sat in his office at the Ministry of Defence, and showed me, province by province, the military reports that came in each day.

'Here, you see,' he said, picking up a daily report from Cibitoke. 'We have yesterday in Cibitoke. Three people killed, including one soldier. Two civilians wounded. Those are the figures that I give out to the press when asked. If the human rights monitors say that two thousand, five hundred people have been killed in Gitega in ten days, I have no option but to read the military reports. Their figures will be different, obviously.'

He picked up the military lists for Gitega. Only small numbers of civilians were reported dead, caught in 'crossfires'. Nearly fifty rebels were reported dead in the marketplace at Bukirasazi. Colonel Fyiritano had been buried with full military honours, killed, as Nibizi said, 'on the field of battle'. The files of 400 soldiers charged with human rights violations and excesses against the civilian population were available for inspection by the human rights monitors. That, he said, was all.

I walked past Lieutenant-Colonel Minani's office on my way back to the car. I remembered my first visit five months before. Even the Burundian military had felt that Minani was not really serving their best interests, so he had been put out to grass. I'd seen him in a restaurant the week before, showing off in front of a crowd of civilians.

'We'll line them all up like this,' he said, putting five Amstel bottles in a line on the bar.

'Then we'll go along the line and shoot them unless they talk. Finished. No questions. That's how we'll win this war.'

Gaston was waiting outside. We pulled up the hill towards the university, where all afternoon I sat and listened to President Ntibantunganya speak to an assembled population of students, army officers and politicians. The options he outlined formed almost perfect sound-bites.

'The country is thirsty for peace . . . innocent people are

dying . . . the UN must accelerate all possible options . . . we're in a state of war . . . is there still time for another effort?'

Two seats away from me, a colonel snored quietly in the afternoon dark of the auditorium.

'The forces of order will punish all those who step out of line . . . we need help from the international community . . . the army must be reinforced . . . the actions of the CNDD, FROLINA and PALIPEHUTU must be condemned.'

'Gentlemen,' he concluded. 'The hour is grave.'

His bodyguards bundled him into his car, their pistols drawn. It was to be the last time I saw him.

The following afternoon I sat out at the airport and listened to the response of the international community. Yet another UN special envoy, this time a man called Marrack Golding, had arrived. I stood in the VIP lounge listening to his proposed solutions.

'There is no military solution, only political . . . the secretary-general and the Security Council are worried . . . there could be an explosion . . . the possibility exists of a humanitarian disaster . . . there is a war going on . . . it is possible to save the situation . . . at the moment the international community is not ready.'

It was nothing but talk. I could see very clearly how the Rwandan genocide had been allowed to happen.

'The secretary-general shares the suffering of the Burundian people.'

Golding was excelling himself.

I waited for him to finish and walked off. It would hardly make a line for Reuters. Such was the frequency of my reports of killing, that Reuters had installed a limit. Fifty people or more had to die before it constituted a story, they said. Unless there was a politician or a senior military figure involved, in which case an exception was made. It was getting dreary and dispiriting, I thought. I walked upstairs to the airport terrace-bar and bought a hot cheese-and-ham sandwich. I sat down on a plastic beach-chair in the shade and started to compile my list of security incidents for the last fortnight, enjoying the warm sun on my face. It was nearly the end of April. Perhaps it was time to leave while the going was good, while I was ahead. I felt that if ever there was a mission for a journalist in Burundi, it was to alert the policy makers in Washington and Europe to the situation, and let them take some action. Everybody knew what was going on here. Everybody knew that the army and the Hutu rebels were equally to blame. Everybody had sat back and watched the Rwandan genocide happen. What would they do about Burundi? I ordered an Amstel, and listed the options in my notebook.

i. Coup d'état by the army. Most likely possibility. Get rid of Sylvestre, put in hardline army colonel. Evacuate majority of expatriates. Close airport, don't allow any journalists or human rights monitors into the country. [Get rid of Jennings immediately, I thought.] Carry out massive programme of Hutu exterminations in the hills. Chase Hutu politicians out of power. Take break. Order much Primus.

ii. Depose Sylvestre. Put in moderate army officer. Reduce level of killing in country. Keep hold on power. Forcibly repatriate Rwandan refugees. Take break. Order much Primus.

iii. Watch as country taken over by military intervention overseen by UN Security Council mandate.

The only pointers I had as to what might happen had come from an accidental meeting I'd had the week before. I'd gone to see Charles Mukasi unannounced, and had walked in on him, former President Pierre Buyoya, Lieutenant-Colonel Jean-Bosco Daradangwe and a fourth person I did not know. I was in the doorway for approximately fifteen seconds. (Daradangwe was the Colonel who in 1993 had been part of the triumvirate of army officers who had briefly taken power after the coup.) I heard only a snatch of conversation, which came from Daradangwe.

'We must let the Americans know about it.'

The four of them saw me, so I apologized, and walked out. What were they plotting? It was like a scene out of a Tintin book. I felt that whatever was going to happen was underway already. 'Let the Americans know' about what? Colonel Daradangwe had used a French verb, *se rendre compte*.

It appeared that the pace was going to quicken in the coming weeks, and I did not want to be an unwitting victim of any upsurge in violence. What should I do? I had nothing to leave behind in Burundi. There were friends I could see again, elsewhere. I felt that I had done as much as I could for Reuters, given the security constraints. It would take me two hours to pack my bags. I could be back at the airport for the next Kenya airways flight to Nairobi before anybody knew I was gone. Another correspondent could be flown in, somebody with an unblemished record, somebody whom the army didn't know.

That afternoon I telephoned Reuters in Nairobi and spoke to Nicholas Kotch, the bureau chief. He solved my dilemma, temporarily, by announcing that he was going to come to Burundi and assess the situation for himself. I should stay put in the interim, and leave for Nairobi only if I judged the situation untenable. My bags, as it were, should be packed. So in the late heat of that afternoon, I sat down on the sofa at the house I was then living in, and made out what I thought would be one of my final reports. It was, not surprisingly, an update on the fighting.

I laid out my rough notes in front of me, gave them a title and picked up a pink highlighter. Death by machete, bullet, rape, drowning, knives, spears, mortars, clubs, stonings, and burning alive. It went on and on. In one massacre Hutus had been found hacked to death with kitchen cutlery. I stood up, stretched, and went to fetch an orange Fanta from the fridge. How many had died? What percentage of the total number of incidents had I witnessed, counted, or been informed of? Twenty-five? More? Less? Did it matter? Aziz Hani reckoned that between himself, Christophe and me we were managing up to 35 per cent of incidents. This extrapolated into a figure of approximately 4,320 people killed in the month of April. Even if I said that the UN estimate of the casualties in Gitega was erroneous (there was nothing to suggest it was) then I was left with 1,820 dead. If this was 35 per cent of the total, I was left with a total figure that read thus:

$1,820 \times 2.86 = 5,199$.

If UN Human Rights figure added then 2,500 plus 5,199 = 7,699 dead.

This was close to the figure of 7,500 people per month that Aziz and Christophe reckoned were dying.

Reading this list, I felt more than ever that Burundi was at a turning point. What, though, would push the UN, the United States, whoever, over the edge and make them act?

The army provided the answers. On or around the night of 27 April, a small group of Hutu rebels attacked a large group of displaced Tutsi peasants on the hills at Buhoro. This small village lies north of Gitega, on the main track to Ngozi. The Hutus were trying to 'tax' the Tutsis, most of whom were fleeing the fighting in Karuzi province. The Hutus killed twenty of them. By six-thirty on the morning of the twenty-seventh, soldiers started arriving from Bugendana and Ghihogazi. The Hutus had vanished. The soldiers took their revenge on the locally displaced Hutus, many of whom had moved from hill to hill to avoid the influx of Tutsis. The killing started at eight o'clock that Friday morning.

In the valley below the hills of Buhoro lay the mission station of Mutoyi. An order of Italian priests ran a hospital, a school, an orphanage, a pottery and a seminary. A small river ran through the valley. It was cut off from the surrounding area, almost lost in time. Father Luciano Farina first knew something was wrong when hundreds of Hutu peasants started pouring into the open area in front of his hospital. The army, they said, were killing in the hills. By the time night fell, the army had moved their operations over to the other side of the river, behind the mission station. Father Farina waited until the light began to fail before he took a tractor and trailer and drove up towards Buhoro. The Hutus were burying their dead. Forty-seven shelters had been burnt, one hundred and thirty-three women had been killed, along with eight-three children and twelve men. Another fifteen people had been killed in the valley. Father Luciano counted the dead and spoke to the local people as they dug. Two hundred and forty-nine people had been killed by the military. Thirty-five wounded were in the mission hospital. Father Luciano drove to Gitega the following day, and passed a written message to an expatriate from UNICEF. They in turn brought word to the UNICEF office in Bujumbura. By Tuesday I was driving towards

Mutoyi, along with Ferdinand Ferella from Voice of America, and Joseph from Studio Ijambo.

We drove fast. The army knew we were heading towards Buhoro. So tense was the situation, so nervous was the army, so fragile its relation with the international community, that both Ferdinand and myself felt the news of this massacre had to be the final straw. Several people whom we told about our trip reckoned the army might try and ambush us. If we were not back in the capital by dark then it was to be assumed that we were in trouble.

By lunch time we were at the seminary. Everything, the grass, the pine trees, the people and the buildings was covered in red dust. Two and a-half thousand displaced people were gathered in the valley outside the hospital. We told the priests why we had come. True Italians, they looked at each other, and asked if we had eaten. We hadn't. We were waved into the refectory.

'Pasta. Eat.'

Father Luciano gave us ten minutes once we had finished lunch. The story was told. Then we visited their orphanage in an attempt at camouflage. Half an hour later we were taking the dirt track back to Gitega and the capital.

The following morning Ferdinand and myself were having breakfast with Lieutenant-Colonel Daradangwe at the Novotel. My story had moved on Reuters the night before, as well as on the BBC. It was while we were drinking coffee with the colonel, an urbane, calmly spoken man, that Ferdinand's story ran on VOA. The three of us listened in silence. Then Daradangwe reached for his mobile phone. I hadn't heard it ring.

'It doesn't ring,' he explained. 'It just itches.'

Colonel Isaie Nibiz was briefed to receive us immediately. Within hours a commission of inquiry was set up, consisting of three army colonels: Lieutenant-Colonel Marcel Sinarinzi, the chief permanent secretary at the Ministry of Defence, Lieutenant-Colonel Nicodeme Nduhirubusa, whom I suspected of having called me the 'son of Leonard Nyangoma', and a third officer I did not know. When he heard our evidence to back up our massacre story, he realized it was time for some damage limitation. Within days, Assistant US

Secretary of State for Democracy, Human Rights and Labour, John Shattuck, was on his way from Washington with a message that many thought would be the last for the Burundian government. The American Embassy was saying that each massacre in Burundi pushed the country's agenda further up the daily schedule at the State Department. They had close links with the military. They were running a military justice training scheme with various senior officers. Some of the more intelligent and humane officers had been trained in the United States.

But before Under-Secretary Shattuck could cross the equator, the hardliners in the army struck again. In the northern half of Bubanza province, on the way to the Rwandan border, lies the small conglomeration of houses known as Kivyuka. On the first Sunday of May, it was incredibly busy. An open-air market had been set up there and at Bukinamyana, further down the road. Everything was for sale: cloth, batteries, salt, vegetables, fresh meat, tools, wood. But there was a lot of tension. Two days before, soldiers had opened fire on market goers in Bukinamyana and killed many people. So when about twenty-eight soldiers gathered around the Kivyuka market that Sunday, it didn't take long for people to panic. The soldiers first said it was illegal for the market to be open on a Sunday. Then they said that Hutu rebels were hiding among the people. Then they threw sixteen hand-grenades into the crowd and opened fire. The priests from Kivyuka, along with local witnesses and the local authorities, counted the bodies afterwards. The army coerced sixty Tutsi displaced people into burying the bodies; an estimated 320 of them. In follow-up operations the same day the army killed a minimum of another 200 people. Many were thrown into pit latrines to hide the evidence, at least 55 in Kivyuka, and an estimated 200 in Bukinamyana. I spoke to seven survivors who managed to reach the Prince Regent Hospital in Bujumbura. Their descriptions of events matched the claims of the local clergy and administration, and cross-matched with the number of graves, the number of people disappeared, and the number that the Tutsi displaced claimed to have thrown into latrines and buried. In three days in Bubanza, 920 civilians died at the hands of the army.

'There is a severe danger that Burundi is at risk of committing political suicide,' said Under-Secretary John Shattuck at the airport, the day that my Reuters report on the killings appeared. 'I repeat the warning that the United States will not support any government that comes to power by force. It will deny any assistance to, and seek to isolate, such a government.'

'The United States condemns in the strongest possible terms the violence by Hutu insurgents and Tutsi radical groups. I urge a swift publication of the reports into the incidents at Buhoro and in Bubanza, and the prosecution of those responsible. I urge that the human rights monitors be given full access to those areas.'

The United States seemed to have decided what it would do about Burundi. The following day, I had breakfast at the Novotel with two British defence attachés from the Kampala embassy. A major from the Coldstream Guards and a colonel from the Light Infantry, they affected an insouciant chumminess. In reality, one asked questions and the other took down the answers in his Filofax. What were the bridges like on the Route National Seven? How deep were the rivers? Could they be crossed by armoured vehicle? And airstrips in the south of the country? What about Bururi? Could helicopters land at Gitega and at Ngozi? What did I reckon to ambush sites on the road from Bururi to the capital? Plans were afoot for Burundi and moving fast. Nobody was taking chances.

The trio of army officers charged with investigating the killings at Buhoro got their answers in very quickly, long before the team of UN human rights monitors had had a chance to reflect on their findings.

'The military commander who led the operations on the ground at Mutoyi was not available to give testimony,' said the report. 'We were not permitted to uncover the bodies, but the local population to whom we talked said that 118 people only had been killed. The local population told us that the killings were carried out by a mix of displaced Hutus, people speaking Kinyarwanda, and some soldiers.'

I could imagine the reaction of a small group of Hutu peasants on the far-flung hills at Mutoyi before three senior army colonels and their bodyguards. They would say that spacemen had carried out the killings if it meant they could escape unharmed.

'One of the Italian priests, Roberto Monti, apologized for simple, unverified reporting, and for taking unconfirmed testimony from the local people. Our interpretation is that Hutu rebels and displaced people killed those who refused to join in with them in killing Tutsis. The matter is closed.'

Fathers Luciano Farina, Roberto Monti and one other left the country shortly afterwards. Just after they did, the United States played the last card in its diplomatic hand. US National Security Adviser Anthony Lake repeated Shattuck's message almost verbatim.

'The United States is planning for any contingency. Our central message is that the violence must stop. Those on the extremes will not benefit from political suicide because this will prevent their ability to function. We urge Burundi to reject violence. I repeat the warning that the United States will not recognize any government that comes to power by force. We will deny assistance to and isolate any such government.'

I was standing in a knot of journalists, next to one of Lake's security men. The man's arms were as thick as my legs. His fingers seemed tightened into claws, ready to grab a gun the moment any threat materialized. I wonder what he had been told in his briefing before arriving in Burundi? An automatic rifle lay half covered in the shoulder bag at his feet.

'There are striking parallels with Bosnia: I've seen the same kind of brutal ethnic cleansing as I saw in Bosnia . . . this is ethnic cleansing and this is every bit as serious and it needs just as much attention.'

I moved house again the following day. It was getting too dangerous to live away from the company of other expatriates. I had had another death threat – predictably – just after my report on Kivyuka.

'There is only one explanation, Jennings. You are a white Hutu. And we know what happens to Hutus.'

I moved into the Hotel Source du Nile, just behind the Novotel. The remainders of the UN commission of inquiry were still staying there. I felt some security. I could feel time running out, however, and had asked Whisky about the possibility of firearms. He had said that he could get me either a handgun, or a pump-action shotgun. He warned me that should I actually be seen carrying it, the military or the gendarmerie would no doubt use it as an excuse to expel me. So at night in the hotel, during the long, hot hours of candlelit power cut, I would sit outside in the darkness of the corridor, waiting in the corner, watching my hotel-room door. Night after night, they didn't come. Whisky told me that if I had the money – which I did – he could get me an Uzi sub-machine-gun, which would ensure some sort of security.

'Look at it this way,' he told me on the last occasion I went to his office. 'If they come to get you, you'll need a bit of muscle.' He slotted six hollow-nosed rounds into his .357 Magnum and spun the chamber. 'It'll be a bit late to start asking questions. An Uzi and ninety rounds of ammunition will give you breathing space. Out of your hotel room, down the stairs, hole up in the garden. Just call me: I'll come with my boys.'

That night I regretted not taking him up on the Uzi.

I was sitting in the candle-lit gloom of the hotel bar, talking with some of the delegates from an MSF team. They had moved out of their house in the capital after a particularly violent armed burglary. My phone rang.

'Jennings. It's us. We're coming for you tonight in the hotel.'

All the shapes in the gloom took on a menace. I went and looked in the lobby. Nothing. Out in the dark of the garden the palm trees waved in the warm wind coming off the lake. Nothing. I went to reception and told them that if anybody came looking for me, I had gone to stay at the Novotel. In the car-park I stared at the deserted presidential palace next to the hotel. That was where President Melchior Ndadaye had been arrested by the army during the coup in October 1993. There was nobody to be seen. Nothing moved in the late-night breeze. I sat in the bar till midnight, and then crouched in a corner of my fifth-floor corridor, watching my door, wishing for an Uzi and ninety rounds of ammunition. Dawn came and I was asleep. My head was leaning against a pot-plant. When I went for breakfast at the Novotel, Vicky told me in a cheery voice that three men had come looking for me at eleven o'clock the previous night. That was it. As soon as my bureau chief's visit was over, I decided that I would leave the country. The whole operation would have to be carried out extremely covertly, because I reckoned that if the Tutsi militias realized I was planning to jump ship, they might pre-empt me.

The visit of Nicholas Kotch, my boss from Nairobi, started uneventfully. I organized a schedule for him. We did interviews. He saw Anique from MSF, he saw the ICRC, he saw Gordon Duguid from the American Embassy. Colonel Nibizi showed himself to be the voice of military reason. We had dinner with Bryan Rich and Sandra Melone from Studio Ijambo, and he met Pirjo Dupuy from the UNHCR. We spoke to Hutu politicians, and Aziz Hani from the UN. Nick met Charles Mukasi, and tried to get to grips with the intractable convolutions of the peace process in Mwanza. He was surprised and shocked when he discovered that all of the interviews he had done were off-the-record. He began to understand why my Reuters pieces contained no names but my own. On the third day we drove into the country.

The story that day had started with an unconfirmed report of large-scale killings, some rumours, messages passed to the capital. All was as normal as the Studio Ijambo white Land Rover cleared the outskirts of Bujumbura. On board were Nick, me and two journalists from the Studio. Our destination was Kiganda, an isolated cathedral town in the highlands of central Muramvya province.

Kiganda was the town where you arrive in your nightmares, where everybody knows the terrible secret apart from you. The cathedral was huge and empty, far too big for the small collection of buildings around it and the lycée. The local mayor and an army officer greeted us as we stepped out of the Land Rover. There was, they said, little to be seen. Yes, five people had been killed a few nights before in a Hutu raid, but that was it. A few shops had been looted. In the cathedral, the floor had been cleaned, and rows of lighted candles stretched down the aisle. There were very few people to be seen. But in the red-brick classrooms of the high-school, some 300 pupils sat attentively in class; they stood politely when we entered. A sign on the noticeboard forbade the wearing of ostentatious jewellery.

Nothing, the school's headmaster said, was out of the ordinary. Yes, he admitted, a girl had been suspended for a month after she had given birth to an illegitimate child, which she had drowned in a well. But nothing else. There was a small gathering of displaced Tutsis behind the school building. Wood-fires smoked; maize was pounded. Rain crept in over the eucalyptus forests on the surrounding hills. I felt very far away from the rest of the world, and wanted to be done with Burundi.

We climbed back into the Land Rover, and headed back out of town. The mayor and the army officer waved as we turned out of the square in front of the cathedral. Perhaps, we thought, the rumours had been false. Perhaps there had been no attack. We turned to head back to Bujumbura.

It was only when we accidentally bumped into a four-wheel-drive vehicle full of local staff from an aid agency that we discovered there was something that everybody had been hiding from us.

'Go five kilometres down there,' said the vehicle's driver. 'Ask for Martyazo hill.'

Three kilometres further on, we parked just off the track. We asked a local farmer what was going on. He beckoned us to follow him.

'It started here,' the farmer said, pointing into a patch of runner beans where the plants had been flattened, the earth freshly turned. 'It started at one o'clock, in the school lunchbreak.'

The man stood in the drizzle, a grease-stained corduroy hat red with earth sitting on his head. He was, he said, one of several hundred Hutus who originated from this hill, and from Renga, close by. They had returned to pick their beans.

'It was students from Kiganda lycée who did most of the killing,' he explained, showing us some blood-stained bean plants. 'They killed as many people as they could; they took weapons from the families they attacked. Knives, clubs, locally made weapons. Some had pistols. It was the boy students in their lunchbreak.'

Fifty-one people were confirmed killed on Renga hill. Onesphore Mkeshimana, the *chef de colline* from Martyazo said the total could be as high as 300.

241

Geography during class-time; killing in free-time. No ostentatious jewellery but don't worry about throwing your baby down a well. Stand up when visitors enter, and don't forget to bring your machete into the classroom in case it's needed for extra-curricular activity. Burundi, that early summer, was a country where everything that you understood and took for granted was stood on its head and made a mockery of.

Back in the capital news came that the governor of Cibitoke province had been murdered. Lieutenant-Colonel Nrutse had tried to take a moderate stance; word was that he had got in the way of the gold-smuggling syndicate run by the army. His bodyguards had shot him as he sat in his jeep, then claimed it had been a Hutu ambush. They killed five civilians who happened to be at the side of the road, just to make things look authentic, then stole the car. The moderate military commander of Muramvya province was also hit and wounded in an ambush. Under immense pressure, the civilian governor of Gitega province resigned. Salvator Nsabima, a Hutu, said he had no means to govern the war-ravaged region. At the United Nations, Marc Faguy was protesting because the human rights monitors were not allowed to go to Kivyuka. A military escort was mandatory, the army said, and they just didn't think security was satisfactory. Storm clouds were over Lake Tanganyika as I paid up at the Hotel Source du Nile, and booked back in at the Novotel. If it came to a last stand, I thought, at least I should do it somewhere with colour television.

Charles Mukasi came out first with a response to Anthony Lake's warnings.

'We're against FRODEBU. Tutsis have been in the process of being massacred and accused of carrying out genocide since 1965. If there is an intervention in this country, UPRONA, my party, would go off and turn itself into a guerilla army. If the President can't govern the country it's because he has an army he can't control.'

Up the hill past the Presidency, Nick Kotch and I listened to the riposte of the Hutu Jean Minani, leader of FRODEBU.

'There is a plan of extermination for the cadres of FRODEBU, planned with the cohesion and knowledge of the forces of law and order. The governor of Cibitoke was killed by his own guards and tortured, Lieutenant-Colonel Hwaye in Cibitoke is thought to be implicated.'

We ate lunch at the Tanganyika restaurant with Colonel Jean-Bosco Daradangwe. It was a civilized affair. I had cold Vichyssoise soup and the lemon sole. Daradangwe spooned soup into his mouth, and patted away bread crumbs with a linen napkin. We were alone in the restaurant. To our right, the lake glimmered grey. I sat between the two, hardly speaking. After the sycophantic, nervous Belgian owner had allowed the colonel to sign the bill, we stood for a moment on the steps outside. Daradangwe flicked imaginary dust off his hound's-tooth check jacket. A plane climbed away from the airport overhead. I wished I could be on it.

'So, Colonel,' said Nick, shaking his hand. 'You can really say that you can assure Christian's security?'

Daradangwe laid one hand, Lucifer-like, on my shoulder.

'Nicholas, you can leave him here under my benediction.'

Nick left for Nairobi that afternoon.

I went to interview the French ambassador. His concerns that afternoon were for the security of the 360 French expatriates in Burundi. As a first measure he had closed the French school and advised all the pupils and their parents to return to France unless their presence in Burundi was vital.

'Plans,' he said, 'are underway for an evacuation from Bangui in the Central African Republic.'

And for military intervention?

'We are going to wait to see how the situation develops here; all I can say is that Bangui, N'djamena, Djibouti . . . they're within a few hours flying-time.'

Christophe had seen a copy of the plans for any intervention to rescue French nationals. First in would be a company of the Legion's 2e Régiment Étranger de Parachutistes from Bangui (at that point on stand-by). Then would follow three or four companies of Legion and regular army paratroopers from Djibouti City, Chad, Bangui, Gabon or Réunion. Jaguar ground-attack aircraft would hit the airport, securing it off for a ground-landing of the paratroopers. Once the airport was secured, the three-kilometre drive to the airport would be taken. The expatriates would be gathered at the Novotel (I imagined screaming children, teddy-bears falling in the pool), and transported to the airport by any means available for air-evacuation. Any person hindering the evacuation in any way, civilian or Burundian military, would be shot instantly. I wondered if I would still be in the country, dead or alive, when such a rescue operation took place.

Crisis had one very noticeable effect in Burundi: people started saying exactly what they had meant all along.

'The closure of the school is part of Burundi being re-colonized by France,' ranted Deogratias Niyonzima, the leader of the SOJE-DEM Tutsi youth militia. 'Burundi will never accept being the slave of another power. Patriots will rise up and fight against the slavery plan of FRODEBU, FROLINA and the Hutus. In effect, the French intervention that is being prepared will be accompanied by a desire to achieve a genocide of all Tutsis, and non-FRODEBU Hutus. Rumours of a coup d'état are not to be discounted.'

I dutifully noted it down. All of it would be the predictable barmy rantings of the politically marginalized, I thought, if it weren't for the fact that this man had the ear of every armed Tutsi fanatic in the capital. And there were thousands of them. What he was assuring, however, was that by including the French in his list of enemies, he was condemning himself and all his followers to a swift and violent death at the hands of French paratroopers if they ever arrived.

That evening I went to the airport to watch the crowd of French and Belgian expatriates board the Air France flight. The white Boeing 747 stood out on the tarmac; a dozen stewardesses, elegant and beautifully made-up, stood at the souvenir stand buying carvings, coffee and pottery from Mutoyi. To one who had been in Burundi and Rwanda for eight months, they seemed impossibly civilized, clean, shiny. The departures hall was crowded: all the expatriates who weren't leaving seemed to have turned out for all those that were. The fact that it was French and Belgian families leaving upped the emotional stakes considerably. These were, for the most part, families who had not left the capital for two years; families who had attended the same round of polo club parties, Christmas celebrations and gymkhanas since long before the 1993 coup. These were not people who took the road to Bugerama junction, or drove north to Cibitoke, or to Bururi. For most of these families, the country's problems were something abstract, vague and African that took place in that vast green yonder. For the teenagers, Bujumbura, with its lake, its sun, its bit of beach, the polo club, could have been Réunion, Mayotte, Martinique. Unfortunately 'they' were always shooting, 'they' were always killing each other, 'they' ruined it for everybody else. Anyway, they were all black, and isn't that what black Africans do to each other? Kill each other all the time? Burundi, unfortunately, played up to every European stereotype of black Africa.

As the departure time of the flight approached, small gangs of teenage friends said goodbye to each other. The twelve and thirteen year old girls, with their teddy-bear rucksacks, first lipstick, and subterfuge Marlboro Lights, embraced each other with every bit of fervent Gallic hyperbole they could muster. There was much kissing, many promises of unending friendship. Girls wearing Asterix t-shirts, their gymshoe laces patterned with multicoloured hearts, tried to inhale their cigarettes. They burst into tears in the confusion, not knowing who they'd miss more: their new pony or their best friend. Some children refused to be separated.

'*Écoute*, Chantal. They can do what they like – passport or no passport, I'm getting on that plane, and they'll have to drag me off.'

'*Eh, Veronique. Mon p'tit stowaway. Tu es adorable.*'

Through the throng of embarking travellers moved the body-guards from the French Embassy, their holstered weapons concealed under their untucked shirts. I went to stand upstairs on the terrace. Sandrine and Nicolette from Médecins du Monde had been saying goodbye to one of their team

'*Eh alors*, Christian. It's the end of an era.'

I smiled.

'So,' asked Nicolette. 'When do you expect the coup?'

'I don't know,' I answered, sitting beside them and ordering three

Amstels. 'Things are getting pretty tight. The military are squeezing this country. I think they'll try for a coup.'

'When?'

'The Americans have, I think, delivered their final warning. The army moderates, the prime minister, they want the violence to stop. Leonard Nyangoma said in Rome that the Hutus might be prepared to talk. It's all up to the army hard boys.'

'They've got too much to lose,' said Sandrine. 'It's gone too far. I wonder whether we all ought to be on that flight. Especially you.'

Three days later a Burundian army Land Rover blocked the road three kilometres short of the church and hospital at Butezi. An armoured car was parked next to it.

'Where are you going,' asked an officer, as I got out of the white Studio Ijambo Land Rover.

'We're journalists; Reuters, BBC, *Washington Post*.'

'It's all up ahead. You can't miss it. But I warn you, it's pretty disgusting.'

We accelerated along the track.

'Given what lies before us,' I ventured from the front seat. 'Shall we eat our pizza now?'

'No,' said Stephen from the *Washington Post*. 'Let's leave it till afterwards. Less to sick up if it really is that bad.'

We drove forward. To our right was the valley of the Sanzo river, clusters of huts speckling the hills along its edges. We drove into a eucalyptus forest, and then emerged into a clearing where the smoke from burning huts climbed up through the branches. Knots of soldiers, policemen and peasants were gathered in front of a red-brick building.

'There are the bodies,' pointed Alexei.

We climbed out of the Land Rover, introduced ourselves. I moved forward. On the verandah of the building fifty-one bodies lay covered in grey blankets. On top of each blanket a name had been written on a slip of paper cut from a school exercise-book. I went along the line, lifting each blanket as I listed name, sex and cause of death. Callixte Karombo had had the front of his skull cut off with a machete before he was burned. His jaw-bone and jellied face had slid onto the front of his Roger Rabbit t-shirt, his yellow teeth stuck like full stops in the sticky brain-matter. I moved along the line. Gerard Ngendakumana and Isadore Sindituma had both been burnt alive, their limbs cracked where the petrol-roasted flesh had turned black and carbonized. Fifteen women, six men, fourteen little girls, and fifteen boys. Fifty-one. All Tutsis. A man lifted the corner of a blanket for me. A child had been burned into a black, carbonized shape.

These were Tutsi displaced people who had been attacked by rebels hidden among the local peasant population. An army position had been attacked at the same time. In the mud and scorched bricks of the burnt-out huts, there were melted yellow jerry-cans, pools of sticky dried blood, and the frizzled carcasses of dogs and goats. The Hutus had attacked first with machetes and Kalashnikovs, then poured petrol into the huts and torched them.

We were at Butezi, five hours away from the capital. The displaced persons camp lay two kilometres short of the church and hospital on a windblown ridge overlooking Tanzania. A group of thirty green-uniformed prisoners from Ruyigi had been brought in to dig the graves. Being Tutsis, the dead got a grave each. No mass pit like the Hutus. The bishop of Ruyigi had got out of a Land Cruiser; three bodyguards in army camouflage were setting up a small speaker for his prayers.

'These people are the result of sin and fratricidal hatred,' he said, his words blowing on the wind that came through the trees. 'We thought that little by little the situation was going to get better, but we now see that these people are incapable of living together.'

The bodies were lifted up and taken to the graves. Two prisoners hefted the corpse of a woman. From underneath her blanket, one breast, sliced off and only attached by a stretch of skin, flopped out and dragged gummily in the red dirt. Fifty-one people were buried by the time we drove along to the hospital where hundreds of local

Hutus had already taken refuge from the army reprisal they knew was coming.

'We can't let you in,' a nurse hissed through the gate. 'The army has already killed one of our staff this morning.' We turned and drove slowly back along the ridge. Three soldiers were walking towards the valley: behind came two Tutsi men, one wearing a moleskin headband and carrying a spear. In his other hand he had three assault rifle magazines lashed together with blue UN tape. These belonged to the soldier who walked in front of him. The other Tutsi peasant carried a belt of machine-gun ammunition.

Back along the road, we found the Land Rover and the armoured personnel carrier still in place, the officer watching the action in the valley below us through binoculars. Our fan-belt chose that moment to break, to his utter fury. For fifteen minutes we had a grandstand view of the military reprisal in the Sanzo river valley, as the military shot their way from house to house in each village.

A few days later I left the capital for the last time. Along with Alexei, Bryan Rich and an English cameraman called Jeff, I travelled north into the war of Cibitoke province. The ICRC had sent three vehicles up the road already that morning: they estimated 100,000 people were without water, food and shelter in the very north, almost on the Rwandan border. The drive to Cibitoke was eerie and ghostly that day. Normally there were road-blocks every five kilometres, with lengthy car-searches and cigarettes smoked in the shade while the driver went through the contents of his boot. Today was different. At one point a patrol of soldiers flashed across the road, looked briefly at us and then vanished into the head-high grass. Half way up the road another patrol led eleven Hutu men off into the bush, their hands clasped on top of their heads. The patrol shouted at us to disappear. I suspected the men were shot minutes later. Three huts on the verge smoked from where they had been attacked an hour earlier. Piles of broken beer bottles were smashed on the road in a sticky pool of Primus. A lorry had been ambushed. All of us had a very bad feeling by the time we got to the town of Cibitoke itself.

We interviewed the six Red Cross delegates as they distributed their jerry-cans and blankets to the population. We watched rather perplexedly as a gendarmerie Land Rover followed us around the town wherever we went. At lunch time we sat outside the officers' mess while the ICRC delegates had a meeting inside. By two o'clock we decided we could wait no longer. There was a choice of options: go south back to the capital, and check out the military operations on the way. Or go north with the three ICRC Land Cruisers towards Mugina and Rugombo, and see if we could find the estimated 100,000 displaced people. Neither story was particularly urgent. It was that or more complicated, messy politics back in the capital. We argued the toss for a moment or two. Go north? Go south? Finally, Jeff said that he needed a bit of time to get some pictures, so we slipped into first gear and rolled back down towards Bujumbura.

We went for a drink when we got back. Jeff, Bryan, Alexei and myself were just sitting back when my mobile phone rang. It was the bureau in Nairobi.

'Christian, we're just getting reports out of Geneva that the ICRC delegates have been ambushed in northern Burundi. Possibly three dead. What have you got?'

I told the others. We started to ring round. We hadn't got very far when Ulli Muller, the deputy head of the ICRC turned up. He was crying.

'Juan; Reto; Cedric.'

He slashed a hand across his throat.

'All dead.'

Chapter 8

White Hutu

The ICRC Land Cruisers had driven north from Cibitoke town. At the small village of Rugombo, two of the vehicles turned right up into the mountains towards the displaced persons camp at Mugina. The third vehicle stayed in Rugombo. The first two Land Cruisers allegedly saw a dead soldier and a dead civilian at Rugombo market, along with four wounded civilians. The local population told them that the route to Mugina was heavy with Hutu rebels. They turned right anyway. In the lead vehicle were three Swiss and Italian ICRC delegates. One of them, Juan, was the boyfriend of my ex, Charlotte. According to the army, the vehicles passed a military patrol which informed them that there were rebels in the area. Just past the village of Muyange there was heavy firing from one side of the road. The first vehicle rolled over several times. The second vehicle overtook and accelerated towards Mugina. A lorry following in the same direction picked up the bodies to take them to Mugina. The three corpses, including one that had been decapitated by a hand-grenade thrown into the Toyota, were left at the village's military position.

The army's official report was compiled by three senior military officers, including Colonel Marcel Sinarinzi, who had carried out the official whitewash after the massacre at Buhoro. The report claimed that when a military patrol arrived at the ambush site, the bullet-riddled Land Cruiser was in the ditch. The elephant grass at the side of the road was nearly head-high. Written in white chalk near the vehicle, and near one of the dead bodies, was the following message:

FNL-PALIPEHUTU, TSINDA NDUWAYO ARABAHENDA MURIHURIYE
NA FNL NANI

Loosely translated, it means: Beware [Prime Minister] Nduwayo,
you have just met the FNL-PALIPEHUTU.

It went on:

ABAZUNGU MWANSE KUGENDA HAKIBONA MUZOGENDA NDA
MUTIKIRONKA INZIRA

To other white people will happen the same as has happened to
these.

The military report said it was convinced that the ambush was
carried out by the Hutu rebels.

Patrick Berner, head of delegation of the ICRC in Burundi, told
me after their own inquiry that he was 'ninety per cent convinced it
was carried out by the army'.

Why would the army want to force the ICRC to leave Cibitoke?
For three reasons. First, and most directly, they were seen to be
supplying food and relief supplies to the local Hutu peasant
population. As far as the army was concerned, this translated into
direct material support for the PALIPEHUTU rebels.

Second, the province of Cibitoke was run like a mafia operation by
a cartel of army officers. They were Colonel Celestin Ndayisaba,
who had given me my death threat at the Novotel, Colonel Lucien
Rufyiri, who controlled Bubanza, and a Lieutenant-Colonel Hwaye.
Rufyiri was one of the officers implicated in the planning of the 1993
coup. Hwaye commanded a battalion of the Groupe d'Intervention
Léger Anti-Terroriste, or GILAT, a quick-response army unit.
I had been told by a Hutu politician that he had been behind
the killing on 13 May of Sylvain Nurutse, the previous, moderate
governor.

The army had much to hide in Cibitoke. There were the gold and
opium smuggling operations between Zaire and Burundi that I'd
been longing to report on. In connection with a company called
AFIMET, they were allegedly smuggling Zairean gold into Burundi, and then shipping it to Europe. Outside of Bujumbura airport

there was a small compound, called the Tax-Free Trading Zone. Heavily fortified, this contained the headquarters of AFIMET, and a small bank that dealt in offshore accounts.

The gold and raw opium were taken out of Bujumbura's tax-free trading complex into Europe on Air France and Sabena. Some of the material was used as direct payment for arms shipments coming into Bujumbura.

The third reason the military were opposed to the presence of the ICRC was that the colonels wanted to be able to impose harsh law-and-order programmes on the province. These kept the area free of Hutus, then kept the border area with Zaire secure, and they allowed the army and their Tutsi henchmen to keep safe their money-making operations. For colonels like these, keeping power in Burundi was about controlling access to very meagre resources, and the power to oppress the Hutu in every way possible kept this access secure.

The Burundian transport minister, as well as one of the dead delegates from the ICRC, had led people to understand that they knew about a recent assassination attempt on the president in Cibitoke, which had allegedly been organized as a prelude to a coup d'état. One of the delegates from the ICRC had said that Colonel Hwaye had led the attempt on the life of President Ntibantunganya during a recent visit to the province. Sylvestre had been due to return to the capital by helicopter, but on this particular occasion, the chopper had broken down. He was told that he would return to the capital by road. He was ushered to the convoy by the military hierarchy who had planned his death, and shown the lead vehicle. He refused to get in, taking the third car instead. Five kilometres south of Cibitoke, the first car in the procession was blown to pieces by an RPG anti-tank rocket.

But power struggles, smuggling and the oppression of the Hutu rebels were all small fry compared to the biggest operation taking place in Cibitoke. The Rwandan government was planning to hit the refugee camps in eastern Zaire, and sort out the problem of ex-FAR and interahamwe infiltrations once and for all. For eighteen months they had watched UNHCR fail to separate the innocent refugees from those guilty of crimes committed during the 1994 genocide.

They had decided to do something about it themselves. In this task they were assisted by the considerable diplomatic clout of the United States. American Special Forces soldiers were also training the RPA and the Zairean Tutsis in counter-insurgency operations, ready for their final assaults on the refugee camps around Bukavu, Uvira and Goma. Their passage into Zaire's South Kivu province was through Cibitoke. The last thing the Burundian army wanted was for the ICRC to find Rwandan troops, or worse, Americans in Cibitoke. So they had decided to solve the problem the only way they knew how, without consulting anybody else. The Rwandan army, the Burundian army and the Americans all knew that for the refugee problem in Zaire to be solved, Burundi had to be stable first.

The end began for me three days after Juan, Reto and Cedric were killed. I'd been sitting at a barbecue drinking beer in the sun, chatting with three friends. My phone had rung with the news of another massacre. Two American Mennonite missionaries based in a rebel-heavy valley outside Gitega had just watched the army kill seventy-three civilians. I'd arranged to meet them the following morning.

I moved the piece on Reuters at Sunday lunch time, and on the BBC mid afternoon. The BBC Kirundi service broadcast the names of the two officers who had led the massacre. It was a wearingly predictable tale. I visited the valley where the missionaries, Keith and Susan, lived. It was near Kiganda, where the schoolchildren had killed the Hutus in their lunchbreak. The valley of Kigemba was used by the Hutu rebels as a crossing-point in their movements across central Burundi. Susan had even seen a column of rebels once, one of the few Europeans ever to have laid eyes on them. She described them: two dozen ragged Hutus, mostly barefoot, two wearing army boots and uniform, and one wearing an old brown laboratory coat. Seven of them were carrying land-mines, sacks of food, water and ammunition on their heads. The other five held, respectively, an RPG-7 rocket-launcher, two Kalashnikovs, and two German G3 rifles. Three were women. It was a far cry from the Death's Head Batallions of Minani's nightmares, the squads of highly equipped killers who were in imminent danger of bringing the capital to its knees.

Christophe and I often had discussed the military composition of Leonard Nyangoma's rebels. It was of enduring interest to both of us why they could not get their act together to attack the capital. After all, they could infiltrate anywhere they pleased. They could massacre thousands of people, ambush roads, cripple the power supply of a whole country. They had displaced three-quarters of a million people, killed at least another 100,000, and faced down a well equipped army. Could they not go that one mile further and properly assault Bujumbura? In truth, both of us suspected that their disorganization was total, and their logistical supply-chain weak. They were a very effective guerilla army – they'd spread terror through the whole of Burundi – but they would never conquer it.

In the valley at Kigemba, the soldiers had started killing the previous Thursday. They were led, Susan said, by a particularly notorious and vicious lieutenant. Susan and Keith were genuinely good people, the kind of people who, in the Bible, will inherit the earth. I'd paid a visit to their farm once, and found them teaching the Twa cattle-rearing techniques. I had a vivid memory of a row of pygmies sitting on a wooden bench, none of their feet touching the ground. I suspected part of the reason that the local military were so hostile was because Keith and Susan were so popular. The Hutu and Twa civilians were chased by the soldiers towards a river. They couldn't swim. They were hit with bullets first, and then, Susan said, the soldiers dropped their guns and went in with machetes.

On the Sunday afternoon, I could feel things closing in. I'd gone out for Sunday lunch with a friend who had a house near the beach. As the sun bounced off the lake we'd had roast beef and Yorkshire pudding. Then we'd worked our way through a crate of Primus. Chris Baker worked for the World Food Programme as a logistician. It was he who negotiated the transport of thousands of tons of grain on barges up Lake Tanganyika from Tanzania and Malawi. By tea time I was drunk. When Lieutenant-Colonel Jean Bikomagu, chief of staff of the army, rang me to accuse me of telling lies, I don't think I took it in. The tide seemed to be ebbing out fast. I didn't care anymore. I felt numb. By supper time I had moved on to vodka and orange at a dinner party, then more Amstel at the Novotel. Around ten o'clock, I was arrested briefly by three Burundian gendarmes while trying to negotiate the ten feet of pavement between the Novotel and the Meridien in violation of the curfew. By eleven, I was back at the Novotel bar, on Jack Daniels and Coca-Cola. I was almost speechlessly drunk. That was when I burst into tears.

In a second, tipping back my glass, all my confidence seemed to disappear. It really was like a slippery carpet being pulled out from under my feet. All the bravado, all the courage, all the self-confidence and slightly affected jauntiness disappeared in the time it took to burst into tears. Then my phone rang.

'Christian!'

It was Jane and Greg from the BBC in Nairobi. I could hardly speak. I muttered and snuffled and sobbed a little bit, and then cleared the call. Then I ordered more bourbon. I had never felt such complete terror in my life. I felt that death was extraordinarily close. I should have left Burundi with Nick Kotch two weeks before. Naming the army officers on air had pushed the army too far.

'It was as though somebody had squeezed a pair of pliers around your bollocks and was twisting them,' said Bryan Rich the following day. 'After they had forced you to eat a gram of heroin. You were squealing.'

'Not making much sense at all, my dear,' said Sandra.

'You were,' laughed Bryan, 'shit-faced and crying.'

By Monday lunch time I was sitting at their terrace table, nursing a monumental hangover. They had prepared what they called a 'last lunch'. Sandra was arranging smoked salmon, opening a bottle of cold chardonnay. I was shaking so much I could hardly hold my cigarette. This was no ordinary hangover. This was fear. My confidence had not returned. I could hardly eat.

'I think, Christian,' said Bryan, 'it's time for you to go. Word around and about is not good. People think they'll try to kill you.'

We sat through the meal. I picked at my salmon.

'What should I do?'

'Go to the American Embassy after lunch. Tell Gaston he doesn't need to pick you up. We'll take you there.'

We left in their Land Rover shortly afterwards. Instead of going to the embassy and throwing myself at the mercy of their diplomatic protection, their squad of Marines, we went to the United Nations building. I explained the situation to Aziz.

'Ring the American Embassy. See what they have to say.'

For two months I had formulated careful plans for what I should do in this eventuality. There was no British Embassy in Bujumbura; diplomatic representation was through the ambassador in Kigali. The Belgian Embassy was, theoretically, looking after British citizens, but I had forged closer links with the Americans. I had been exchanging information on a regular basis with one of their political officers, Steven Fox, and we had established a good quid pro quo relationship. Should my life be in the balance, I could think of nothing I would rather have beside me than ten Marines from their Marine Guard detachment stationed in Bujumbura. Also, the Burundians had a completely exaggerated fear of the United States' military capacity. Several expatriates had been told by Burundians, in complete seriousness, that the US Navy had a nuclear submarine on standby in Lake Tanganyika. The Burundians thought that if they ever offended the US, the Bujumbura skyline would suddenly blacken with the thwack and hover of sixteen Cobra helicopter gunships.

I rang Mark Hunter, the US embassy security officer who had chided me constantly about security, suggesting that one day I would get killed travelling on Burundi's roads. As he had not left the capital for a long time – if at all – I had never been sure about his advice. He said he couldn't guarantee my security on the trip from the UN building to the embassy. Word was already out as to my whereabouts and intentions. The Sans Échec militias had let it be known that they were after me. How was I going to get out of the country? First things first, I thought. Assume that you are going to be allowed to leave normally. Then work up to a more extreme scenario. I rang the office in Nairobi, and told them it was all over. It took them a few minutes to understand; they thought at first I meant I'd be returning at the end of the week. I told them what was happening, adding that it was certain that I would be killed if I didn't leave the country the following day. I asked them to be prepared to send a charter from Wilson to pick me up if things got that bad. The Kenya Airways office was in the same block as the UN. I walked down and booked a ticket for the following afternoon. I had less than twenty-four hours to go. I had only to keep my cool till then. It was all out of my hands.

Back at the UN office I paced up and down. Every time my phone rang I was convinced that it was the Tutsi militias outside at the gates. Eventually one of Sandra's staff gave me two valium tablets. Within thirty minutes, the world seemed to calm down, and I sat in a warm blur, letting events take their course. I spent that night at the house of Aziz. We drove from the office to his house with his bodyguard, Leonidas. This man was a former sergeant in the Burundian army, and moved very stealthily. Sandra called him 'the Panther'. He shadowed Abdul Aziz wherever he went, and guarded the house at night. One evening, Aziz told me, there had been heavy firing in town. The rebels had come in from the hills and were clashing with the army. Aziz had told Leonidas to take extra precautions. Just before bed, he had walked out onto the terrace to find Leonidas crouching behind the firing mechanism of a belt-fed Browning machine-gun, mounted on a tripod. The following morning, Aziz instructed me to go straight to his office, wait there until the flight was due to leave, and then drive with Leonidas and some other armed men to the airport. I made the fatal mistake of stopping at the hotel for my things.

I was leaning on the reception desk when the five Burundian paramilitary policemen turned up at the hotel to take me away.

'Where is the room of Jennings?' asked one, undoing his pistol holster.

I thought of making a run for it. Gaston was outside. I could be at the American Embassy in under five minutes.

'That's him,' said the manager, pointing at me.

'Jennings,' said the officer. 'It is time. We have come for you.'

I thought I was going to wet myself. I wondered whether I would be tortured before being shot. But first they wanted to search my room. The six of us crushed into the lift; I was surrounded by Kalashnikovs. On the fifth floor I started unlocking my door but they lost patience and booted it down. I was forced to stand against the window at gunpoint while they ransacked seven months' worth of Reuters reports, personal files and letters.

'You are planning an outrage against the Burundian army,' said the plainclothes officer. 'You and your Zairean spies.'

He picked up my five most recent reports. I winced. All of them detailed massive slaughters of civilians, mostly by the army.

'You are spreading lies about the Burundian army. We have seen enough. Take him away.'

I had been in the swimming pool, and was wearing nothing but shorts and a towelling robe. With angry prods of their AK assault-rifles, they gestured that I should get dressed. What, I had wondered in that long, slow-motion second before the fear kicked in, do you wear to your own execution? Would the Gap jeans do another day?

While I dressed, two soldiers were searching the bathroom. One walked out with my tube of Colgate stuck on the end of his Kalashnikov bayonet.

'You can forget the toothpaste,' said the officer.

I used a few seconds of confusion to pick up my mobile phone and speed-dial seven digits. It rang once.

'Hello, James Shepherd-Barron.'

'James, Christian. I've got six goons in my hotel room. I'm being arrested. Get onto the US Embassy and UN security.'

The plainclothes officer grabbed at my telephone and barked at me.

'Hurry up! No talking!'

I was led downstairs behind two armed men carrying two boxes of papers. In the lobby were gathered half of the hotel guests, including three TV crews. I was filmed by CNN as I was led out to the dark-blue van outside. Two bullet holes starred the glass on the driver's side. I was pushed in the back and driven off to the army barracks behind the Hotel Source du Nile. There I was escorted out of the vehicle, still clutching my phone, and led into an office. Opposite the room into which I was taken were two barred cell doors. A mass of half-naked, ragged men were pressed against the bars. All of their faces were bloated, swollen and covered in blood. Hutus, I thought. Inside the office, a uniformed military officer was sitting at a desk. He stood as I came in.

'Jennings from Reuters. Or should I say Jennings from Zaire. The traitor. Sit down.'

He laid his Kalashnikov on his desk and turned to the plainclothes officer.

'He has questions to answer, no?'

'He must sign the statement first,' said the plainclothes man.

A side of A4 paper covered in writing was pushed in front of me. I was not allowed to read it. There was a dotted line at the bottom.

'Sign here,' said the man in uniform.

I pushed the paper away and started to stand up. I was pushed back into my chair.

'Sign here, Jennings of Zaire.'

'No. I refuse to sign anything. You know who I am. Why have I been arrested?'

'Jennings,' said the uniformed officer. 'It is we who ask the questions. Now . . .'

He reached behind his chair, and brought out a pickaxe handle which had been leaning against the wall. One end was wrapped with lead; thick, rusty nails had been hammered through it. The plain-clothes officer shut the door. The man in uniform took the club and came round to stand beside me. He looked at the plainclothes man.

'Do you want to start, or shall I?'

Then he looked at me.

'Are you frightened? You're shaking. Have you not eaten properly this morning?'

'I'm fine.'

At that point another man arrived, and I was taken to stand in the sun outside another office. My phone rang.

'Jennings. You've finally got what's been coming to you all along. If you get out of this, which you won't . . . don't ever leave the capital again. Your body will be found in pieces in a ditch.'

I pressed Clear.

Give the Burundians credit for one thing, I thought. They gave good death threat. But for some reason I no longer felt so afraid. I thought that if I was going to be executed, they would have done it by now. And then I noticed, standing outside another door, a freelance Belgian cameraman I knew. He'd also been arrested. I felt relieved. At least there were two of us in this. Marc Hoogsteyns worked occasionally for Reuters. He said he had wives in Kigali and Thailand; he said he'd been a Belgian paratrooper. My phone rang again.

'Christian.' It was the Nairobi office. 'We hear you've been arrested. Can you give us some details?'

I told them that I was about to have my phone taken away, but that I was fine, and hadn't been harmed. Then I cut them off. I wanted to hold on to my mobile as long as possible.

'Come in, Jennings.'

It was a dapper-looking man at a desk inside the office. I walked in and sat down.

'So. Jennings. And your colleague Hoogsteyns.'

Oh God, I panicked again. Marc had committed one of his regular monumental *faux pas*. Was I to hang for one of his blunders?

'Tell me, Jennings. Your mission started in Zaire. Before you infiltrated Burundi, who briefed you in Kinshasa?'

'I work for Reuters, an English-language news wire agency, which has offices in most of the major . . .'

'Jennings. We know about Reuters. It forms part of the Zairean intelligence network. Tell me; who is your controller?'

'I am the Reuters correspondent for Burundi. I am here to provide accurate, independent and objective news reporting on a daily basis of every aspect . . .'

'Jennings. Come, come. We know who you are. You and your henchman Hoogsteyns. We know you infiltrated Burundi by night, across the Rusizi river, with the rebels. Tell me, how did you blow up those electricity pylons.'

I knew that this whole interrogation was a complex exercise in humiliation, and that by now, Abdul Hani Aziz was probably working to get me out. On my side I had two things: I could speak perfect French and I was a lot more used to this kind of experience than the Burundian interrogator thought. In a moment of bravado, it flashed through my mind that everything in my life to date had been preparing me for this moment. English public school, solitary confinement in the French Foreign Legion, Her Majesty's Prison Service.

'Answer me, Jennings of Reuters. Reuters of Zaire. President Mobutu's news service.'

What did they say, those intelligence blokes who'd trained with the Joint Services Interrogation Wing? Simple true answer? Repeat it till they get bored? Or cut your testicles off with a penknife.

'Reuters is the world's leading English-language wire service news agency, providing millions of subscribers worldwide with up-to-the-minute news, photographs, television pictures and financial information. From a complex network of interlinked bureaux on six continents, the subscriber may access a variety of services, primarily through a desk-top terminal through which . . .'

Fuck, I thought. I just said all of that in French.

'Jennings. We know what Reuters is. We know who Reuters is. We know where Reuters is. In Kinshasa.'

He paused, and drew in a deep breath.

'RUN BY PRESIDENT MOBUTU WITH THE SIMPLE AIM OF EXTERMINATING TUTSIS!'

Flecks of white saliva hit my face.

'I think you can have time to reflect now. Remember. What you fear is that we will expel you from the country. What we know is that we can prevent you leaving. And you know what will happen if you stay . . .'

He nodded at my telephone.

'You need to understand, Jennings, we arrested you for your own protection.'

I want to go home. Even if I get out of here I've got to get past the Sans Échec. Get to the airport. Take off without being shot. They'll be announcing on the radio any minute that it's every Tutsi's rightful duty to try and kill me. Please. I'll go and be based in Scandinavia for ever after this.

'And now, I shall leave you.'

He closed the door.

By lunch time my interrogators had made things a little clearer for me. I had been arrested by the gendarmerie on the orders of Lieutenant-Colonel Pascal Simbanduku. My offence seemed to be twofold. Marc Hoogsteyn's room had been searched and papers discovered linking him to the Hutu rebels. He had been stupid enough to contact the Brussels office of the CNDD and ask to be allowed to accompany their men on an insurgency mission from Zaire into Burundi. A response had been faxed back. The CNDD Brussels fax machine was tapped, and a print-out came through in Bujumbura. When Hoogsteyns arrived in Burundi, intelligence had been waiting for him. He was now in the office next door to mine, and was not helping his own case by arguing, shouting and refusing to be cooperative. I had, over the course of an hour, persuaded my interrogator that Hoogsteyns was simply a freelancer for Reuters, and that I had relatively little to do with him. My case had been strengthened late morning by the arrival in the courtyard of a tall, lanky white man wearing a beige linen suit.

'*Bonjour*,' he had said, taking off his sunglasses. 'Steven Fox. United States Embassy. I believe there is a problem.'

I could have hugged him. It was like the US cavalry coming to the rescue in a western. The Burundians immediately started acting in a deferential manner.

'Christian; I can't tell you which way it's going, but we're onto it. So is Aziz at the UN. We're going to try and get you on that Kenya Airways flight.'

My interrogation resumed afterwards, but it seemed more of a formality. The interviewing officer, who turned out to be a lawyer, knew exactly what was happening, and the moment the tables had been turned in my favour by the arrival of Steven, he had seemed to back down. My major preoccupation now was that even if I was released, how was I going to get to the airport safely?

At lunch time I was taken under armed guard to the Novotel, where I ate an omelette. Vicky at reception told me that at least three different groups of people had come looking for me. I couldn't wait to get back to the safety of the gendarmerie. By mid afternoon, it was clear that I was not going to catch my Kenya Airways flight. My terror was having to spend another night in Burundi. Unless I spent it in a US Marine house, or guarded by Belgian paratroopers, I reckoned that I'd had it. The lunchtime news had run a lead item saying that I had been arrested by the army and the police while trying to leave the country. They added that the team from Reuters had been intending to carry out a mission with the PALIPEHUTU and FDD rebels from Zaire. I was now being held at a central barracks. Then the telephone rang again.

'Jennings. We will get you on the way to the airport.'

Steven Fox and the Americans had negotiated my release. Hoogsteyns they had left to the Belgians, who were not being quite so assiduous. The Burundians were going to get their pound of flesh from him. As for my saviours, by the time the attorney-general had signed my release, Christophe Boutonnier and the Panther were outside. The Panther had his Kalashnikov, Christophe his Magnum. We drove fast to the UN office. Nairobi and the British Embassy in Kigali were informed that I was safe. Then it was time for the run to the airport. Downstairs in the UN car-park was Christophe in one Land Cruiser and Mark Hunter in the other. I had missed the Kenya Airways flight, but there was a late Cameroon Airlines 737 *en route* from Kinshasa to Nairobi. Aziz had spoken to the colonel at the airport: the flight could wait for me on the tarmac. Mark Hunter took one vehicle with Aziz. Leonidas, who had now added a Makarov pistol and a hand-grenade to his armoury, came in the other. Whisky laid his Magnum on his lap, changed into first, and we roared out of the car-park, spraying gravel.

The ten minutes it took us to get out of the city were the longest of my life. Whisky pushed the car as hard as he could, splashing through the ruts on the untended road, overtaking along the verge, scattering pedestrians. We hit 130 kilometres an hour after the roundabout with the mango tree. There was a military road-block just short of the airport. Two soldiers stood by the ubiquitous Primus crate in the middle of the road. About ten men in civilian clothes were standing on the gravel verge, looking at the two oncoming vehicles. Christophe blew the horn long, and accelerated. Leonidas cocked his Kalashnikov in the back seat, and pointed it out of the window. Mark pushed up closer behind us. At the last moment the soldiers moved the crate and we blew past.

Inside the departure terminal they had closed the gate for the Cameroon flight. I shook hands with everybody, and told them I would see them again. I gave one of the women from the airline two hundred dollars; she gave me a boarding-pass. I hooked my arms through my luggage and my body-armour, and ran through the departure lounge and out onto the tarmac. The plane had its engines running, the back door down, a pilot standing waiting for me. I ran on. Behind me on the terrace I could see four people waving. I stopped for a moment out on the hot tarmac and waved back. Then I was in under the warm rush of aviation fuel from the jet engines. The pilot took one of my bags and ran up the rear steps; I followed. They started to close as I was half way up. I was still making my way down the inside aisle as the plane started to taxi. I stowed my luggage, and flopped into a seat. As I did up my seatbelt, I took one last look at the terrace. Mark, Aziz, Leonidas and Christophe were waving. The pilot opened up the engines, released the brakes, and we screamed down the runway towards Lake Tanganyika.

Part III

Chapter 9

Dateline: Zaire

Five months later I stood on top of a Toyota Land Cruiser and watched half a million Rwandan refugees walk past me. A column of people fifteen kilometres long blocked the road. The inhabitants of the Goma refugee camps were going home at last. Men, women and children of every age had put their bundles of possessions on their heads, walked out of their shelters of blue plastic sheeting, and were heading back towards the border. From a satellite telephone at the side of the road, I had just sent a bulletin to the Reuters office in Cyprus.

'Four hundred thousand Rwandan refugees quit Mugunga camp – heading back to Rwanda.'

It was the moment that the Kigali government and the UNHCR had waited for since the middle of 1994. In front of me an old Hutu woman was walking slowly. On her back was one child, she was leading another two by the hand, and all her possessions were on her head. Next to her, a Hutu farmer balanced a load of firewood on his back, while carrying a crate of empty Primus bottles in his arms. He had, he said, bought the beers in Ruhengeri in 1994, and was taking them back for his returnable deposit. He was wearing a t-shirt which showed a pig skiing down a snowy slope, wearing sunglasses. 'I'm a real boar on the piste,' read the caption. Another man had balanced a small pirogue canoe on top of his head and had a live turkey in each hand.

'The road is blocked by a twenty-mile wave of people,' a UNHCR spokesman told me. 'All the camps have emptied. Most of them are heading back to Rwanda.'

Opposite, a woman gave birth on the gravel verge. Three other Rwandan women gathered round. One cut the umbilical cord with a knife, the child was smacked, and the mother washed down with a bottle of dirty water. Then both parent and baby rejoined the flow of people.

'All Rwandan refugee camps around Zairean border town of Goma have emptied,' I dictated to Reuters. 'UN refugee agency and World Food Programme estimate between four and seven hundred thousand people on the move. Rwandan refugees say Mugunga camp with four hundred thousand people attacked over-night. Most moving back to Rwanda. Camp empty.'

At the side of the road lay the corpse of a man killed during the night's attack. His body lay sprawled in a scatter of brass cartridge cases and empty rifle-grenade containers. A mortar lay in the ditch. I stood two feet away from the flood of tramping, rushing feet and noted down all the details I could. Mattresses on heads, filthy blue plastic sheeting wrapped around bundles of possessions, yellow jerry-cans, maize sacks, sticks, logs, chickens, children, cooking-pans and machetes. One woman had both breasts hanging free from her cotton dress: a child sucked at one nipple, while a small goat licked at the other.

'Impasse broken; most refugees moving Rwanda-wards, says UNHCR. Interahamwe and militias retreating west into Zaire. Very few young men on the road. Mugunga and Lac Vert camps deserted. Rwandans keeping border open. No checks being made on returnees.'

I moved into the crowd. Mugunga refugee camp was at least five kilometres away and I was on foot. I couldn't move too far from the car because I needed to return to the hotel soon to file a longer report. Five hundred metres further on, a group of soldiers had formed a road-block. I slipped past and elbowed my way forward. A Browning machine-gun on a tripod lay on the verge, tipped side-ways. Next to it was a pile of cartridge cases. Three corpses stank in the ditch, tipped on their heads in a tumble onto the volcanic rock. The people moved on, their eyes fixed either ahead, or on the road beneath their feet; bowed under their loads, they trudged forwards in total silence. The only sound was a shush-shushing of half a million calloused feet brushing the warm tarmac. A vehicle from the Associated Press nosed through the mass, honking its horn. I sat on the tailgate for a kilometre. I needed to see for myself how far this stream of people stretched. I hopped off and stood on a large rock at the side of the road. As far as I could see, there was one, huge swarming mass of Rwandan refugees heading back home towards me.

I stood for five minutes and tried to make an accurate head-count. I worked out that twenty people were passing me every two seconds. If I stood there on my rock for fifteen minutes, 9,000 people would go past me. Or would it be 20,000? Or 15,000? It was impossible to make an accurate estimate, so dense was the mass of people. Perhaps, I thought, watching an old woman push five babies in a wheelbarrow, I should do it like this: if each metre of road was occupied by twenty people across, and they were on the move over fifteen kilometres, there were 300,000 on the move. Plus 30,000 at the Rwandan border already, another 30,000 still in the camp, that made 360,000 people heading back to Rwanda. Figures of a hundred thousand up or down would be impossible to estimate today, I thought. But who cared? The deadlock was broken; no international intervention force would be coming to Zaire to free the refugees from the interahamwe and former government soldiers. In one morning, the situation in the Great Lakes Region had shifted completely.

I walked still further up the road. The volcanic rock of the lava plains started at the edge of the road: there were the same eucalyptus trees, banana plantations and mango trees as in Rwanda and Burundi. On the horizon were the peaks of the three active volcanoes of the Virunga National Park. To my right was the grey sheen of Lake Kivu.

We'd been asleep in the hotel in Goma the night before when the camps had been attacked by Rwandan troops and the Zairean Tutsi rebels they had trained for the operation. It was clear that the interahamwe and ex-FAR had made some sort of a stand. The outer perimeter of Mugunga camp was surrounded by little bunkers made out of volcanic rock. Corpses of FAR and interahamwe were scattered here and there. So too were those of civilians whom the interahamwe militias had killed in an attempt to force the refugees to flee with them into Zaire. A hundred metres further on, sunflowers grew by the side of the road and the air smelled. In among the big yellow flowers was a pile of eleven bodies; refugees who had been caught trying to leave the camps. On top of the pile was the naked, headless corpse of a woman who had had her stomach cut open. Green-grey ropes of intestines snaked down among the corpses underneath her. These people had been killed several days before because they were rotting and bloated. The woman's possessions had been emptied out of a suitcase on top of her; the ten other people in the pile had also been mutilated. I climbed back up onto the road and walked down to meet my driver, Christian, coming the other way.

Back at the Hotel Frontières, in my room overlooking the lake, I switched on my computer and started to write:

GOMA (Reuters) – 350,000 Rwandan refugees quit their camps outside the Zairean border of Goma on Wednesday and headed back to the border with Rwanda, officials from the UN refugee agency said.

Mugunga camp, which until today had held over 400,000 refugees was empty by mid morning after a night-time attack by troops belonging to Laurent Kabila's Democratic Alliance. Rwandan and Ugandan troops are also believed to have joined in the assault.

Nearly half a million refugees have been held hostage in the camp by soldiers and militiamen loyal to the regime of the former Rwandan government which presided over the slaughter of an estimated 850,000 Tutsis and politically moderate Hutus in the spring and early summer of 1994 . . .

It was just over two years since a million people from Kigali, Gisenyi and the north of Rwanda had fled into Zaire. And now, twenty-six months later, they were pouring over the border back home at the rate of three hundred a minute. For the RPA in Kigali, and General Kagame, it was a triumph. The camps had been emptied by force and the threat to Rwanda's security had been removed. The militias and the ex-FAR had either fled further west into Zaire, or had come back home. The task that the United Nations and the international community had never been able to achieve, of separating the true refugees from the genocidal war-criminals, had been carried out. It had, in the final reckoning, needed a vast amount of force, as everybody had known it would, but international intervention had not had to be mobilized. The Rwandans and the Zairean Tutsis had done it for themselves.

If the logistical and military support behind the Rwandan government army and the Hutu power youth militias between 1988–1994 had been French, then that required to break their stranglehold on the Zairean refugee camps was American. The genesis of the attack on Mugunga camp had started in the early summer of that year.

In July 1996, weeks after I left Burundi, the Burundian army carried out its long-expected coup d'état. I was on holiday in England when I read an article in a Sunday newspaper about Burundi. There had been yet another massacre, this time of some 360 Tutsis by the Hutu rebels, carried out on the wind-blown plain at Bugendana, on the way to Gitega. The slaughter had coincided with the presence in the country of a team of journalists. There was extensive coverage of the massacre. On the front page of the *Independent* had been a photograph of a dead Tutsi. A few days later, President Sylvestre Ntibantunganya had travelled by helicopter to Bugendana for the mass funeral. Tutsi hardliners, troops and militiamen were in place. The ceremony had dissolved into chaos; stones and bricks were thrown. Sylvestre was escorted back to his chopper by his bodyguards, and on his return to the capital, had taken refuge in the American Embassy. Two days later the army had formally declared a coup d'état. The Tutsi former president, Major Pierre Buyoya, had taken power. This, then, had been the plan that Colonel Daradangwe and his henchmen had been plotting that day I had interrupted them in Charles Mukasi's office.

Buyoya took power, and among the first tasks he addressed was the repatriation of the Rwandan refugees from Burundi. By August I was back in Rwanda as the Reuters correspondent. The Burundian army surrounded the four camps in the north of their country, around Ngozi, and announced that they were going to push the 150,000-plus refugees back to Rwanda. Hitoshi Mise and his team from UNHCR protested, as did Geneva, but as soon as they realized that the Burundian army were serious, they closed the camps. For two weeks at the end of August, I travelled backwards and forwards from Kigali to Butare, and the Burundian border, watching the UN trucks roll home. Reports from the camps at the other side of the frontier were that the repatriation was not quite the voluntary idyll that UNHCR was making out. It had been carried out with the full cooperation of the Burundian army, which had beaten refugees to make them board trucks, burned their shelters, and shot those who tried to flee into the hills. But by-and-large, the repatriation was peaceful, if not exactly voluntary, and by the beginning of September, some 200,000 people were trying to settle back into the communes they had left over two years before.

For Major-General Paul Kagame and his high command in Kigali, it was time to turn attention to Zaire. Kagame had made a visit to the United States in July 1996, explaining that the international community had one last chance to do something about the camps in Zaire, with their populations of intimidators, militiamen and former Rwandan government soldiers. It was clear that the UN were not, by now, going to undertake the task of separating those Rwandan refugees who were holding the innocent refugees as hostages.

During September and early October, my reports from Kigali started to include accounts of fighting in eastern Zaire's South Kivu province. This was taking place between a large group of ethnic Zairean Tutsis and Mobutu's corrupt, looting rag-bag army, the FAZ, or Forces Armées Zaireoises. There were frequent clashes in the area of Uvira, on the northern tip of Lake Tanganyika. Refugees were starting to get restless. Zairean Tutsi refugees started to appear on Rwanda's borders. By late September, a man named Muller

Ruhambika had taken to calling the large house in Kigali in which I lived, claiming to be the spokesman for this group of ethnic Zaireans. The Mulenge, he said, were a people almost entirely made up of Zaireans – with full Zairean nationality, rights of residence, identity papers – who had lived in the region for over three hundred years. They were Zairean Tutsis, many had come from Rwanda in the troubled years between 1959 to 1994, and almost all of them spoke Kinyarwanda.

I met Muller for a cup of coffee at Kigali's Hotel Mille Collines. I explained that I had been in Burundi for nearly seven months that year, and my view of Rwandan events in particular, and the Great Lakes Region in general, had become blinkered by events in Burundi. (This was true. When I arrived in Kigali in August, I was astounded to discover that it was a country where UN staff were bringing their children. There were even backpackers on the streets of Kigali; life was, as a rule, peaceful and social.) I told him that I had become too immersed in the massacre politics of Burundi, the constant paranoia of the Tutsi militias and the curfew culture. He said he understood. The Tutsis in North Kivu province, from the hills above Goma, had been having a difficult time of it recently. The ex-FAR and the interahamwe from the Goma camps had set about chasing the Tutsi from the fertile, agricultural heartland of North Kivu's Masisi region, an area of high, grass pasture and forest, stretching back along the far western shore of Lake Kivu. A variety of ethnic sub-groups – Nande, Hunde, Tutsi – had coexisted in comparative harmony prior to the arrival of the Hutu cadres with the refugees in 1994. But recently, he said, things had dissolved into anarchy. Interahamwe militiamen and FAR soldiers, as well as rogue Zaireans, were trying to carve out a new homeland for themselves, a new Hutu state, on the lush heartland of the Masisi. There had been massacres, populations had been displaced, the machete, as it were, had been removed from its scabbard. It went without saying that the United Nations agencies, whose personnel had been involved full time since 1994 in catering to every logistical whim of the *genocidaires* in the Goma camps, were untouched by the situation in the Masisi.

The UNHCR tended to deal in polarized situations: the words

black and white, good and bad, refugee and persecutor, came from the vocabulary they understood. The majority of the UNHCR's officials in eastern Zaire between 1994 and 1996 found the complexities of conflicting Zairean ethnicities went beyond their comprehension. There were Rwandan refugees, they had to be looked after, and Geneva and Sadako Ogata had to be kept happy. That, for UNHCR, was life.

By October 1996, said Muller, taking another cup of coffee, these anomalies had taken their toll on South Kivu. With the camps around Bukavu and Uvira, there were some 500,000 Rwandan Hutu refugees in South Kivu, as well as a large detachment of the FAZ in Bukavu town and Uvira. The local Zairean Tutsis, the Banyamulenge, were suffering at their hands, and at the hands of the Rwandan interahamwe. The offices of a Banyamulenge NGO, called MULIMA, had been burnt; churches, offices and businesses had been attacked. But the Banyamulenge were fighting back. There had been fighting in and around Uvira with the Zairean soldiers and their militia henchmen. In September I had driven south to Gitarama for the day, to a church courtyard where forty widows from South Kivu told how they had been forced to take refuge in Rwanda after the Zairean army had drowned and hanged their husbands.

For the Kigali government, the situation in South Kivu provided part of the answer to how they might solve the problems posed by the refugee camps near their borders. The Banyamulenge were Kinyarwanda-speaking Tutsis, and thus deserving of Rwandan government help. If they could be recruited and trained by the RPA inside Rwanda, and sent back into Zaire with Rwandan officers, then a force would be in place to demolish the camps. Furthermore, General Kagame saw that President Mobutu Sese Seko's corrupt, anarchic and sprawling Zairean republic would always pose a distinct threat to Rwandan stability. Why not try and kill two birds with one stone?

Since late spring of 1996, the Kigali government had been in negotiation with Laurent Desiree Kabila, the gold and opium smuggler who did business with the Cibitoke colonels in Burundi. Kabila was from the Shaba area of Zaire, and did not speak Kinyarwanda; he certainly was not one of the Banyamulenge. He had fought against the Kinshasha government in the 1960s under the rebel leader Mulele. He claimed also to have fought briefly under Che Guevara in the Congo. He based himself in South Kivu, selling illicitly mined, unlicensed gold, and small amounts of opium, to any buyer who came along. By 1996 this included, of course, the genocidal Tutsis of Burundi's army. He drank too much, was unprepossessing, unreliable, severely overweight and none too bright. However, he hated Mobutu, had the ear of the breakaway Zairean factions and he was available. By the end of October, he had welded the four main groups together. The Popular Revolutionary Party of Shaba, the National Resistance Council for Democratic Kasaii, the Revolutionary Movement for the Liberation of Zaire and the Democratic Alliance of the Banyamulenge people became one. The Alliance of Democratic Forces for the Liberation of Congo-Zaire, the ADFL, was born.

'Effectively,' said Muller, that day by the pool in Kigali, 'the aim is to continue the fight against the Zairean army. One day we will sweep to Kinshasa and see the Atlantic.'

Yeah, yeah, I thought, smiling and waving for the waiter.

By the last week in October, fighting between the ADFL and the Zairean army was cracking backwards and forwards across the Luberizi plateau, north of Uvira and along the western edge of the Rusizi river. Rwandan instructors had trained the ADFL cadres in camps set in the Kagera National Park, on the Tanzanian border. The RPA in their turn had been assisted by American Special Forces teams brought in from one of the Green Beret battalions from Fort Bragg in North Carolina. These soldiers had actually crossed into Zaire with the RPA, through Cibitoke province in Burundi, and had clashed with the Zaireans. The Zaireans in and around the town of Bukavu had responded to Rwanda's hostilities by trading fire across the Rusizi river between Bukavu and Cyangugu. I had spent three nights in Cyangugu, three hundred metres away from the lake, watching Zairean anti-aircraft fire coming in towards Rwanda.

On 8 October, the deputy governor of South Kivu, Ngabo Lwabanji, had given the Banyamulenge a week to quit Zaire. He had rescinded their Zairean nationalities. It was the last card to be played. If they had not left after a week, they would be considered to be in open war with the Zaireans. Major-General Kagame's last appeal to the international community came the following week during an emotive visit to Israel, where he burst into tears at the Holocaust memorial at Vad Yeshem. With Ezir Weizemann and Shimon Peres at his side, he made one last request, that the UNHCR deprive all the suspects in the Goma camps of any weapons. The government also declared itself surprised to see humanitarian relief being given indiscriminately to innocents and to criminals. It called, for the last time, on the international community to take action to break the deadlock around the refugee camps.

By 18 October, Rwanda, the RPA and the ADFL had made their move. After a week of continued fighting between the Alliance and the Zaireans in South Kivu, the ADFL attacked all eleven of the refugee camps around Uvira.

'Two hundred and twenty-one thousand of them are moving north towards Rwanda,' said UNHCR's Paul Stromberg. 'There are sizeable military incursions from Rwanda.'

By the following day attacks had begun on the camps around Bukavu, including Panzi with its huge continent of ex-FAR and interahamwe. The United Nations and other aid organizations fled to Kigali. By 27 October, the United Nations in Rwanda, under the auspices of its charming head, Omar Bakhet, was still making plans about what to do if there was a sizeable return of refugees to Rwanda. He prided himself on understanding Rwandan thinking, yet he seemed to be blind to what was going on in front of his nose. However, in the time-honoured UN tradition of confronting crisis with vacillation, he told me that day:

'A logistical plan is going to be put together whereby all the UN agencies and implementing partners (NGOs) will put together a plan . . . to be presented to the UN Department of Humanitarian Affairs.'

Meanwhile his beloved UN staff recruited to work in hazardous situations were scrambling onto Beechcraft at Bukavu airport as the refugee camps on the hills outside town came under fire. The UNHCR in Kigali was still talking about basing the Uvira refugees 'further' inside Zaire, seventy kilometres away from Rwanda, from where repatriation would be difficult. They didn't add that such camps would, of course, require increased numbers of UNHCR staff, increased budgets, increased dependency on the Zairean army, not to mention the questionable wisdom of camping quarter of a million people, a large proportion of them guilty of genocide, in the middle of a jungle.

As soon as the refugees began to move from the southern stretch of Bukavu camps towards Rwanda, the Alliance started northwards using every stolen aid vehicle on which they could lay their hands. They had camouflaged many of the white four-wheel-drive Nissans and Toyotas by splashing on zebra stripes with black house paint. The Alliance Forces, commanded in many instances by Ugandan and Rwandan officers, drove up the track on the far side of Lake Kivu. Soon they were within a few kilometres of the Goma camps of Katale, Kahindo, Kibumba, Mugunga and Lac Vert. Katale, Kahindo and Kibumba were swiftly attacked, one after the other, and their refugee population of 500,000 moved in all directions. Some went west into Zaire, some north along the Ugandan border, and a pathetic nine individuals asked the UNHCR to take them back to Rwanda. But the vast majority followed their intimidators, the interahamwe, the ex-FAR and their former communal leaders, and settled in and around the outskirts of Mugunga camp.

'There are around five hundred and thirty thousand refugees in Mugunga,' UNHCR's Paul Stromberg told me on the twenty-seventh. 'There are the populations of Kahindo camp, some from Katale and Kibumba, and the population of Lac Vert has joined them as well. There are an estimated two hundred thousand refugees outside the camp. And another three hundred and twenty thousand in the rest of eastern Zaire.' He paused for effect. 'Mugunga camp is now the largest concentration of refugees in one camp in the world.'

He paused. He was one of very few people within the organization who seemed to have a decent sense of perspective. All of us wondered why he worked for them. Still, even this late in the day, when the

UNHCR's battle was so clearly lost, their largest Great Lakes operation a failure, Stromberg tried to keep their ragged, compromised standard flying.

'We're doing what we can . . . Hygiene is going to be a problem, but we are working on CDAs.'

'CDAs?'

'Communal Defecating Areas.'

Plane-loads of Zairean reinforcements started arriving at the airport in Goma. Sixty thousand refugees were still straggling down the approach road from Katale. The thousands of heavily armed interahamwe, ex-FAR and the FAZ moved north to three kilometres south of Kibumba. From there they encircled Mugunga, surrounded the hundreds of thousands of refugees, established defensive positions and prepared to fight it out with the Tutsis on the volcanic lava plain at Mugunga.

I drove north to Gisenyi that day and camped in the Meridien Hotel on the shores of Lake Kivu. It was calm and quiet for a couple of days, and I and four others had the run of the rooms. Then our reports started to be picked up and the hotel filled with journalists from every corner of the earth. First in were the wire agencies from Nairobi, along with the BBC and French radio and newspapers. Then came the British newspapers, also from Kenya, along with CNN and the major American printmen. Reinforcements arrived from Johannesburg, and after that it became anybody's guess. Suddenly there were American TV networks, radio journalists from Bavaria, a newspaper from Mexico. Even the Swiss managed to get somebody in. October turned into November and the Alliance soldiers mortared their way into Goma. One evening I stood on the lawn listening to a Greek TV correspondent ask which country he was in.

The Alliance forces, with their Rwandan and Ugandan colleagues, spent nearly three weeks preparing the final attack on Mugunga camp. The showdown on the Goma lava fields was being organized like a game of military and diplomatic chess. The journalists, who by the beginning of November numbered 139, were allowed across the frontier into the town of Goma itself, where they duly pitched camp at the Frontières Hotel. Run by a small, nervous Belgian expatriate called Marcel, the hotel charged the dollar-laden correspondents up to a hundred and fifty dollars each per night, in many cases to sleep five to a room. There was no access to Mugunga camp, and little to see or do. While the world's aid agencies sounded warnings that the half a million refugees could be perishing from famine and cholera, the UN cobbled together a plan for an international intervention force. Why half a million people who had lived together for two years without succumbing to mass epidemic should suddenly start dying was never explained. They were refugees, said the UN, and therefore vulnerable. They had limited food-stocks, there were an awful lot of them crowded together in one place, so *de facto* disaster had to follow. The refugees were the final card in the hand of UNHCR: their continued presence in Mugunga meant the continuation of the UNHCRs' presence in eastern Zaire. The UN Security Council formulated a number of options, none of which came to fruition. To allow the return to Rwanda of the innocent refugees meant attacking the camps and using physical force to kill or displace the ex-FAR and the interahamwe who were using the mass of bedraggled Hutus as a human shield. Who would carry out this onerous task? Kabila and his henchmen sat in Goma and Bukavu declaring that they would resist by force any attempted intervention by the French, who had, they said, a hidden agenda. US troops, Canadians, British paratroopers, all were put forward as potential saviours of the Hutus. I leant one night on the bar in the Frontières with Sam Kiley from the *Times*, discussing the massive free-for-all firefight that would result in any confrontation between the interahamwe and the British Parachute Regiment. No greater cultural clash could be imagined. It would be the basis of a TV series, we decided: *Great Moments of Violence* – Part One. Festus and Clovis from the Interahamwe meet Nobby and Ginge from 3 Para Mortars.

The Hutu militants had the Alliance positions in Goma under surveillance. The rocket-positions and observation posts of the Tutsi gunners were on Mount Goma, a 300-metre-high rise set just behind the Hotel Frontières, and exactly in the line of fire from any incoming fire from Mugunga. Artillery and mortar rounds landed close to the building; some journalists took to wearing flak-jackets in the corridors. My first experience of mortar-fire had come two weeks previously on the Zairean border when the FAZ had lobbed five 82mm mortar-rounds into the town of Gisenyi. Three had landed short, within a hundred metres or so of where six of us were lying in the cover of a deserted customs post. The incoming whistle and thump as the volcanic rock was blown to smithereens was frightening in the extreme. The artillery fire coming in over the hotel was little better.

The Rwandan government were denying that they had dispatched any of their troops across the border into Zaire. The fighting was, they claimed, being carried out by the forces of Laurent Kabila. Major Emmanuel Ndahiro, military spokesman to Major-General Paul Kagame, held a press conference in early November at the Meridien Hotel in Gisenyi.

'We have categorically no intention of going into Zaire,' explained the languid major. 'We have limited our response to our borders. We do not, however, support any idea of military intervention.'

Ndahiro was not speaking the truth. I had been among a small party of journalists that had crossed the border in the first days of November, while the fight for Goma was still going on. We had ducked under the Rwandan frontier barrier, and moved very cautiously forward. This was the no man's land between the two countries where, two years before, I had arrived in Zaire with Beverley. We scuttled up the fifty metres of road while anti-aircraft rounds, machine-gun bullets and artillery rattled overhead. The border-post was deserted. A team of Rwandan commandos landed from Lake Kivu in a small rubber boat to our left. We filmed them touching down in Zaire.

Later in the day, we went back into Rwanda and then back to Zaire. This time a Rwandan government information officer came with us. He had dressed for the occasion. In ninety degrees heat, he had put on a brand-new pair of black Wellington boots. He accompanied us across into the first kilometre of Zairean territory, proudly saying that the Rwandan soldiers we had seen land that morning were not Rwandans but 'indisciplined elements from the lake'.

When I reached the UNHCR building in Goma an hour later I was by myself. The gates to the compound were open. I went in. Firing was going on all over the town. I hugged the wall and ventured onto the lawn. There, sprawled unconscious, was an Alliance rebel soldier. A Primus bottle had flopped into the tropical grass at the end of his outstretched hand. He was snuffling quietly in his sleep through the largest pair of nostrils I had ever seen. He was wearing a faded camouflage uniform, blue and red tennis shoes with no laces, and a green cotton hat. His Chinese machine-gun lay across his chest, its linked brass cartridge-belt rising and falling with his deep slumbering breath. I walked on. The main door had been smashed in, and the building looted. It was from this building that UNHCR had held sway for two years over the lives and fortunes of a million refugees. It was from this building that their catering operation had been run from which the ex-FAR and the inter-ahamwe had benefited so profoundly. It was from here that their humanitarian empire, with its own self-justifying rules and regulations, had been governed. That was all over now. It was with a sudden jump of childish pleasure that I noticed a long, curling brown turd that somebody had laid right in the centre of the head delegate's smashed desk.

Suddenly there was a crash behind me; I turned quickly. The soldier was standing in the broken door-frame, dragging his weapon, his trousers slipping down. He was smiling.

'I,' he said, 'I am the man.'

I smiled back.

'I am the man that liberated this building.'

Then he fell over again. After a bit, he walked on into the building and the two of us went through the broken UNHCR safe to see if there was anything of interest in it. Nothing. Just tens of thousands of UN telephone cards for their own integral communications system. We left them, and after a bit wandered out into the sun. We sat on the steps, I gave him a cigarette, and we smoked silently together for five minutes. It was one of those moments that occur often in Africa; neither party was thinking of anything apart from the fact that the sun was warm, the town was liberated, and smoking made you feel good.

By the time the Alliance was ready for its attack on Mugunga, no firm decisions had been made with regard to an international intervention force. Canadians had arrived in Kigali, as part of a reconnaissance effort, but that was it. Most of the journalists suspected that the United States, at the request of the Rwandans and the Ugandans, had blocked the idea of intervention at the level of the UN Security Council. The Alliance were able to complete their preparations for their assault on Mugunga without the irksome presence of any international monitors getting in the way.

A week before the camp was attacked, five of us skirted the Alliance and interahamwe road-blocks and drove to the empty camp of Katale. It was a forty-eight-kilometre drive, moving northwards at a right angle to Mugunga. We drove through the back streets of Goma and then cut through the banana plantations. Mugunga was now on our far left. This was uncharted territory; the interahamwe could be anywhere. We were, in fact inside the huge offensive ring that the Alliance forces had constructed around Mugunga camp, but outside the Hutu defensive ring. In other words, no man's land. I was disobeying one of the three primary safety rules of journalism:

  i. Never film or photograph a retreating army.
 ii. Never get caught between two front lines.
iii. Never refuse Slivovitz from a rebel commander. (This had been invented in Bosnia, so didn't really apply.)

We were caught between two front lines as we drove. The road up from Goma to Katale camp was mined; I watched the wheels of our Land Cruiser slide past the holes in the road from which two anti-tank mines had been removed. The offending devices sat on the gravel verge, like large, grey iron cowpats. There must be others ahead buried in the surface of the road. We drove forward slowly, Innocent, the driver, keeping exactly in the tyre-tracks of the vehicle that had gone before us. Had the mines been laid before or after that vehicle had driven this way? Had the vehicle that had gone ahead of us been blown up? Who had laid the mines? Had they been properly fused? Did I want to die? Would it hurt? Common sense told me that if you are sitting at the bottom of a road in rebel-held territory between two opposing African armies in the middle of a vicious ethnic conflict, then you are in quite a bad way. If you have discovered, but only after driving three kilometres of its length, that the road up which you intend to drive for forty-eight kilometres has been laid with anti-tank mines, then you're in a really bad way. You're also stuck. How many mines are there ahead? How many behind? If you are three kilometres up the length of this forty-eight-kilometre road, and you've discovered that it is laid with anti-tank mines, and probably anti-personnel mines as well, and you insist on driving on, then you're nuts. If you insist on driving the full forty-eight kilometres, then you have a death wish.

There were six of us driving up this road, in two vehicles, all in varying stages of fear. These stages could be listed as follows:

i. Least afraid, or best capable of hiding it: Sam Kiley, *The Times*. His theory was that loads of people had driven up this road, it wasn't really mined, and anyway, there were local people walking up and down it so it was probably safe.

ii. Quite afraid, but phlegmatic, and calmly gung-ho: James Furlong, Sky TV. He thought Sam was probably right, and anyway, you don't know what's going to happen unless you move forward.

iii. Reasonably afraid, but acting as the voice of reason: Mariella Furrer, agency photographer.

iv. Frightened, but having no choice: Innocent the driver. It should be added that Innocent had seen his house in Gisenyi take a direct mortar hit a week before, and had shrugged it off, saying 'It's only a house. I can get another one.'

Also travelling with us that day up the road was Mark Chisholm, one of Reuters TV's top cameramen. While displaying a jaunty calmness and sang-froid in the face of adversity, South African Mark admitted that it was still a rather risky venture.

v. Routinely terrified, desperate to turn back, making no pretence at hiding fear: Christian Jennings, Reuters.

We drove on. Presently we swished past a lone Zimmer-frame standing deserted in the middle of the road. Alongside it was the rush and detritus of tens of thousands of refugees who had passed this way. The frame would have made a good photo, I thought, stark against the skyline of volcanoes, mountains and forests. Five kilometres later we still hadn't driven over a mine and had already passed the empty camp of Kibumba. No other journalists had been this far, I thought. Hmmm. Perhaps we won't run into the interahamwe. Another three kilometres and we ran into forty-seven-year-old Denis Manibaho, jogging along at the side of the road after a morning of light looting.

'Kahindo camp is empty. I haven't seen anybody hostile on the road.'

I said nothing as the others decided to drive on. At the beginning of the Virunga forest we stopped sharp. There had been an ambush here. An open-backed truck had swerved across the road, blown-up and burnt out. The road was scorched, the gravel blackened by burning fuel. The smell of corpses hung in the air. We counted four bodies lying in the ditch, and another two lying at the edge of the road. Five hundred metres further on was a large green 'Safari Bus Express' coach burned to pieces. It was full of rotten corpses and several hundred-weight of carbonized potatoes; we guessed the interahamwe had tried to escape from Kibumba camp in this vehicle, and run into an Alliance ambush that had outcircled them. Shell-cases lay on the road. Two more bodies lay at the entrance to the woods. GIFT OF JAPAN TO RWANDA, said the lettering on the side of the bus. The militias would have fled to Zaire in this two years before. We pushed on, through the dense green forest overhang, our tyres singing on the crisp gravel road until we saw Kahindo camp to our left. Then, ahead, was Katale. I breathed in hard. We'd got there. No mines. We were fifty kilometres ahead of everybody else. It was time to have a quick look, scout around a bit, then whizz back to Goma.

As recently as ten days before, the refugee camp of Katale had held anything up to 200,000 people. Now it was empty. Thousands and thousands of trashed, rotting, looted shelters stretched to the horizon. Their roofs had been stripped of their blue plastic covering, the ubiquitous material marked with the UNHCR symbol, known to Rwandan refugees as *le sheeting*. I walked around the edges of the camp. A bloated woman's corpse lay face down in the water of a stream. Underfoot was a rain-soaked pair of dead rats, a broken machete and a teddy-bear. There were bamboo shops and houses, two-storey video parlours, aisles, alleyways and lanes dividing up the little hutments. Everything was made of sticks, wooden poles and bamboo. Here and there was a metal support. The mud around the shelters had been churned by the flight of thousands. Above the trickle of the stream, over the maggoty humps of the occasional corpse, only a vast silence lay in the lunchtime heat. The air burned yellow-grey to the horizon. The refugee camp had been kept vibrant and functioning for two years by the presence of thousands of people. What was left amounted to little more than looted stands of bamboo and firewood blowing rotten and deserted in the calm rise and fall of the African breeze.

I stood in the mud, poked in the stream and scraped my boot in the ashes of a hut before it was time to go. There were reports of a massacre further on, but there was a knot of Alliance rebels at a road-block 200 metres away and I didn't want to get stopped. Innocent spun the wheel, I lit up, and Mark, Mariella and I were back at the Frontières for lunchtime filing and a cheese-and-ham sandwich.

The Hutu Power militants in Mugunga camp were slamming 120mm mortar rounds into the area around the hotel two days later. There was a mid-morning flurry of rumour, whispers of a press conference. Somehow, most of the journalists scattered around the environs of Goma got wind, and we all turned up to meet Laurent Kabila. The rebel leader of the Alliance chose a fitting place to meet the press: President Mobutu's former Goma palace. Three kilo-metres out of town on the edge of the lake, the dictator's Goma residence was a three-building complex set behind barred gates. There was a scatter of cartridge cases, some discarded weaponry, half-burnt scraps of paper lying in the dust of the entrance, but otherwise the building was intact. Sam Kiley and a band of other early birds had arrived some days before for a spot of looting. Kiley called it 'affirmative shopping'. The despotic president's eastern palace was the ultimate in dictator chic. There were the white marble floors, the sunken bathrooms, the king-sized beds that might be found in the Surrey lounge of some gilded porn-magnate. There were the revolving sleeping-areas, the conversation pits in mock white Chesterfield. There were the beige sliding-front wardrobes that still held the sequinned gaudiness of some long-fled Zairean mistress. The bathrooms had catering-size bottles of Aramis and Chanel, eight litres at a time. In the back rooms were cases of high-velocity ammunition, racks of M-16 assault rifles, sealed boxes of rifle-grenades. But the most fitting metaphor for the dying, decaying president and his dying, decayed republic were in the bathroom cupboards. There were perhaps one hundred maxi packs of Always sanitary towels, in an absorbency that could probably only be described as international. Alongside them were a few packs of Pampers. Mobutu had prostate cancer, and was doubly incontinent. As journalists stretched their wings across the vast country of Zaire in the next few months, and more and more of Mobutu's summer houses, dachas and temporary residences fell to the rebels, so the absorbency and bulk of the nappies and sanitary towels increased.

'Our target is to reach Kinshasa,' said Laurent Desiree Kabila, rebel leader, gold and opium smuggler, and puppet of the Rwandan government.

Sitting in a gilt-trimmed armchair, the plump, cannonball-headed man in the beige safari suit looked every inch the African dictator he was to become. His correspondent brown leather-and-canvas shoes fitted the image he wanted to project: friend of the people, egalitarian leader, liberator.

'We are very clear about what we are doing here. If we attack the camp [of Mugunga] to push out the killers, the international community will start crying again. The solution may be that the UN can come through our corridors and negotiate with people in those camps. But they . . . must stop people shelling us; how can we continue to be silent when they are killing people here? In a few days, if the shelling continues, we might have to do something.'

Such as?

'Our next step is to launch an offensive.'

There was a scribble of notes.

'We need impartial soldiers to come and help us, countries like Sweden, Mali. But can we wait two weeks for them?'

The answer was no, he couldn't. Nobody really took Laurent Kabila seriously: everybody could see the hands of the Rwandans, the Ugandans, the Americans at work behind him. What mattered was that there was seen to be an African solution to the problem. Kabila's message was: we're doing this ourselves. The US, backing and observing every move, hovered everywhere. Literally. Orion reconnaissance aircraft buzzed over Goma and Lake Kivu tracking the refugees; satellites phased over the region taking images. Refugees were quantified, estimated, the figures and their locations passed to Kabila. The perimeters of Mugunga were clearly delineated; the Alliance forces moved into place.

The attack on Mugunga took place at night. The Alliance put their strongest forces to the west of the camp, with their backs to the Zairean interior. This allowed a weaker exit line on the east for all the refugees to move back to Rwanda. The plan worked perfectly. Five days after the attack, 600,000 people had upped sticks, hit the hot, tarmac chippings, and taken the road east back home. Those were the days I spent driving up and down the road between Goma and the village of Sake; sitting in a purring Toyota Land Cruiser crunching up and down the miles of road that had once been the heart of Mugunga.

Two days after the camp fell we drove right through it. The outskirts of Mugunga started about three kilometres from Goma. The camp then stretched for sixteen kilometres. From there to the village of Sake was another three. For two weeks that stretch of road became my life. The ex-FAR and the interahamwe had mostly taken up positions facing west towards the village of Sake. When we went through the camps, this is where we found the majority of their traces, the military equipment, the defensive positions. There was one stretch of road which turned out to be particularly interesting.

The moment the camp had come under attack, the interahamwe and the FAR, especially the officers, had tried to flee. They had commandeered the green Japanese buses, cars, donkey-carts, anything with which to flee westwards into the Masisi, into the centre of Zaire, anywhere away from the area of the Rwandan border. As one UN official put it, 'they are heading due west into the heart of darkness'.

And many of them had run straight into the extensive ambushes that the Alliance, under their Rwandan tutors, had put in place for them. On one particular two-kilometre stretch of road near Sake, it looked as if the tens of thousands of Rwandan men, women and children terrorized by the interahamwe and FAR into accompanying them westward had dropped everything they were carrying. The road was buried, covered, piled with thousands and thousands of different, strange items, relics of two years in a refugee camp.

There were old white bras, new red knickers, army-issue gasmasks, tripods for 60mm mortar-tubes and biology textbooks from the 1970s Rwandan curriculum. There were three buckets of a hundred dead yellow chicks, some volcanic rock placed in an ammunition box and several maps of Rwanda. There were tens of thousands of condoms, some in and some out of their foil seals, there were pairs of army boots, tins of black paint, a jigsaw puzzle of Canada. Under a broken Uzi sub-machine gun was a huge portrait of President Juvenal Habyarimana. There were boxes, opened and unopened, of female Microgynon contraceptive pills, including one pack where the owner had taken the first of the month the previous Thursday. (The interahamwe had treated the camps as mobile breeding farms, and had taken to raping any unpregnant Hutu girls they found, urging every woman to breed more Hutus for the great new Rwandan empire.)

There were sacks of maize, tins of oil with bullet holes in them, bows, and arrows tipped with barbed, iron points. There were Italian assault rifles with the working-parts taken out, Uzi sub-machine-guns, live rounds everywhere, and three anti-tank mines. There were axes, rolls of linoleum, old military berets and items of military uniform, filing cabinets, and a wheelbarrow full of bath-plugs. There was a dead FAR soldier lying in the middle of all this, among medical documents, blackboard chalk, posters of the different breeds of cow, instruction manuals for Spanish anti-personnel mines, and a pencil drawing of a prawn. It was as though an entire second or third world civilization had been upended and left on the surface of the road, which was a foot deep in junk in some places.

And that was before we all got to the three green 'Gift of Japan' buses.

When, in 1994, the Rwandan government army – the FAR – had fled their country with the interim authorities and the interahamwe, they had taken the entire contents of the country's treasury with them. The country had just been taxed, so this amounted to several billion Rwandan francs. On top of that was a considerable sum in American dollars, all of the country's gold reserves, and any other money they could remove from the foreign exchange safes of the capital. This money had moved from Kigali to Gitarama, and thence on to Goma and Bukavu. Also removed from the country, and spread out across every inch of the road were thousands and thousands of papers of every description. Two of the buses were knee-deep in papers, documents, maps, folders and files. It was the national archive of the former Rwandan government, coupled with all the documentation that had been kept by the exiled leadership while in the camps. Here were detailed all the movements of the inter-ahamwe, all the training operations of the ex-FAR, all the arms purchases from abroad. It was a gold mine.

If ever proof was needed that the Hutu administration had been planning to reinvade Rwanda, then here it was. Here were the invoices, the order-forms, the confirmation of deliveries of arms sales. Here were the details of how UNHCR aid supplies had been sold and the profits used to buy weapons. Here were all the requests from former members of the FAR to their commanding officers for authorization to go on missions into Rwanda. One former sergeant in the FAR had been sent into Gisenyi province, across the lake by pirogue, with a mission to recruit 'Hutu intellectuals'. His report back was simple: he had not found any Hutus who could be considered remotely intelligent. Another FAR non-commissioned officer requested a transfer for training purposes to one of the refugee camps in Tanzania. The reply told him to put his application in writing to the UNHCR, claiming that he had family in Tanzania, and he would be duly transferred.

There were hundreds of such requests, hundreds of formal applications for 'duty'. It reminded me of the French Foreign Legion, where punishment reports had to be filled out in meticulous handwriting, with carefully measured spaces between the lines, and only a certain number of centimetres in the margin. In the mud and grime of Goma, the men of the former Rwandan army had made out their applications to return to fight in Rwanda. All of them were addressed either to Major-General Augustin Bizimana, the former defence minister, Augustin Bizimungu, the former chief of staff, or Theoneste Bagosora. The latter could not have received his letters of application. As the Defence Ministry cabinet head, and a leading member of the akazu of Agathe Habyarimana, he was a wanted man. The French Special Forces had evacuated him from Butare by helicopter in May 1994.

The FAR had kept its command structure completely intact for two years. It had separate divisions, based in Bukavu and Goma, and in Ngara and Benaco, Tanzania. There was a constant flow of men from one camp to another. Military training courses were held regularly. The army continued to function in the camps much as it had done in Rwanda. Logistics and transport was laid on by UNHCR, without their apparent knowledge. There were detailed lists of refugees, commune by commune, detailing how their village structure had been recreated in the Goma camps. Alongside these lists were figures showing the number of people claiming food from the UN and the actual number of people to whom it was being distributed. The interahamwe sold the surplus, pocketed the difference, and spent it on weaponry.

If one section of the camp contained 5,000 people, the interahamwe would claim for 5,500. In a camp of 130,000 people, for instance, this meant that 13,000 non-existent people were being supplied with food every week. The Hutu power structure operated markets in each of the camps where the local Zaireans would come to do their shopping. On sale would be maize, beans, oil, medical supplies, tools, seeds, farming equipment, plastic sheeting. Everything, in fact, that the refugees received free from UNHCR and its 'implementing partners'.

There was an absolutely direct commercial line that could be traced between the new weaponry and equipment carried by the FAR and the militias on their missions in Rwanda, and aid handouts from the UN.

As the teams of journalists picked through the remains of the refugee camps, the interahamwe and the FAR fled deeper into Zaire, fighting all the way. They went north towards Rutshuru and Butembo, along with the FAZ, and they went south along the west side of Lake Kivu, through Minova. They bomb-bursted all across the vast arable plateaux of the Masisi, killing as they went. The Alliance had laid concentric rings of troops around the camps through which the Hutus had to fight. A week after the camps had emptied, the Alliance were battling the fleeing gangs of militiamen and ex-FAR soldiers across the whole of North and South Kivu provinces. We followed behind, slowly. Most of the journalists sat behind in Goma in the Frontières Hotel, and once the refugees had gone back to Rwanda, they went back too. That was the story in which their editors were interested. How were hundreds of thousands of Hutus going to re-settle into the communes they had left two years before? Many were guilty of slaughtering their neighbours. How was this extraordinary social dynamic going to work?

Soon there were little more than ten of us left in Goma. Every day we would drive up to Sake, through the ruins of Mugunga, and try to follow the Alliance troops and the trail of bodies. On the first day we had arrived in Mugunga, thirty corpses of women and children, mainly little girls and boys under ten, were discovered lying in a jumbled heap by the Oxfam water tanks. They had been macheted by the interahamwe, and left to die. An American photographer discovered baby twins still alive, and took them to a Médecins sans

Frontières Land Cruiser on the road. Two days later, I passed the pile of corpses again. A stream of clear water was running over them from a pipe attached to the tanks. One of the boys, perhaps eight or ten, had been revived by the flow. He had a massive head-wound from a machete, but was groaning quietly in the pile of death. The heap of bodies occupied a patch of volcanic rock perhaps three metres by three. Even standing directly over them it was difficult to count how many dead there were, so intertwined were the smashed limbs, the eviscerated stomachs, the crushed babies' skulls. I passed the boy on to an aid doctor. Almost nobody was left in the camp who could say why the women and children had been killed. One old man told a journalist that they had come from Katale, and were strangers. Another man, standing by the pushed-over weaved bamboo of his shelter said it was the interahamwe who had done it. Part of an operation to terrorize the other refugees into following them into the heart of darkness. Twenty metres further away there were another four corpses.

Along the edges of the roads lay the dead and dying refugees who did not have the strength to make it any further. The sun was hot. Many of them were dehydrated and some had walked from Bukavu. Journalists and aid workers driving back and forth from Sake took into their cars those they reckoned had a chance. What could be done was done. I tried to resuscitate a dehydrated old man lying by the side of the road. His throat was too dry to swallow, however. The litre of mineral water I was pouring into his mouth went straight into his lungs. He drowned two minutes later.

Under a large mango tree on the outskirts of Sake lay the corpse of a woman, half covered by a stretch of sheeting. In a deep crevice in the volcanic rock ten metres from the road there was a familiar stink. Five foot down, through the stalks of the sunflowers, there was a man's corpse, his arms tied behind his back with coarse rope. One forearm was chopped off, and lay beside him. By a collapsed tent at the edge of the refugee camp lay the bloated green corpse of a woman who had been macheted while giving birth. The baby poked half way out of her. On the beginning of the tarmac and dirt road that led into the foothills of the Masisi, there was the evidence of flight curtailed. Here was a group of eight women and children, scattered face down in the road, macheted. A tiny baby strapped to its mother's back had its skull smashed open like the top of a boiled egg. Their bundles of possessions were everywhere. This could have been the Alliance, it could have been the interahamwe or FAR. Perhaps they had been killed because they couldn't keep up. Further on were two burnt-out four-wheel-drive vehicles. The tarmac was blackened and greasy; the tyres had melted and caught fire. Four rotting corpses lay twisted in the road. A dusty crow had pushed its head up the trouser-leg of one body. It was tugging something out.

Mass death has an energy born of the urgency and extreme chaos that it brings with it. Around every corner was the sodden, decapitated, disembowelled, macheted, hacked-up, limbless, amputated and eviscerated detritus of violent ethnic polarization. Up a steep track, where the bramble bushes and honey-suckle flowered close to the path, there was a road-block. Two teenage Alliance soldiers in snow-washed denim jeans, black Wellington boots, black berets and t-shirts stood at a crest in the path. It was too narrow to reverse. They blocked the way forward. Their Kalashnikov assault rifles swung lazily towards us. There was movement, noise, in the village ahead of us. Something was going on.

'Please; you must go back. There is nothing to see here.'

The bushes formed a solid barrier at the side of the road: the only way off the track was through a narrow gap in the vegetation, two feet wide, which led down the side of the hill. I moved towards it, motioning to open my flies.

'Do not go down there. If you go down there you will have problems.'

The teenage soldiers did not move, just stood in front of us. I undid my flies, shuffling forward inches at a time. A narrow path rose up three feet through the gap in the hedge, then curved down; just around the corner of it I could see the first bodies.

'Do not go down there. Not at all going down there, Sir. Problems.'

The soldiers were a completely unknown quantity; we didn't know if they would open fire, arrest us, steal our cameras, or what. I moved forward, craning my head. I could see three children, one woman and one man lying in the lolling, hurled-about way that corpses have. They were on the edge of a large pile of bodies. I moved forward six more inches.

'No!'

The soldier moved forward. I moved back. We reversed the vehicle and left.

'How many?' asked Alistair the cameraman.

'I saw five. Right on the edge of a huge pile. Perhaps forty. Perhaps two hundred. Couldn't say.'

'They were killing in that village,' he said, lighting a Marlboro. 'You could just tell. Just doing everybody.'

At Kirotshe hospital, south of Sake, twenty wounded patients told me that on the night Mugunga was attacked, three hundred ex-FAR soldiers had fled through the village. The interahamwe had followed, shouting, stealing anything they could. They'd quarrelled over the price of some bottles of soda, then killed three people with their machetes when they'd got bored of arguing. They'd moved up behind Kirotshe, into the Masisi, said the patients. Two hours further along the deeply rutted track, two hours of painfully slow driving, of liquid mud splashing up to the windows, we came across several thousand refugees. They were mostly men, camped briefly at the side of the lake on their way west. A young man in pink tracksuit trousers and muddy bedroom slippers stood under a tree. He was flicking a Bic lighter, trying to smoke a Tampax.

'You don't understand,' another fit young man said to me, watching an old woman slump exhausted at the side of the road. 'We'd go back and do it all over again. And we're going to.'

The woman sat with her head in her hands, a bundle of sugar cane propped beside her, tied with grass. A muscular man wearing beige corduroys dropped his trousers next to her. He squirted five seconds of yellow diarrhoea over it, and walked on. His eyes bulged and were mad. The woman stood and picked up her bundle. The liquid shit dribbled down her back.

The road-blocks that day were all run by child soldiers. They seemed to be everywhere. Minova, the point from which we were returning, was half way down the western side of Lake Kivu. In between there and Sake, which lay at the top of the lake, there must have been five road-blocks. The armed children in their ragged, oversized camouflage manned all of them. The 'Maji-Maji' had arrived. The war, and the killing, was now going to get even more extreme, more mad and more chaotic, if these boys had now allied themselves with the Alliance.

The Maji-Maji came from the forests of the seven-hundred kilometre-long escarpment that runs north all the way along the Zairean and Ugandan border, and from the high plateaux of the Masisi. Originally they were the armed groups of male warriors, from the Hunde and Nande tribes, aged from seven to sixty, who defended each little village. They had their own complex set of rules and rarely ventured beyond their communities' territorial boundaries. Like most things, these delineations had been ruptured and shifted by the war and by the Zairean army. The Maji-Maji were now essentially mercenaries, switching allegiances like the wind, and terrifying their enemies.

For the Maji-Maji thought they were superhuman. They were 'vaccinated' by their mwami, or one of his witch doctors, with a serum supposedly to have magical powers, one of which was to make the recipient invincible and bullet-proof. In reality, the children were probably given injections of glucose or distilled water. The result was the same, for their combination of youth and faith in the powers of their magic made them utterly fearless. Their name drives from the Kiswahili word *maji*, meaning water. It was often shortened to 'Mai-Mai'. Like all self-respecting African fetishists, their witch doctors had introduced a set of rules designed to prevent the magical powers from backfiring on them. The warriors tended to get terribly cross when they discovered that they were not impervious to the rounds of an anti-aircraft gun, or assault-rifle and got wounded or killed like the rest of mankind. Eastern Zaire being a busy war zone in 1996, this was a fairly regular occurrence. So the mwamis told them that if they got wounded, it was because they lacked belief in the proper spirits. Nevertheless, the FAZ were terrified of them. The interahamwe saw kindred insanity, but were cautious of them because the

Mai-Mai were essentially warriors, while the interahamwe were just civilians recruited to slaughter other civilians. The Rwandan and Ugandan soldiers who provided the backbone of the Alliance looked on them with paternal irritation, but did not hesitate to send them into battle in the front line. The Zairean Banyamulenge regarded them as a mad essential. Between 1994 and 1996, a round of temporary allegiances had existed between the various factions. But by November, the Mai-Mai had been brought up by the Alliance, and were fighting the interahamwe, the FAR, and the FAZ.

The Mai-Mai were armed with every variety of automatic weapon they could lay their hands on. Large assault rifles and belt-fed machine-guns were too big for most of the children, but they used them anyway. A Belgian FN-GP machine-gun is meant for use by a strong, fit infantry soldier, trained in its use. Put into the hands of a ten-year-old, the consequences were disastrous. But it was all part of the experience for them. Like most children, they were very enthusiastic about new things: meeting journalists was no exception. The CNN crew were invited to film a demonstration of the magic of *maji*: a warrior was to be tied to a tree and an RPG-7 anti-tank rocket was to be fired into him by his colleagues while he was filmed. CNN declined.

We drove back to Goma through the empty camp of Mugunga. An MSF team were treating the wounded and dying refugees staggering out of the forest from their vehicle at the side of the road. These were people who had hidden when the camps were attacked, and not come out until Mugunga was empty and the interahamwe had fled.

Françoise Hakizimana sat on a lump of volcanic rock and stared at her baby. Under a screen of plastic sheeting and canvas an arrowhead was being extricated from its back. She had fled Katale camp two weeks before and had hidden in the forest with the rest of her family. Four of them had died. Those who had stayed behind in the forest were also dying of lack of food. She had been sent ahead with the child to see if conditions were safe to come out of hiding. She was going to pick up some food, make the day's walk into the jungle, and rejoin her relatives. Flies crawled in and out of her mouth as she sat there. In front of her two Pygmy women were having their feet dressed by Spanish nuns.

Behind her was an old Hutu man, at the end of the line. Life had let him down. He had left his village north of Kigali in August 1994 and walked north to Ruhengeri, before crossing the border into Zaire. Some of his family had died there of cholera, and he had moved to live in Katale. After the camp was attacked he had hidden in the forest, and had then walked to Mugunga, around the lower slopes of the Nyamulagira volcano. He had been dehydrated for more than two weeks; his feet were cut and crawling with flies. He was wearing all his clothes, including two dirty turquoise anoraks, which meant that he was almost hyperventilating with the heat. Nibbling at a biscuit, a second sachet of oral rehydration salts flowing into his arm, he described how the interahamwe had urged everybody to leave the camps with them.

'They said that we had to leave with them to go into Zaire; those who returned to Rwanda would be killed by the *inyenzi*, the cockroaches. It was a plot to capture people they wanted to kill. All the white people were involved in the plot. We had to prepare to leave immediately.'

Next to him, listening and translating into French, was a relative.

'Many people said they didn't want to leave, that they thought they should return to Rwanda. The interahamwe became angry; they said this would happen to those who returned.'

He waved his hand slowly through the air and made the swishing noise of the machete blow.

'The camp was attacked from the back. The interahamwe said we had to leave with them to the west. We stood there; we wanted to have the usual people tell us what to do.'

The man spoke slowly and painfully, swallowing carefully. Crumbs from the biscuit stuck to his lips.

'Then they took three families and put them in front of us in a line. We were all standing there. They lined them up and said this is what will happen if you return to Rwanda.'

He waved his arm again.

'A group of interahamwe walked behind the people they had lined up and suddenly started to hack at them and hit them with machetes till they fell down. There were huge cuts. It took them three or four minutes to kill everybody, and then four of them finished with a woman who didn't want to die. After that we followed them and I hid and ran away with my cousin at night.'

And the interahamwe?

'When they left the camp at the back they were all together, with women and children, their families. The soldiers were waiting. There was a huge killing.'

A Zairean aid worker had told me about this incident. When the interahamwe fled from Katale with the FAR, there was allegedly a huge Alliance ambush. Over 4,000 Hutus had been killed; their bodies were still lying by the forest. We moved slowly back to Goma in the Land Cruiser that I had hired as part of the Reuters mini-fleet. There were two cameramen, two photographers and myself. Each time I returned to the Frontières hotel from the road or the forest, I hitched up the satellite phone to the computer, beamed it into the satellite over the Atlantic Ocean, and filed another story. I had been doing this a minimum of four times a day for a month. I was exhausted. The hotel had not had hot water for three of those weeks. Lack of electricity for refrigeration meant that there was a lot of food-poisoning, and we were not getting much sleep. Still, I was out in the sun and rain and wind all the time, was well tanned, and probably very healthy.

That evening we went to the Church of Spiritual Combat in the centre of Goma town, above which was a nightclub. The room was crowded and sweaty when I arrived with a handful of English aid workers. It was very dark, but even so, the three Alliance soldiers who stood by the DJ's booth cradling AKs were wearing sunglasses. In the centre of the dance floor a large Zairean woman was shaking her bottom, waving her hands in the air. The strobe lights reflected neon blue off the white rubber surgical gloves she was wearing.

'It's the first dance since the revolution,' she shouted in my ear.

For most Zaireans, the arrival of Laurent Desiree Kabila and his Alliance forces really had made a difference. For a while, it seemed that perhaps there was a possibility that the ruined country could start afresh. By the beginning of December, Kabila's troops were occupying all of North and South Kivu. The Zairean army and its Rwandan Hutu associates were being chased out of the north-eastern corner of the country, the province of Haut-Zaire. Secession was not a word on Kabila's lips: he wanted Kinshasa. He wanted his troops to see the Atlantic Ocean. The interahamwe and the FAR were moving south-west, towards the town of Walikale. One sign that Goma was under new occupation was that for the first time in years the streets were swept, the verges trimmed and cut, rubbish was collected. The citizens could move at night without fear of the Zairean army. At the other end of Lake Kivu, in the town of Bukavu, a local woman explained to a fellow Reuters journalist how her life had changed since the Zairean army had left.

She was the secretary to the managing director of the brewery in Bukavu. It was a good, salaried middle-class job. Every day, she said, she got off the bus at the end of the road near the brewery and walked to work. Opposite the brewery was a Zairean military position.

'In a normal week,' she said, 'I would be raped once. In a bad week, every day.'

Nothing she did – smearing charcoal or mud over her face, wearing filthy clothes – made any difference. Then the rebels arrived at the end of October, and Bukavu fell. The drunken, despotic Zairean soldiers fled in panic.

'Now the rebels have arrived, I can go to work without being raped.'

The following day we loaded two vehicles and drove north to follow the fighting. By nightfall we were nearly 300 kilometres north, in the town of Butembo. We checked into the Auberge Hotel, a deserted tourist lodge set on a hill above the town. Butembo was controlled by the Mai-Mai, and they were in the middle of an enthusiastic funeral of one of their warriors when we arrived. Two of them – aged about ten and twelve – had got into our vehicle, at gunpoint, and insisted we went for a drive. They wanted to fire their guns out of the windows but we prevented them. They really were like truculent children. Truculent children in uniform with guns. The fighting had swept through Butembo some days before, so in the morning we headed further north for the next town up the road, called Beni. The dawn was cold and damp on that high escarpment, and the mud still wet on my jeans as we loaded the vehicle, shivering.

We drove north. The road to Beni was controlled by the Mai-Mai, but their tempers seemed to be fine that morning, and we were not stopped. The procedure at their road-blocks had been established. They had been recruited by the Alliance, but it appeared that they had not been paid. They were, therefore, hungry. Each time we approached a group of them at a road-block, our driver stopped. There would be a bang on the car door and a child's head would appear. Cigarettes and UNHCR biscuits normally sufficed. You had to get out of the car, lay the gifts on the ground, and stand back. The Mai-Mai would then sprinkle a little dust over them – to remove the evil spirits – and then pick them up. They would never take them direct from one's hand.

Beni was a morning's drive from Butembo. Buildings were still smoking and graves still being dug when we arrived. The Zairean soldiers had been driven out two days before. They had fled north towards the town of Bunia, an important trading post complete with airport, into which the Zaireans were funnelling reinforcements from Kinshasa. The town was said to be cut off. In the attack on Beni, the Mai-Mai had been deployed in the front line of the advance. Ninety-six Zairean troops had been killed, two child soldiers, thirty civilians and none of the Banyamulenge.

Kakule Kinsonia was in charge of the radiology department at Beni hospital; in the absence of any electrical supplies to run his department, he had been deputed to help run the casualty department.

'The Zaireans fired mortar-bombs as the little soldiers attacked,' he said. 'There were black explosions in the air, but they couldn't kill anybody because the power of the Mai-Mai defused the bombs.'

Five of the children were in bed in the hospital, all with bullet-wounds. A total of thirty-eight had been hit, thirty-four by each other as they struggled manfully with their adult automatic weapons.

We found the Mai-Mai at the far end of the old, ruined town. A posse of them had gathered just before the buildings petered out and the road continued north. It appeared that they had recently looted a shop-full of bathroom fittings. One teenager was wearing camouflage trousers, a t-shirt, and carrying a World War Two vintage Garand rifle. This weapon was standard-issue for US troops in the war, and was considered heavy and clumsy even by them. The young warrior was dragging his along the ground by its sling. Around his head he had weaved a sprig of purple flowering wisteria, and on his feet was a pair of white abattoir gumboots. He had slung a chrome-plated double mixer tap around his neck. Another warrior had hung a lavatory chain, including the handle, from his epaulettes, while a third was swishing a shower curtain backwards and forwards across his body, Zorro-style. We were told that anything that touched water was sacred and bullet-proof.

We gathered around the thirty-strong gang, hoping to film them. There was a little bit of ritual dancing going on; tiny gymshoes and Wellington boots shuffled in the dust. Assault-rifles were waved, there was some whooping. Miguel the cameraman and Ricardo the photographer, both from the Associated Press, started to film and take pictures. Ricardo was about six-foot five though; the children probably felt a little intimidated. They stopped jiggling up and down. Voices were raised.

'The cameras,' I was told in a hushed voice by an old woman at a fruit stall next to me, 'they will not work if the children say the word *maji*.'

Ricardo and Miguel, with a bit of translation from their driver and fixer, started to discuss the possibility of doing some more filming.

'You see that warrior,' said the toothless woman, pointing at a twelve-year-old standing in a dirty puddle. 'You cannot film him if he is standing in water.'

Filming and taking of pictures recommenced. There was more whooping, and the oiled clicking of weapons being cocked. Some of the Mai-Mai started pointing and laughing at Miguel, and then suddenly their voices turned to anger. This is just what I do not need, I thought, looking at the group. I do not want to be shot by a ten-year-old in pink flip-flops wearing a loo-chain around his neck. It seemed they were cross about the cameras. They stopped dancing, then started again. Then they said we couldn't get back in our cars, that we had to stay there with them.

'You are all spies of the Mobutu regime,' said one, pointing at me.

Oh-oh, I thought. That'll get them going. The tension was now high. The group of thirty were under the head-masterly command of a Rwandan officer in ironed combats, a Belgian pistol at his waist. They seemed to do what he said, but with reluctance. When we had tried to drive past their last road-block at the exit to the town, the Mai-Mai warrior guarding it had cocked his M-16 assault rifle – admittedly with difficulty – and aimed it at us. We turned round to negotiate. The Rwandan officer upped the tension some more by whipping the little soldier across the face with the aerial of his radio handset, right in front of us. A sort of whisper went through the armed gang. I do not know what the Mai-Mai response was to losing face in front of a white man, but I suspected we were going to find out. For one brief second I thought I should stand in a puddle of water to protect myself. But perhaps it wouldn't work if I wasn't vaccinated. They started dancing again. Wisteria blossom and bathroom-fittings waved and clinked. Whooping recommenced.

Leaning against our vehicles was another member of our team. William Scully had arrived in the Frontières Hotel several days earlier, bag in hand, saying he had come to do some freelancing. He had the build of a soldier, and the nose of a boxer. Women seemed to notice his eyes. He had served in 'D' Squadron of 22 SAS in Hereford, and had come to Zaire, he said, to try and make some money. Regardless of intention or plan, he was a welcome addition to our team. He had an even temperament and a finely tuned sense of humour. He was standing in front of our Land Cruiser, watching the children shuffle in front of us. One of them suddenly unscrewed the bottom of a stick-grenade, turned to me and made as if to throw it.

'Do you want to play?' he asked in French.

As I dived into the side of the old womans' fruit-stall, four of them opened fire. Five seconds-worth of Kalashnikov bullets sprayed everywhere as they loosed off their weapons. I felt a moment of weightlessness as I lost contact with the ground, then hit earth. I was on my side in the ditch. I felt a line of pain shoot up my spine. I landed on my sunglasses. Then I heard the laughing behind me.

'Oh shit,' I shouted. The laughing continued. The white men, it seemed, had been duly humiliated.

I'd been away from my base in Kigali for forty-three days. Suddenly, the prospect of driving across half of Zaire chasing the Alliance didn't appeal. It seemed unlikely that we would get anywhere near Bunia, and we would remain stuck ten miles behind the front line. The weather was drawing in on the escarpment; the heavy rain was turning the roads to mud. However, I still felt slightly sheepish the following morning at breakfast when I told my colleagues that I was heading back to Goma, and home. There was, I said, a story I wanted to check out on the road back. The incident with the hand-grenade had spooked me, as well. I felt that luck and chance were tilting a little too far the other way. The bridge was creaking under my weight.

The church and convent at Maboya lay twenty kilometres south of Beni. Christian and I arrived in the middle of a rainstorm that lashed the puddles in the courtyard into a brown earthy froth. CONVENT OF THE CONGRESS OF THE LITTLE SISTERS OF THE EXPOSITION OF OUR LADY OF PEACE, read a sign on the door. I left Christian to shelter the Toyota and dashed across into the church. It was deserted, but calm and clean and peaceful with the rain hammering down outside. The light burned in a red glass lamp over the altar. God was at home. Suddenly a priest coughed behind me.

'You have travelled far?'

He took me through the rain to the convent kitchen and made tea. Two Zairean nuns came in; one, in a grey wool dress, sat down with me. She was young and quiet; no more than thirty.

'It was the tenth of November when the soldiers and gendarmes fled through here,' she said, leaning closer to make herself heard over the noise of the rain. 'The Mai-Mai troops were two days to the south still. There was fighting.'

A picture of the Virgin Mary hung on the wall. There was a crucifix, a picture of the head of their order. A robed and balding man, the photo was sepia-tinted and old. My tea was scorching in its plastic mug.

'Two lorry-loads of the Presidential Guard from Goma drove up the road; they had fled. They wanted petrol, they attacked the sisters. They beat them.'

The Zairean soldiers had broken into the pharmacy of the church hospital, smashed the room up, stolen drugs, and then rounded up the nuns. Six soldiers went from room to room; they hit one of the nuns who didn't give them any money. They found François, a male seminarian, waiting in the dining room. Typically inventive with cruelty, the Zairean paratroopers had tied a large, ripe pineapple to his scrotum with wire. Then they pulled it repeatedly, hard.

'Sitting down is still uncomfortable for him,' said the young sister.

François was also beaten with a Kalashnikov butt. Some of the nuns fled onto the slopes that surrounded the church and convent, where rows of coffee grew.

'The soldiers then went through our rooms, taking our habits, our clothes, and two pairs of white, high-heeled shoes. These were loaded into one of the trucks.'

And then?

'And then there was the incident with the older sisters. Sisters Salome, Martine, Lauretie, and some of the others, those aged over sixty. Come I'll introduce you to one of them.'

Outside under an awning of the tiled roof, old Sister Salome was stirring a vat of white porridge. Eucalyptus sticks fed the fire. The Zairean soldiers had made the older nuns undress, and stand, naked, in front of them.

'Sister Salome here, she has arthritis, and couldn't run very far. She also had malaria that day when they raped her and the others.'

Over her tub of maize meal the old nun smiled. The younger sister shook her head.

The destruction of the convent's facilities complete, and the patients in the hospital beaten, the seven much older nuns raped, the soldiers then tried to set fire to one of the five or six younger, prettier girls. But they lost interest. The last glimpse the nuns had of

President Mobutu's soldiers was of six of them standing in the back
of a truck, reversing out of the courtyard. They were pulling the grey
habits on over their camouflage uniforms.

That night, the night of my thirty-fourth birthday, I stayed alone
in the Auberge Hotel in Butembo. At dusk, I pointed the satellite
antenna skywards. The tale of Sister Salome and the fleeing Zairean
army was dispatched into the stratosphere. Birthday supper was a
completely silent affair, the only noise the click and tink of my
cutlery through the leg of my Zairean fried chicken. I drank thick red
wine to keep a cold at bay.

At breakfast, the sun had come up and burned some of the damp
off the escarpment. The Auberge Hotel was one of those places that
you only visit properly once in life, I decided as I sat in the early sun,
smoking a Marlboro Light and waiting for the bill to be made up.
Christian arrived from his lodging in the town promptly at seven-
thirty. The fresh mud slicked under our tyres as we sped south
towards Goma.

We stopped once; looking west from the escarpment. The whole
of the equatorial interior of Zaire was laid before us. Rainforests, lost
jungles, trees to the far horizon. It was green. Very green. Somewhere out there in the thousands and thousands of square kilometres
of bush was the mighty Congo River.

The volcano exploded that night. I was back in Goma, and had gone
up towards Mugunga and then Kahindo to have a look at the
situation on the roads. I crossed paths with a UNHCR press-officer
coming the other way.

'The volcano's going up, you know.'

'Never.'

'It is.'

It was. Four kilometres north of its main crater, the Nyamulagira
volcano was throwing a hundred and thirty-metre-high jet of bright
orange lava into the air. Thick grey smoke rose from the jungled
slopes where a ten kilometre river of lava was burning its way
through the trees. The volcano was one of two live ones set in the
middle of the Virunga National Park; it was forty kilometres from

Goma, and there were no refugees anywhere near it anymore. Unfortunately, we all thought.

'Please,' said Chris Tomlinson from the Associated Press. 'Just let that lava catch up with the interahamwe.'

We stood at the side of the road, looking through binoculars. Somehow it wasn't that much of a surprise. It was as though after all the madness, unpredictability and danger, all the fighting, the bullets, the hundreds of bodies and the firefights of the last month, the eruption of the volcano was par for the course. I removed to my room, and put through a call to Reuters in Cyprus.

'Volcano, eh?' asked the woman on desk duty. 'Erupting you say? Well, all I can say is it's all go in your part of the world.'

That night the western sky burned orange. All the journalists who were left in the hotel stood outside and watched in silence. It was a supremely calming moment. One entire half of the compass was on fire. Nothing but orange light hanging above the earth, illuminating the whole of the north and west. The jungle stood out sharply in the light. An American photographer joined us. He had been smoking dope. He took one look:

'Hallucino-fucking-genic.'

The lava was still rocketing skywards the following morning as I headed north with Christian, Celine Dion playing on the stereo. In the back seat was Matthew Bigg, a Kenyan Maasai of English education who had come to replace me.

'Where are we going?' he asked.

'Katale.'

An hour later we stood in a semi-circle with a group of Zairean aid workers and an English doctor in the middle of the deserted camp.

'This,' said the doctor, 'is what I think you are looking for.'

In front of us was a large pit, dug out of the volcanic rock. It was about fifteen feet wide by twenty long, and was covered with planks. Twenty-four holes were drilled in rows in the wood, each hole separated from the others by a wooden framed screen of plastic sheeting.

'They started building these pit latrines in August and September 1994,' said Doctor Nick. 'This one's probably been here since then – Katale was the biggest and the first camp to get organized.'

The Zaireans around us advanced with crowbars and spades, and started pushing the little cubicles over. Then they examined the corner of the planking at one side of the pit. It had been prised open recently and hammered back down.

'Stand back,' said Nick, as the Zaireans started to pull the planks off with a tearing, creaking snap. As soon as five or six planks were removed, one man came forward with a long eucalyptus pole, stained to three-quarters of its length. Nick motioned me forwards with his eyes.

'When we first started uncovering these pit latrines in the camps, several days ago,' said the Zairean with the pole, 'we didn't know what to do or how to empty them. It was always difficult, especially when there were bodies. We started off trying to empty them, count the bodies. But there was always the danger of disease, drowning. Plus, it was always hard deciding which poor sod would be roped up and lowered in. Now we just pour lime on them.'

Through the uncovered strip where the planks had been removed came the smell of hell. It was a warm day, but the air that gushed and wafted upwards from the pit latrine seemed even warmer. It was the final rotting stink of bodies that have not decomposed, where every bit of the body is putrid, actually falling apart. It was the smell of twenty feet of compacted and rotten human excrement that has lain for two years in a pit of volcanic rock, where it cannot drain away or decompose. It was the smell of freshly killed corpses that have been allowed to rot in that sludge.

The light from the sun fell across the grey-green bubbles and black-brown lumpen glue of the surface. Through the fecal mass poked an arm, raised in supplication, its fingers crooked in agony. There was a foot, wearing a black sock and lace-up shoe, poking up from the horrible depths. There was a rotting face on which half the black flesh had yellowed and fallen off sideways, mouth opened in a last scream. The teeth were huge. A pair of trousers bloated and inflated with gas had kept one man afloat, his shirt dashed open, his ribcage and intestines pouring forth from where he had been macheted. There was a half-submerged back, red and rotten yellow where it had been cut in two.

The Zairean man with the eucalyptus pole pushed it through the crust of the surface and down through the depths. There was a crackle and splinter of bones snapped, corpses barged, bodies impaled by the searching pole. The smell that came up from the depths through the crust was worse, far worse than the one before.

'I reckon we've got fifty on the surface, then about six layers minimum underneath that. Three hundred I'd say. Half killed first with machetes, then pushed in to drown. Boards nailed back on afterwards. In Kahindo . . .'

'Yes?' I said, lighting up.

'In Kahindo camp we found one latrine which was nearly full. When we took the boards off there were bodies with their fingernails and faces sticking to the undersides of the planks. Interahamwe. Fuckers.'

Half the boards had by now been removed. Sacks of lime were being cut open when the workers stopped and pointed. I walked over; across the splatter and ooze of the surface of the pit was walking, very dirty, a bit disorientated, a large white Muscovy duck.

'What the hell?' asked one Zairean man, readying a shovelful of lime.

'It must have got in when the interahamwe shoved the bodies in, just before they fled the camps.'

The duck splashed and waddled its way across the corpses, then just sat there. The lime went in. My colleague Matt shuffled his glasses up his nose, and looked quizzical. He turned to me, and then looked back at the duck.

'What on earth is a nice bird like you doing in a place like this?'

We followed the Zaireans around Katale for another hour. Twenty bodies were found hidden under some straw. The Zaireans were from a local organization, intent on cleaning up their area. The British aid workers were giving them food and milk every day to do it. Just before getting in the car and going back to Goma, I was told about the other bodies, the interahamwe corpses, lying at the other side of the camp.

'There are about three thousand four hundred of them,' one man told me. 'They were there the day before yesterday. Killed by the Alliance. Lying on the rock by the forest.'

I looked at the sky, the trees and back at the camp. I'd report on the bodies; three hundred and twenty was enough for one day. I'd leave these 3,400 dead with the 500 and 300 that I'd just missed seeing and counting two weeks before in the Masisi.

'I'll take your word for it,' I said, getting into the Toyota and winding down the window.

While Matt was settling in that afternoon, arranging his satellite dish, sending test messages to Nairobi, I took a last drive to Mugunga. Christian pulled off the road into the deserted camp somewhere near Lac Vert. I walked away from the car a bit. There were no clouds overhead, the sky was a clear, fierce blue and there was a warm wind coming off the lake. A kilometre away, a tipper truck rumbled through the volcanic rock hutments, looking for rotting bodies. The dozens of women who had come to loot firewood from the camp in the previous weeks seemed to have disappeared. It was very quiet. I walked around, stepping over a body lying under some plastic sheeting. On the crunchy rock underneath my feet was all kinds of rubbish. A Kalashnikov butt, a dead dog, a small woven crown of grass used to cushion loads carried on the head. There were hundreds and hundreds of rats flicking brown and lithe through the ruins. I walked further, into the bashed ruins of a little hut. There was a broken boot and a badge from a FAR commando unit. Shit was everywhere underfoot.

But over all the ruins, the decay, the destruction and the death were growing thousands upon thousands of flowers. There were wild orange marigolds, huge sunflowers on seven foot stalks, daisies pushing up white and yellow, bindweed crawling furiously over the stones. There were gladioli pointing up to the sky, where three eagles soared and drifted. Underfoot the rats scurried for spilt maize, but as you stretched your eye, the grim, steely grey volcanic rock was becoming covered, so fast you could almost watch it happening, in creepers and flowers.

'If aliens landed in these places from another planet in a hundred years time,' a Zairean doctor called Freddy Moakata had said to me, 'wouldn't they wonder what a strange kind of civilization it was they had found?'

Chapter 10

My Rottweiler Will Take a Scotch

Rwanda in January 1997 was spare on humour. It was a country where people's sense of reality and memory had become very blurred. But one day, a Rwandan driver, half-Hutu, half-Tutsi, told me a new joke. A Rwandan man and a Rwandan woman are sitting on the Sabena flight, returning from Brussels to Kigali for the first time since fleeing the country in 1994. They're affluent, middle class. Both are Tutsis. They do not know each other, and are sitting on opposite sides of the aeroplane aisle. After a while the woman notices that the man is reading a magazine in Kinyarwanda. 'Penises of the World', it says on the cover. Perplexed, she moves over towards the man.

'Excuse me,' she says, 'but I couldn't help noticing the magazine. You're one of us?'

'Why yes,' says the man, shaking her hand, admiring her hair braids.

'Do you mind, I couldn't possibly have a look at your magazine, could I?'

And so the two Rwandans look at the photos together. The woman is amazed. Arranged in alphabetical order are penises from Australia, America, China, Japan, Mongolia, Peru – everywhere she can think of. And they are all the same shape. Long, thinnish, covered in skin, and straight. All straight. Every country in the world has a penis which is straight.

Except Rwanda. The man turns to 'R', and shows her the colour illustrations. On facing pages are two chocolate brown penises. One is shaped in the form of a capital T, the other a capital H. The two

Rwandans shake their heads in approval. They say nothing. The woman stares out of the window for a while, then turns to the man.

'You know, the rest of the world.' She sighs. 'Isn't it strange?'

Rwandans would laugh at this joke – I tried it on several – but then nod their heads on serious agreement. It was true. The rest of the world was strange. Perhaps, they'd say, it was just them being Rwandan. The country was exceptionally insular and cut off from the outside world, and always had been. After the takeover of the country by the Tutsi, this tendency was exaggerated. Rwanda in 1997 was having to deal with the fact and the trauma of the genocide, and all it left behind. Its other major problem was deciding how to deal with the outside world.

The genocide appeared to have left behind one or two of its relics in the house where I lived. Set in a compound behind high gates, it sat in the suburb of Kimihurura, overlooking Kigali. From the garden there was a view of the centre of town, the diplomatic and government buildings half hidden in the green of the trees, and the opaque yellow-and-red shimmer of dust hanging over the city. There were bullet-holes in the gates, scraps of masonry blown out of the compound's walls. The house was the property of a wealthy Rwandan woman. Several members of the family had been killed there when the genocide started in April 1994.

There were five of us living there. Me, Chris Tomlinson, a Dutch doctor who worked for UNICEF, Chris's girlfriend Rebecca Dale, who worked for the UN Development Programme, and Gary Stahl. Gary was a senior UNICEF bureaucrat who liked his creature comforts. Silk dressing-gowns, a well-stocked cocktail cabinet, tennis balls bought by duty-free mail-order. There was Augustin the Hutu cook, a Tutsi housemaid who had lost a husband at Kabgayi in 1994, and a rolling staff of gardeners, gate-boys and security guards. There was also the unwelcome presence of Fidette the rottweiler puppy. She barked all day and night at the neighbours, and tore around the small garden compound. After a few weeks of sleep constantly interrupted by her barking, I had learned how to encourage her to drop off in her basket. A nightly saucer of mixed beverages from Gary's cocktail cabinet normally did the trick. By mid January, Fidette was lapping up half a bowl of Harveys Sherry a night, normally splashed with a taster of Kahlua, red Martini or Crème de Menthe. *In extremis* I found that Stolichnaya mixed with Grappa would send her down.

Fidette could not go out of the compound to play or stretch her legs. We thought that the Rwandans would kill her. Dogs were getting a bad press in Kigali after their orgy of human flesh during the genocide. When the RPA liberated Kabgayi mission station, they found the dead bodies being wolfed down by stray dogs. They shot them, much to momentary horror of Samantha Bolton from MSF.

'They can't shoot dogs!' she'd exclaimed, before realizing that they could, and were.

If let out into the red dirt road, Fidette would all too often return with a terrible little trophy, especially after the rain had churned up the muddy track. A bit of collar-bone, a fragment of cranium, a hip bone would be deposited on the living room floor in a little gluey puddle of saliva.

We were joined in late January by William Scully, formerly of the Special Air Service. He'd gone walkabout in eastern Zaire after I'd last seen him in Beni, and had a close shave after being arrested by Alliance troops somewhere in the heart of darkness. He'd been stripped, temporarily imprisoned, threatened. Things had looked bad but he'd got out. He was now ensconced in one of the many bedrooms of the house.

One day he reported that he'd had an unexpected visitor during the night. His bedroom door had been locked. Nobody could get in or out without him knowing, and the room was small. He'd woken during the night to discover an unbearable weight on the back of his legs; he couldn't sit up. He opened his eyes to see a small child kneeling on his knees, staring down at him. He thought he was dreaming. He closed his eyes, then opened them. The child was still there.

He didn't mention the incident for a few days. His background had left him nothing if not phlegmatic. It was when a camerawoman from Zimbabwe claimed that she too had felt the presence of somebody standing in a doorway, then moving to look over her in bed, that we felt something was wrong. It transpired that Wills' bedroom had been the children's playroom, the camerawoman's bedroom the place they slept. On or around 8 April they had been killed inside the house, parts of them allegedly dumped in the well in our back garden. Tutsis had also hidden in the false ceiling of the corridor, concealing themselves from the interahamwe.

Rwanda was full of survivors, full of memory and full of faces freshly returned from the refugee camps. Our housemaid asked me one day if I would adopt her two children. As a widow of the genocide, she said there was shame attached to her status in the eyes of other, newly arrived Ugandan Tutsis. If I was only to adopt the children – they were, she said, doing well at school – then things would be simple. She would continue to do the house, but felt that if I was to be the patron of the children, then it would only be fitting if she moved into my bedroom. My shoes, she said, would be kept shined. I declined. Nothing more was said of the matter until she approached me one day later the same week.

'Monsieur Chris,' she asked, just before breakfast. 'He has no wife, although . . .' she looked around furtively, 'there is Madame Rebecca. Perhaps in his country of Texas they would be happy to have me?'

I said I thought not, but would check.

I imagined what it might have been like adopting her children. Little Anaclet and Phocas, or Fulgence and Dafrosa, playing in the yard, while their newly arrived sister Ascension lies strapped to her mother's back as she irons sharp, irremovable creases in my jeans. Me returning from a hard day's reporting in the north-west, dusty from the body-count at the ambush site. The last story filed to Reuters, then my lager poured cold and ready, a crisp shirt for the evening out. The other Tutsi couples, all genocide survivors apart from me, the white stranger who married in. Audifax and Corona, Florida and Porteur, Dieu Donne and Jean d'Arc and Christian. Learning Kinyarwanda, moving to a tin-roofed house before the arrival of baby number four, Hypax. A diet of maize meal and goat. Beer all day. Long, one-sided conversations with Fidette as she lapped her terrible nightly dash of Cointreau; then the tearful subservient heavings and night-memory of the bedroom. Sought out by white journalists as the one who stayed behind. The sharpened machete always ready in the Toyota Corolla; lost and dated memories of a Europe never to be seen again? I shuddered. No, I didn't think it would be for me. Imagine, for one thing, the traumatized in-laws. There would be terrible drunken one-upmanship as to who lost the most direct family in the genocide. Awful bogus claims to be related to some mwami, and weekend trips to granny in the Masisi. Evenings spent throwing darts at pictures of Juvenal Habyarimana.

That day I paid one of my regular visits to the Ministry Of Information. Genocide trauma and the tricks of fake memory seemed to have taken up residence in this building. I needed to renew my monthly yellow press pass, without which I could not renew my visa to work in Rwanda. But, of course, lesson one of any self-respecting bureaucracy was that no press pass could be issued without a visa. And I didn't have a visa. The office that issued press passes was on the second floor, and had been since the RPA took over Kigali in 1994. One of the first actions of the RPA had been to officialize the exploitation of the international media. Tutsis were not, by and large, a people who believed in an equal swap, of providing goods for payment, or value-for-money. The genocide had turned them into accomplished smash-and-grab merchants. For twenty, or fifty, or seventy-five, or a hundred dollars a month, depending on when you arrived in Rwanda, you received a yellow folded card bearing your photograph, authorizing you to work as a journalist.

The process of obtaining your card could vary from the occasionally effortless to the wildest bureaucratic nightmare. In the early days, in 1994 and 1995, it had been easy. The RPA had been happy to see journalists. Journalists had, after all, told the world about the genocide, and, by and large, sympathized with the Tutsi raison d'être. Press cards were a formality. After a few hundred million dollars had been spent by the UN and aid agencies helping Hutu cholera victims in Goma, the RPA's nostrils began to twitch. Things got a bit harder. After the Tutsis massacred a few thousand interahamwe along with their women and children at Kibeho camp in April 1995, press coverage of the tiny country became, dare we say it, a little hostile. It wasn't long before the RPA discovered that they did not have a monopoly on the world's sympathy. Two years later, when I arrived to get my press pass, the situation had just got stupid. As the resident correspondents in Kigali for Reuters, AP, the BBC and Voice of America, Chris Tomlinson and I were on the receiving end of it more than anybody. When it came down to it, when all vestiges of prejudice and accusations of bias were stripped away, the Rwandans simply did not understand the idea of an objective, free press. They also did not understand how the mechanics of journalism worked. So it was never any surprise to enter the chamber of horrors at the Information Ministry and become acquainted with the latest bureaucratic monstrosity they had spawned.

The office was run by a man and a woman. He was called Ladislas, and she, I think, Véronique. Or that seemed to be her name. And in Rwanda at that moment, seeming was sometimes as close as you got. I had rung the day before to check that they had received word from the Immigration Ministry that they could issue me with a press pass even though there was no visa in my passport.

'The head of cabinet, he is out,' I was told. 'This is his secretary, Natalie.'

'Hello, Natalie.'

'You should ask Véronique in the "Bureau d'Exploitation de la Presse".'

Ladislas' colleague said that her name was not Véronique. That was the name of the secretary opposite. No, I said, that was Natalie. Ah, no, that was Marie-Vièrge.

'But she said that you were called Véronique, and her Natalie.'

'That is somebody different.'

There were four actions that had to be completed: typing of form, gluing of photograph to form, writing of receipt for fifty dollars, and transport of completed form across corridor to Minister's office for signature. This could take twenty minutes; it could take three days. First objective when arriving in the office of Ladislas and Scarface, as we all called her, was to divert their attention from the TV. This was a set with a twenty-nine-inch screen, volume turned high, on which they would watch anything they could lay their hands on. Ninja movies dubbed into Turkish, Algerian Sports Channel dog-racing, Bass fishing in Hawaii. There were endless family videos. One day in August I had made the mistake of turning the set off in front of them, telling them that it would speed up their work. I didn't receive my press pass for fourteen days.

On this particular visit, the two of them were watching a home-video of one of the many Tutsi weddings that took place every weekend. Ladislas had his hand on the pause button, his colleague was pointing at the screen.

'Doesn't that look like Hilaire and Aphrodite?' she said, pointing at the wedding couple.

'It is Hilaire and Aphrodite,' said Ladislas. 'It's their wedding.'

'No, it isn't,' said Véronique–Natalie, 'it just looks like them.'

A white African friend – the one who had seen the ghost standing over her bed – had told me that this was common. Many Africans were incapable of decoding a two-dimensional visual image into a realistic translation. Véronique was watching what was happening on the video, but couldn't make the jump between action and recorded recollection.

It was in this atmosphere of removed reality that I tried to track down a story I had been told about one of the girls who worked at the Information Ministry. The story was rapidly approaching the status of an urban myth, and in Rwanda, where daily reality was so extreme already, a mythical version had to be far, far worse. It went like this: a Tutsi woman returns to the wastes of Kigali in 1995, trying to find where her husband was killed. She has been in exile in Nairobi for a year; things have not been easy. She feels that all she has to do to start getting over her trauma is to find her husband's body, retrieve it and give it a proper burial. She starts her search. It transpires that he was killed with three others and thrown down a well in the garden of a house. In due course the house is located, and yes, there is the dreadful stink at the end of the garden. The little water that is remaining is drained from the well, and the rotted, semi-decomposed skeletons removed with a rope. She recognizes her husband's body somehow, and finally grieving can begin. But first, she says, before the funeral she needs a last photograph.

The picture is posed, with her in her wedding dress, holding the remains of her husband beside her. The shutter clicks. Somebody I knew had seen the photograph, or so they said. All the widowed bride in her wedding-finery is holding is what was retrievable from the well: her husband's bottom half.

Did it happen? Three people in all claimed to have seen the photograph, but nobody could produce a copy. Then they said that the woman in the photograph was a relative of one of the girls at the Information Ministry. Urban myth or true story? In Rwanda after the genocide it did not need to be either. One could guarantee that a worse incident had happened to somebody, that somebody had witnessed an act even more extreme, an act still further beyond the realms of what is considered psychologically manageable. Out there were hundreds of thousands of survivors shuddering beneath the burden of traumas beyond the realms of categorization.

When the Rwandan refugees came home from Zaire the previous November, their President, Pasteur Bizimungu, had been there at the border to meet them and to welcome them home. The innocent and the killers, all together. Peace and reconciliation were his message. For many thousands of Rwandans, though, this meant having to cope with the return to their villages and their hills of people who they knew to be the killers of their families. Rwanda's overpopulation was such that there would not be room for any space between the innocent and the guilty, the victim and the perpetrator.

Rwandans were very unsure about how to deal with their immediate past. The official reaction to what had happened, at a governmental level, was to provide some sort of security, reassurance and stability within the country. But it is almost impossible to comprehend the magnitude of the problems facing Rwandans at the beginning of 1997. Try to imagine, for instance, that between the months of April and July 1994, seven million people had been slaughtered in Britain by a hardline, ultra-right-wing political faction. Imagine the Royal Family, the entire Conservative and Labour parties, most middle-class intellectuals, politicians, teachers, artists, sportsmen, doctors, dentists and architects were all killed in public places by mobs, soldiers and militias created out of disenfranchised unemployed youths. Imagine that all Pakistanis, Bangladeshis, West Indians, Africans, Indians and other immigrants were slaughtered. Think of Tony Blair, Ian Botham, Will Carling, Prince Andrew, Sarah Ferguson, Peter Mandelson, Linford Christie, Jeremy Paxman, Chris Evans and the entire staff of the BBC being publicly crucified along the Mall in one night. Imagine going to the local bank to discover that all the staff had been slaughtered at their desks with swords and automatic rifles. Imagine 80 per cent of all your brothers, sisters, cousins, grandparents, aunts and uncles being killed at road-blocks set up at every service station on every motorway. Imagine every banker and member of the London Stock Exchange crowded into St Paul's Cathedral, all the women raped, and then anti-tank rockets fired inside before it was burnt to the ground.

Imagine that as this started happening, eighteen thousand Chinese, Ecuadorean and Mauretanian soldiers stationed in Britain under a United Nations mandate watched as the killing happened, and then drove to Gatwick airport along the M25 motorway where people were being killed every five yards. Imagine that these same soldiers had rescued their nationals and then departed, leaving five hundred, mainly Taiwanese, Red Cross workers, eight of whom spoke English. NATO did nothing. Every road, every building, every moor, every office-block and every town square was occupied by right-wing mobs, killing anybody suspected of being remotely middle class, or having voted Conservative or Labour at the last election.

Then imagine that a small army based in Holland invaded the country, chased out the killers, and set up a government. Think of the killers going to base themselves in Belgium, aided by Singapore who intervened under a humanitarian guise. Then think of how you would feel if the United Nations proceeded to spend eight million dollars a day feeding, clothing, housing, educating and providing medical care for these killers, while the world rearmed them. Meanwhile the UN is patrolling every road in Britain, discussing with the new government how the returning killers should be allowed immediate NHS care on their return to Britain. And then imagine thirty-five thousand Mongolian, Icelandic, Japanese and Zimbabwean troops arriving and trying to tell you that you should live in peace with the people who killed your families.

It was almost impossible to extrapolate. British people used to find the idea unthinkable. The Americans were always more horrified, especially when you told them that it was the equivalent of thirty-five million people being slaughtered by extremist members of the National Rifle Association on the basis of skin colour, political adherence and education.

But this, or something like this, is what happened in Rwanda.

The enormous question of what should be done about justice and retribution for those guilty of offences committed during the genocide was being addressed that January. A genocide bill, debated for over a year by the Rwandan parliament, had been passed, and the first trials for genocide had started on 27 December. Rwanda's most-wanted list was made up of 1,950 suspects. The bill divided the crimes committed into different categories. Category One was reserved for those who had taken an active part in the organization and implementation of the crimes. The hundreds of thousands of returning refugees had provided the RPA with thousands of suspects.

That December, the Tanzanian army were forcibly repatriating around 400,000 refugees from the camps around Benaco and Ngara. They had now re-settled in the former communes in Kirundo and Byumba, as well as Kigali Rurale, and 2,609 of them had taken their places in the prisons and communal lock-ups of Kibungo province. Many of these people, said a report from the UN human rights monitors, had handed themselves in for their own protection, while others had been brought in to communal detention centres by the local population. The report added that seven hundred refugees had been arrested on their return from Zaire in December.

Some former members of the interahamwe and ex-FAR did not get the chance to give themselves up. Just before Christmas, in a small commune south of Gikongoro in the far south-west of

Rwanda, a former member of the FAR was publicly executed. A UN staffer told me that it was alleged the man had killed a survivor of the genocide, who he feared might be able to testify against him. He had been picked up by the RPA, who took him back to the village in which he had killed, and asked the local population what they wanted done with him. He was tied to a tree and executed by the soldiers.

Genocide memorials were constructed in four different places. One of these was at the church of Ntarama, which I had not visited since 1994. Once again I set off in a hired Toyota Corolla and spun south.

The caretaker of the church, Marc Nsabimana, said he thought that the trials would take some time.

'It's only two and a half years ago that all this happened,' he said, gesturing behind him at the genocide memorial, where some three hundred skulls lay piled on a wooden stand.

'It is good the trials have started, but they will take time. So many of these people have been out of the country for so long.'

He showed me the visitors' book that he kept. By the first of January 1997, 3,019 people had tramped around the tiny chapel and its outbuildings. The remains of 1,500 people and their possessions still lay where they had fallen. The smell had diminished considerably since my last visit; it was now more of a sulphurous, dusty reek, rather like the smell one would expect to find in a sarcophagus. Next to the chapel itself, a series of wooden tables had been laid out, on which were several hundred skulls. (It was from here that the two Australian UNAMIR soldiers had tried to steal a couple of them.) There were a few bones, some ribcages, a few dozen tibiae and femurs, but that was it. A dried wreath lay against one table leg. Plastic UNHCR sheeting had been stretched over some wooden struts to keep off the rain. Marc brought over the visitors' book for me to sign.

'Get the bastards who did this,' was the message from a couple of Australians who had passed through the year before.

I wrote 'Until the next time,' implying that I would be returning, that I was a visitor whose trips to Ntarama were frequent. A regular.

'That is disgusting, how can anybody write that?' muttered a Belgian woman who had arrived at the chapel behind me. She was in a party of three who had come down from the capital. Genocide tourists, as it were. I realized that she had misinterpreted my message, reading it as a wish that the genocide might reoccur. I'd had enough of people like her, I decided suddenly. Drooping, rich Europeans indulging themselves in other people's misery, without putting in the spadework of having to live in their country. Just one of hundreds of irrelevant Europeans who had cluttered up the country since 1995, when they had considered it physically safe, but rather *risqué*, to visit Rwanda. I could see why the RPA wanted to get rid of them all.

'When was the first time you visited Rwanda?' I asked.

She bristled.

'I arrived after Christmas,' she muttered in guttural English.

'Well,' I said, turning to face her, blocking her path. 'I arrived here for the first time in 1994. I live in Rwanda; I'm a journalist. And it is likely that the reason you know about Rwanda is because of other journalists.'

She recoiled, and started to speak. One of her companions started to try and pull her away, saying that she shouldn't bother.

'So the next time, darling,' I said in my finest Foreign Legion French, 'you feel like airing your lack of intellect, don't, you tired lump of lard.'

I turned round, pissed off. Yahya, my driver, was smiling. I pulled the red iron gates shut. We headed south.

The next closest memorial was at Nyamata, on the road towards Bugesera. The government had rather grandiose plans for this church. Physical structures provide solid and lucid anchors for memory. In this manner, rather like the Israelis with their memorial at Vad Yeshem, the Rwandans were formalizing the genocide as a cornerstone of national identity. The country could never be allowed to forget the genocide, some said, because to forget it, and consign it to the unreliable and gradually fading territory of memory, would be to rob Rwanda of one of the most powerful and unique parts of its national identity. Genocide memory, in the late 1990s, was what

Rwanda had instead of history. The country had applied for the official copyright on suffering.

Nyamata church sits in a sandy market place, just over an hour's drive south of Kigali. In 1994, there had been a large massacre here. Tutsis had locked themselves into the church: the interahamwe and the gendarmerie had blown the doors off with Kalashnikovs and hand-grenades. They had killed 1,600 people. In January 1995 I'd come down here when the mass graves still stank in the sun, and the earth was fresh. There had been half-rotted childrens' skeletons in the latrines of the neighbouring school. In the long grass I'd surprised a cat, crouched by a pile of eucalyptus leaves, chewing a shoulderblade. But now, the inside of the church had been excavated. There was a huge hole where the pews had been; the bullet holes that had peppered the roof threw a colander of light on the interior. The earth was heavy and red. Eventually, it was planned to take all the bodies that had been excavated from the mass grave behind the church and lay them in the floor. A catacomb-like structure was envisaged; there would be steps down, heavy glass would be laid on top. Meanwhile, as digging and other preparations went ahead, the bodies of some 1,250 people had been stacked at the back of the church in black plastic bin-liners.

It was as though the Rwandan people needed a tiny percentage of the victims to be set in stone, to be permanently un-dead, to be constantly looking over the nation's shoulder.

The other two memorials were at Nyarabuye, on the road towards Tanzania, and at Musongo school outside Gikongoro. Here the skeletons of the pupils and adults who had been killed had been returned to their classrooms, stretched across the floors in the positions in which they died.

Yahya and I returned to Kigali. Since the new year, the Rwandan soldiers at the barracks behind our house had been parading around in new uniforms. Gone were their East German camouflage and Wellington boots: they had American tiger-stripe camos, and brand new Chinese assault rifles.

'We think the uniforms are chic and different,' one of them told me that afternoon. 'We are more noticeable now.' He had tied a small furred teddy-bear to the cocking-handle of his Chinese AK-56. 'Happy Rwandan New Year,' he waved.

Kigali sweltered in the heat. Yellow and red dust hung in the air over the valley. Fidette was lying on the lawn, panting. I swung into the cool of the house, rang through a short report to Nairobi, and went into the shower.

Late that night, sweating lightly in the heat, I sat on the doorstep and drank a last cold Mutzig. The air was very clear now and there were lots of stars. Will Scully and I had made a night of it. There had been drinks at the American Club, pizza at the Cactus restaurant, and then dancing at the New Cadillac. It being a Saturday, there had been a long line of four-wheel-drive vehicles parked outside. The bodyguards from the British Embassy were down, as were the American special forces, MSF, UNHCR, UNICEF, a Toyota from the ICRC sporting several radio aerials. All were there. We danced a little, watched a Tutsi man playing air-keyboards to a Dire Straits song, had a few drinks. Then we drove back up the hill and home.

I swigged my bottle of Mutzig and watched the stars. I wondered how much longer I was going to stay. My unspoken agreement with Reuters was that I would remain in Rwanda for at least a year. I was not on staff, and if I wanted to go on with Reuters after that, there would be courses to be done in London. Economics would have to be assimilated, company writing style brushed up. Perhaps a spell on the Commodities desk. I laughed to myself in that self-indulgent, contented way one has when one's drunk. I knew myself well enough to know that I'd last about eighteen minutes in London learning about equities and futures; the table packed with eager graduates, the office windows that didn't open, the no-smoking building. Every morning at nine in some bleak financial information purgatory. Forty-five minutes for lunch elbowed into a pub surrounded with people who took it seriously. Then the terrible afternoon trying to keep awake in the lecture on derivatives, before the cold pavement home under a sky that saw no stars.

I fetched another Mutzig and grinned to myself. The Reuters bosses on the ground were good. They had to be. With fourteen countries to run, Nairobi was a difficult bureau – most of its fiefdoms were at war. The office had taken casualties in Somalia, and on the noticeboard, signed by former bureau chief Jonathan Clayton, was a poignant message. After the deaths in Mogadishu of three of its staff, nobody should ever feel they had to undertake an assignment they weren't comfortable with. There would be no repercussions. Clayton had been a good leader; his successor, Nick Kotch, an African analyst of repute. A new man, Fox, had been posted in as deputy from Brussels. A tight ship was run; people knew where they stood. The platoon, as it were, was steady under fire.

I sort of knew it wouldn't be quite like this in London. So I thought I'd finish Rwanda in August, then go to Uganda and Sudan for a year, then apply to be roving correspondent, Africa, for a year. Then home. Demob. Perhaps try and bite the bullet and stick with the company; a transfer to Copenhagen or Vienna, perhaps. Drinks with the girls from Sales. A soft Nordic presence during those long northern nights. I stood up, and threw my empty beer bottle over the wall into the road. Then I said goodnight to the black, starlit canopy and went inside to pour Fidette her night-time constitutional. I thought she deserved a treat as it was a weekend, so I opened the cupboard and reached for the Tia Maria and Cassis.

The trial of Froduald Karamira, one of the former vice-presidents of the Kigali interahamwe, began the following week. The capital's first genocide trials had opened in a small courthouse in the capital with room for no more than a hundred people. A small crowd had gathered in the dust in front of the building; speakers attached to the building's pillars relayed the proceedings to those crowded outside. Karamira arrived in a pick-up truck, guarded by three orange-uniformed prison guards. He was wearing neatly ironed pink shorts and a tunic; handcuffed to him was another prisoner. He was led through the crowd and took his place at the front of the courtroom. The proceedings were brief. Karamira's defence lawyer called for a postponement; his client had not had time to study the papers detailing the charges against him. I pushed my way forward to the front of the court, and leant over to talk to him.

'As a politician,' he said, 'I have no confidence in the system of justice. As a man, I would say the same.'

There were nine witnesses that day to detail the evidence against Karamira. One of them was Gerard Ngendahimana, who said that he lived near the defendant in Kigali. This man had heard Karamira speaking on the telephone to one of his colleagues, ordering him to present himself for duty at a neighbourhood road-block, to carry out 'actions'. The man had refused, so Karamira had sent interahamwe to his house to kill him. Gerard had fled with his wife to Karamira's house, where militiamen shot first his wife, then him. He showed the court the wounds around his eye.

Another man, Jean-Baptiste Sebudandi, a neighbour, said that he knew Karamira as one of the heads of the MRND(D) 'Power' factions. One of his deputies in the party said that Froduald had not only killed during the genocide but before it. Through his broadcasts on Radio Mille Collines, on which he described Tutsis as 'cockroaches who shouldn't be allowed to go into government', Karamira had played a direct part in inciting the genocide. He had armed interahamwe attackers, coerced them into attacking Tutsis, and incited them to kill. He had given greetings over the radio to groups of interahamwe, congratulating them for having carried out successful killings. In the commune of Runda, he had announced, the people were to be congratulated because not a single Tutsi was left alive.

Froduald Karamira had been arrested in Ethiopia, and was the most senior member of the Hutu Power leadership in Rwandan custody. He had been detained after arriving on a flight from India. During the three days of his trial the proceedings against him were broadcast on National Radio. In our house, the staff stood in the shade outside the kitchen door and listened to the radio all day. Augustin cooked without looking at what he was doing, his head cocked to the wireless. Yahya, my driver, was translating for us. He was gripped by the case.

'I was illegally arrested,' said Karamira, sweat shining on his bald pate as he stood to give evidence.

'There was no international arrest warrant agreed between India and Ethiopia. The footage of my speeches on the radio has been edited to show me in a bad light. Most importantly, I am a Hutu, from the MDR party; here I am, being judged by the RPA. How can this be fair? All parties involved in the Arusha Accords should have a say in how the trials are going to be carried out.'

By January of 1997, it was nearly three years since the days of the genocide. Here, at last, the wheel seemed to have come full circle. A process of justice was moving forward. One of the senior instigators of the mass slaughter was being tried in a court of law. Rwanda, at last, was sorting out Rwandan problems its own way.

Several days before, I had travelled south-east to the town of Kibungo to visit the prison. Those arrested by the Rwandan Army since the summer of 1994 had, largely, been confined to detention without trial for nearly three years. Over 50,000 inmates were being held in fourteen major prisons countrywide. Another 26,000 were detained in 182 communal lock-ups known as *cachots*. These were little more than communal buildings pressed into service as impromptu prisons. School buildings, courtrooms, administrative offices, anything would do. In the province of Gisenyi, I'd visited one *cachot* in the small village of Kibilira. A winding dirt track climbed for twenty minutes into the hills off the main road. At the end was a small, scattered village. There was a chapel, and a communal administrative building, on the porch of which were standing four RPA soldiers.

The building consisted of offices opening off a central stone corridor which was open at both ends. I stood talking to the soldiers through a translator, diverting their attention as both Chris, from Associated Press, and I watched what was going on behind them. Thomas, our driver, kept their faces turned towards him, while through their legs I watched another of their number kicking a prisoner along the floor. It was a moment of intense violence. It was as though we were not there. The soldier had the man, who was trying to stand up, by the arm. I could see little except that he was wearing ragged blue trousers cut off below the knee, and a very dirty cream shirt. His hair was scruffed up, and he was bearded. Each time he tried to get up the soldier kicked his legs from under him, and then kicked him hard with short, sharp jabs in the mouth. This continued for perhaps a minute, then the four soldiers in front of us noticed the direction of our gaze. The fifth soldier stopped kicking the prisoner, opened the door of one office, through which I saw a pack of bodies, and then walked back towards us. There was a splash of fresh crimson blood on the toe of one of his Wellington boots. Eighty people were crammed into the room behind him, we discovered. About three per square metre. These were Hutus who had been arrested since their return from Zaire, as well as some who could have been in that room for over a year. Many were people against whom neighbours had borne testimony. The witness of five people in 1994 and 1995 had been enough to get them locked up for crimes committed during the genocide. Many were people whose houses and land had been occupied by Tutsis returning from Burundi or Zaire, or Hutus picked up in acts of revenge by the army. The hills of Gisenyi seemed a long way from the trials going on in the capital.

Floor-space was also in short supply at Kibungo prison. The red brick fort had been built in the 1930s by the Belgians, and sat in the middle of a patch of mud just behind the town's main street. One hundred and nineteen new arrivals squatted outside in rows, just arrived from a *cachot* in nearby Zaza commune. These were refugees who had been arrested coming home. They sat patiently, in lines, waiting to be searched, their little bundles of possessions spread out in front of them: a plastic bowl, a comb, a shard of mirror, a wrap of coloured cloth. Each of these bundles was a life, and although many of these lives had gone appallingly wrong in the last five years, there should still have been the chance to start again. Patrick Mazimhaka, the minister for rehabilitation, thought that the 'seriously guilty' should be punished, with the death penalty if necessary, but that, with a heartfelt confession, a plea of guilty, many of the lower orders of offenders should be released after less than five years. The generally accepted figure was that quarter of a million people actually killed during the genocide. The most guilty had been estimated at just under 2,000.

Orange boiler-suited prison guards with Kalashnikovs led us to the entrance and Corinne the photographer, Patrick the cameraman and I went in alone. There was the same open courtyard surrounded by high walls as in Kigali Central Prison; and every square centimetre of space was taken. In a small cell made for juveniles under seventeen, seventy-three adolescent males swung their feet from the edges of bunks, played draughts, held hands and slept in their crowded quarters, far more cramped than the other prisoners. They looked vacantly at Corinne as she took their picture. There was no lock on their door.

Just across the courtyard, where you had to step over the crouched bodies and be careful not to tread on hands, there was the first of the long rooms where the adult male prisoners lived.

'This is where I live, this is where I eat, sleep and have my possessions,' said Laurent Nzibikamanzi, showing me a four-by-two-foot area of wooden boards on the second level of a three-tier bunk in the communal cell of 160 prisoners.

'There is no privacy. You lie at night with people asleep next to your face, two feet below you, and two feet above you. For a year I have never been more than two feet from another person.'

Around him in the semi-darkness – filled with the pungent stench of sweat, excrement, dirty clothing and stale food – were perched hundreds of men. They jostled for inches of space as they ate their midday meal of manioc and beans. Blankets, tins, scraps of hoarded cardboard, shoes, old t-shirts, and flattened bits of metal were wrapped in plastic sheeting and suspended from the ceiling with orange and turquoise string. The floors were uniformly wet, soaked down with chlorinated water to prevent the spread of disease.

The prisoner governor, a decent-seeming man called Manasse Sebagabo had told us that the main problems were malaria, dysentery and TB. Outside the dark lines of unlit lavatory cabinets, soaked with chlorinated water, dozens of men with diarrhoea queued for a place. In one, three men shared the same hole. In the courtyard, the fierce noontime sun beat down. It left little shade. The prisoners were forced to rotate for space between the indoor cells and the yard, and a complex system of privilege and dominance had sprung up. In charge – of course – were the interahamwe and militia leaders who had come back from the camps, or who had been in the prisons the longest. Discipline was instilled by violence. The Hutu Power inmates controlled all the illicit tobacco, alcohol and food that was smuggled into the prison on visiting days. They also controlled the under-seventeen-year-olds. These were allocated as 'partners' to the militiamen said a prisoner called Anastase, to establish superiority; they were then leased out on a timed rota. Prisoners could pay for twenty minutes under the cover of a cardboard box and a drape of blanket with one of the boys. Different prices for oral sex, anal sex or a combination of the two. Cigarettes, food or, most expensive of all, rights to a place to sit in the shade were the currencies that were bartered.

'But homosexuality isn't too much of a problem,' said the governor. 'This is a rural area, there are many people who cultivate the land, and as we know, it is intellectuals who have the tendency to be homosexual, not peasants.'

Despite their insularity and their monumental arrogance, heightened by the experience of genocide, I felt very sorry for the Rwandan authorities. Each time they asked the international community for help, they got duff goods. Each time any event of importance took place, the UN and the international community cocked up their response to a quite unexpected extent. What was staggering, with the UN personnel, was that such a huge collection of capable, intelligent people, from dozens of different countries, being paid quite enormous salaries, could collectively get it so wrong. The first major disaster was the UNAMIR mission, and its failure to avert the beginning of the genocide. The second was UNAMIR's withdrawal in the face of the mass slaughter of hundreds of thousands of people; the third was French diplomatic and military assistance to the Hutus disguised as humanitarian intervention in the form of *Opération Turquoise*. The fourth was the sustenance, catering, housing and training facilities provided to the ex-FAR and the interahamwe apparatus in Burundi, Zaire and Tanzania. The fifth was the UN Human Rights Monitors Mission in Rwanda, and the sixth was the

UN-funded International War Crimes Tribunal for Rwanda, based at Arusha in Tanzania.

There were one hundred and thirty-nine monitors from the UNHCR in Rwanda. Their job was to assess and report on violations of Human Rights within the country, carried out by both sides. What this actually meant was investigating and reporting on interahamwe and ex-FAR insurgency, the killing of genocide survivors, and the reprisal operations carried out by the RPA, mainly against the civilian population. The monitors were, by-and-large, a conscientious group of people who applied themselves to their job. Relatively few fell into that category of humanitarian groupie who applied for any United Nations contract, regardless of mission or purpose, because it meant a large, tax-free salary, a white car, housing, and a subsidized, relatively effort-free existence in a country where the weather was nice.

No, these monitors seemed to know what they were doing, and every month, or once a week, Chris and I would get a call from their office. There were the beautifully word-processed reports, the gritty factual accuracy, the onerous dependable facts. In short, everything that you really wanted as evidence to prove that either side was up to no good. The problem was that the hundreds and hundreds of thousands of dollars spent on this mission was almost completely wasted. Firstly, the monitors were obliged to operate in the logistical treacle that gunged up every United Nations endeavour, so everything took a very long time. Secondly, nothing was done with any of their reports. They came out between a fortnight and a month after any particular event had taken place, making them of negligible use as news, although their roundups of events did help us with the monthly body-count. Chris and I were always being told how seriously the Rwandan government took the reports, how its *modi operandi* changed as a result of them, how soldiers had been arrested as a result of excesses detailed within them. But we never saw the merest hint of evidence for this.

As for making any difference to interahamwe operations to kill genocide survivors and potential witnesses within the country, they might as well have made paper darts with their reports. Of course, once a month a report was made to the UN secretary-general, with 'recommendations' as to what action he should take. Given the UN's operational history in Rwanda and Burundi, making a report to the secretary-general was as likely to result in effective action as shouting at the sky.

I felt that regardless of UN protocol, sixty of them should have been sent to Burundi immediately, and the rest to eastern Zaire. In Burundi they should have operated outside of the ridiculous, lumbering constraints of the UN system, without army escorts, like every journalist did. We all wondered how many reports we'd see then. As for eastern Zaire, Kabila's Alliance was roaring across the country, slaughtering Hutu refugees, interahamwe suspects, the ex-FAR, Zairean civilians everywhere they went. If the UN human rights monitors wanted a mission with a bit of edge, then there was one. However, the considerations of larger forces were at work. I often wondered how much of a difference 139 journalists based permanently in Rwanda might have made, with a corresponding $200,000 per month budget. Chris and myself probably worked on $5,000 per month each, and it was likely that the combined effects of our reporting, TV pictures and photographs exceeded everything the monitors' mission did. Ultimately, though, it wasn't the people who made it bad: it was as though everything the UN touched in the Great Lakes Region turned to ephemera, to consequence-free sand.

Reporting continued. In the north and north-west of Rwanda, the interahamwe were back at work. Those who had come home with the refugees had hidden themselves among the local population. They continued to lead attacks against survivors of the genocide, against witnesses who might be called to identify them in any trials. Ruhengeri and Gisenyi were once again becoming no man's land, and for the first time in Rwanda, we started wearing flak-jackets on our trips outside the capital. Two human rights monitors were beaten up by the interahamwe in a far-flung village in Gisenyi, their car burnt. The local population had gathered round and laughed as they were beaten on the ground, before being left to walk back to Ruhengeri. An MSF hospital in Gisenyi was attacked. Chinese road-workers took an anti-tank rocket in one of their trucks. International aid agencies started pulling out, rebasing to the capital.

One Sunday in January we drove north to Ruhengeri: a house belonging to an aid agency had been attacked. There were dead and wounded. They were, we were initially told, local staff members. But when we got to Ruhengeri hospital we found an official from the American Embassy organizing the evacuation of a wounded American civilian. There were, he told us, three dead expatriates in a house down the road.

In a clump of banana groves, in a back road of Ruhengeri town, we found the house belonging to Medicos del Mundo, a Spanish medical aid organization. Rwandan soldiers were at the gate, the house was locked. I went around the back to the kitchen door, and found the first body inside. Sprawled on the floor of the kitchen in a pool of blood was a Spanish woman. She had been shot in the head. Behind her in the hall and sitting room were two Spanish men. They had also been executed. The girl's body lay underneath a blanket, blood sprayed up the wall.

Their killers had come during the night. The four people in the house had been asked for their passports; the American had been shot and wounded as he dived for cover underneath a coffee table. The Spaniards had each taken one shot in the head. Their night watchman, who turned out to be a former sergeant in the FAR, had been beaten as he tried to stop the killers entering the compound. He was taken away by the army, and beaten to death in custody. Officially, I was told, he had developed a virulent case of malaria, and the army hadn't been able to help him before he died.

Aid agencies and the UN prevaricated: daytime operations were suspended in the north-west. The army told them they were being targeted; it was time to leave. The UN Monitors had already pulled out of most of Gisenyi, as yet another phase of the counter-insurgency campaign between the army and the Hutus intensified. Their presence in Ruhengeri had had no effect on the army's operations whatsoever. On one trip with Will, I'd found out that the RPA had been conducting a commune-by-commune search-and-destroy mission in Gisenyi and Ruhengeri. In ninety minutes of driving around the area, I'd received preliminary testimony to 132 civilians being killed. On one occasion a local army commander had arrived late for a meeting with the UN; he said he'd had work to do. His arrival at their office in Ruhengeri coincided perfectly with his departure from the site of a killing of civilians a few kilometres away.

'The problem is deciding whether or not this [the killings of the Spaniards] is the interahamwe or not,' said MSF. 'It's interesting for both sides if we disappear. They don't care if medical services pull out; at the moment there is absolutely no evidence of the interahamwe – there were no army casualties. It's very unclear who carried out these killings.'

Killings continued. The RPA were determined to eradicate the Hutu activists who had come back to Rwanda with the refugees. The interahamwe gangs were determined to kill as many Tutsis as possible, and genocide survivors in particular. They slaughtered nearly one hundred in central Rwanda in the middle two weeks of January. In Kibungo prefecture, fifty people were found hacked to death and dumped in a pit latrine. They were returnees from the Zairean camps. Who were the culprits? The army? Local Tutsis taking revenge? The interahamwe? No one knew.

Once again, the energy and chaos of the violence set an entropic tempo followed by the rest of the country. Word was that it was no longer safe to drive outside the capital. Rumour had it that interahamwe road-blocks had been discovered in a Kigali suburb one Saturday night; mines were laid, then removed, around the capital every night. The ring was closing. The expatriates in Kigali reacted accordingly: curfews were imposed, certain restaurants placed out of bounds. Most of the west of Rwanda was a no-go area. UN bureaucrats in Kigali, those who normally never left the capital, were naturally the most scared of all. In our house Gary Stahl found it all a bit too much like hard work. He was finding the presence of people around him a bit trying, he said. There were too many people at home when he came back from work in the evenings. CDs were not being put back in their cases; bottles had been found in the drinks cabinet with their caps not replaced. Something was going to have to be done. He announced, one lunch time of burning heat, that he was going to throw everybody out of the house. Chris, Will, me, Rebecca, Hephke, we all had to go. It was just the last straw, he said, coming home in the evening and finding people drinking and listening to music. For him, Rwanda was getting too much.

So. Camp Gary, as Will called it, was going to be disbanded. We all suspected that what Gary really wanted was to be left alone. Battle lines were drawn at the house. We told Gary that we'd be including him in anything we wrote. Lists of examples were drawn up in our notebooks; Will reckoned that physical violence would be the answer to Gary's tantrums. I thought we all ought to throw his possessions in the garden and burn his silk dressing-gown from the house gates. Deadlock was reached. We awaited his next move.

Will and I had discussed security in detail. White people were being killed. It was, as MSF said, impossible to say who was doing it. It could have been either side. The army felt under increasing pressure from the UN and the various embassies in Kigali to curtail their more extreme commanders in the field. They felt sold out. If only the UN and the aid agencies had agreed to help them search people at the border as they came home from Zaire, none of this would have happened. Things now were almost as bad as they had been before the camps emptied, the RPA thought. The Rwandans were under pressure from the Americans to get their house in order. They felt that they had shown extraordinary flexibility over the whole question of the interahamwe return from the camps, and now they were being criticized when it went wrong. They began to look for a possible scapegoat. Meanwhile, Will and I investigated the possibility of getting hold of some weapons.

A few days later, the killers struck again. Father Guy Pinard was a Canadian priest who had worked in Rwanda for more than two decades. He was saying mass at a small church in Ruhengeri one Sunday when a former RPA corporal appeared behind him. Pinard was giving out communion at the time, so when the man blew four holes through his stomach from behind with a handgun, the priest's blood splashed onto the face of the supplicant kneeling in front of him.

By the time we made it to the north-west Father Pinard was lying in state in an open coffin. Nuns were weeping in the background; incense threaded through the air. His head was wound round with heavy bandage, his nostrils were blocked with cotton-wool. They buried him in the small graveyard of Ruhengeri cathedral, where the dark grey shapes of the Virunga volcanoes sat on the horizon. The church had been full for the service. Round the walls were the pictures showing the twelve stations of the cross. I didn't feel Rwanda had progressed very much since the days three years before when some interahamwe killer had taken his bayonet to the station above my head. Jesus' heart had been slashed with a bayonet.

At Camp Gary the telephone was cut off. We all moved next door, to an empty house just vacated by a friend. Gary refused to get the phone reconnected; he said he was sick of living in a press centre. I tried to get Fidette to piss into one of his favourite bottles of spirits, but she wouldn't go. Augustin came out of the kitchen to find me holding a bottle under her tail. He looked bemused. Across the valley the buildings shimmered in the heat.

Three days later Graham Turnbull, a British human rights monitor, and one of his colleagues were killed in Cyangugu. They were on their way to a meeting in Karengera commune in south-west Rwanda. Graham was with a Cambodian survivor of Pol Pot's regime, Sastra Chim-Chan, and three Rwandan staff. They were driving along a typical narrow, dirt track when twenty people, women included, stepped out of the head-high elephant grass. Sastra's severed head was left on the passenger seat of the Toyota Land Cruiser.

The following day I went to the market to talk to a friend of Yahya's about buying a folding-stock Kalashnikov and a couple of handguns. Will had mentioned hand-grenades and suggested a rocket-launcher, but I thought I had better draw the line. I went out to supper that evening at the Cactus with the heads of UNICEF and the UN Department of Humanitarian Affairs. The lights of Kigali shone below us. They were concerned. They suspected that the Rwandan government was diverting substantial amounts of donor aid from the Education, Agriculture and Health Ministries to their Defence effort. They were pretty sure it was going on; figures didn't add up; columns didn't balance. There were discrepancies. They wanted me to put the question to Major-General Kagame the following day at a press-conference he was holding in the capital. I said I would.

The large hall at the Ministry of Defence was packed the following day. Every ambassador, every head of UN agency, every head of NGO was there. There were dozens of major and minor Rwandan government figures, the normal ranks of Tutsis posing as journalists. The general liked an audience. This was the first time I had ever got to ask him a question – I'd applied to see him numerous times but the Rwandans, well, if they didn't want something to happen, you never heard back from them.

Eighteen questions were asked, in French and English. Nearly half were mine. His responses differed very little from those of any politician facing a sticky line of questioning. He tried avoidance tactics; bland reassurance. Talking in badly disguised riddles. This was a man who didn't really care what impression the international community got of him, in front of an international audience that was beginning to give up caring what he thought. Two sides, I thought, that will never be reconciled. I summed up, I was told, many people's thoughts when I asked yet another question.

'Major-General, we have heard much about your proposed policies, your solutions for the country, your plans. Tell me, there is concern from the United Nations and the European Union that aid given to your Health Ministries, your Education, your Agriculture Ministry, is being diverted to help your – admittedly laudable – war-effort. Can you comment?'

I sat down. I'd had enough.

There was no moon that night over the eucalyptus trees as I walked purposefully out of the terminal building towards the Sabena aircraft, my bags hanging over my shoulder. Our destination was Brussels. The Immigration Ministry officials standing at the bottom of the aircraft steps waved me off, and shook my hand. I turned around at the top of the steps. Yahya and Will were waving from the terrace, Yahya wearing a large white Stetson. I took my last look at Rwanda and turned into the aircraft.

Thirty minutes later the aircraft streaked hard into the air over Masaka Hill, from where the missiles had been fired three years before at Juvenal Habyarimana's plane. I couldn't see the ground below me but I knew exactly what the banana trees, the red dirt tracks and the little houses looked like. I took a large vodka and tomato juice off the stewardess, and wished I could smoke. Before long, the plane flashed over Lake Tanganyika, and we were clear of Rwandan airspace. It was 10 February 1997, and I had been deported.

I'd been lying on the sofa at Camp Gary a couple of days earlier when two plainclothes officials from the Interior Ministry knocked on the door. They handed me a bit of paper and asked me to sign it. It was called a 'Certificate of Undesirability', and it gave me twenty-four hours to leave Kigali. The Major-General, it appeared, had not been amused. Panic set in. Bags were packed, the bureau in Nairobi telephoned. Nick Kotch flew in to make representations on my behalf; I called around. There was a strange silence. Kaye Oliver, the British ambassador, was an object-lesson in unhelpfulness. She had a firmly established reputation as a difficult, obstructive woman, and she lived up to it. Kagame's political adviser, Claude Dusaidi, when asked what her reaction had been to the news that a British citizen and representative of a major multinational news agency was being deported, said that she'd remarked: 'I'm surprised you haven't done it already.'

The government needed no further encouragement. Had she interceded on my behalf, then it is likely I would have been left alone. The Rwandans were just flexing their muscles, looking for a scapegoat, an expatriate on whom to vent their spleen. Oliver had a curiously over-developed affection for the Tutsis. Someone from the British High Commission in Kampala had told me that she was regarded as 'something of an embarrassment' to the British Government. Perhaps the best and most telling judgement that one could pass on this rather unfortunate person came from her own mouth: she had called Lieutenant-Colonel Longin Minani, the barking-mad Burundian Defence spokesman 'reasonable'.

I lay low for a day to see what might happen, but in my heart knew it was all over. I missed the first flight out. At lunch time on Monday, however, two pick-ups full of soldiers from the Interior Ministry came to get me. I was taken to the airport, and all my possessions searched. This was nothing like Burundi, when I thought I was going to be killed. This was just hassle for the sake of it. I had no ticket and the flight out that night was to Brussels. By forty minutes before the departure time, it was looking as though I would not make it on board: the Rwandans were looking forward to this; it meant that they could legitimately make me spend the night in Kigali prison. Me and 3,000 interahamwe. I could not even bring myself to think about the possibility. Nick Kotch, however, discovered what was going on, and flexed the company credit card. Half an hour later it was time for the last walk across the tarmac.

On the plane I pulled out a scrap of note paper that had been given to me that afternoon. It came from Mica Inamahoro, the Rwandan girlfriend of Paul Stromberg.

The events of this day are above all the proof that you've been doing the job properly. They have just let you know this, except in the words of dictators.

On behalf of both countries, as much as for all Rwandans and Burundians, I thank you for the work you've done. I hope above all that you will continue, despite everything, to keep alight the fragile and frail candle of the truth, such as it is, and that one day the darkness and despair will no longer exist.

Signed, Mika, a Rwandan patriot.

This, I thought, was how I wanted to remember the two smallest countries in Africa.

CONCLUSION

Africa's First World War

I saw in the fourth anniversary of the Rwandan genocide in the company of seven former members of the interahamwe. The eight of us stood on a windy hillside in northern Angola and talked about their homeland. It was more than a thousand miles away. They had not seen it since July 1994, and were eager for news. They'd been in one of the camps near Bukavu for more than two years. Then they had made the long retreat in front of the Alliance troops. They'd walked to Walikale, Kisangani, and the diamond town of Mbuji-Mayi. Several months later they'd hit the Atlantic Ocean. There they had turned left. Nobody noticed them as they entered northern Angola. So they kept on walking. Now they were, once again, under the care of the international community in an Angolan displaced persons camp. An NGO was looking after them. The World Food Programme gave them maize. They spent each day sheltering from the sun under their thatch awning, waiting for news.

'How,' asked one man, 'are things at home?'

I'd told them that I had been deported from their country at the behest of the Tutsis.

'Those people . . .' said another man, sucking his teeth.

'They think they can just do what they like.'

His name was Antoine, and he came from Butare. Why had he fled Rwanda?

'There was a fear amongst us all,' he said, looking across the horizon towards the grasslands of Zaire, the Democratic Republic of Congo.

'There was a fear amongst us that what we had done would be misunderstood.'

He then asked the question that had been on every Hutu's lips since November, 1996.

'And is it safe to return?'

I paused. Looked at the group around me. Offered cigarettes. Four years of international care and attention, of UNHCR catering, had made them healthy, almost sleek. One man removed wire-rimmed spectacles and leant forward. There was a shuffling for space, whispers for silence. The sun was hot. Wind blew up from the mango trees in the valley below us.

'The government has started executing people in public,' I said. 'At Nyamata, in Kigali. Tied to posts in the football stadiums. Gendarmes emptying their magazines at point-blank range. Sixty shots each.'

The seven shook their heads, looked around at each other.

'Those people found guilty of crimes from 1994 are dying,' I told them. 'It's become a public spectacle. Everybody's invited. Even the *abazungu*.'

Antoine stood up, and turned away.

'Will it stop?' asked another.

In May 1997, Laurent Kabila's forces of the Democratic Alliance entered Kinshasa. The FAZ laid down their arms. The rebel soldiers had walked across Zaire in their Wellington boots. President Mobutu Sese Seko fled to Togo, then Morocco. In Rabat, his prostate cancer proved too much, and he died. Kabila declared himself president, changed the name of the country to the Democratic Republic of Congo, and settled in. The mighty Zaire river became the Congo again.

Rwandans and Ugandans who had helped him to power settled in to Kinshasa as well, and for a small moment, there was peace. It seemed that the much-vaunted African Renaissance, Africa's new concept of running its own affairs, sorting out its own problems, was working. Post-post-colonialism, as it was called, had proved effective.

The interahamwe and the ex-FAR had spread to the four corners of Central Africa. They were, like Antoine and friends, in camps in northern Angola, in the Central African Republic, Congo-Brazzaville, Tanzania. They'd linked with anti-government rebels in southern Chad. They were fighting on Uganda's western borders with Sudanese rebel deserters. They'd play ball with anybody who had an anti-Tutsi, anti-Ugandan agenda. They formed themselves into one supposedly unified group, called PALIR, or the Party of the Army to Liberate Rwanda. Former commanders of the FAR and interahamwe took control. Basing themselves in North Kivu, the Masisi, the Virunga National Park and north-west Rwanda, they continued to attack Rwanda. They slaughtered Tutsis, attacked the army, and killed genocide survivors.

In December 1997, in a speech in Addis Ababa to the Organization of African Unity, American Secretary of State Madeleine Albright finally apologized for the Rwandan genocide.

'The international community should have been more active in the early stages of the atrocities in 1994, and called them what they were – genocide.'

She then proceeded to Rwanda, where the interahamwe marked her visit by killing more than 300 displaced Tutsis with machetes, clubs and Kalashnikovs at a Displaced Persons Camp in Gisenyi.

President Clinton arrived in Rwanda in March 1998, in the middle of his trans-Africa tour. Barred from Rwanda, I was covering the war from the edge of the ring, dancing attendance from the sidelines in Angola, Tanzania and Uganda. I was sitting in an office in Nairobi when he gave his emotive speech in Kigali.

He didn't leave the airport during his five-hour visit, but his eloquent speech was the most staggering admission by the world's most powerful statesman that Rwanda had been let down.

'Never again must we be shy in the face of the evidence of genocide.'

A year later, Assistant Secretary of State Susan Rice called the war in Democratic Congo 'Africa's First World War'. By mid 1998, Kabila had done a complete about-turn. Accused by his former allies of corruption, inefficiency, nepotism, gross human rights abuses and insincerity, Rwanda and Uganda turned on him, and war broke out again.

A new rebel movement, the National Council for the Union of Democracy (NUCD), sprung up to oppose him from the fastnesses of North Kivu. Sides were taken. Kabila took the unprecedented step of formally recruiting into his national army the interahamwe and ex-FAR cadres scattered across his vast country.

For the Rwandans this was just too much. Rwanda, Burundi, Uganda, the NCUD and Angola faced off Democratic Congo. They were backed in turn by troops from Namibia, Zimbabwe, Chad, the Central African Republic, UNITA and Sudan.

By the fifth anniversary of the genocide, in 1999, the second millennium was coming to a close. Nothing was improving. Northern Rwanda was a war-zone; along the sides of the roads in Ruhengeri and Gisenyi, the houses and the bush had been burnt back for 200 metres to prevent ambushes. Ukranian mercenary pilots were flying Mi-24 Hind helicopter gunships for the RPA. The Rwandan–Ugandan–rebel conglomerate reclosed on Democratic Congo, approached Mbuji-Mayi. Newspapers reported heavy Zimbabwean casualties. Robert Mugabe's home economy was being crippled by the efforts of fighting a war that had its origins at Kigali airport five years before.

In northern Rwanda, and in North Kivu the ex-FAR and interahamwe continued their struggle, excelling themselves in new levels of ethnic violence. Sometimes they joined the RPA in full-scale battles, where thousands of Hutu troops would engage the RPA in massive firefights. At other times they kept to what they did best: remembering that the purpose of terrorism is to terrorize.

One day an old Hutu peasant woman in northern Ruhengeri reported that somebody seemed to be keeping an eye on her plot of land. Somebody, she said, knew her crops better than she did. She reported the matter to the army. The interahamwe were around, she said. The army arrived, and set up an ambush. A couple of nights later, there was a firefight near her house. Two former militiamen were killed. The army moved off.

When the interahamwe turned up two nights later and told her she was a traitor, she knew it was the end. You were either with them, or against them, said her neighbour. This woman found the remains the following morning. The woman had been killed with a machete, but before she died, the interahamwe had cut chunks of flesh off her two children, and forced her to eat them.

And the United Nations? What had they learned from five years of genocidal chaos? What use had their human rights monitors been? Had President Clinton apologized in vain? Had the UN paid any attention to the criticism and witness testimony of the thousands of journalists and aid workers who had tramped across the region from 1993?

Across seven countries, I had personally counted the bodies of up to 2,500 people in three and a half years. Victims of machete, assault rifle, hand-grenade, clubs, spades, bayonets, spears, knives, gardening tools, plastic explosives and mortar fire. The count would have been much higher if the Burundians had not tended to bury their victims immediately. I had probably also reported on the deaths of another 10,000 at least. Perhaps a one hundred and fiftieth part of the death-toll of seven years.

Had it come to anything?

Perhaps the most poignant example of the difference between what it is necessary to do to halt the violence in Central Africa, and what actually is being done at an international level, is illustrated by the following story.

In the International Criminal Tribunal Court at Arusha, Tanzania, the UN made one of its more glaring blunders in March 1999. While the rest of the region was moving forward, they were still wading through their own brand of diplomatic and logistical treacle.

In the dock was Bernard Ntuyahaga, a former major in the Rwandan Presidential Guard, which had been trained and armed by French soldiers. He had commanded the unit that tortured and killed the ten Belgian UNAMIR paratroopers in April 1994. He had overseen the disembowelling and multiple rape of the moderate Rwandan prime minister, Agathe Uwilingiyimana. The Belgians wanted to extradite him. Fearing a Kigali firing squad, he had entered Tanzania from Zambia illegally, and given himself up. The maximum sentence the Arusha court can hand down is life imprisonment. So that he could be extradited to Belgium, the UN court dropped charges against him. Only then did they find out they could not legally extradite him to Belgium. And then they discovered that their legal mandate did not allow them to re-arrest Ntuyahaga. One can imagine the feeling of confidence and trust engendered in Kigali in the international community when Rwandan authorities heard Judge Navanthem Pillay utter the words:

'The tribunal orders the immediate release of Bernard Ntuyahaga.'

Kosovo, 1999

In the last weeks of the twentieth century I stood on a freezing mountainside in far western Kosovo, looking down towards the town of Peja. Nearly six years had passed since the days of April 1994, but there was much about Kosovo that made me think back to the Great Lakes Region: the massive level of violence; ethnic cleansing; the intractable relationships between Albanian and Serb. That morning I'd spent an hour on the streets of Peja, interviewing local Albanians about an attack that had taken place the night before.

A convoy of Serbs had left the town of Orahovac, fleeing ethnic reprisals carried out by Albanians. They'd piled their belongings, their washing machines, their flower-pots and their mattresses into a convoy of old Ladas and battered Yugos, and then hit the road west. NATO armoured vehicles rode shotgun. The convoy crawled through the night. Just outside Peja, one car broke down, the convoy separated, and the twenty-odd vehicles at the tail end diverted into downtown Peja to ask directions to Montenegro.

A crowd of 1,500 Albanians attacked them. Nineteen cars were set on fire, a coach was burnt out, and it was only through the efforts of sixty Italian policemen that no Serbs were killed. It was a close-run thing. A three-year-old Serb child was locked inside a burning car. Old women were beaten with iron bars. The following morning I stood in the pale blue sunlight and watched an Albanian shopkeeper hose the petrol stains and scorch marks off his patch of pavement.

'Until every single one of them has left,' he said, referring to the Serbs, 'we will be obliged to behave in this way.'

I looked around me. The old buildings of central Peja didn't look much like Butare; the trees didn't resemble eucalyptuses, and nobody around me was carrying a machete. But there was something terribly familiar that brought to mind the terraced, red-earth slopes of Rwanda and Burundi. It was the vocabulary. 'Them' and 'us'. A society where your ethnicity, that year, had decided whether you lived or died. Terrified people who didn't understand, who just wanted to be left alone, being forced at gunpoint to pick up all their possessions and hit the road. The Kosovar Albanians had had a horrific time at the hands of the Serbs. 'Operation Horseshoe' – the ethnic cleansing of Kosovo – had seen in action groups of Serb paramilitaries, men recruited from the criminal underclass of Belgrade, the poor, the unemployed of Novi Sad, men who worked on the understanding that so long as they did the necessary killing, they got to loot, steal and rape as much as they liked. These paramilitaries, from gangs with names like 'Lightning', 'The White Eagles' and 'Black Hand,' could give the interahamwe a run for their money.

In the small town of Ishtok in western Kosovo, an eighty-year-old man told how Serbs from a gang known as 'Frenkie's Boys' had cut off his wife's head with a breadknife. In a deserted house ten kilometres from the Albanian border, I'd found the detritus of mass rape. Young Kosovan girls were pulled at gunpoint off tractor refugee convoys, and kept imprisoned in the upstairs bedrooms of houses like this one. Serb paramilitaries and Special Police would finish off a night's drinking and then bundle upstairs, paralytic, wild and burning with a mixture of heroin and brandy, and gang rape the girls. Dozens of notches were carved in the walls with Kalashnikov bayonets. The floor was littered with crushed aerosol cans of Impulse and other body sprays, for when the girls' smell got too bad.

Then, in June 1999, NATO liberated Kosovo, and for a while it seemed that things might get better. Unfortunately not. If it had taken the RPA two to three years to lose their tenancy of the moral high-ground after the Rwandan genocide, then it took the Kosovo Liberation Army, and many other Kosovans, about three months. Their massive campaign of reprisals against the remaining Serbs inside Kosovo saw to that. By the end of the year, the sympathy of the international community had swung against them. In lots of conversations with them, if you closed your eyes you could almost imagine yourself talking to a Rwandan Tutsi.

I spent much of 1999 in Kosovo and Albania, after returning from Africa at the end of 1998. My last stories on the darkest of continents had been of mass famine in southern Sudan, and the bombings of the US Embassies in Nairobi and Dar es Salaam. One of my last memories of Kenya was of the Nairobi City Mortuary, three days after the bombing, with the electricity cut off. The component parts of eighty-four Kenyans hit by two hundred kilos of Semtex littered the interior of the building. A soggy cardboard box held three gluey heads. By early September 1998, after a bout of malaria had left me twenty pounds lighter, it was time to say goodbye. Michela Wrong and I gathered forty friends into the Lord Delamere bar at the Norfolk, and drank ourselves into the night. I finished off the evening watching the sun come up over Nairobi National Park. Three days later I humped two bags on to the overnight Air France flight, and ten hours later was in Paris.

The gang that had covered Rwanda, Burundi and Zaire split to the four corners of the earth. I saw David Guttenfelder from AP in Kosovo, where we watched NATO troops haul the corpse of an old man out of a well. He had had a very narrow escape in Freetown in January, when he just missed death in a road-block shooting that killed Miles Tierney, an AP TV producer reckoned by many of us to be the bravest journalist on the African continent. Then in May 1999 he was sitting on the Albanian–Kosovan border when a Serb sniper shot the journalist next to him in the head. Corinne Dufka from Reuters went to work for a human rights organization in Sierra Leone, and Michela went back to the *Financial Times* in London. Samantha Bolton stayed with MSF, whose efforts in the field were recognized in 1999 with the award of the Nobel Peace Prize. Anne-Sophie from Burundi took her confused sexuality off to northern Chad, while Betsy Greve from UNHCR went to work in Kosovo, and bought a cottage in Yorkshire with her English boyfriend. Nick Kotch from Reuters ended up working on the Financial Desk in London, while James Shepherd-Barron from ECHO took a post in

Tirana. Bryan Rich and Sandra Melone split up, and she moved to Brussels. William Scully of the SAS was awarded the Queen's Gallantry Medal in 1998 for extraordinary courage in defending a hotel in Sierra Leone against rampaging RUF rebels. Chris Tomlinson moved to New York. Fidette the Rottweiler went for a walk one day in Kigali with Will Scully, and was never seen again.

And Rwanda? And Burundi? By the end of 1999, Ugandan and Rwandan troops had finally turned on each other and were last heard of shooting it out in some lost firefight over diamond concessions in the town of Kisangani, capital of the heart of darkness. An AP friend, Hrvoje Hranski, was caught in the middle of it all, and took an AK round in the torso that nearly killed him. Half of central Africa, the interahamwe included, seemed to turn in on itself in an ever-changing series of allegiances, while in Kinshasa Laurent Kabila, the self-parodying African dictator, seemed to go quietly mad. Rwanda denied a visa to Carla Del Ponte, Chief Prosecutor for the International Tribunal, after they released Jean-Bosco Barayagwiza – a Radio Mille Collines bigwig – for lack of evidence. The Tribunal had, by late 1999, managed to convict five suspects in five years.

I shared a bottle of Montenegrin red wine in a downtown Pristina restaurant with Patrick Berner from the ICRC, in the same week that Burundi was hitting the headlines again. A delegation from the UN had run into trouble in a displaced persons camp near Ruyigi. Hutu rebels disguised as military walked into the camp and opened fire on them, and two internationals were shot dead underneath the eucalyptus trees down towards the Tanzanian border. As Patrick and I sat in Kosovo drinking our wine, the Russian army was putting Chechnya through the mincer, and the word 'genocide' had been used again in East Timor. It seemed that just over the horizon there was a permanent glow, as if from a fire, and that if one looked hard, and kept an ear to the news, that the ashes of Juvenal Habyarimana's plane had not yet gone out.